Sorcerer Hunters
Book 6

Sorcerer Hunters

TOKYOPOP Manga

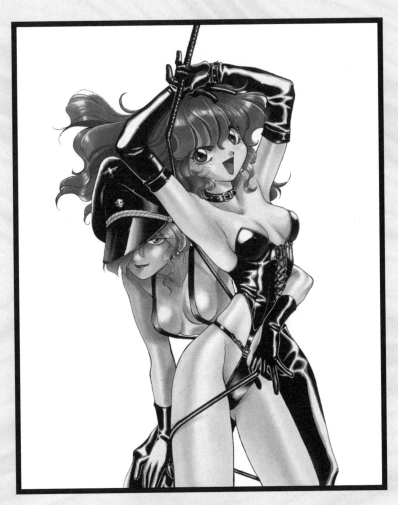

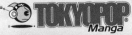

TOKYOPOP Presents
Sorcerer Hunters 6 by Satoru Akahori & Ray Omishi
TOKYOPOP is a registered trademark and
TOKYOPOP Manga is a trademark of Mixx Entertainment, Inc.
ISBN: 1-892213-91-5
First Printing October 2001

10	9	8	7	6	5	4	3	2	1

Translator - Anita Sengupta. Retouch Artists - Ryan Caraan, Roselyn Santos, Wilbert Lacuna.
Graphic Assistant - Dao Sirivisal. Graphic Designer - Akemi Imafuku.
Editors - Katherine Kim, Michael Schuster.
Senior Editor - Jake Forbes. Production Manager - Fred Lui.

Email: editor@Press.TOKYOPOP.com
Come visit us at www.TOKYOPOP.com.

TOKYOPOP
LOS ANGELES - TOKYO

Contents

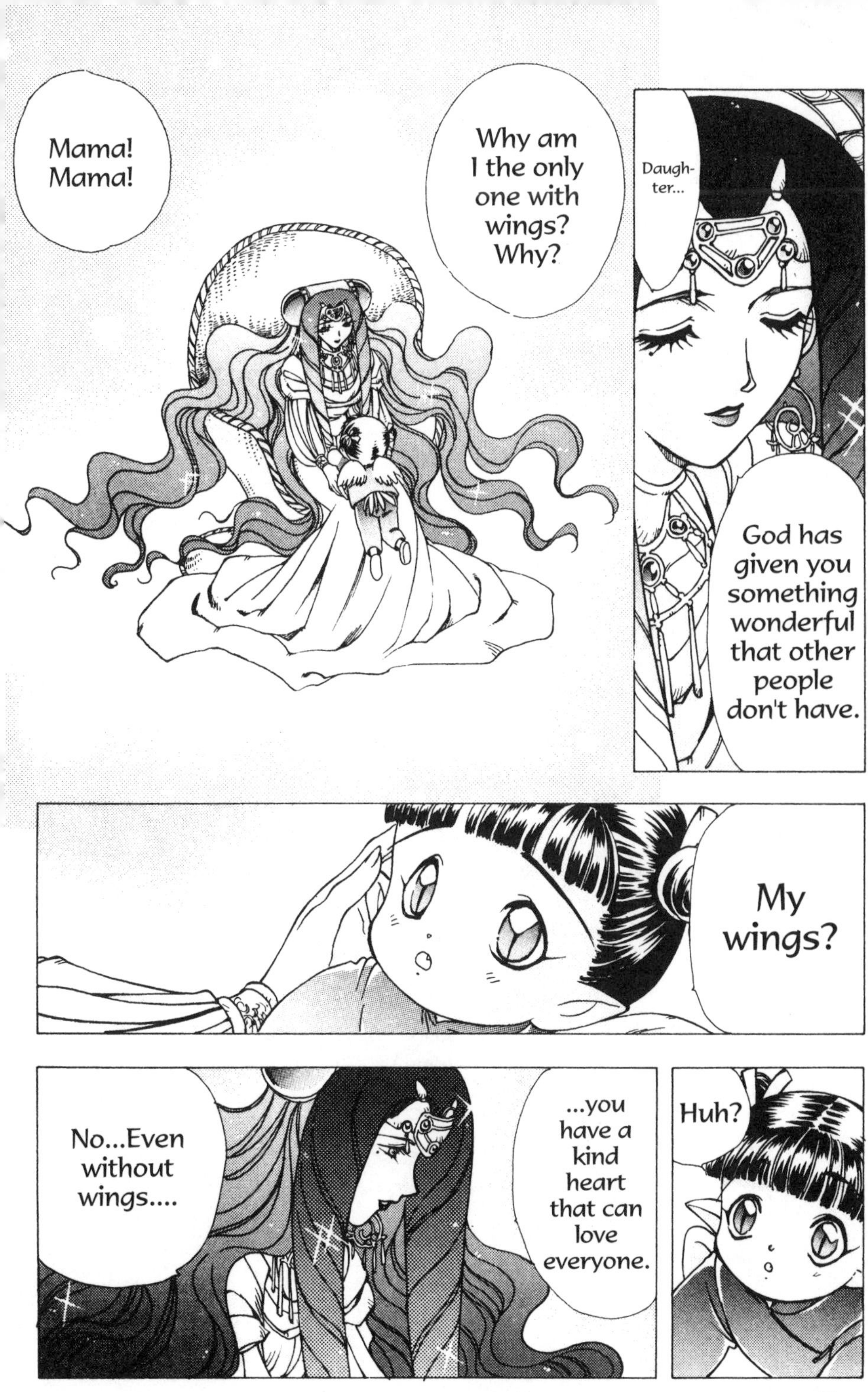
Mama! Mama!
Why am I the only one with wings? Why?
Daugh- ter...
God has given you something wonderful that other people don't have.
My wings?
No...Even without wings....
...you have a kind heart that can love everyone.
Huh?

Daughter in Love (Part 1)

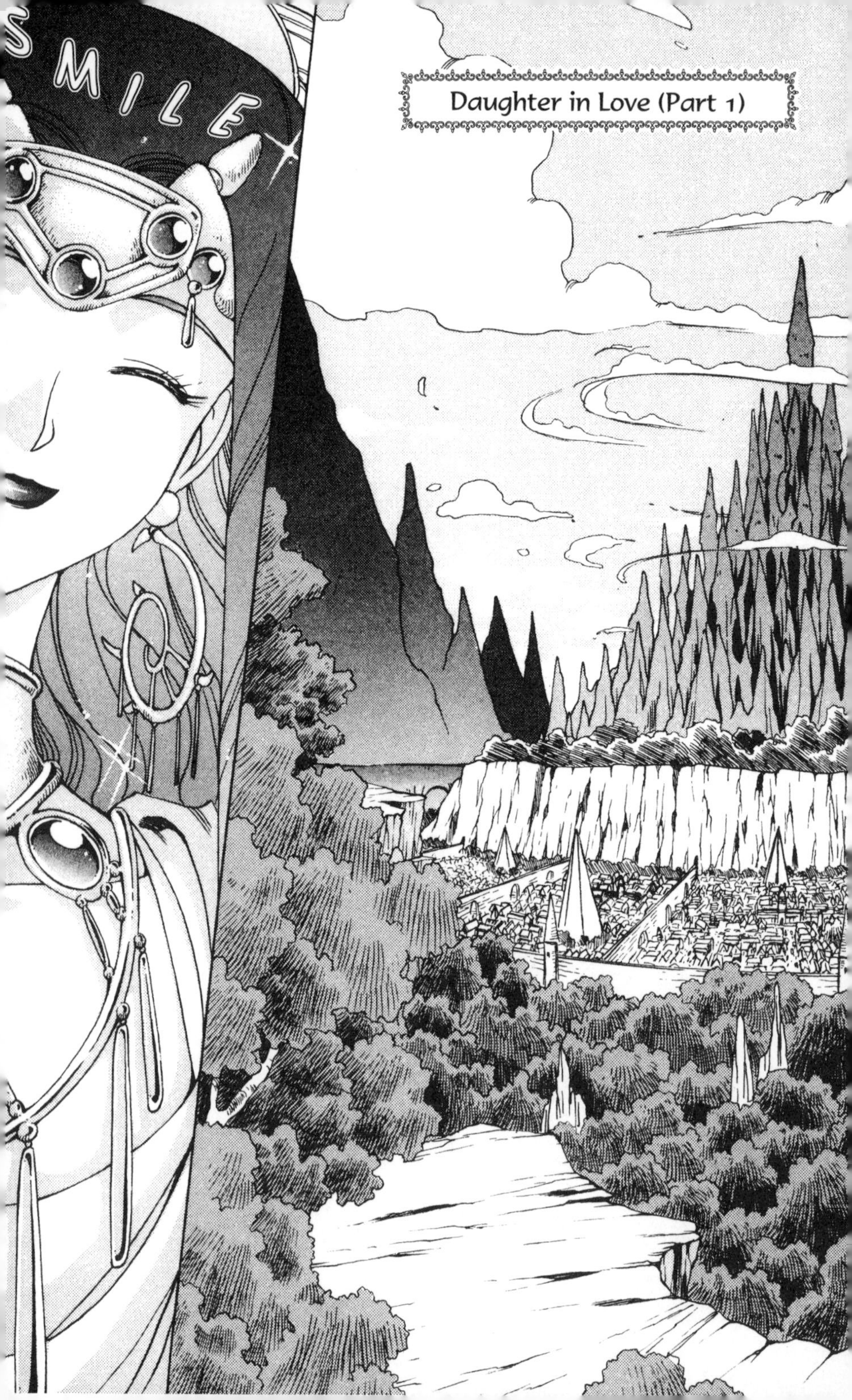
SMILE

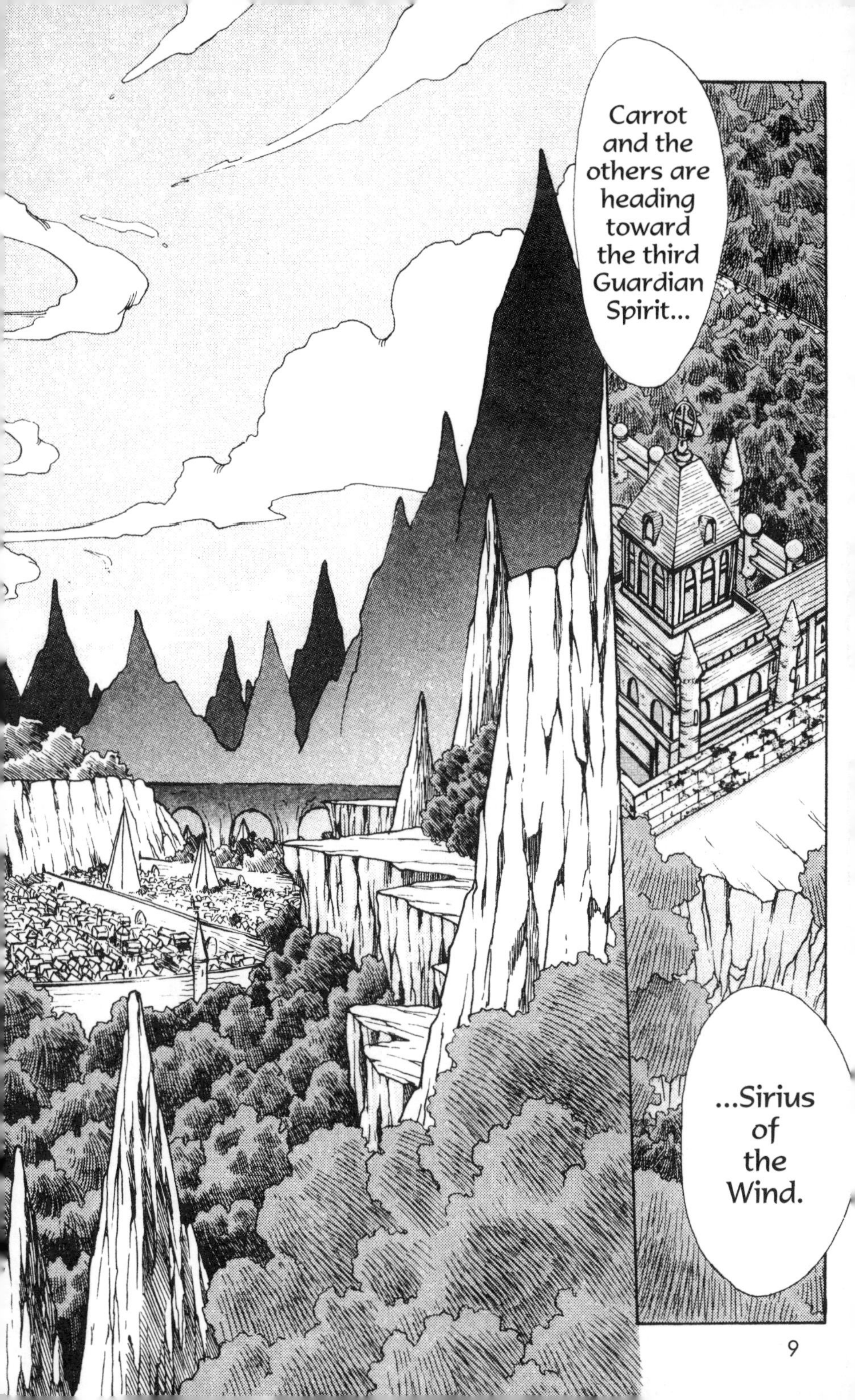
Carrot and the others are heading toward the third Guardian Spirit...
...Sirius of the Wind.

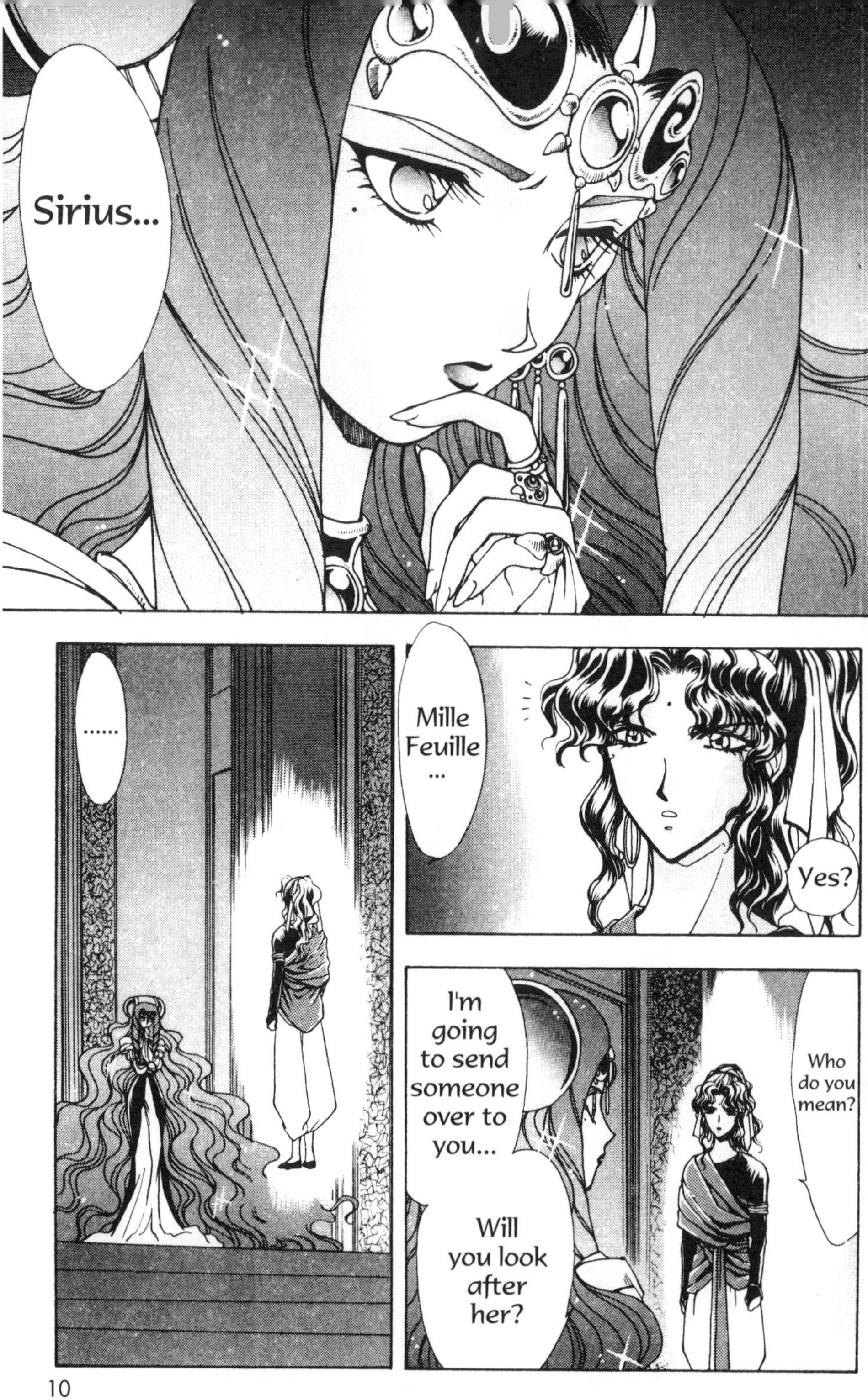
Sirius...
Mille Feuille ...
Yes?
I'm going to send someone over to you...
Who do you mean?
Will you look after her?
......

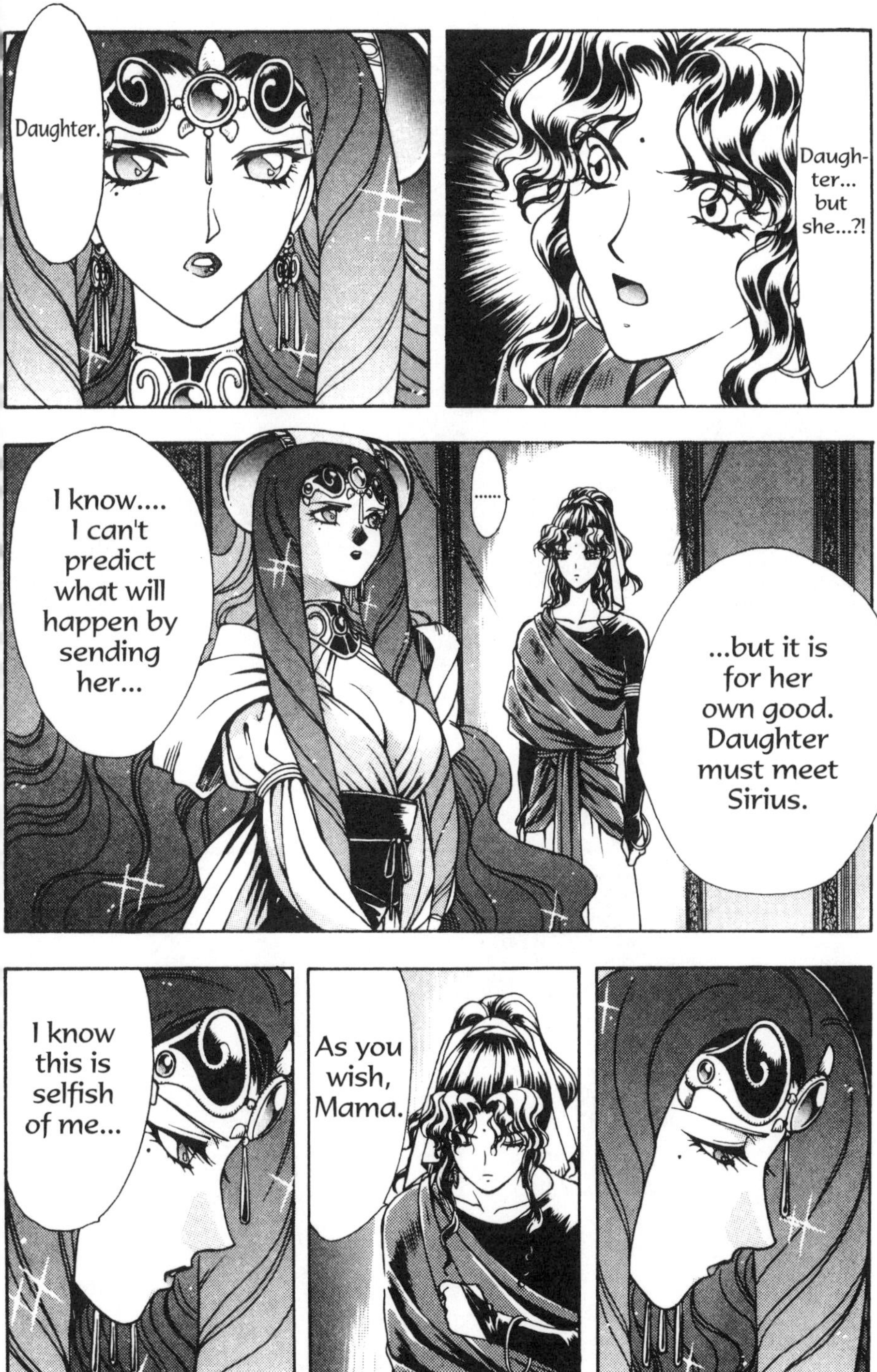
Daughter.
Daughter... but she...?!
I know.... I can't predict what will happen by sending her...
......
...but it is for her own good. Daughter must meet Sirius.
I know this is selfish of me...
As you wish, Mama.

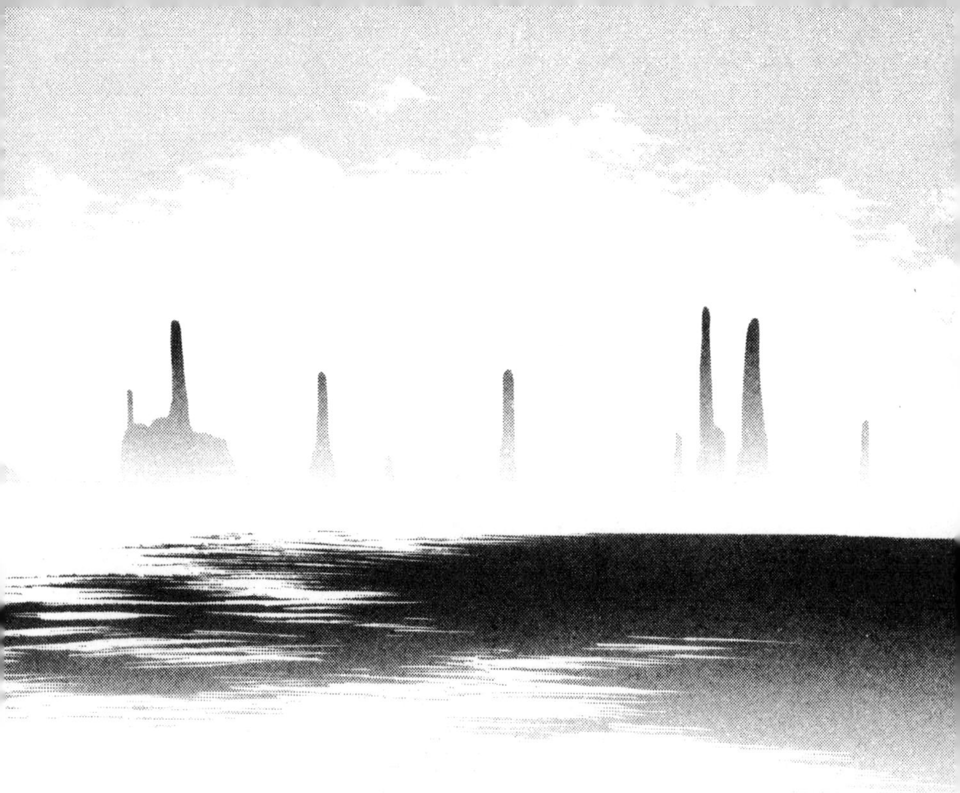

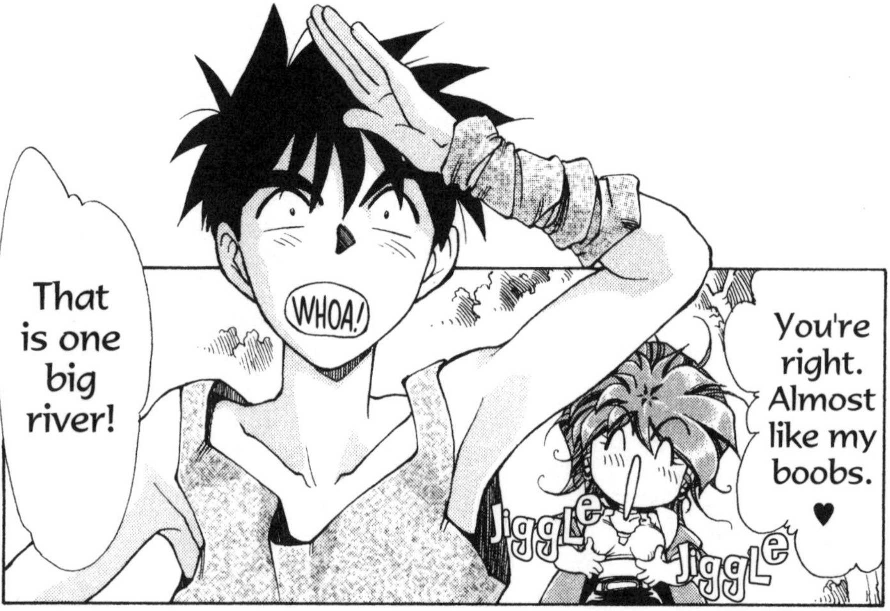
WHOA!
That is one big river!
You're right. Almost like my boobs. ♥
Jiggle
Jiggle

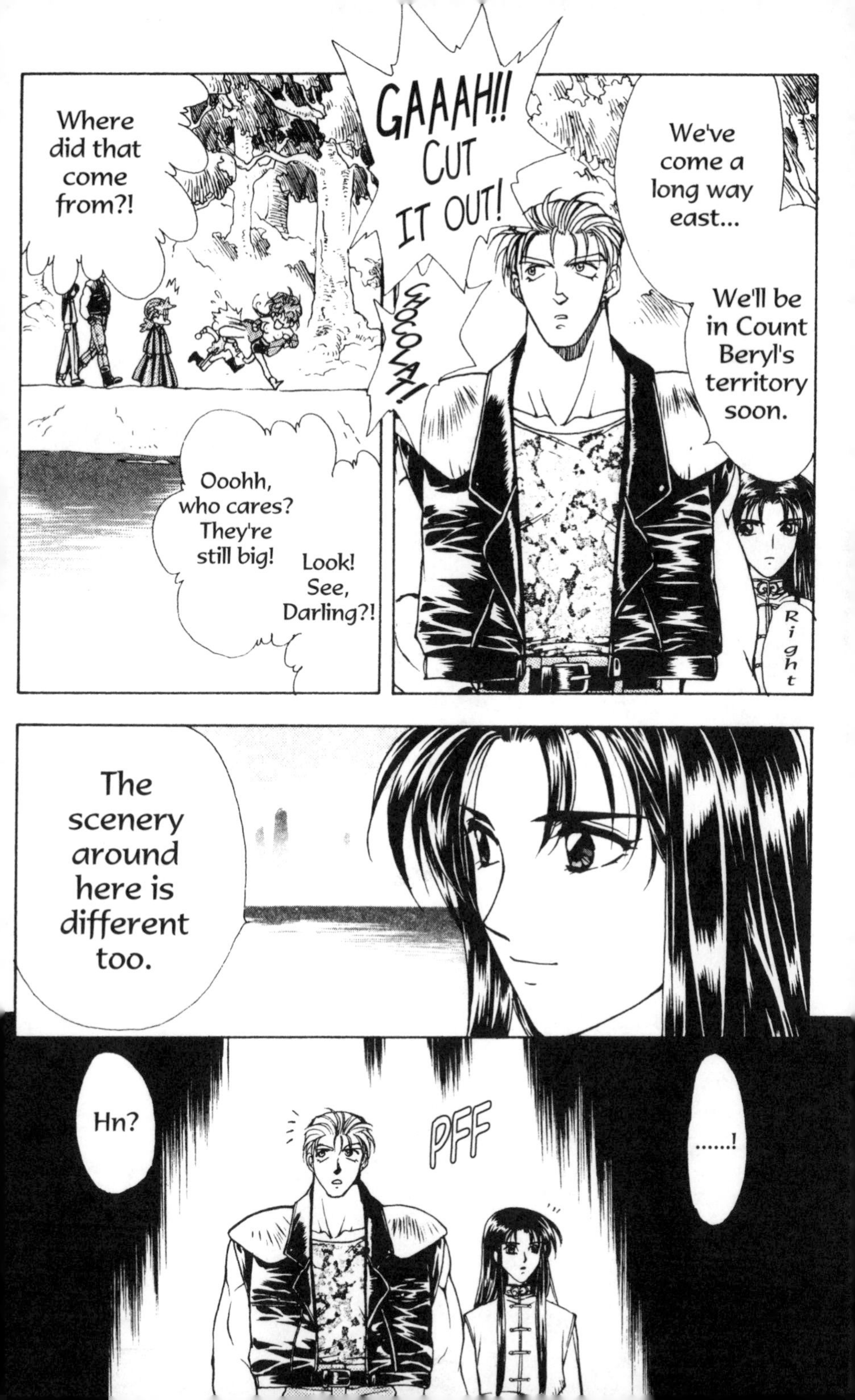
We've come a long way east...
We'll be in Count Beryl's territory soon.
Right
GAAAH!! CUT IT OUT! CHOCOLAT!
Where did that come from?!
Ooohh, who cares? They're still big!
Look! See, Darling?!
The scenery around here is different too.
......!
PFF
Hn?

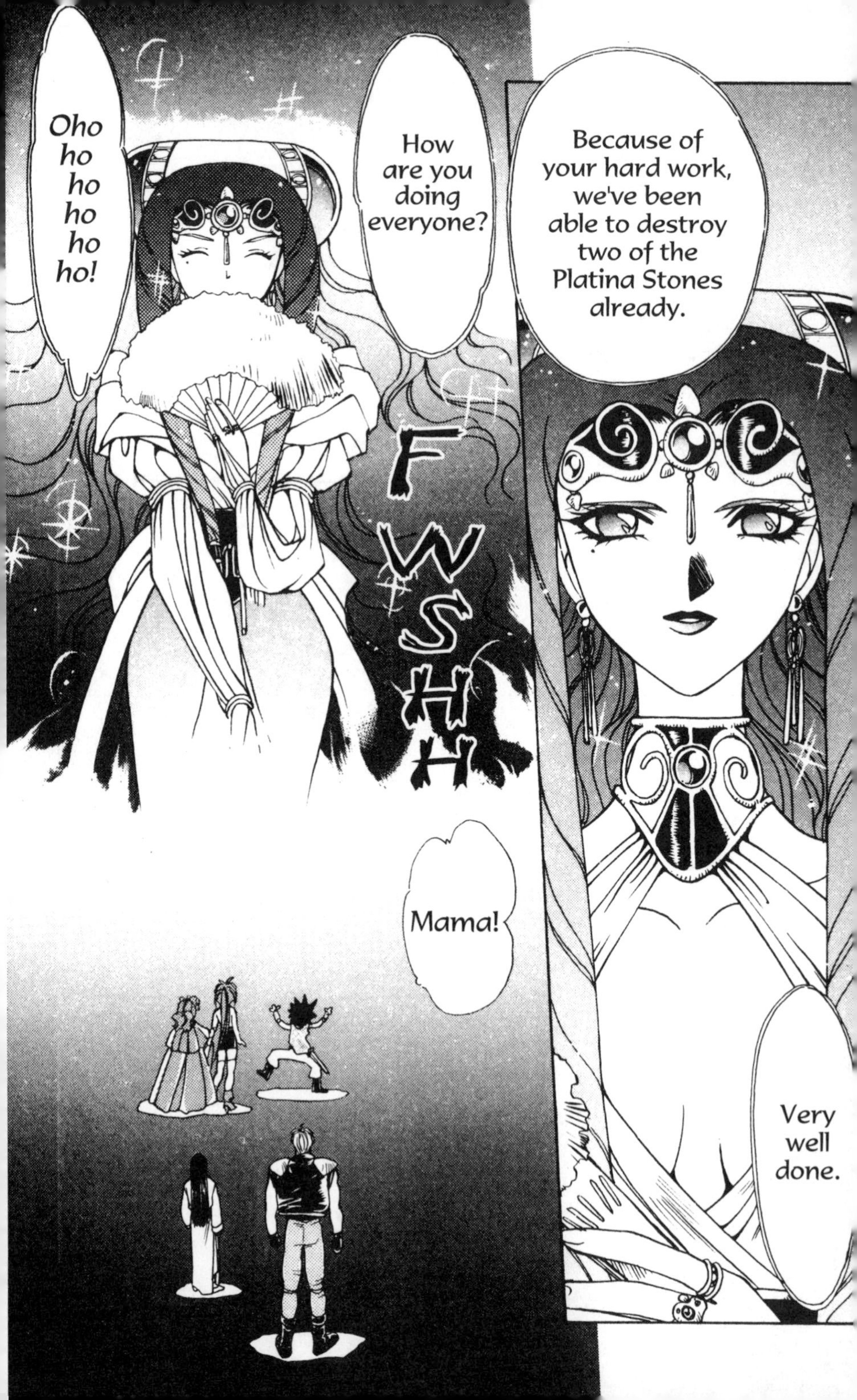
Oho ho ho ho ho ho ho!
How are you doing everyone?
FWSHH
Mama!
Because of your hard work, we've been able to destroy two of the Platina Stones already.
Very well done.

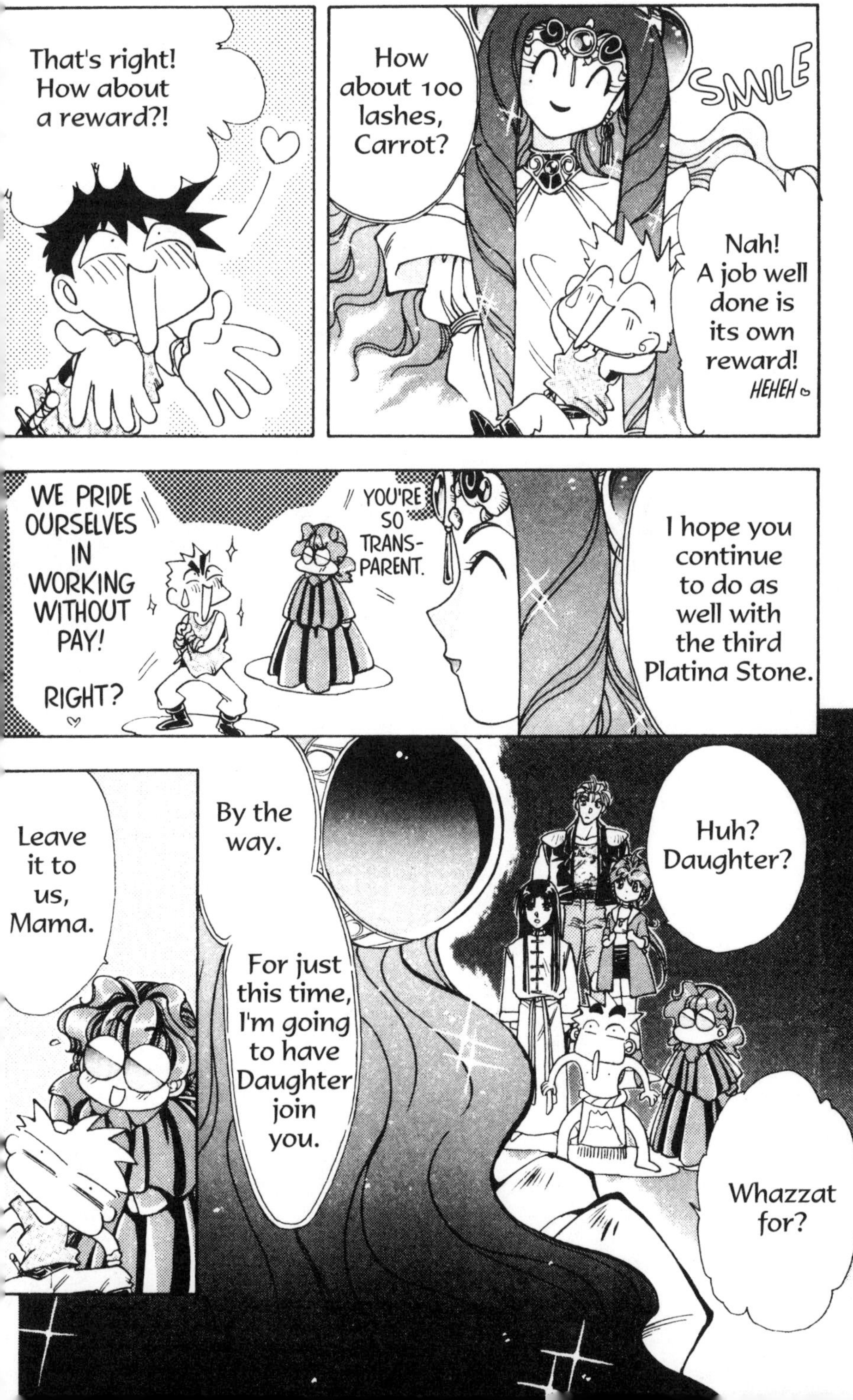
That's right! How about a reward?!
How about 100 lashes, Carrot?
SMILE
Nah! A job well done is its own reward!
HEHEH
WE PRIDE OURSELVES IN WORKING WITHOUT PAY!
RIGHT?
YOU'RE SO TRANS-PARENT.
I hope you continue to do as well with the third Platina Stone.
Leave it to us, Mama.
By the way.
For just this time, I'm going to have Daughter join you.
Huh? Daughter?
Whazzat for?

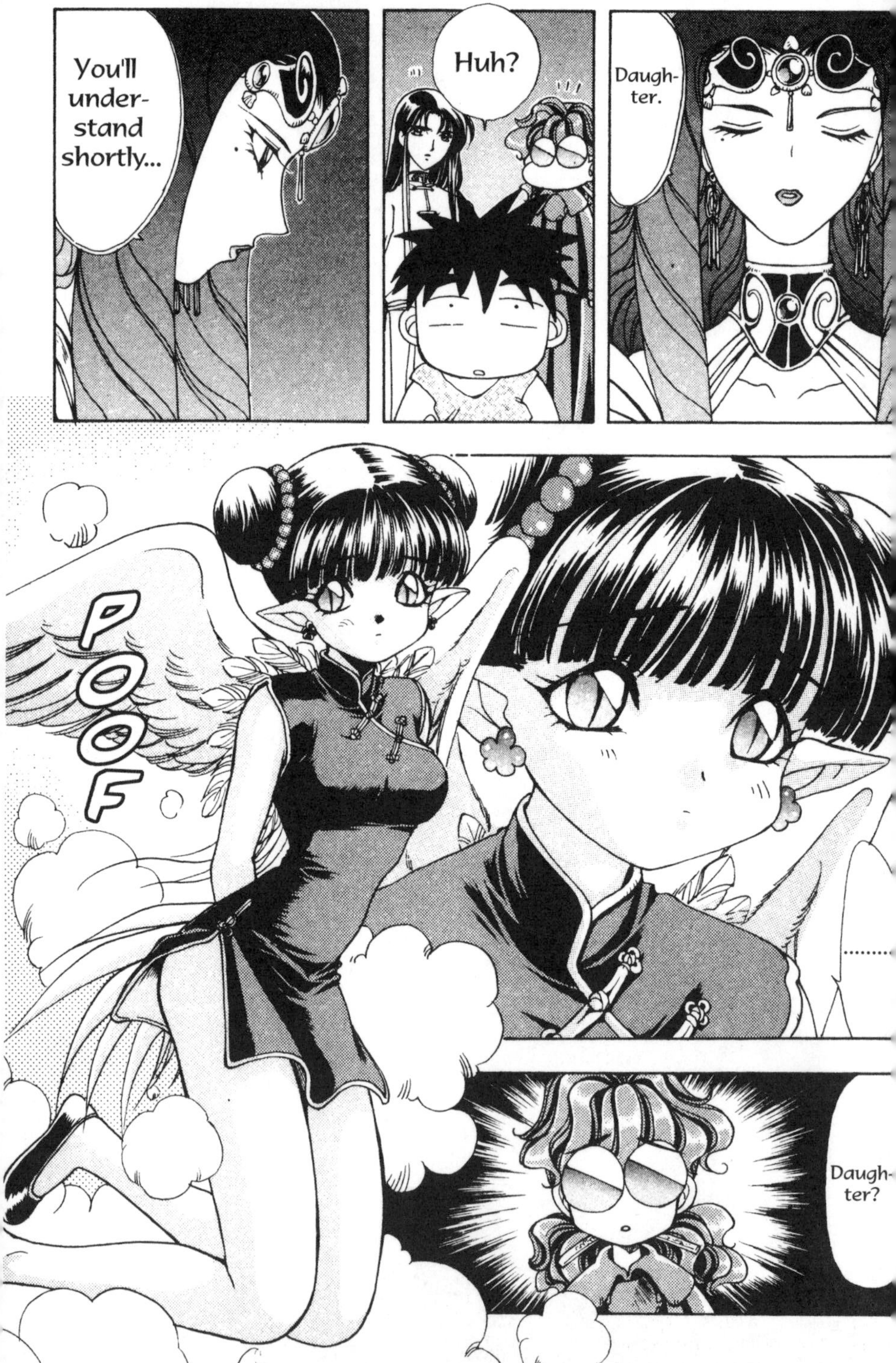

Daughter.
Huh?
You'll understand shortly...
......
Daughter?
POOF

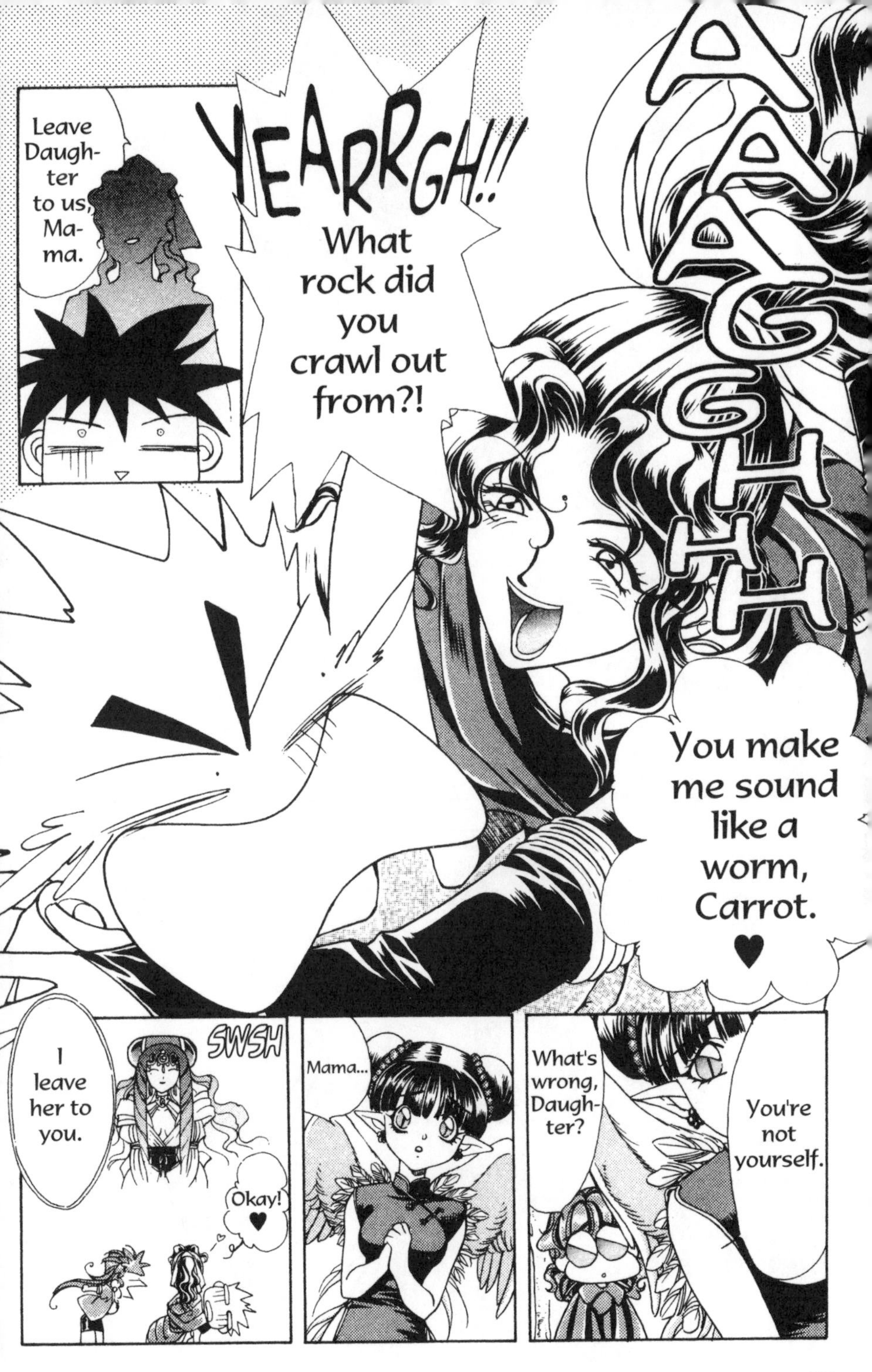
Leave Daughter to us, Mama.
YEARRGH!!
What rock did you crawl out from?!
AAAGGHHHH
You make me sound like a worm, Carrot. ♥
I leave her to you.
SWSH
Okay! ♥
Mama...
What's wrong, Daughter?
You're not yourself.

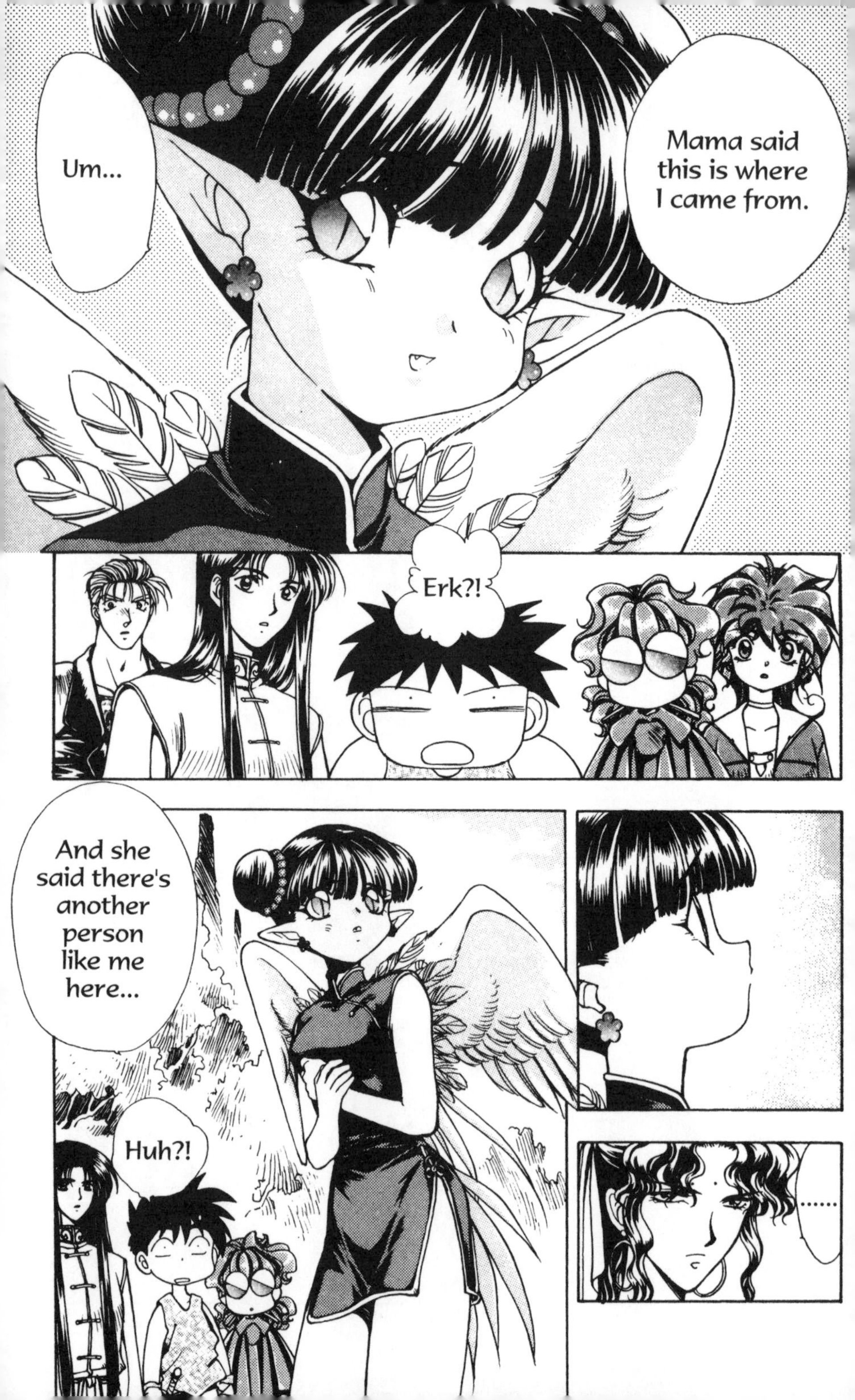
Um...
Mama said this is where I came from.
Erk?!
And she said there's another person like me here...
Huh?!
......

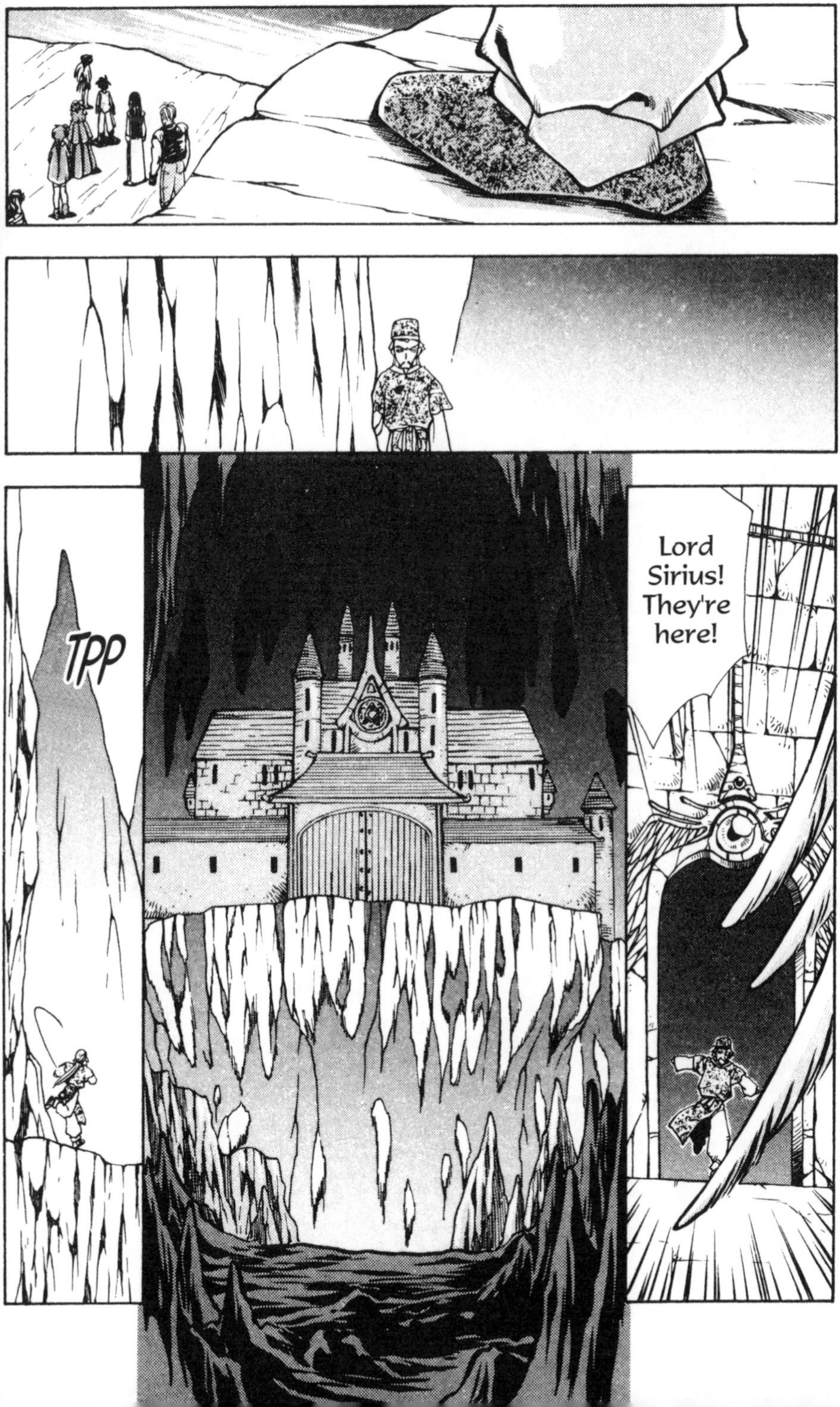
Lord Sirius! They're here!
TPP

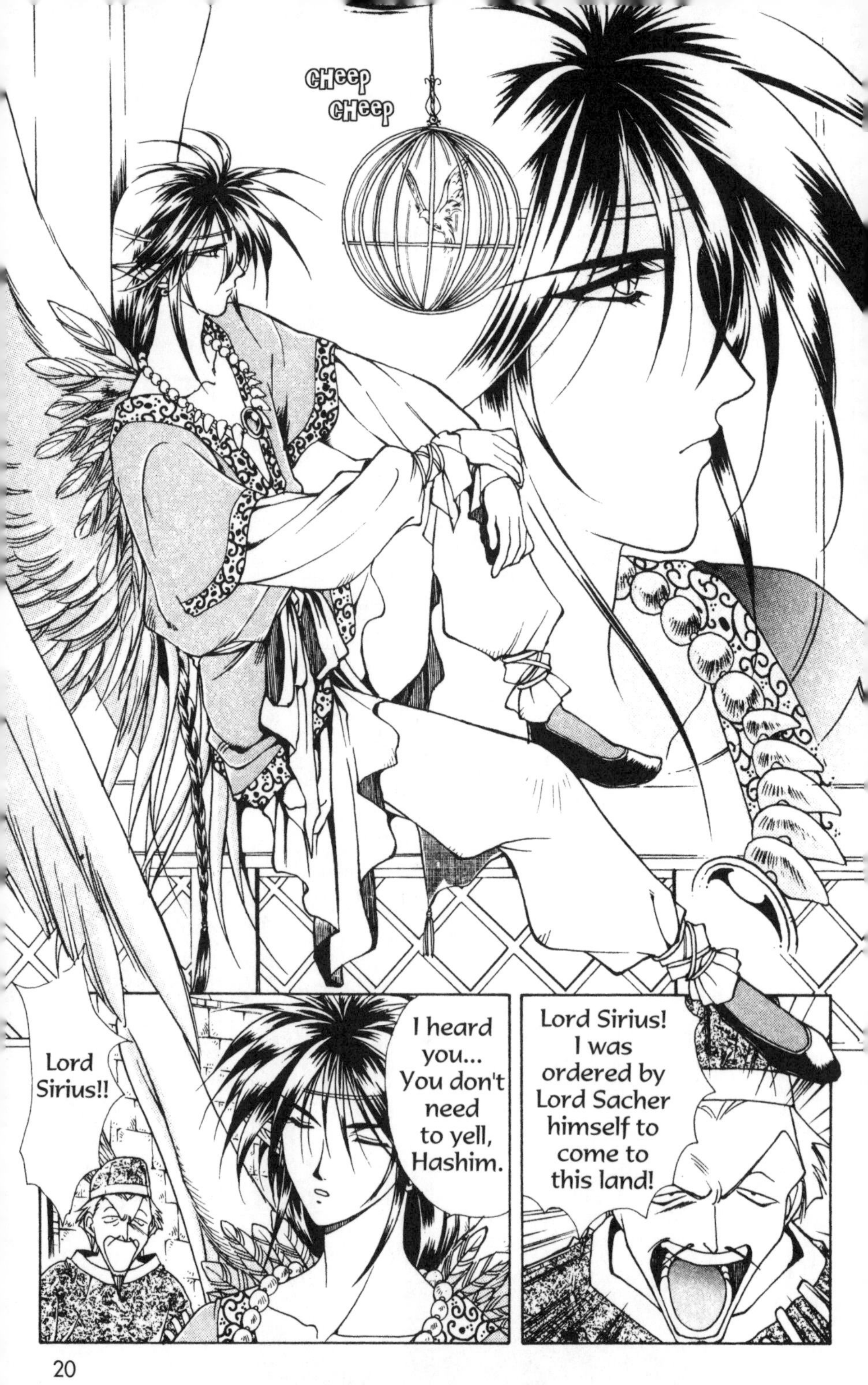
CHEEP CHEEP
Lord Sirius!!
I heard you... You don't need to yell, Hashim.
Lord Sirius! I was ordered by Lord Sacher himself to come to this land!

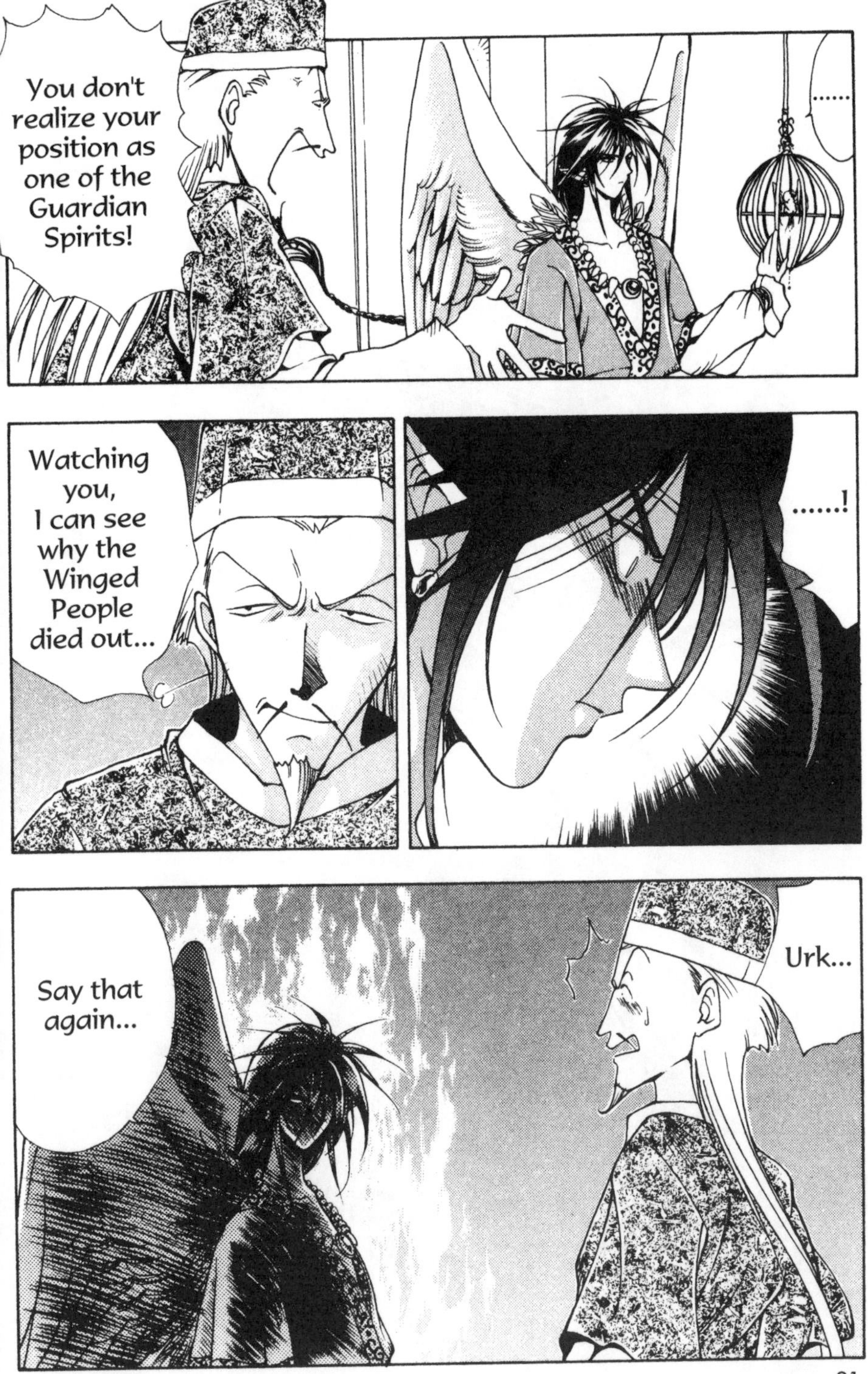
You don't realize your position as one of the Guardian Spirits!
......
Watching you, I can see why the Winged People died out...
......!
Say that again...
Urk...

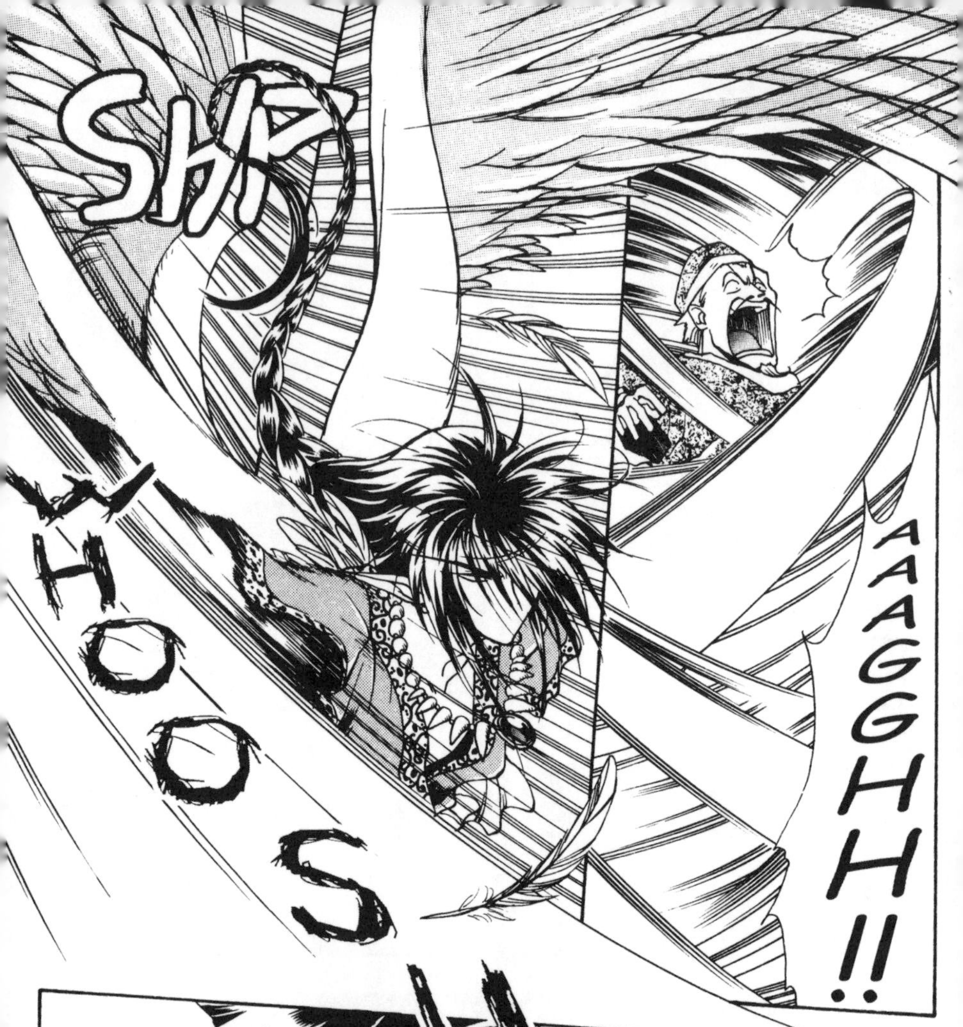
SHP
WHOOSH
AAAAGGHHH!!
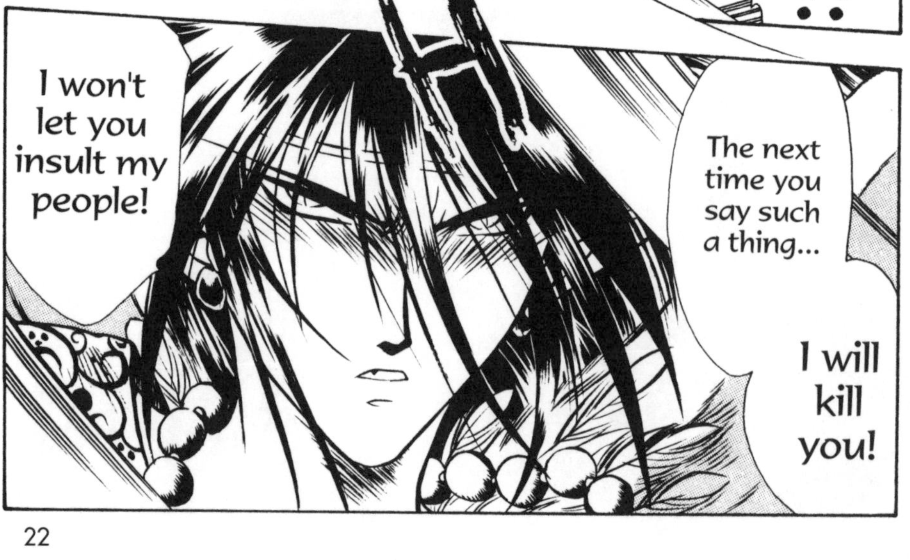
The next time you say such a thing...
I will kill you!
I won't let you insult my people!

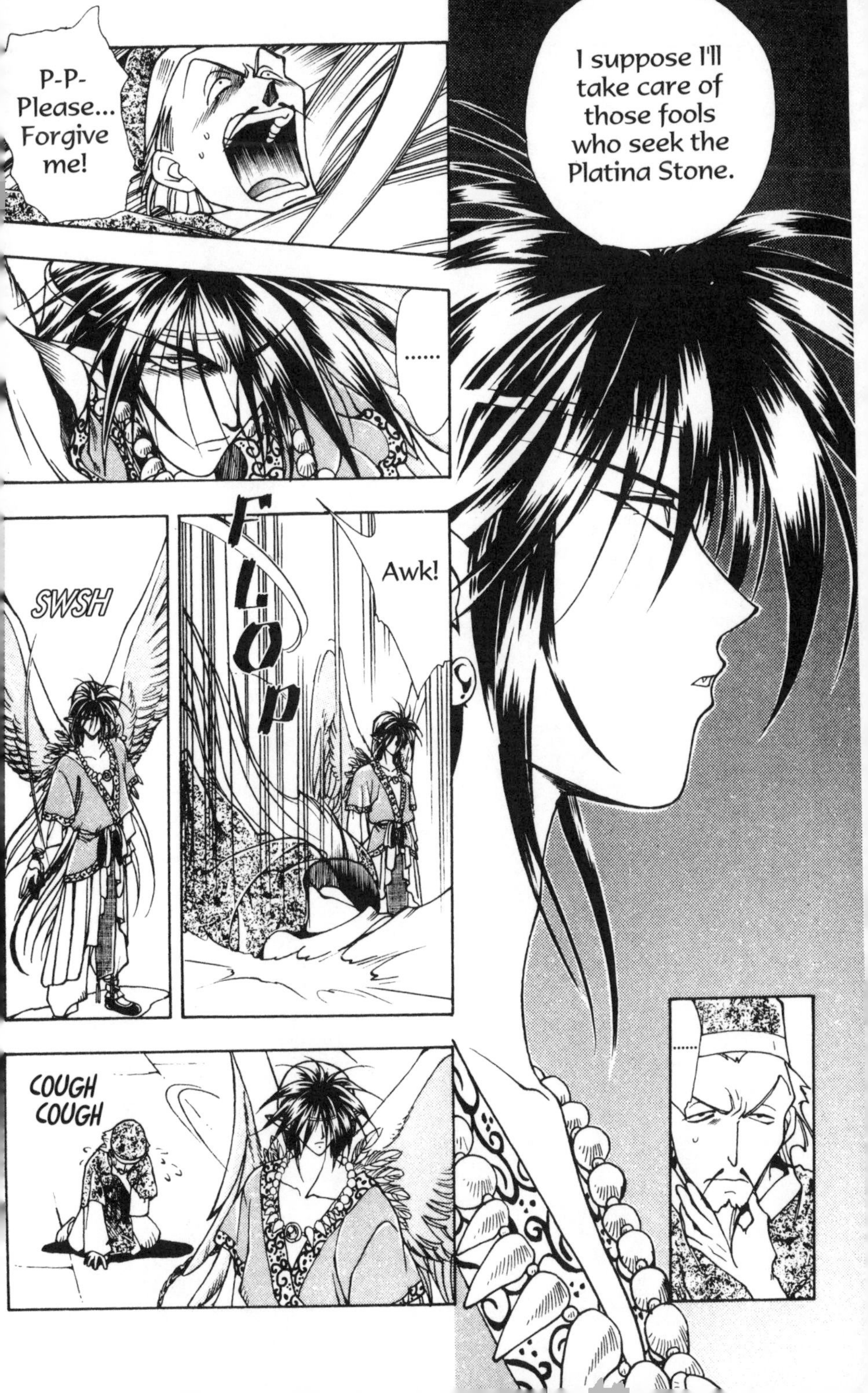
I suppose I'll take care of those fools who seek the Platina Stone.
P-P-Please... Forgive me!
......
Awk!
FLOP
SWSH
......
COUGH COUGH

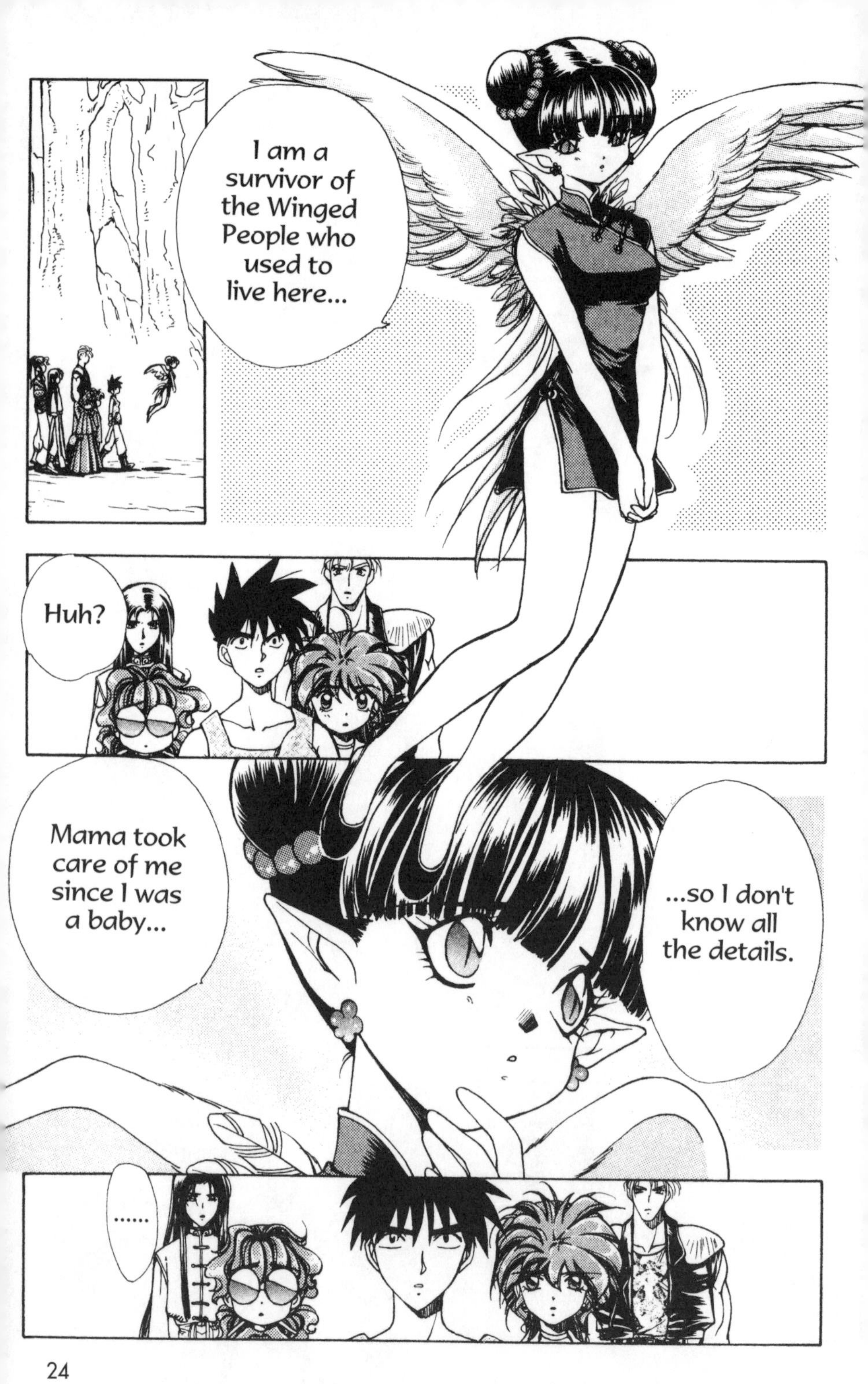
I am a survivor of the Winged People who used to live here...
Huh?
Mama took care of me since I was a baby...
...so I don't know all the details.
......

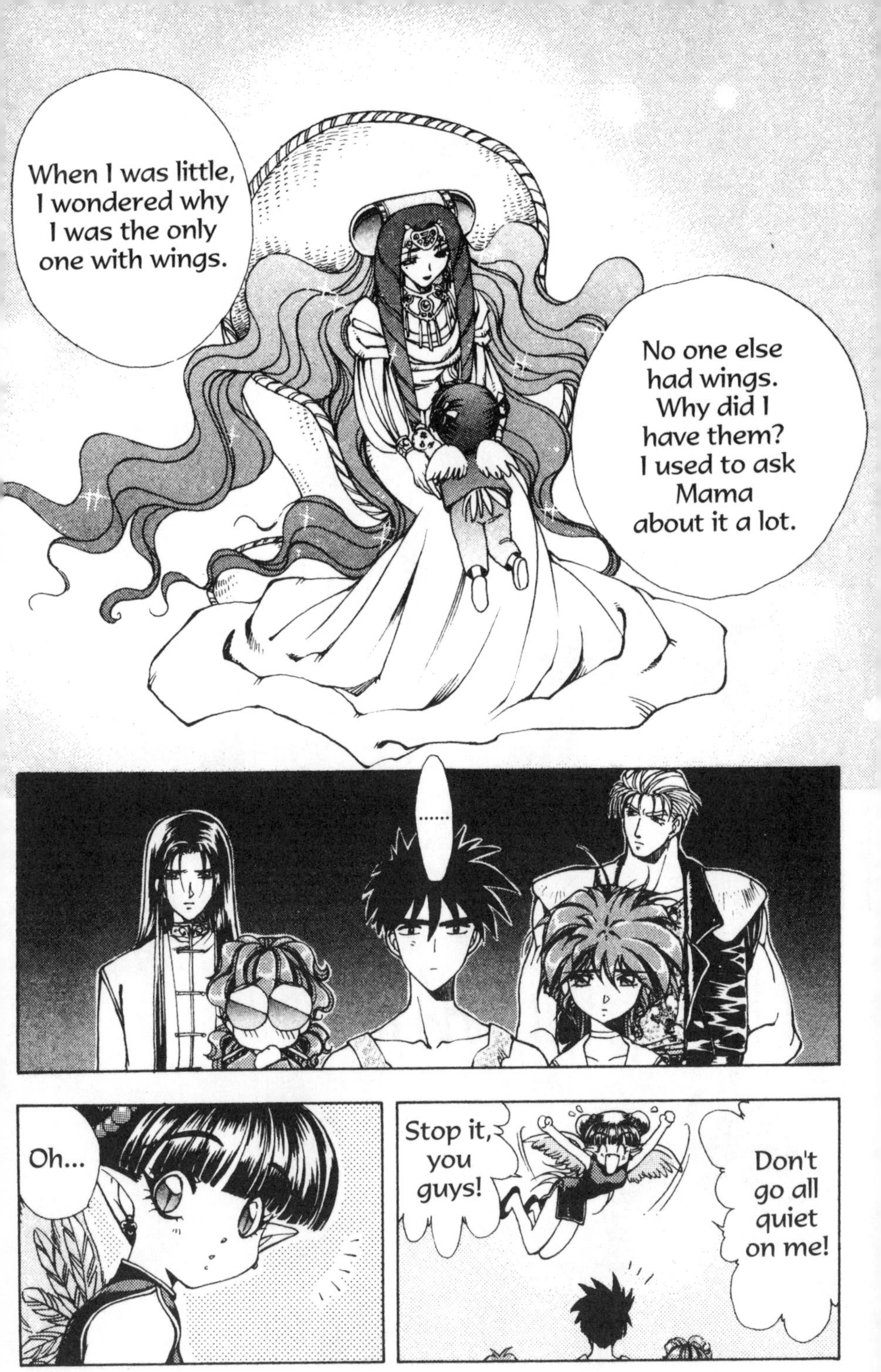
When I was little, I wondered why I was the only one with wings.
No one else had wings. Why did I have them? I used to ask Mama about it a lot.
......
Stop it, you guys!
Don't go all quiet on me!
Oh...

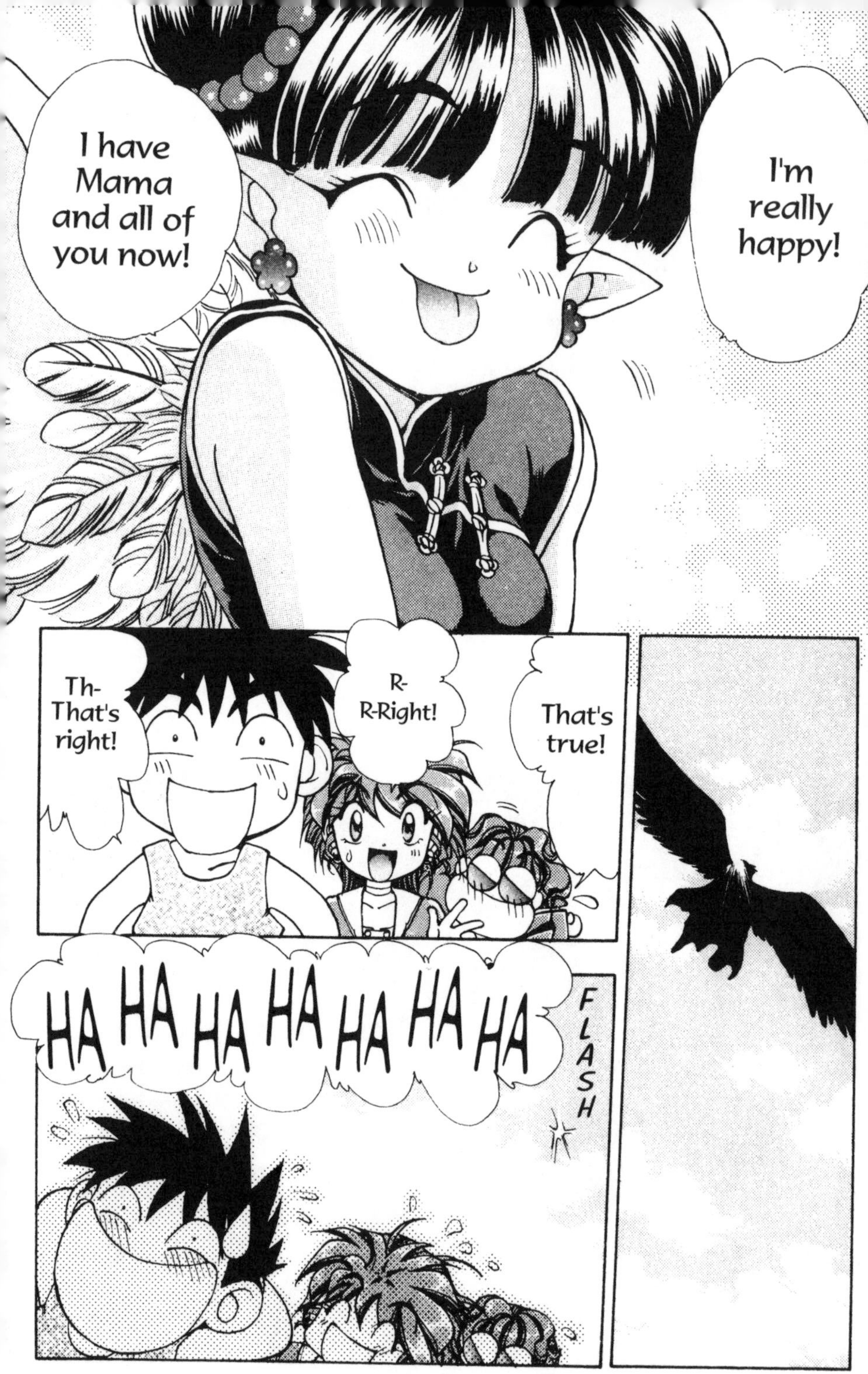
I'm really happy!
I have Mama and all of you now!
That's true!
R- R-Right!
Th- That's right!
HA HA HA HA HA HA HA
FLASH

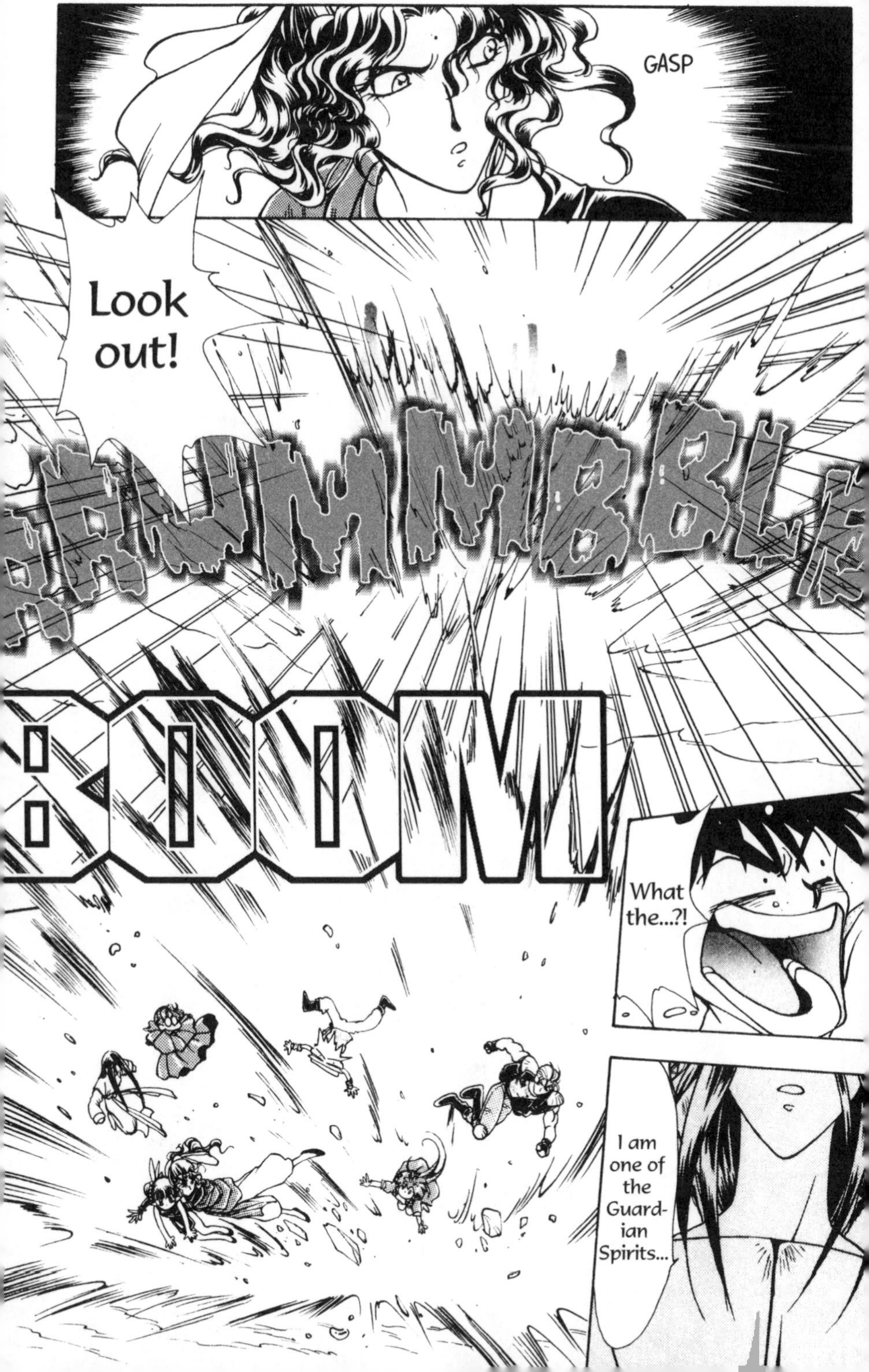
GASP
Look out!
RUMMBLE
BOOM
What the...?!
I am one of the Guardian Spirits...

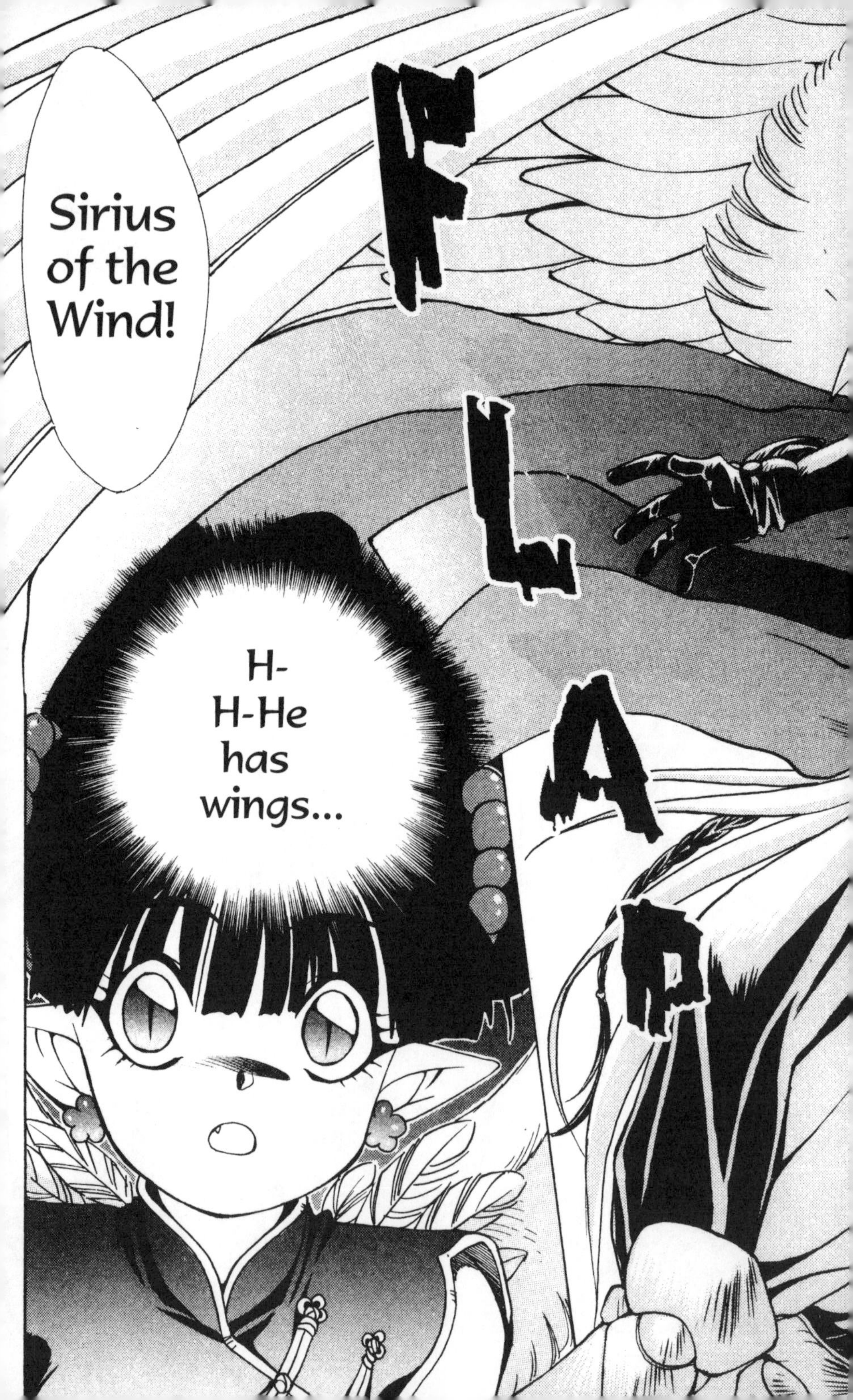
FLAP
Sirius of the Wind!
H- H-He has wings...

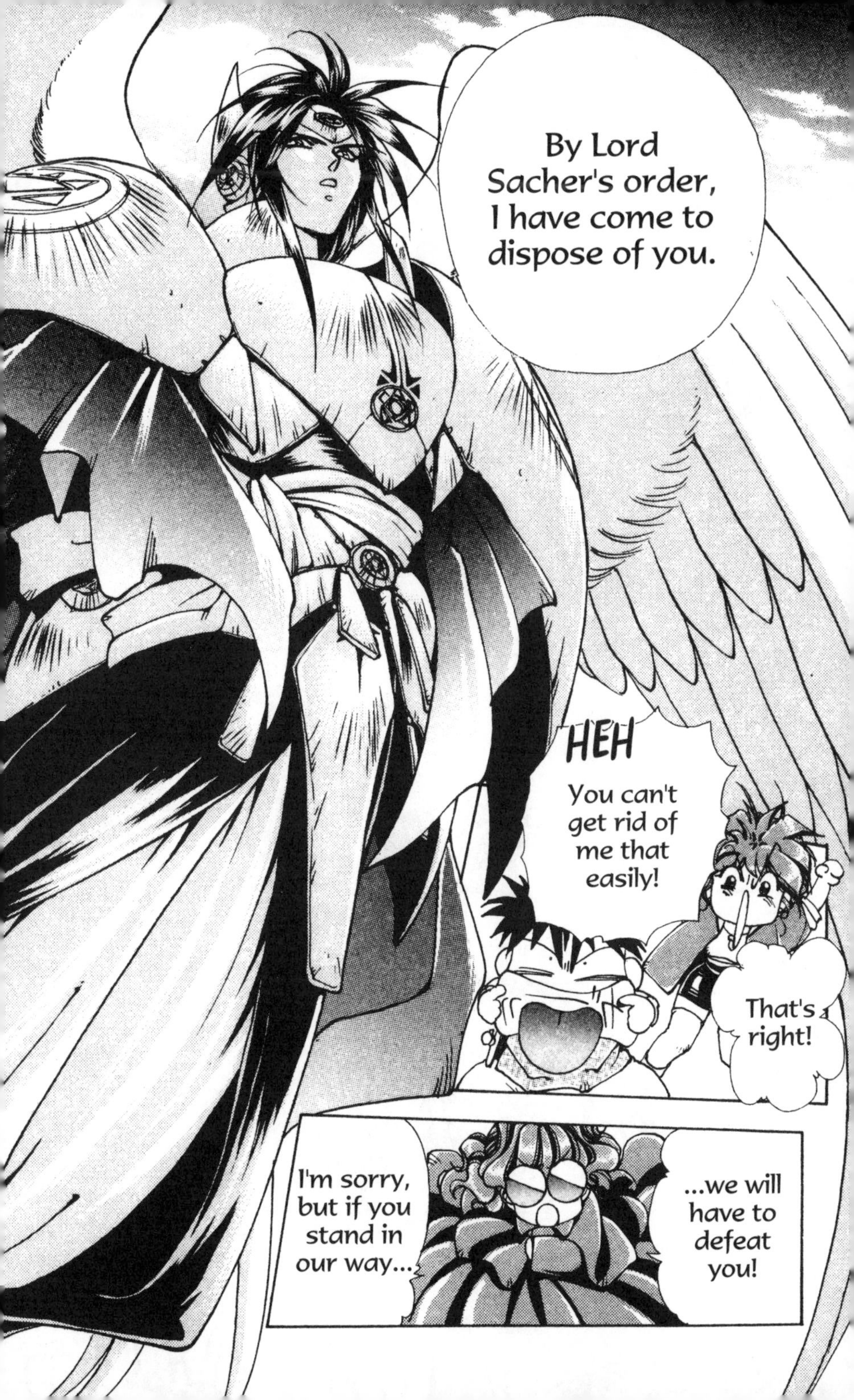
By Lord Sacher's order, I have come to dispose of you.
HEH
You can't get rid of me that easily!
That's right!
I'm sorry, but if you stand in our way...
...we will have to defeat you!

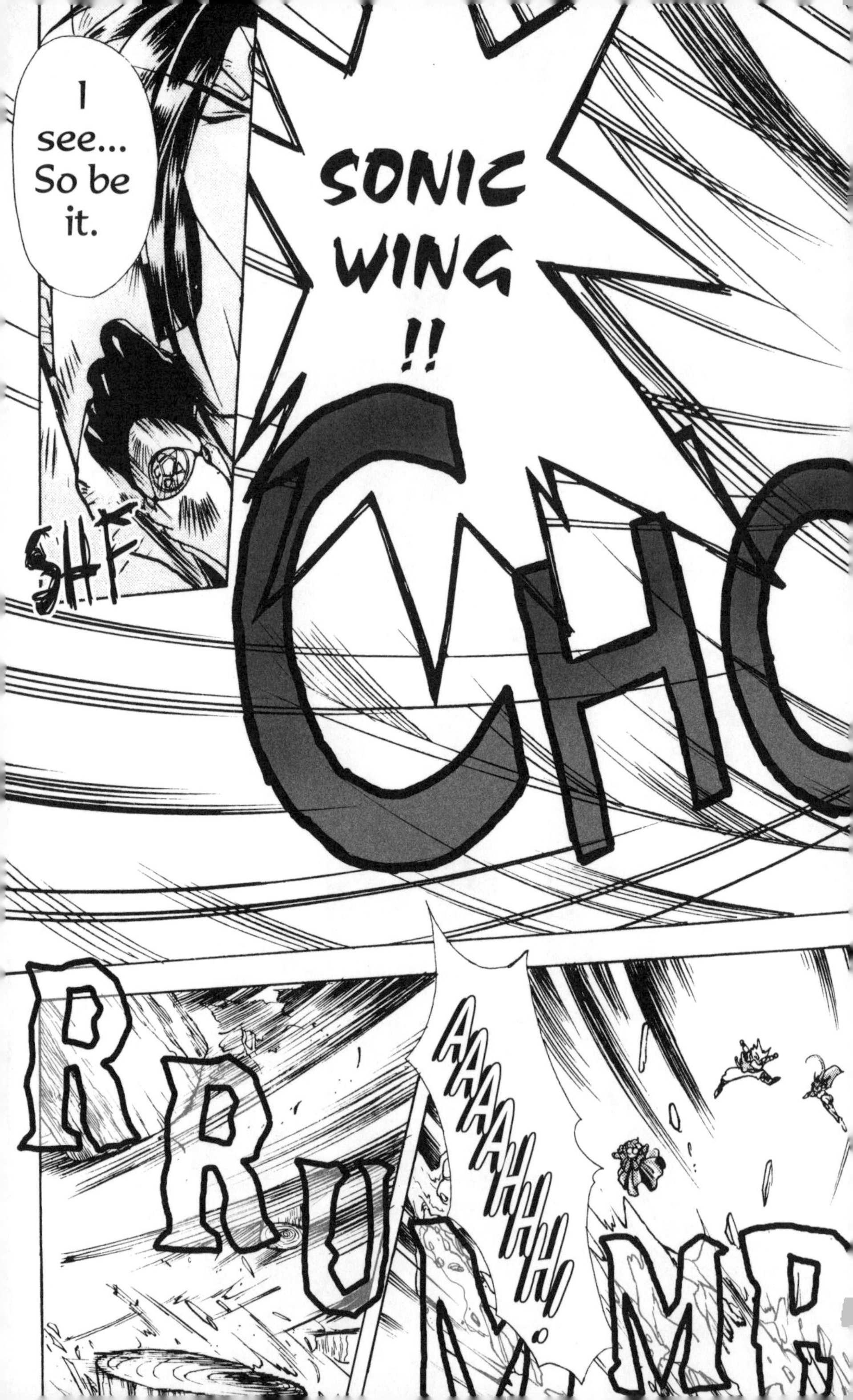
SONIC WING !!
I see... So be it.
SHF
CHO
AAAAHHH
RRUMB

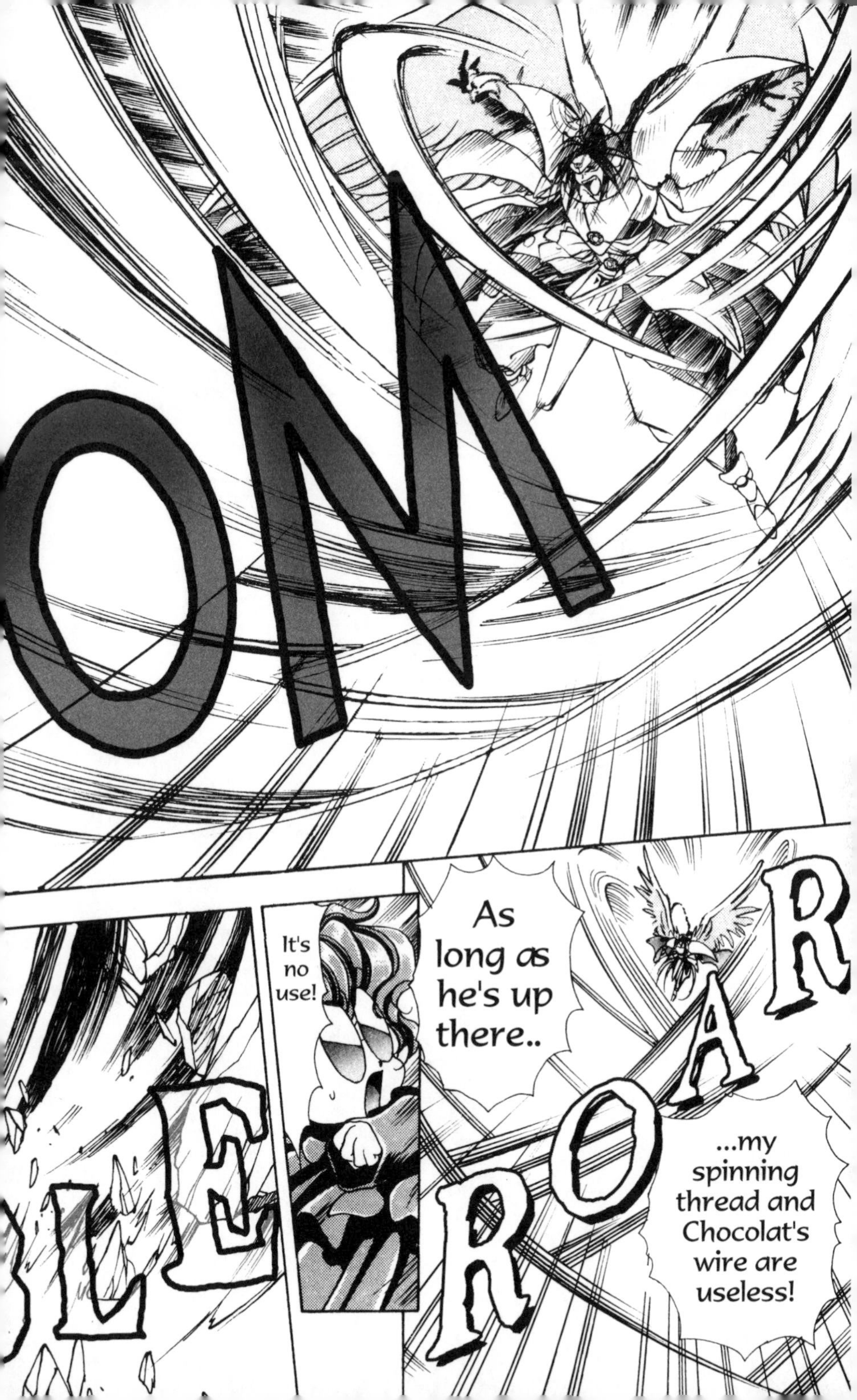
OM
As long as he's up there..
...my spinning thread and Chocolat's wire are useless!
ROAR
It's no use!
LE

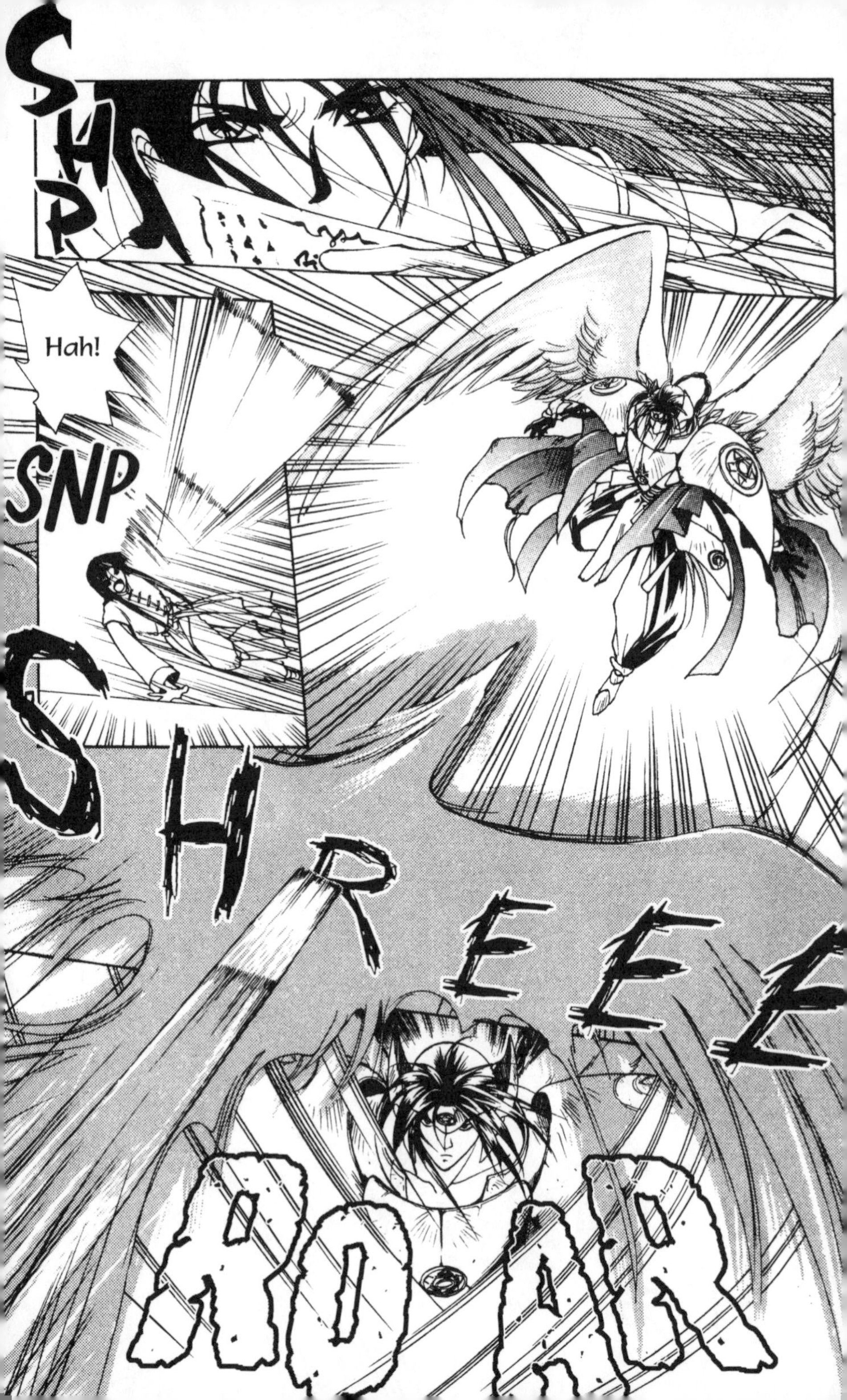
SHP
Hah!
SNP
SHREEE
ROAR

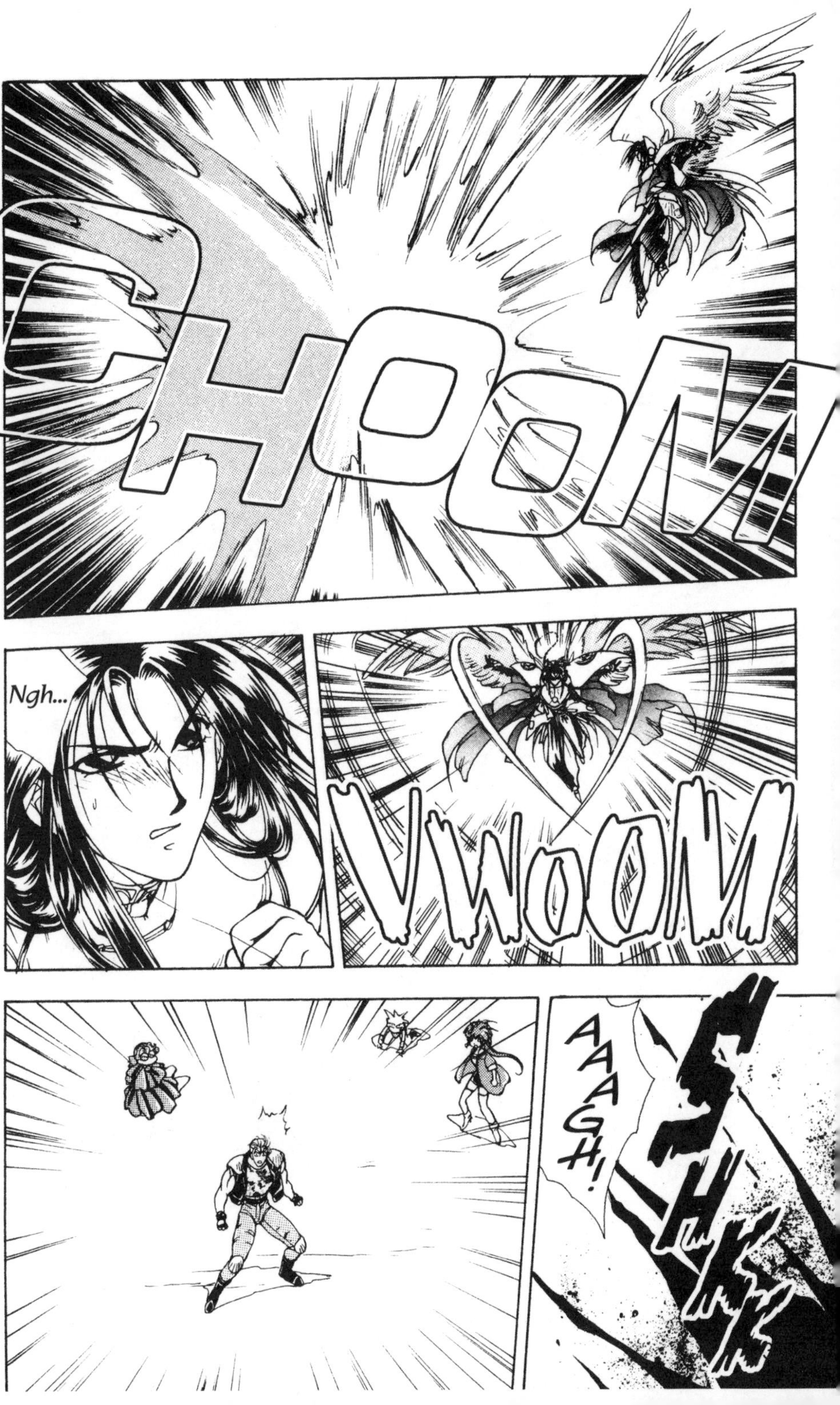
CHOOM
VWOOM
Ngh...
AAAAGH!

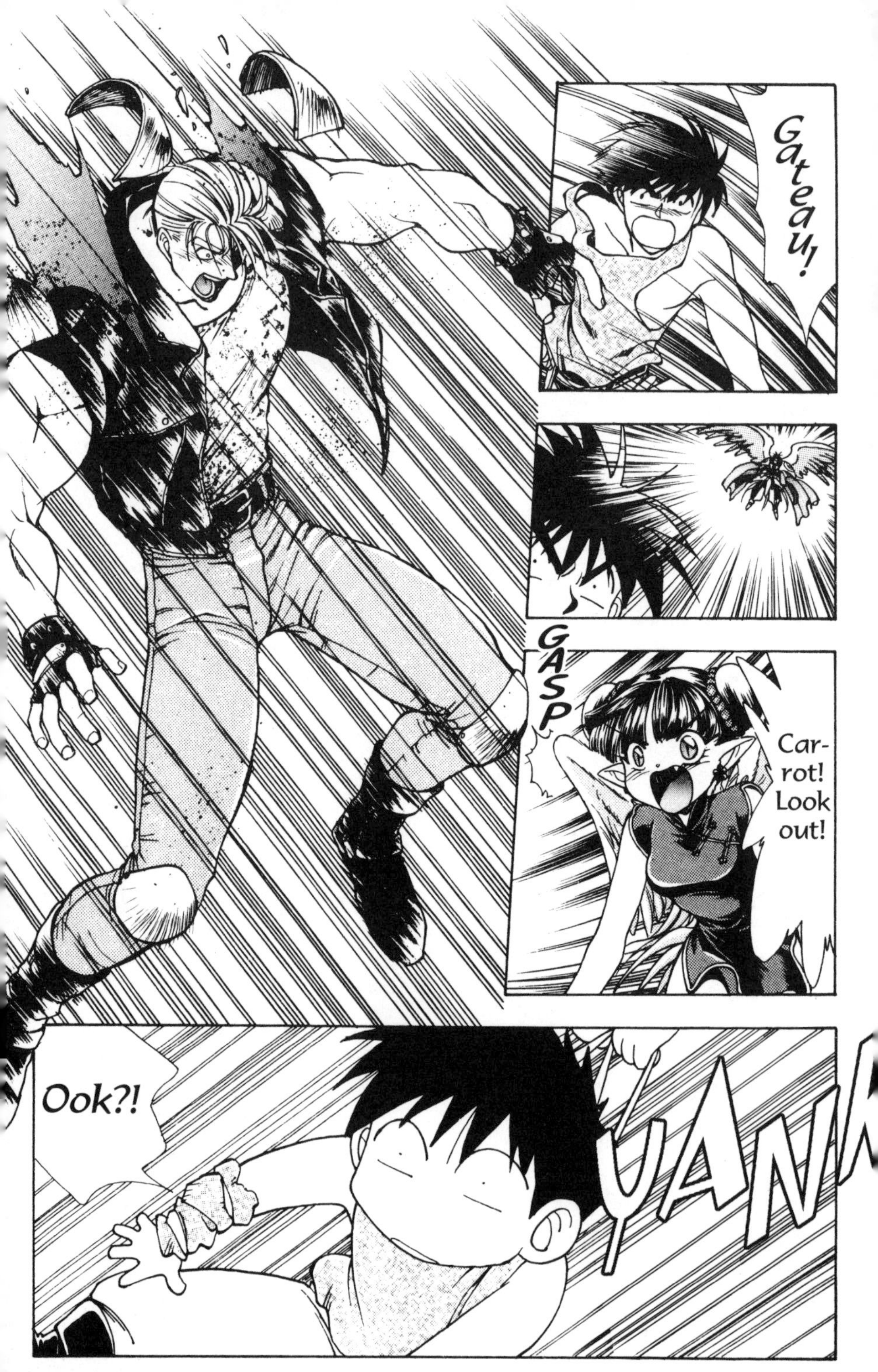
Gateau!
GASP
Carrot! Look out!
Ook?!
YANN

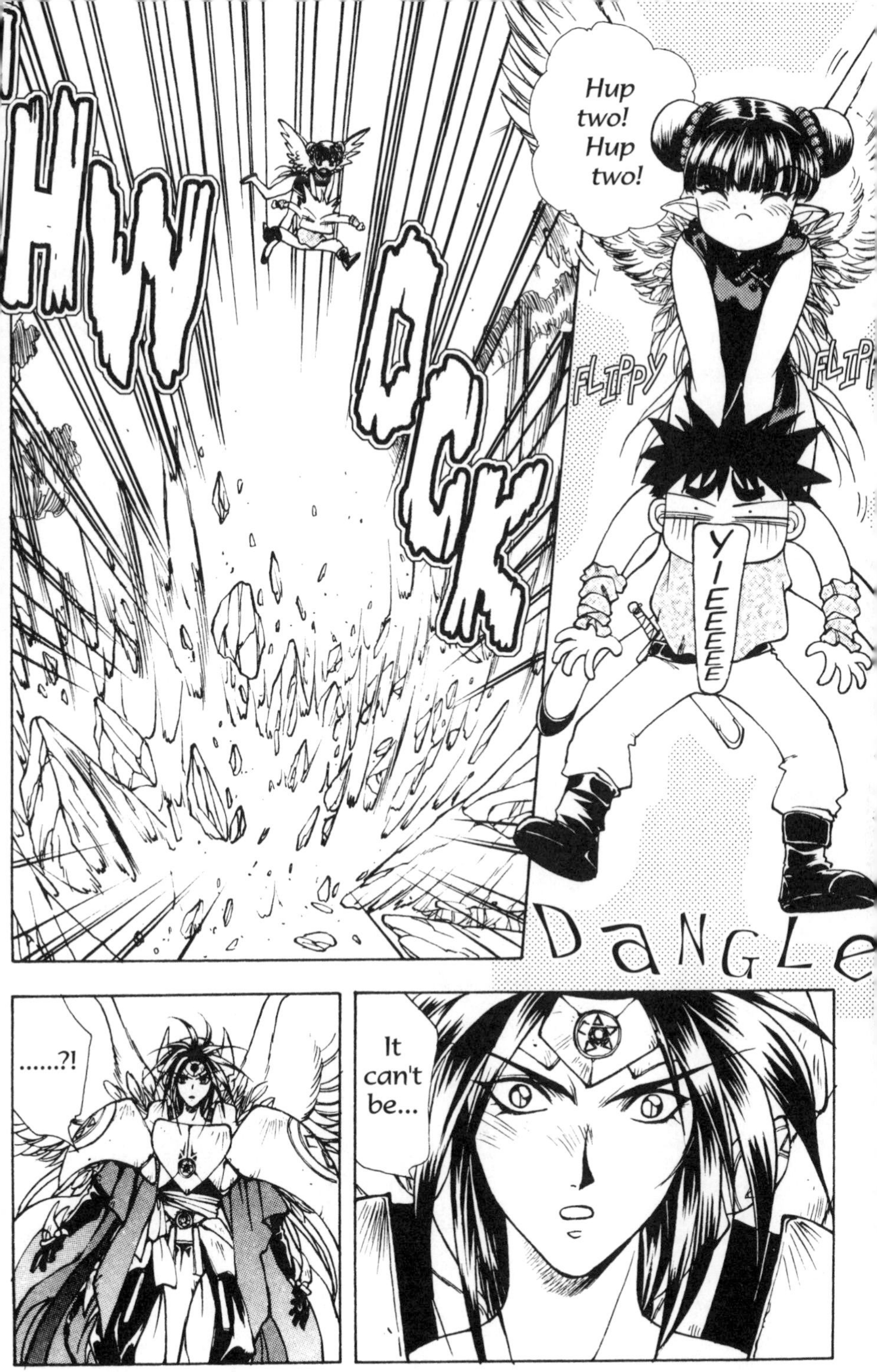
Hup two! Hup two!
FLIPPY
FLIPP
YIEEEEEE
DANGLE
HWOCK
It can't be...
......?!

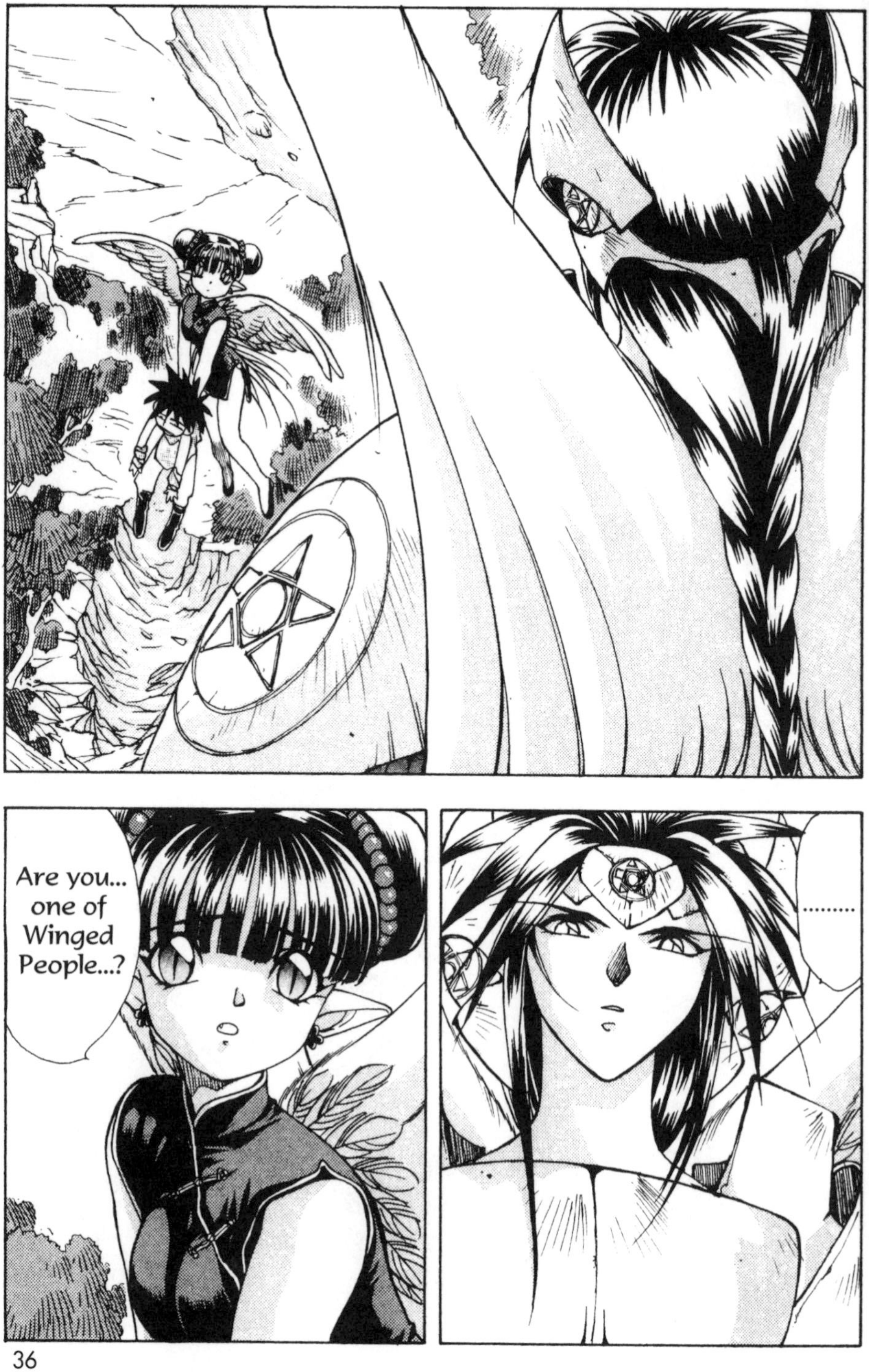
Are you... one of Winged People...?
....

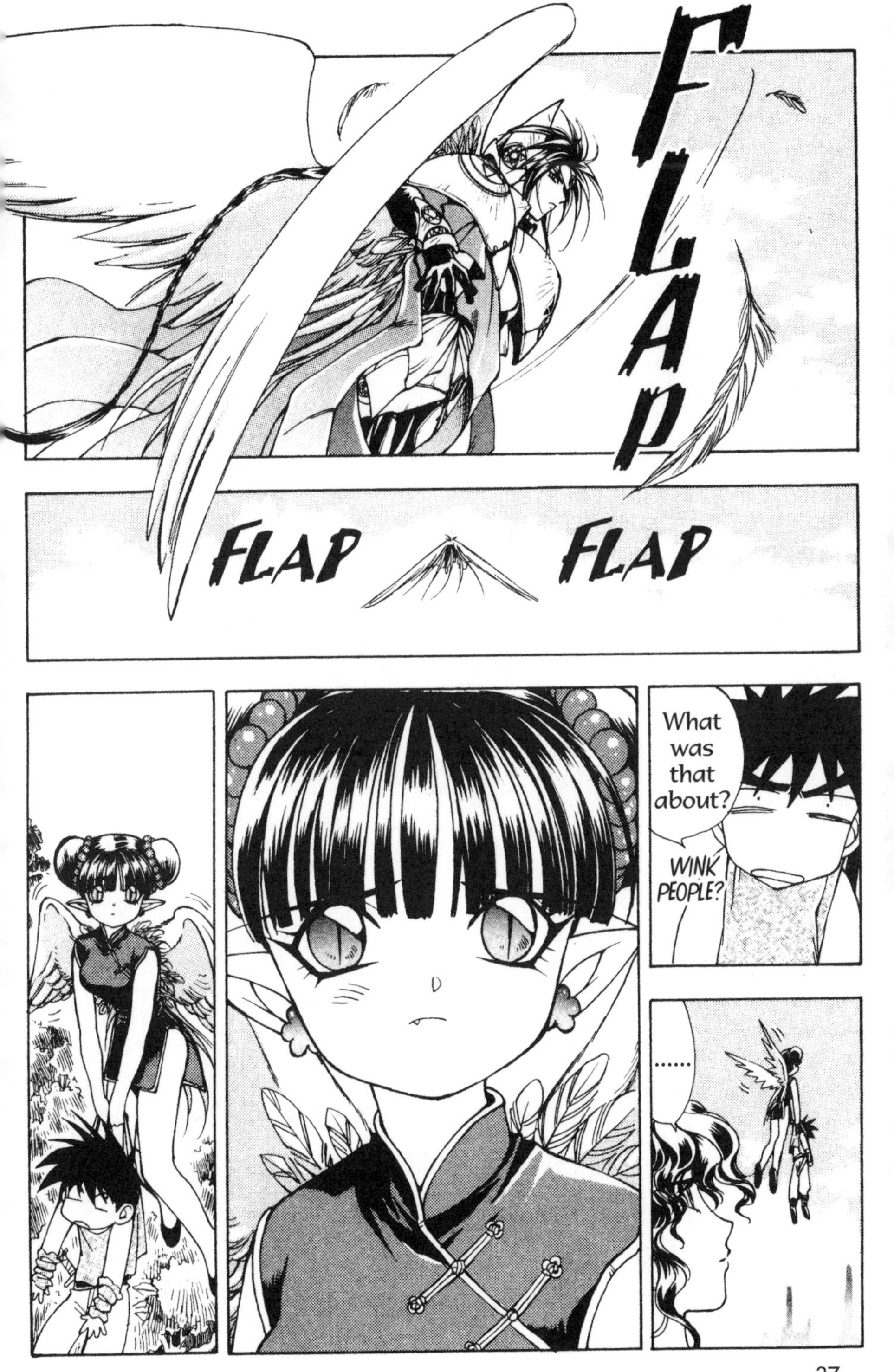
FLAP
FLAP
FLAP
What was that about?
WINK PEOPLE?
......

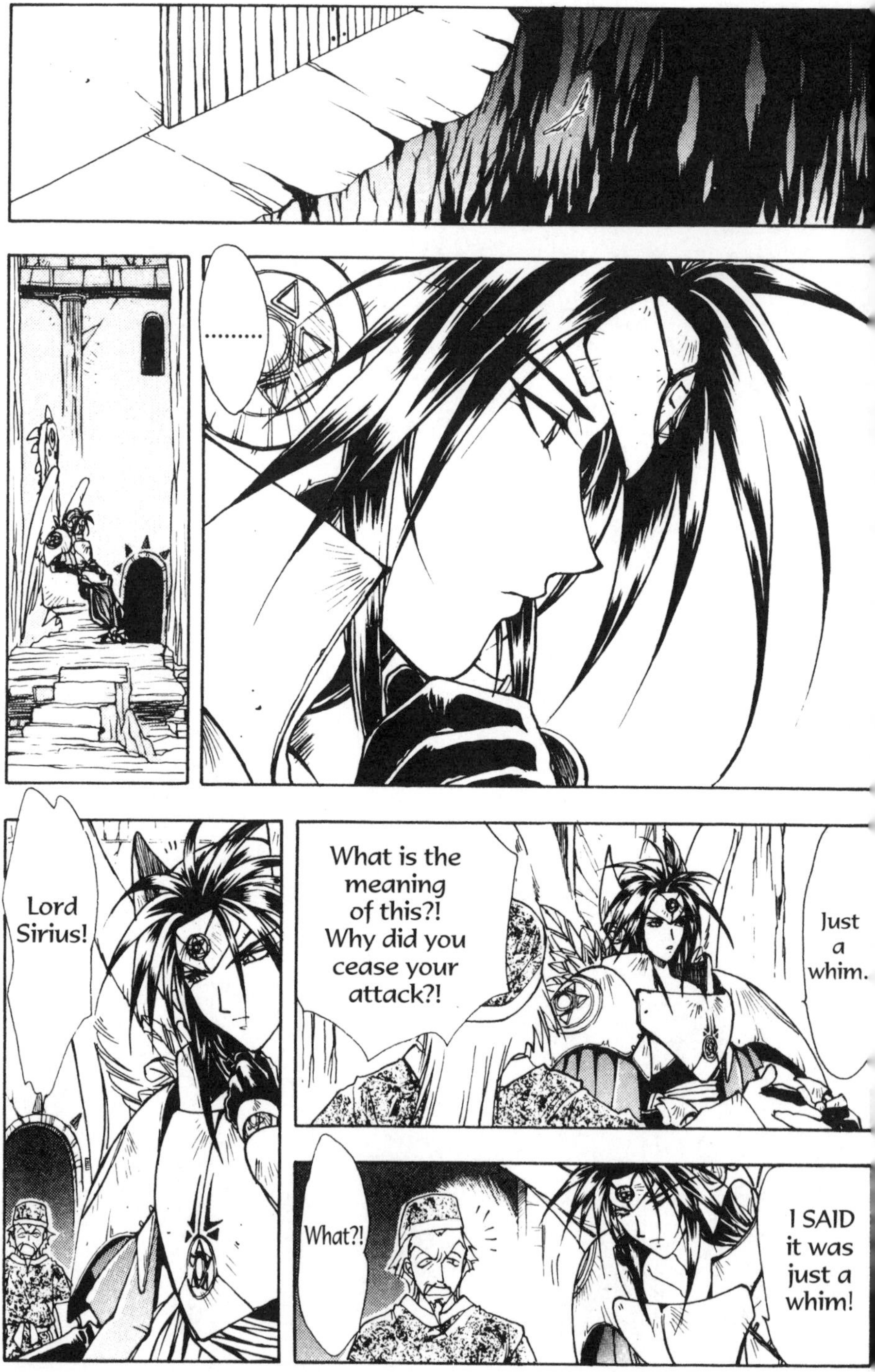

....
Lord Sirius!
What is the meaning of this?! Why did you cease your attack?!
Just a whim.
What?!
I SAID it was just a whim!

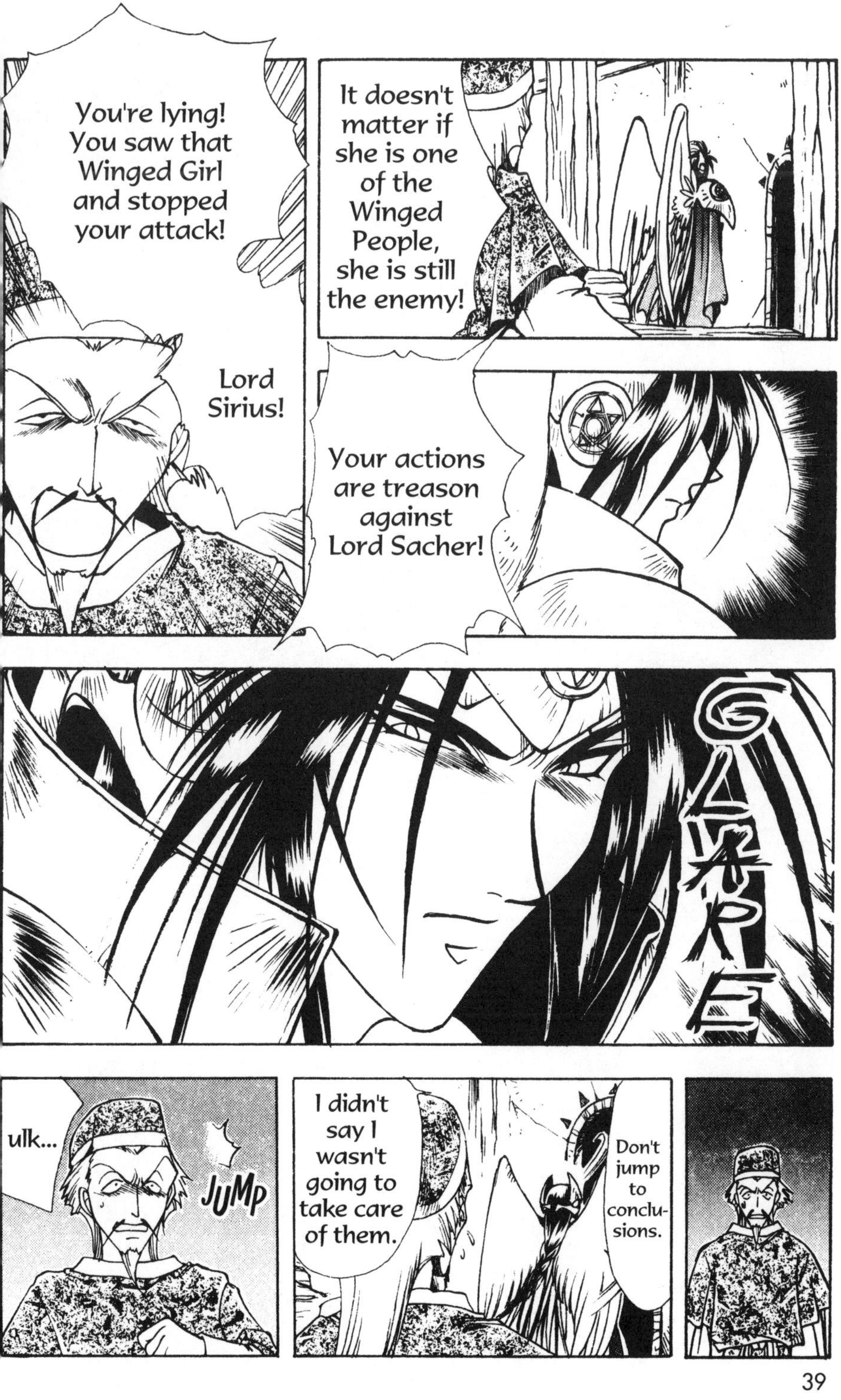
It doesn't matter if she is one of the Winged People, she is still the enemy!
Your actions are treason against Lord Sacher!
You're lying! You saw that Winged Girl and stopped your attack!
Lord Sirius!
GARARI
I didn't say I wasn't going to take care of them.
Don't jump to conclusions.
ulk...
JUMP

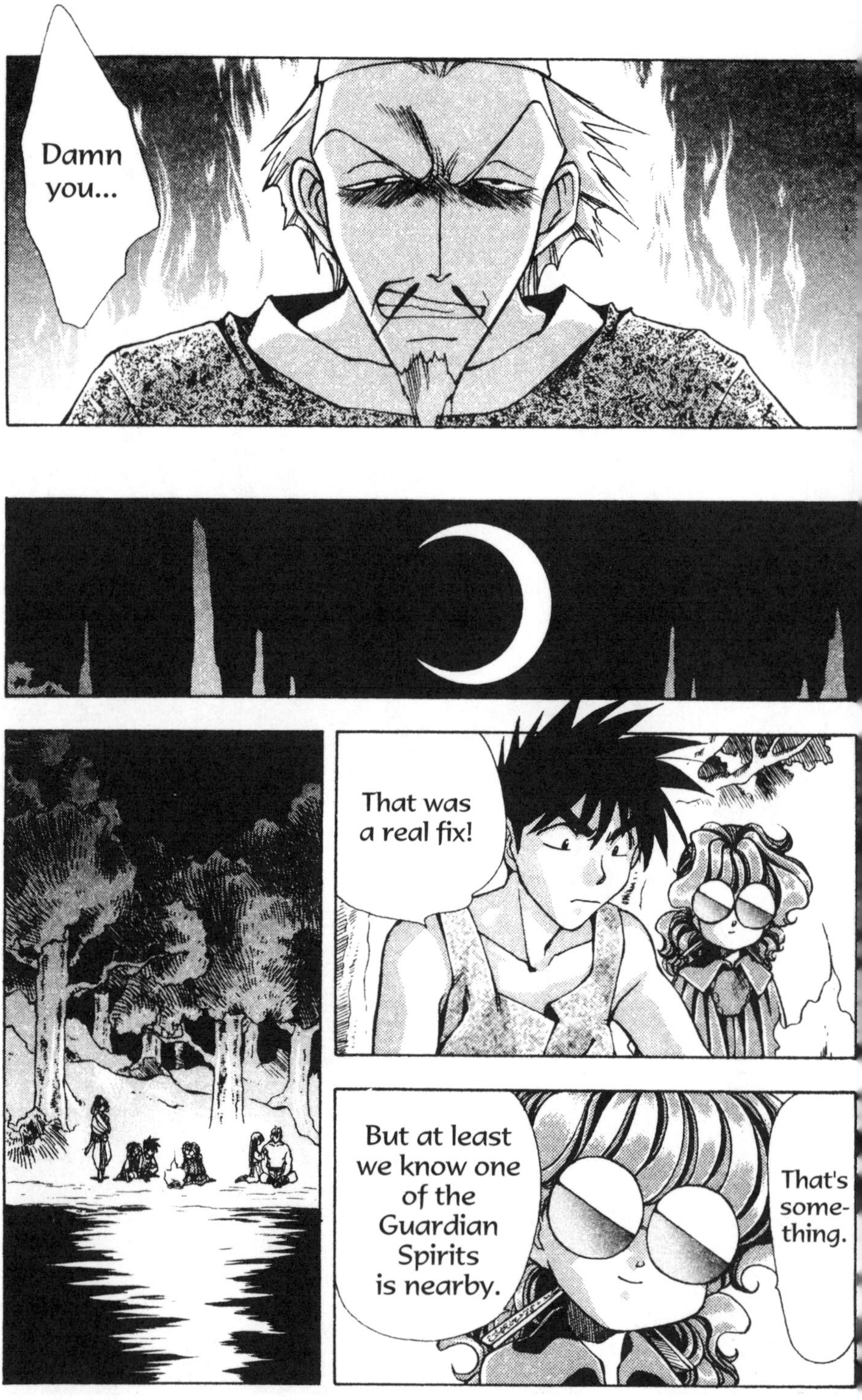
Damn you...
That was a real fix!
But at least we know one of the Guardian Spirits is nearby.
That's some-thing.

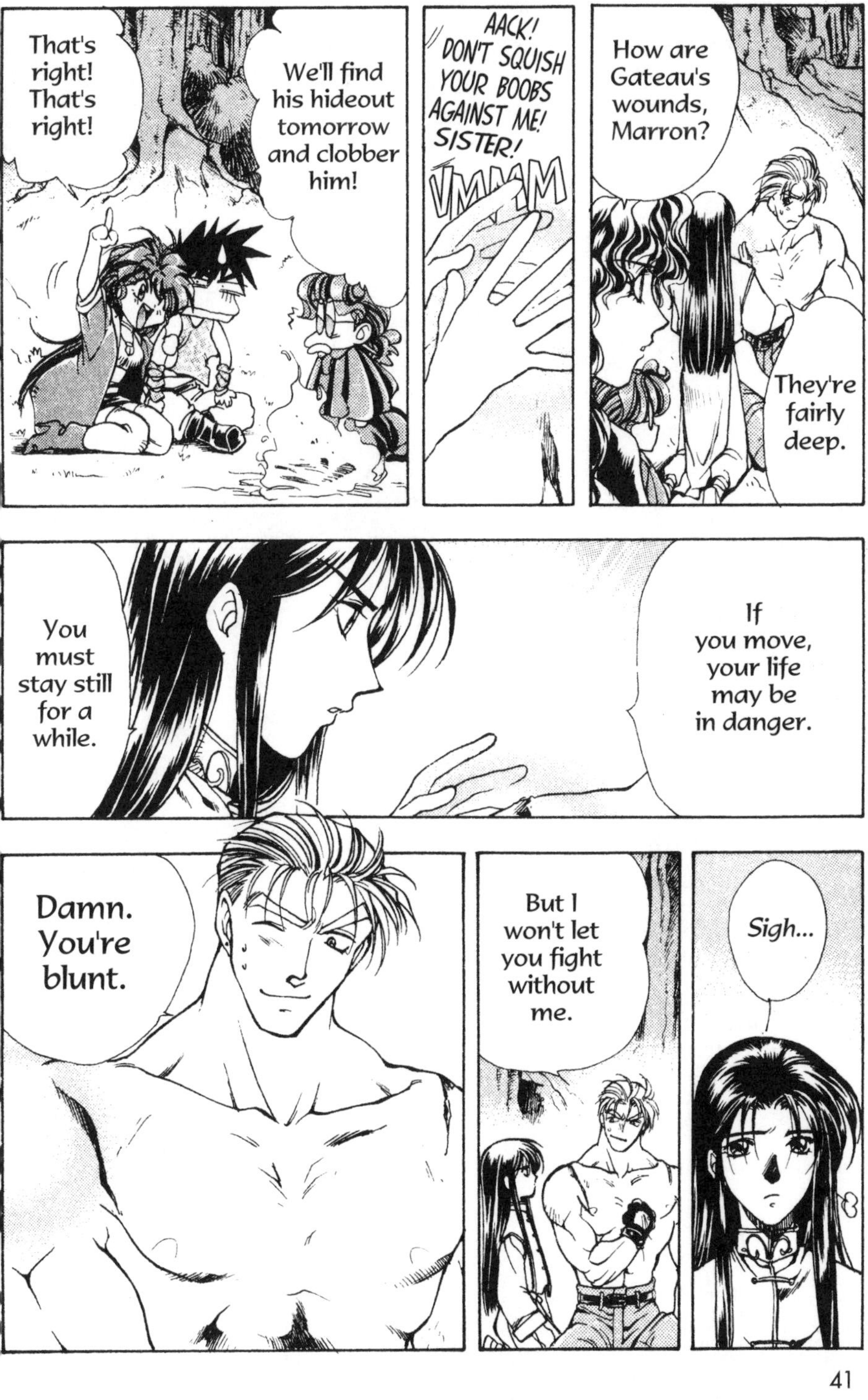
We'll find his hideout tomorrow and clobber him!
That's right! That's right!
AACK! DON'T SQUISH YOUR BOOBS AGAINST ME! SISTER!
VMMM
How are Gateau's wounds, Marron?
They're fairly deep.
You must stay still for a while.
If you move, your life may be in danger.
Damn. You're blunt.
But I won't let you fight without me.
Sigh...

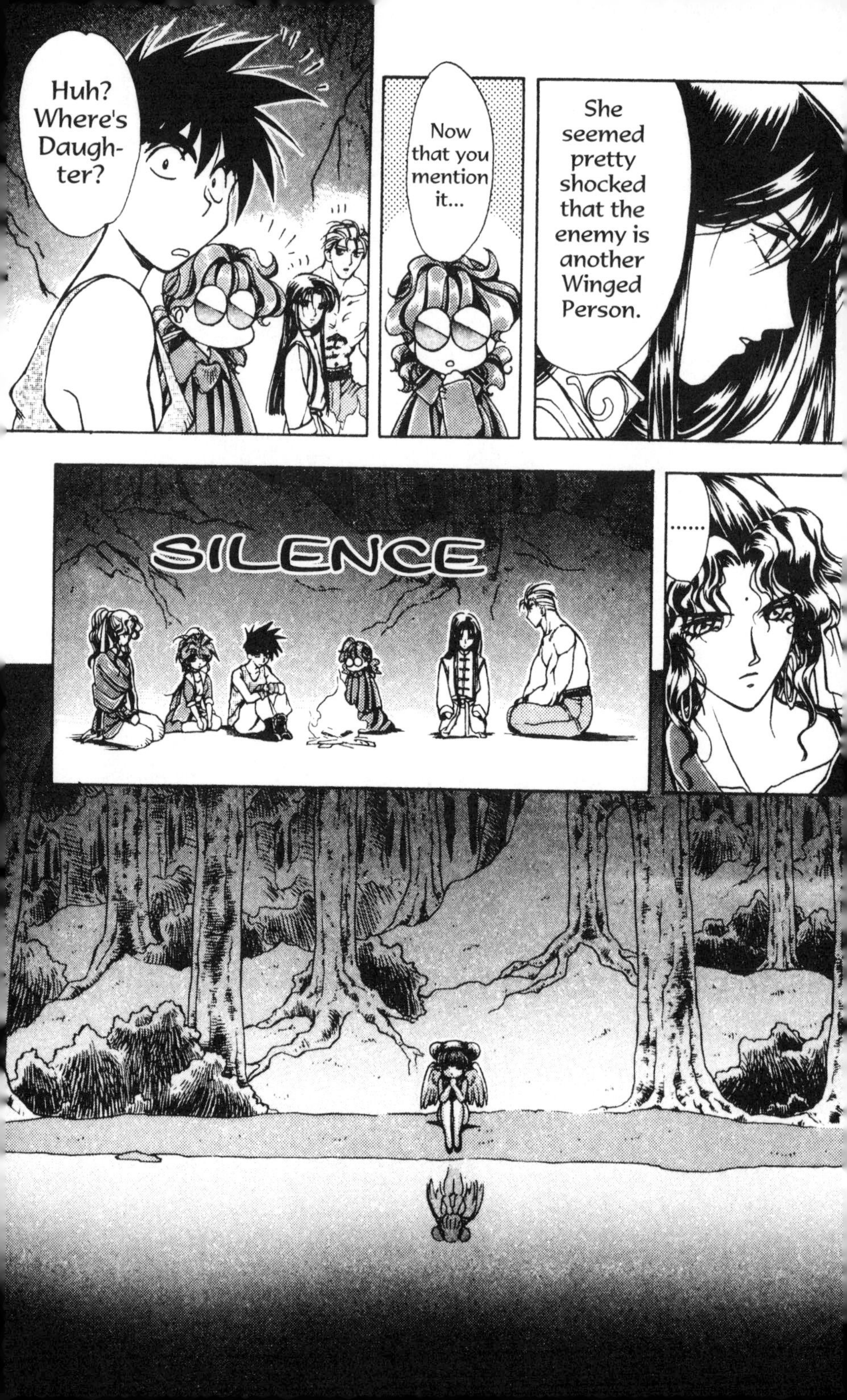
Huh? Where's Daugh-ter?
Now that you mention it...
She seemed pretty shocked that the enemy is another Winged Person.
SILENCE
......

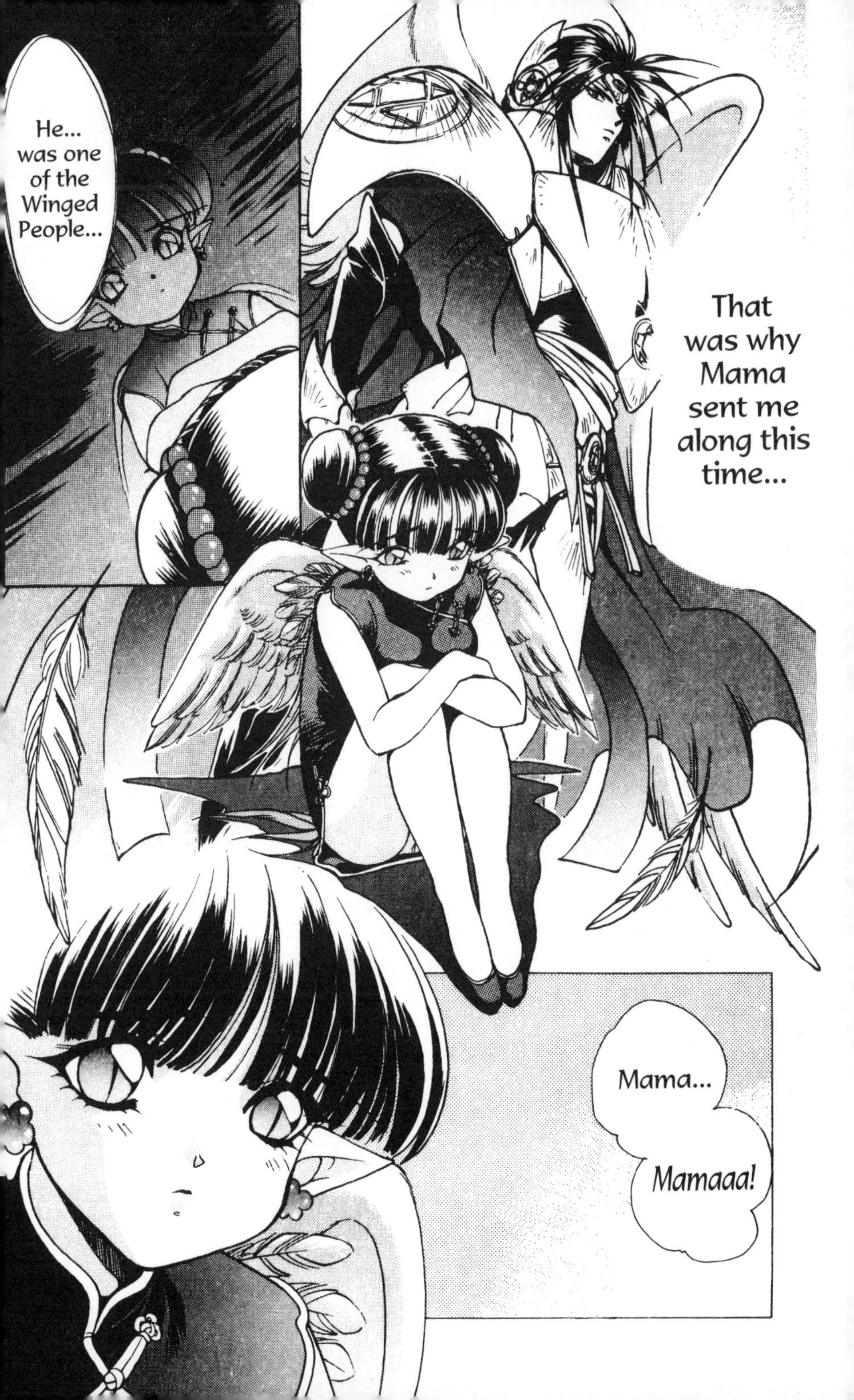
He... was one of the Winged People...
That was why Mama sent me along this time...
Mama...
Mamaaa!

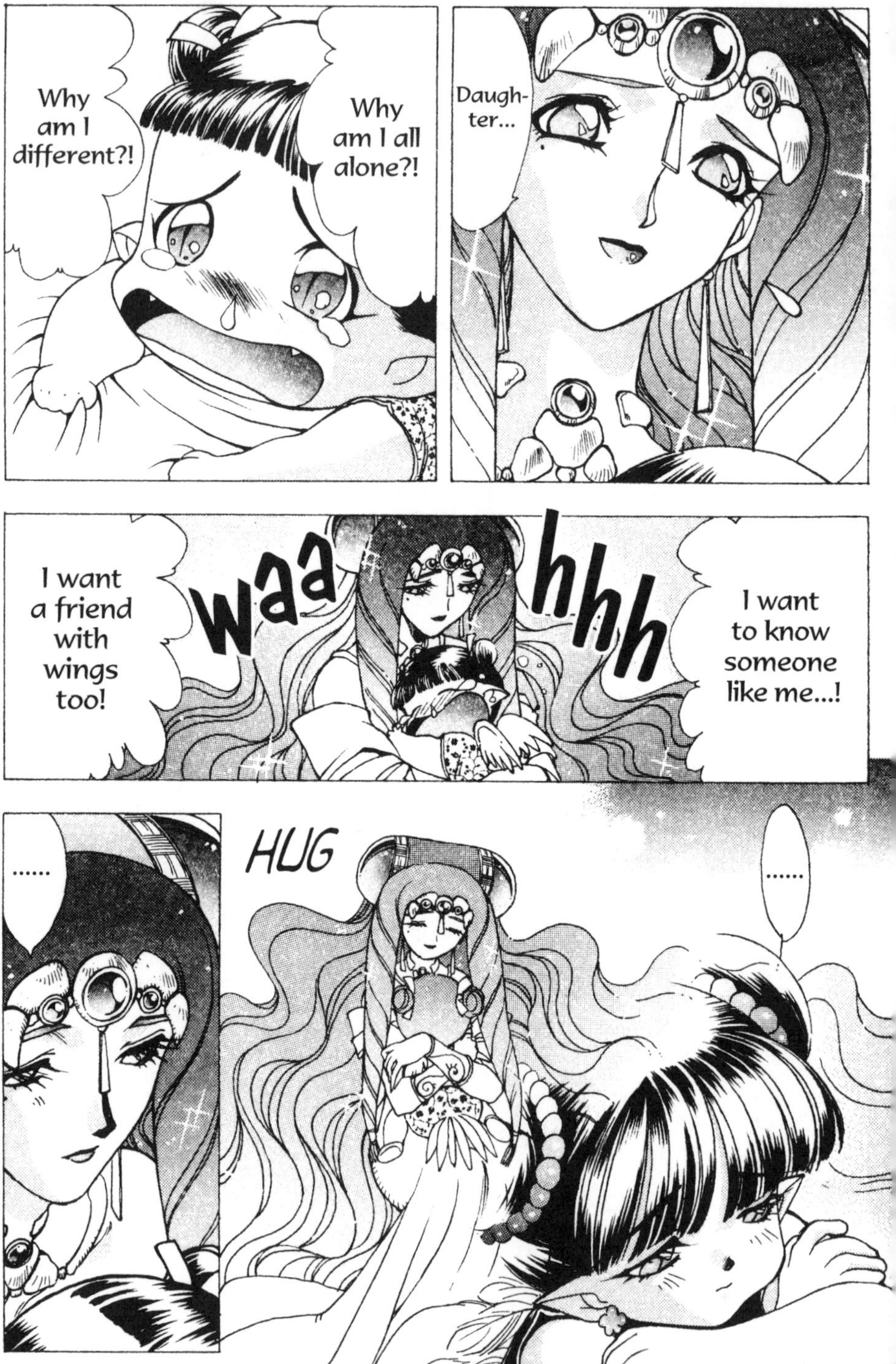
Daugh-
ter...
Why am I all alone?!
Why am I different?!
I want to know someone like me...!
waahhh
I want a friend with wings too!
......
HUG
......

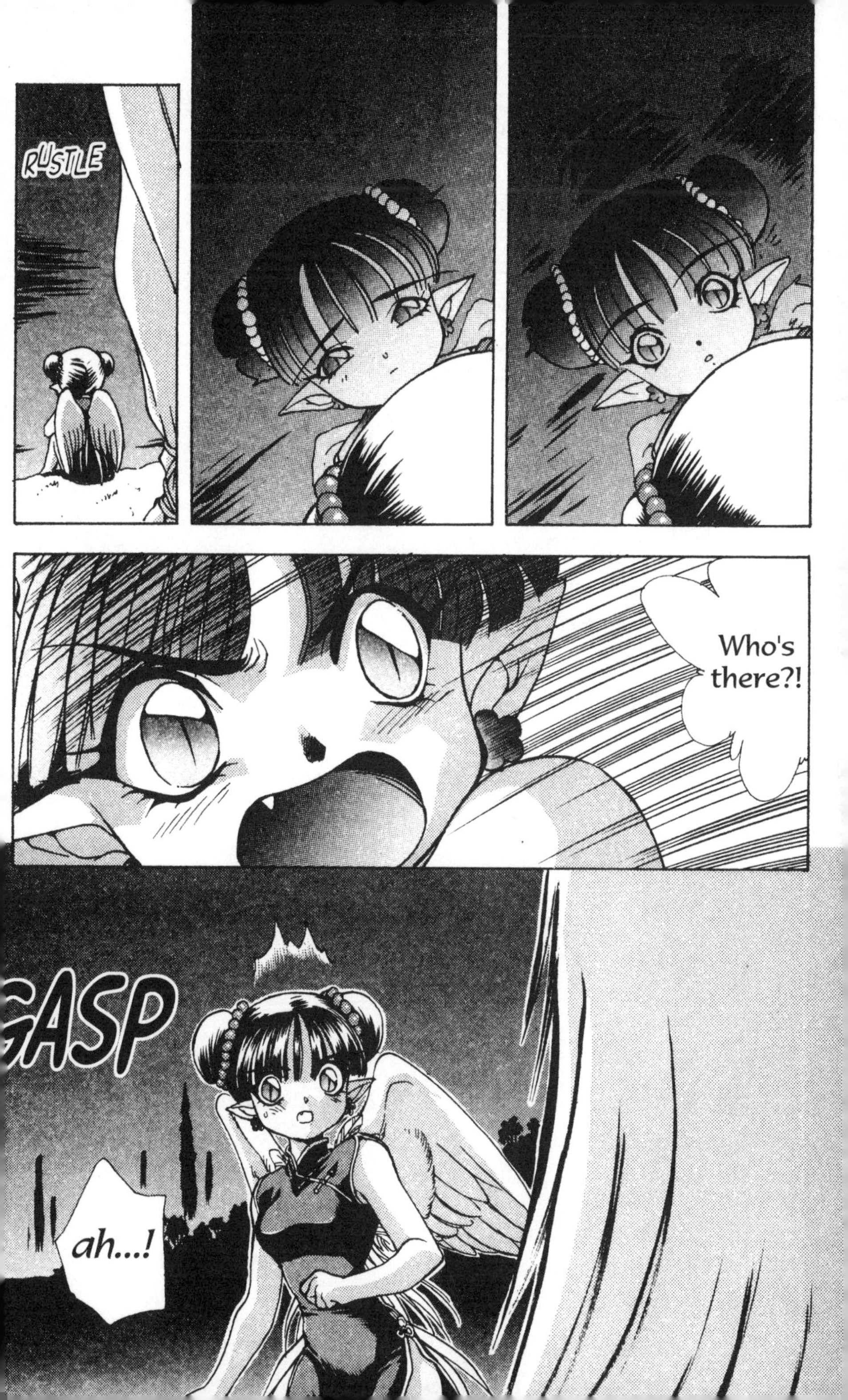
RUSTLE
Who's there?!
GASP
ah...!

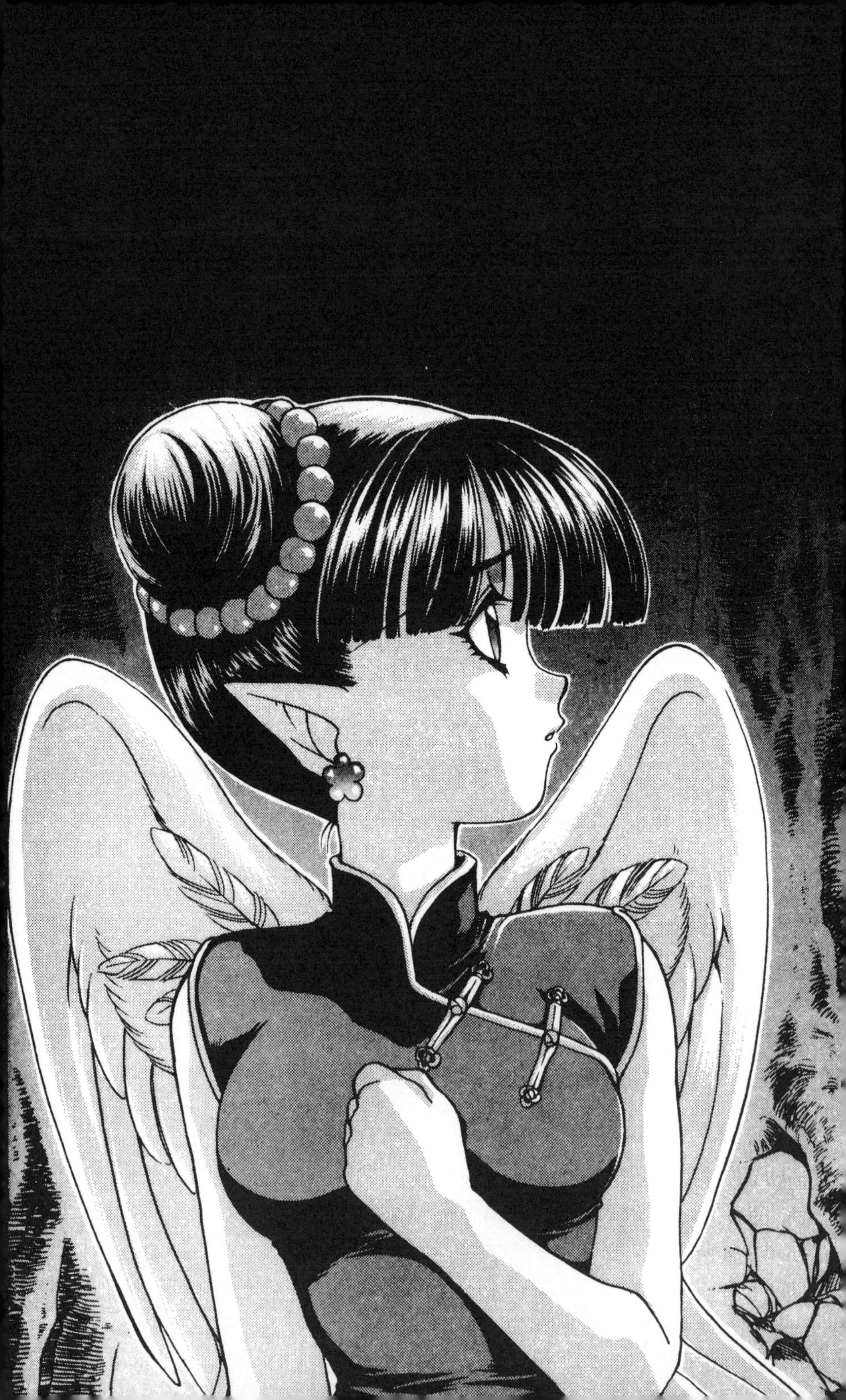

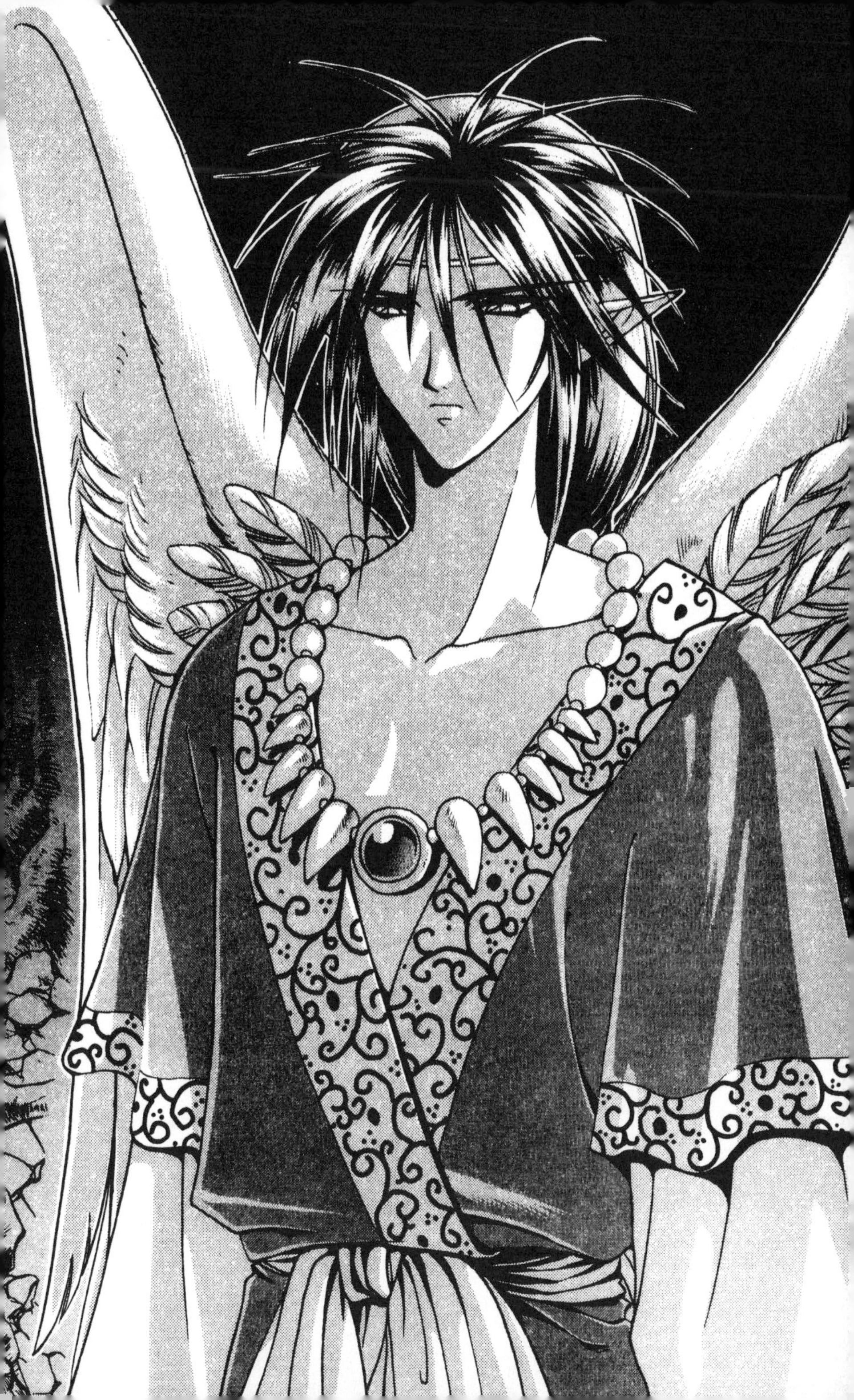

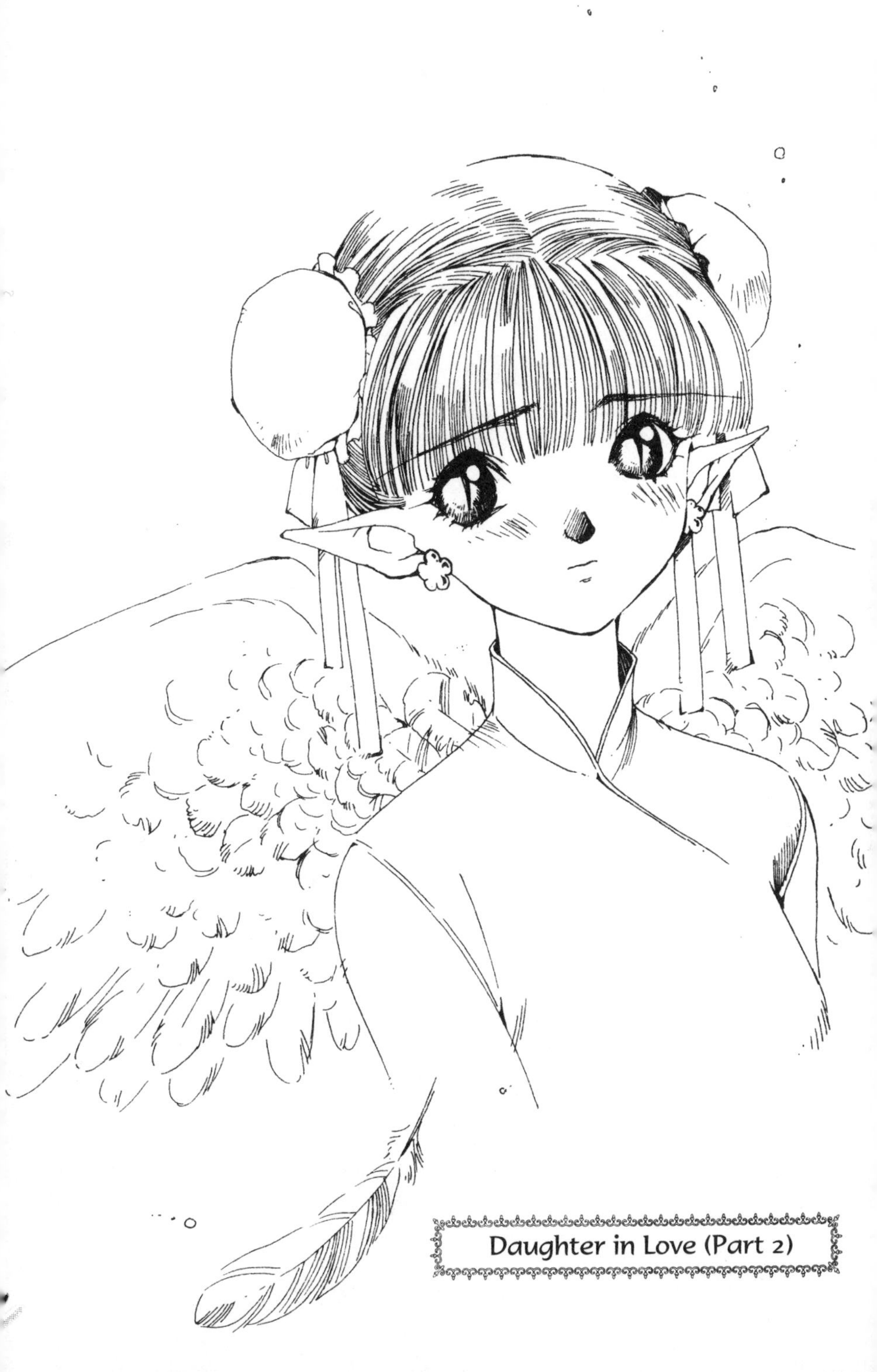

Daughter in Love (Part 2)

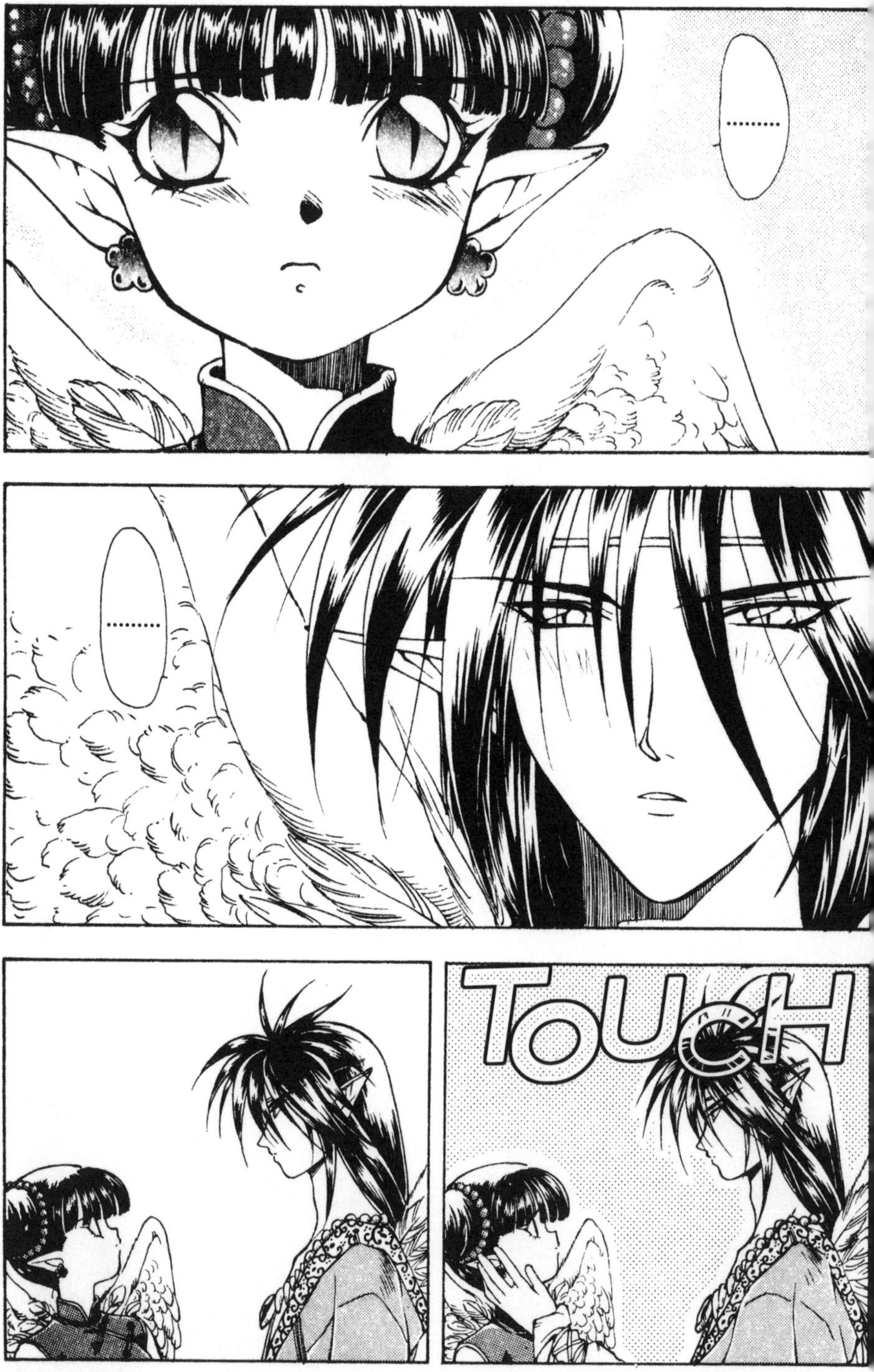
....
....
TOUCH

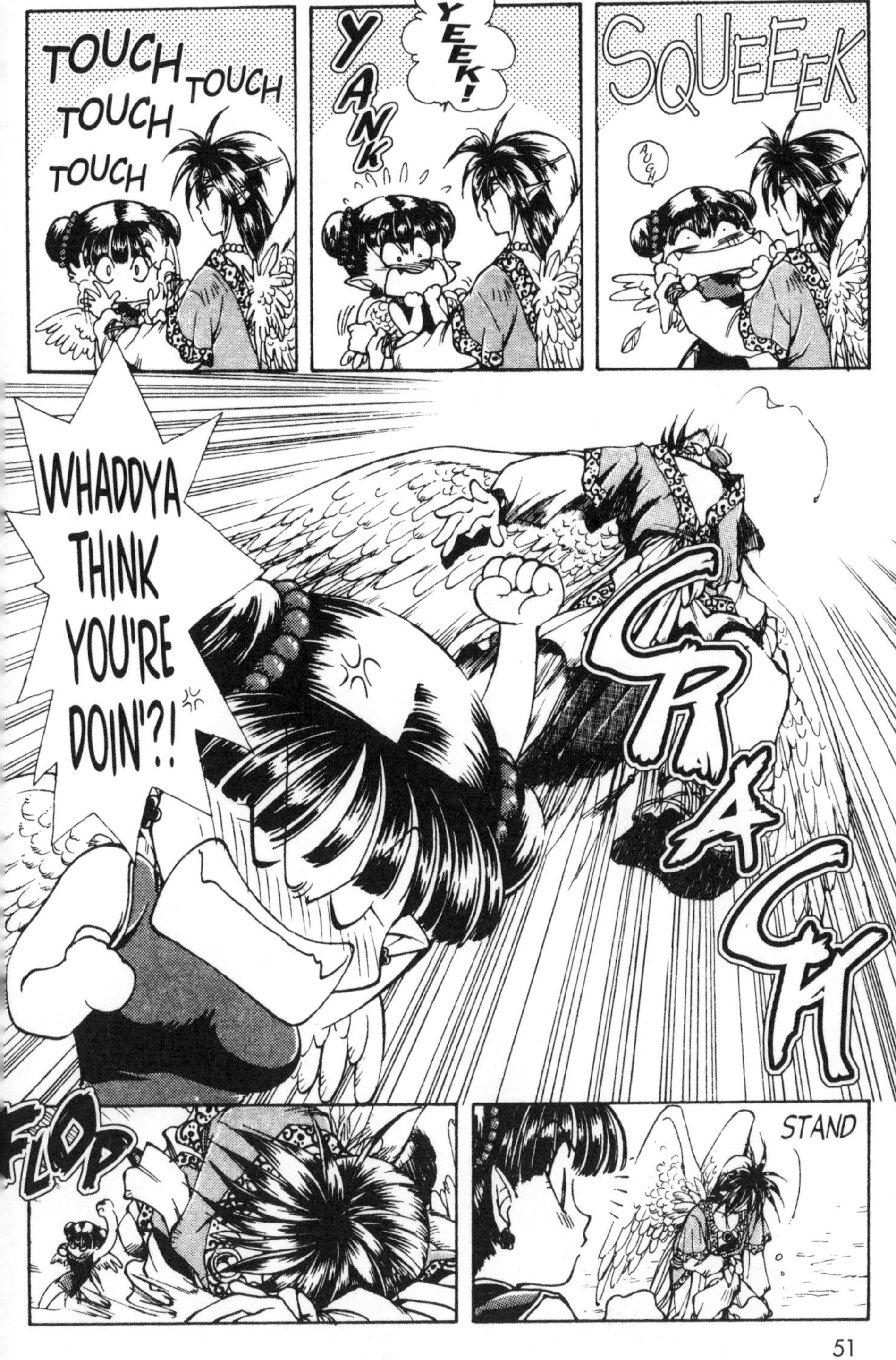
TOUCH TOUCH
TOUCH
TOUCH
YANK
YEEK!
SQUEEEK
AUGH
WHADDYA THINK YOU'RE DOIN'?!
CRACK
FLOP
STAND

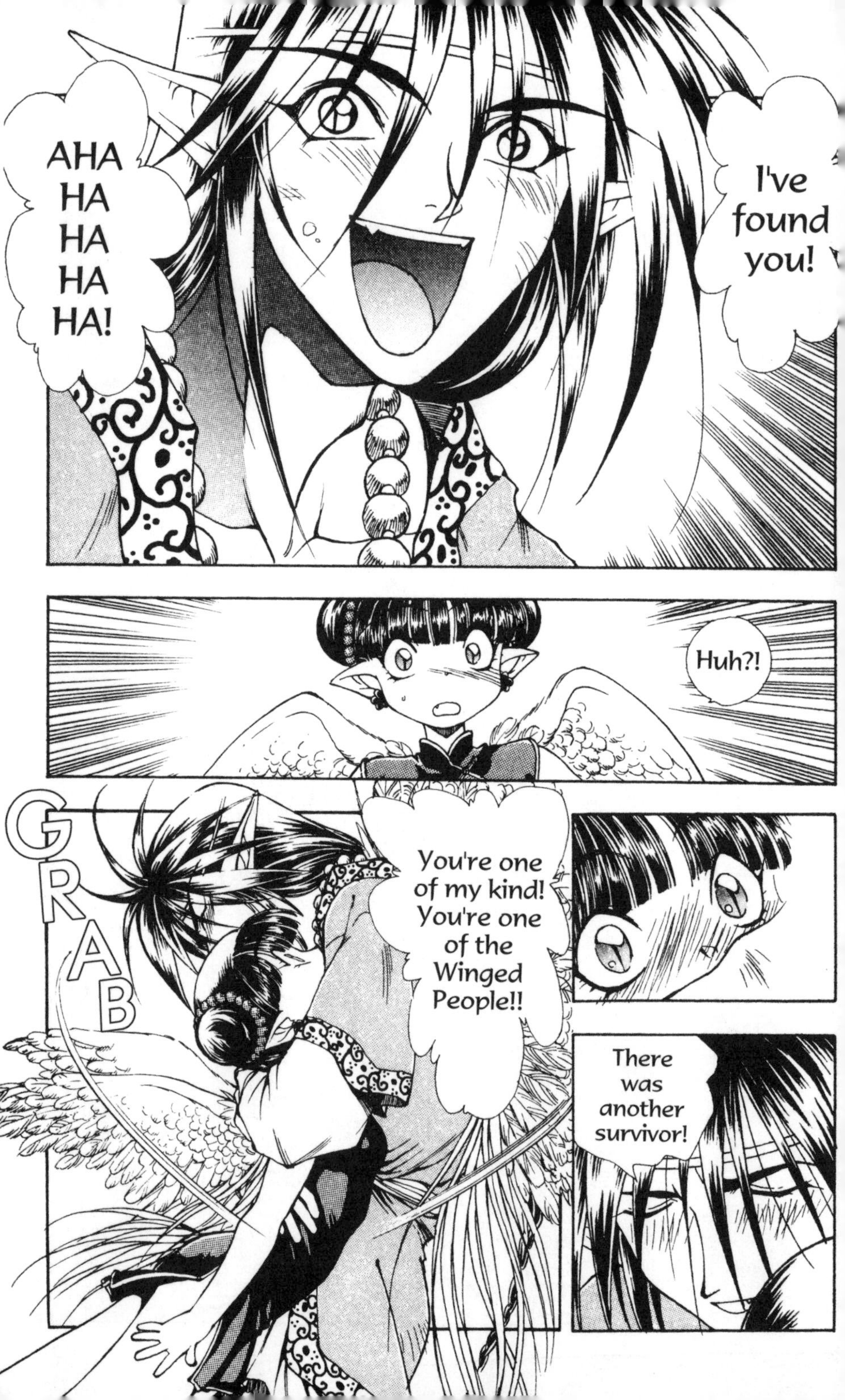
I've found you!
AHA HA HA HA HA!
Huh?!
There was another survivor!
GRAB
You're one of my kind! You're one of the Winged People!!

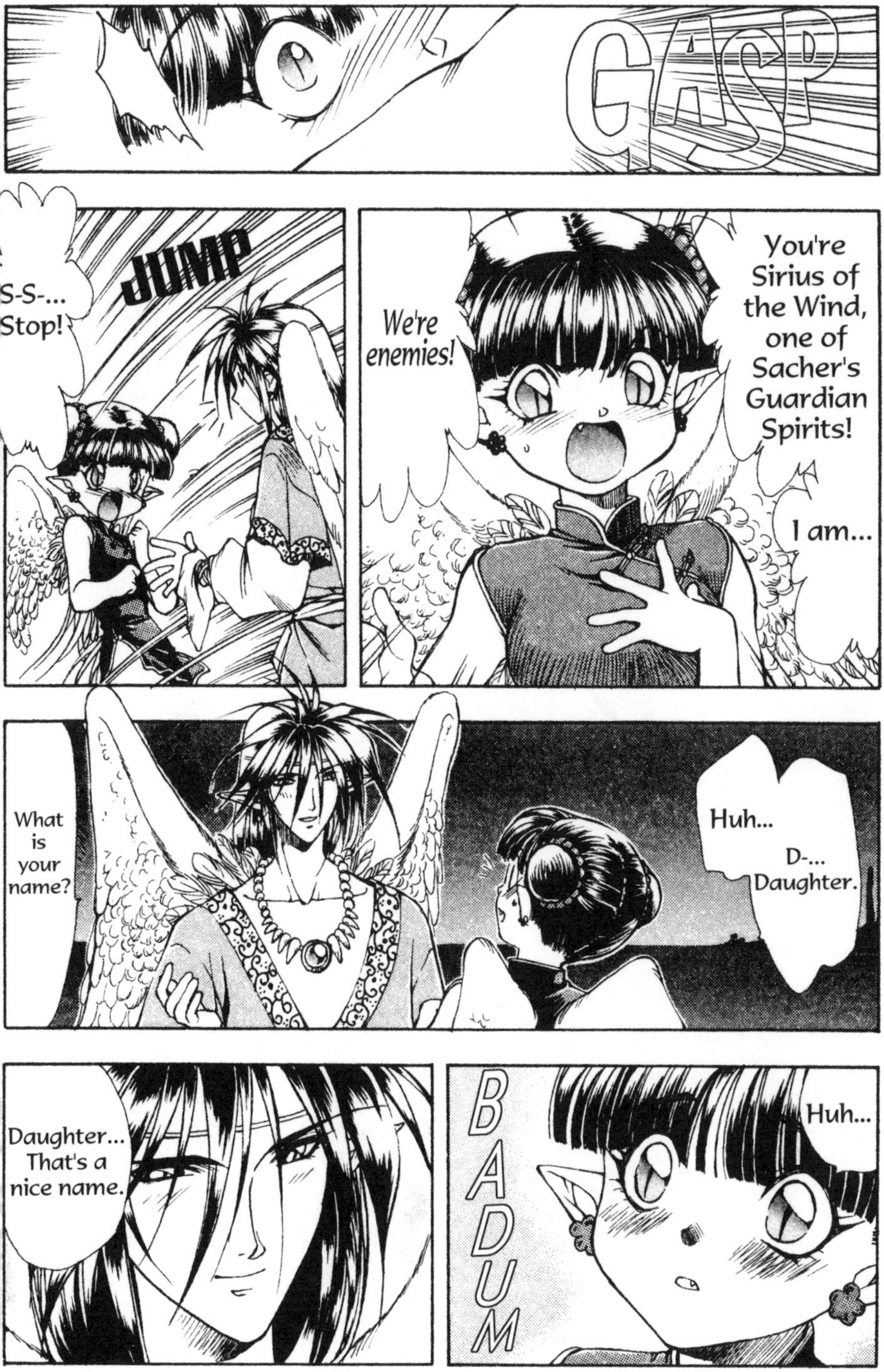
GASP
S-S-... Stop!
JUMP
You're Sirius of the Wind, one of Sacher's Guardian Spirits!
We're enemies!
I am...
What is your name?
Huh... D-... Daughter.
Daughter... That's a nice name.
BADUM
Huh...

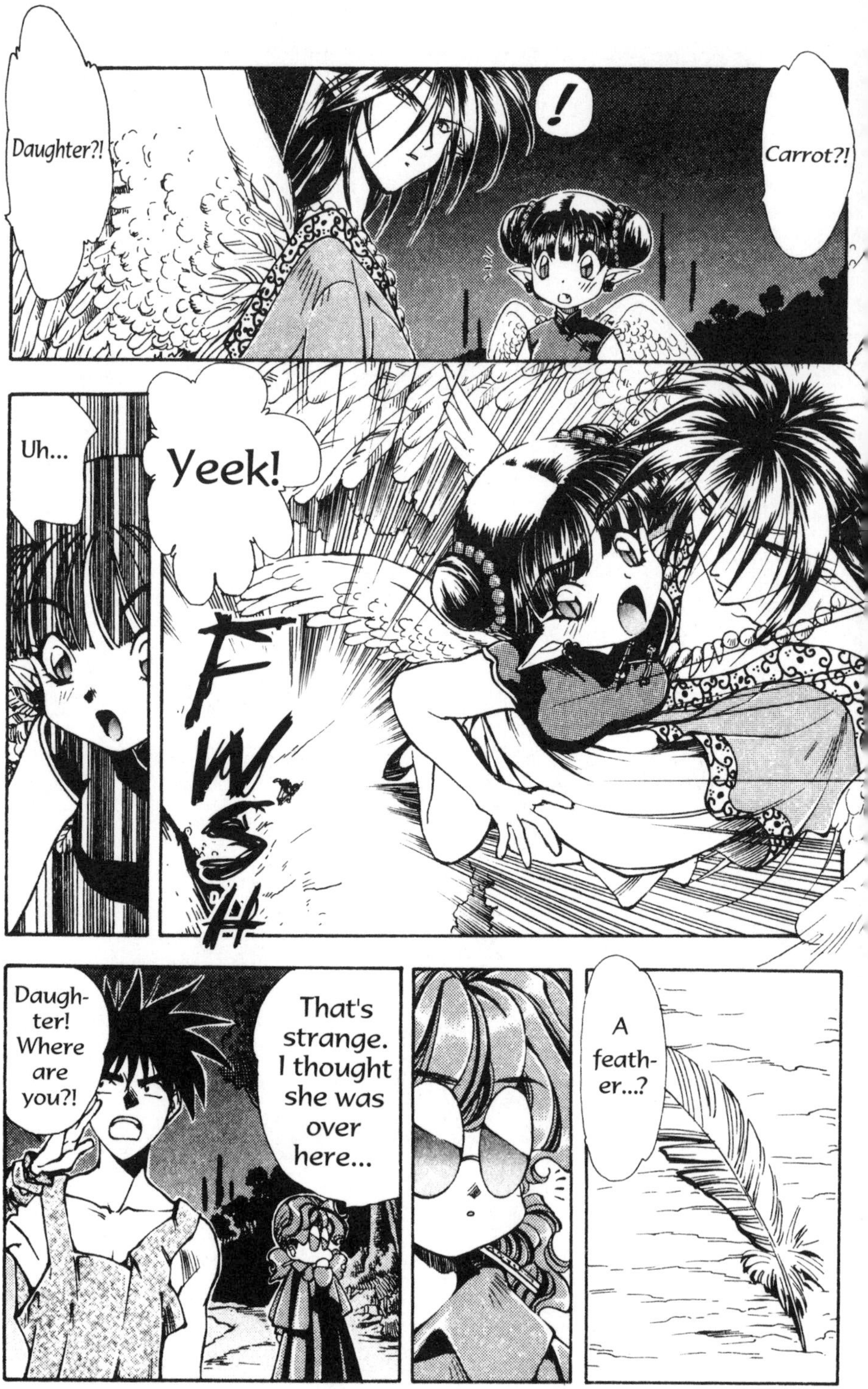
Carrot?!
!
Daughter?!
Yeek!
FWSH
Uh...
A feather...?
That's strange. I thought she was over here...
Daughter! Where are you?!

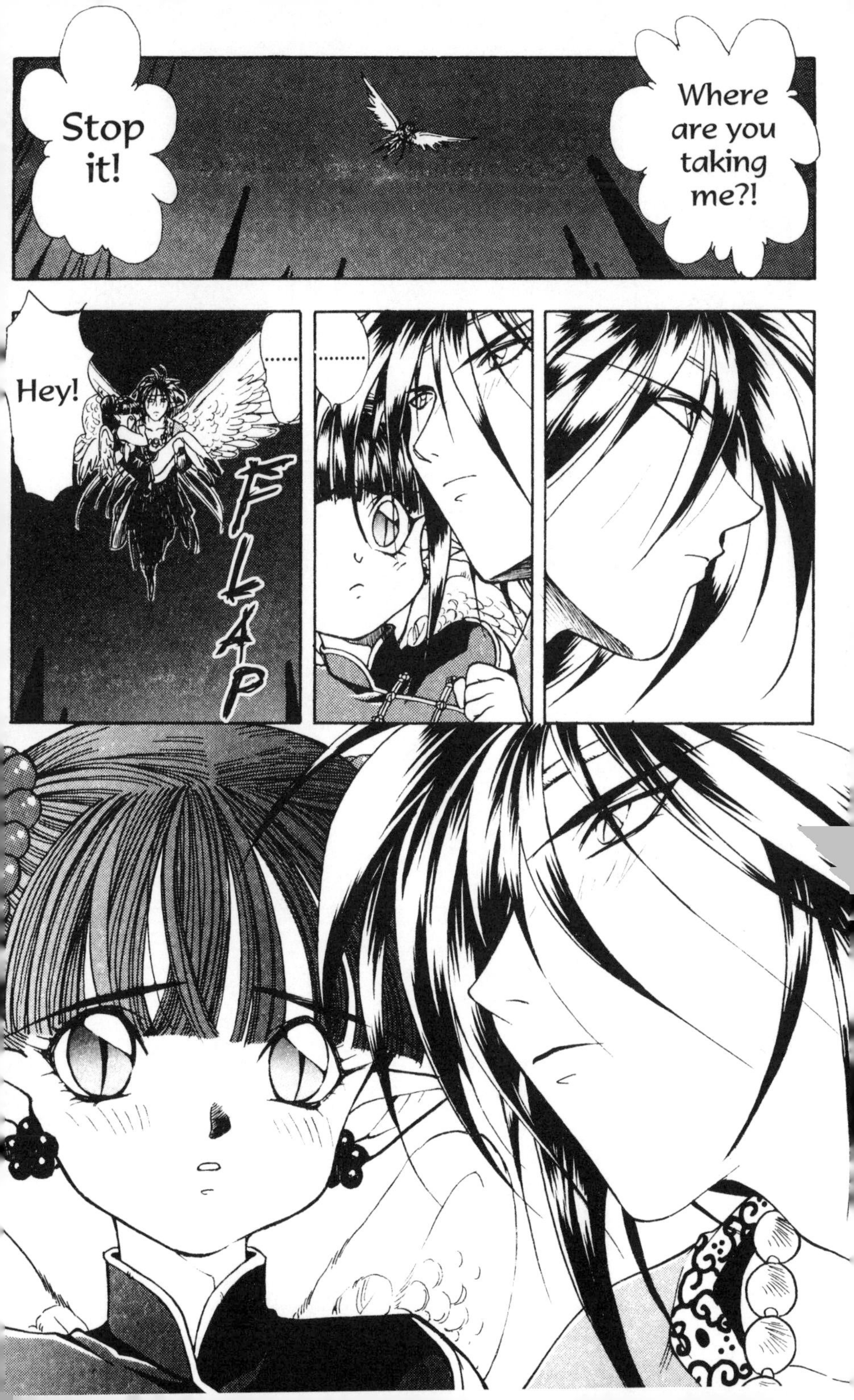

Where are you taking me?!
Stop it!
......
Hey!
FLAP

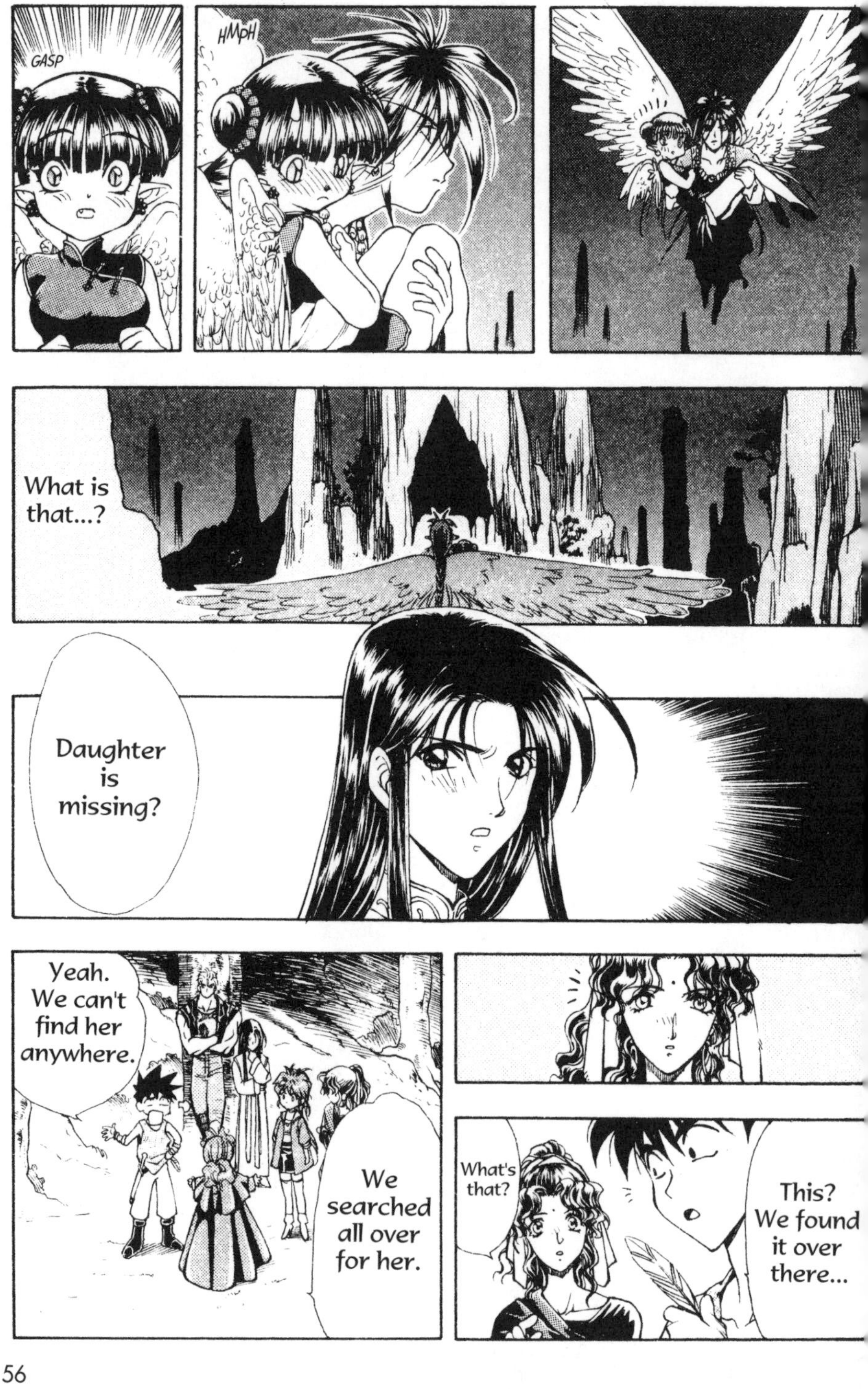
GASP
HMPH
What is that...?
Daughter is missing?
Yeah. We can't find her anywhere.
We searched all over for her.
What's that?
This? We found it over there...

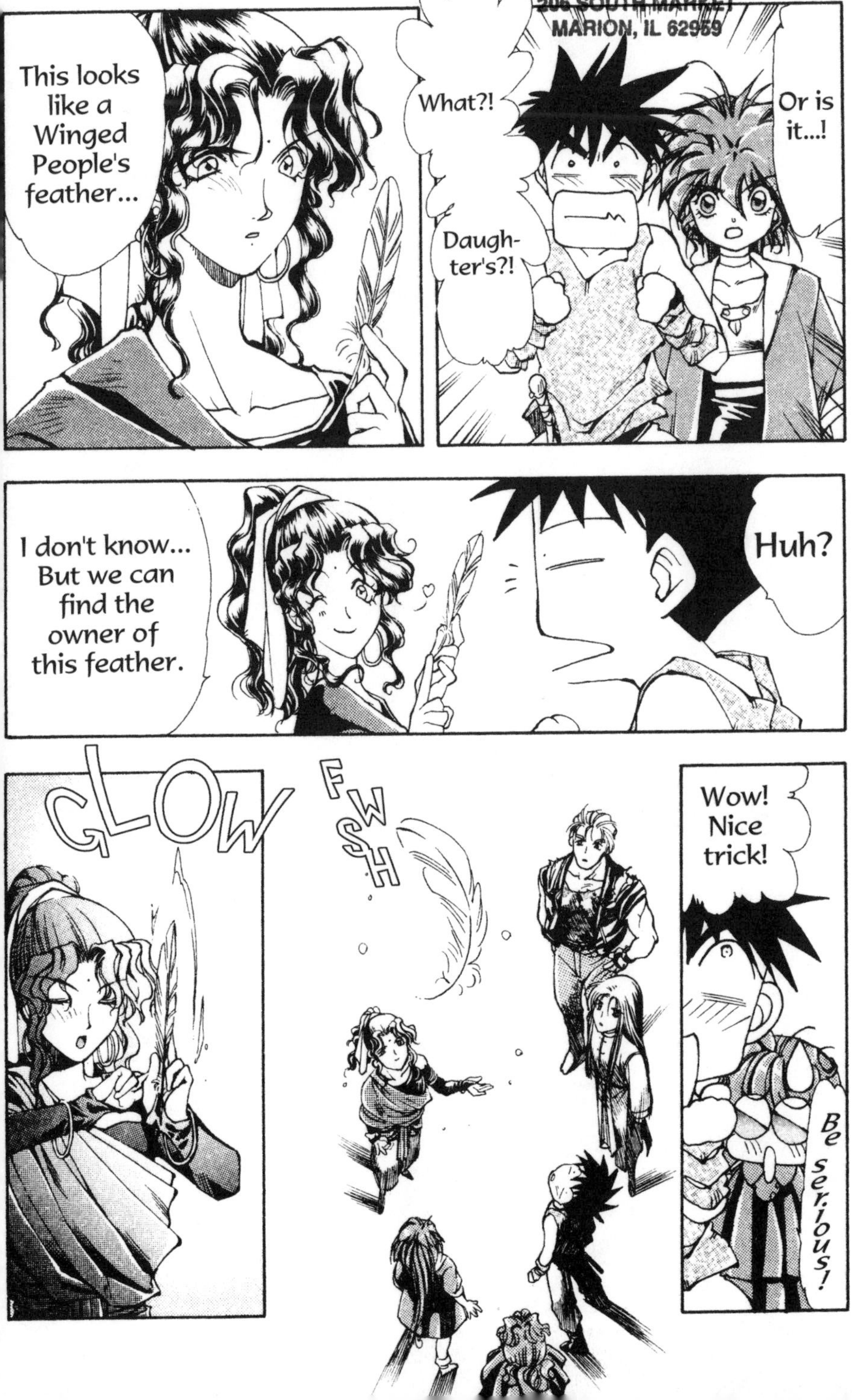
This looks like a Winged People's feather...
What?!
Daughter's?!
Or is it...!
I don't know... But we can find the owner of this feather.
Huh?
GLOW
FWSH
Wow! Nice trick!
Be serious!

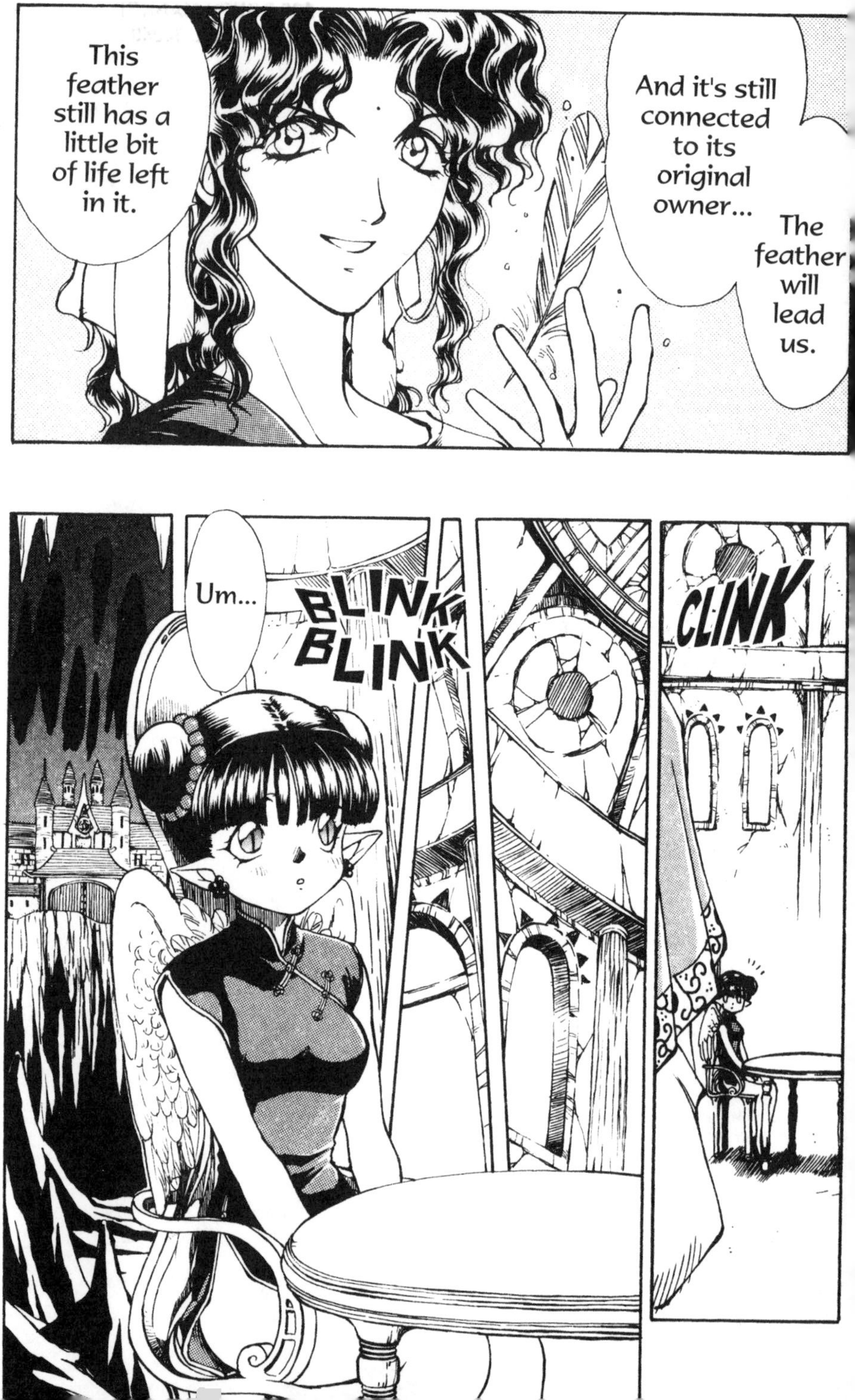
This feather still has a little bit of life left in it.
And it's still connected to its original owner...
The feather will lead us.
Um...
BLINK BLINK
CLINK

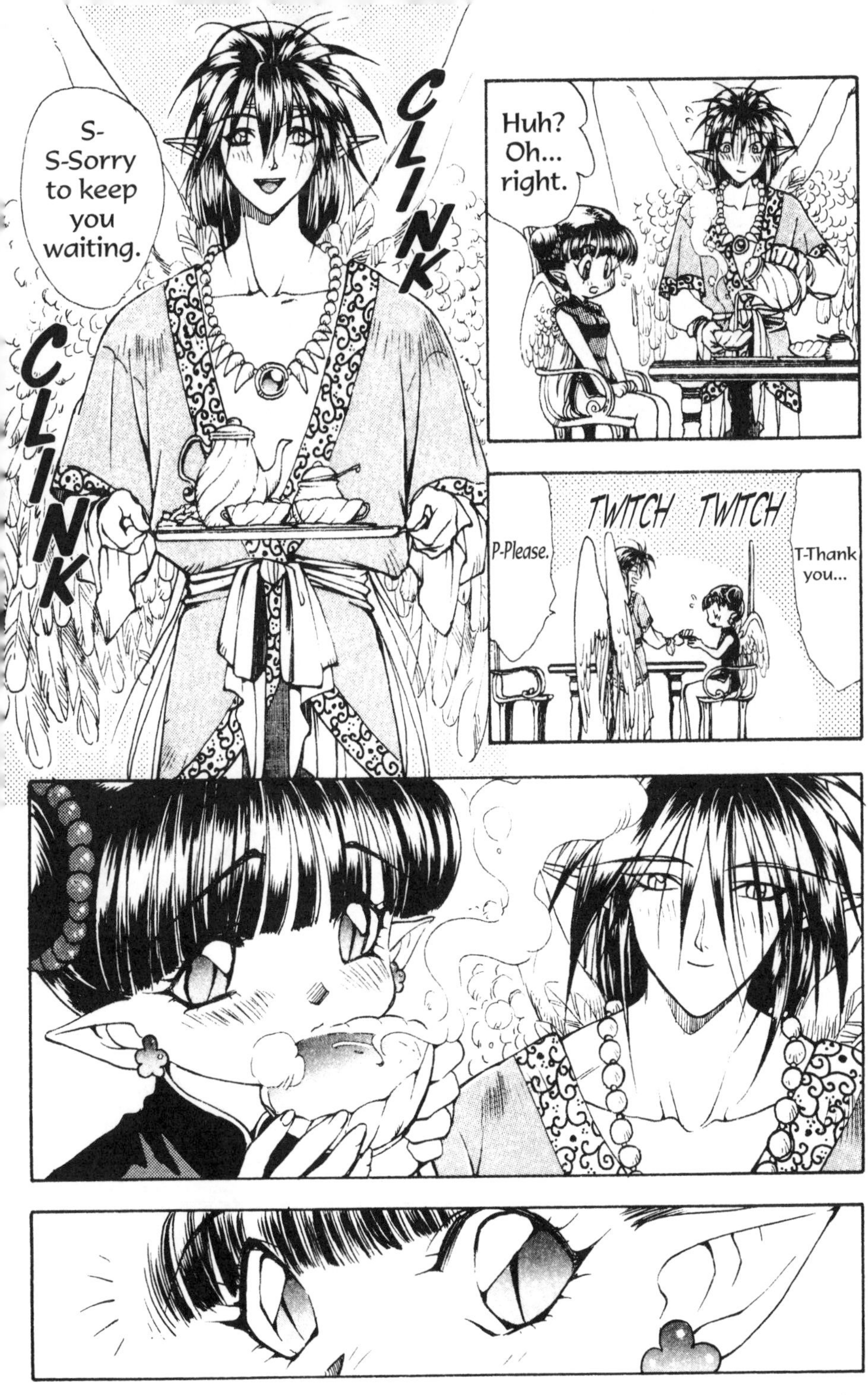
S-
S-Sorry
to keep
you
waiting.
CLINK
CLINK
Huh?
Oh...
right.
TWITCH TWITCH
P-Please.
T-Thank
you...

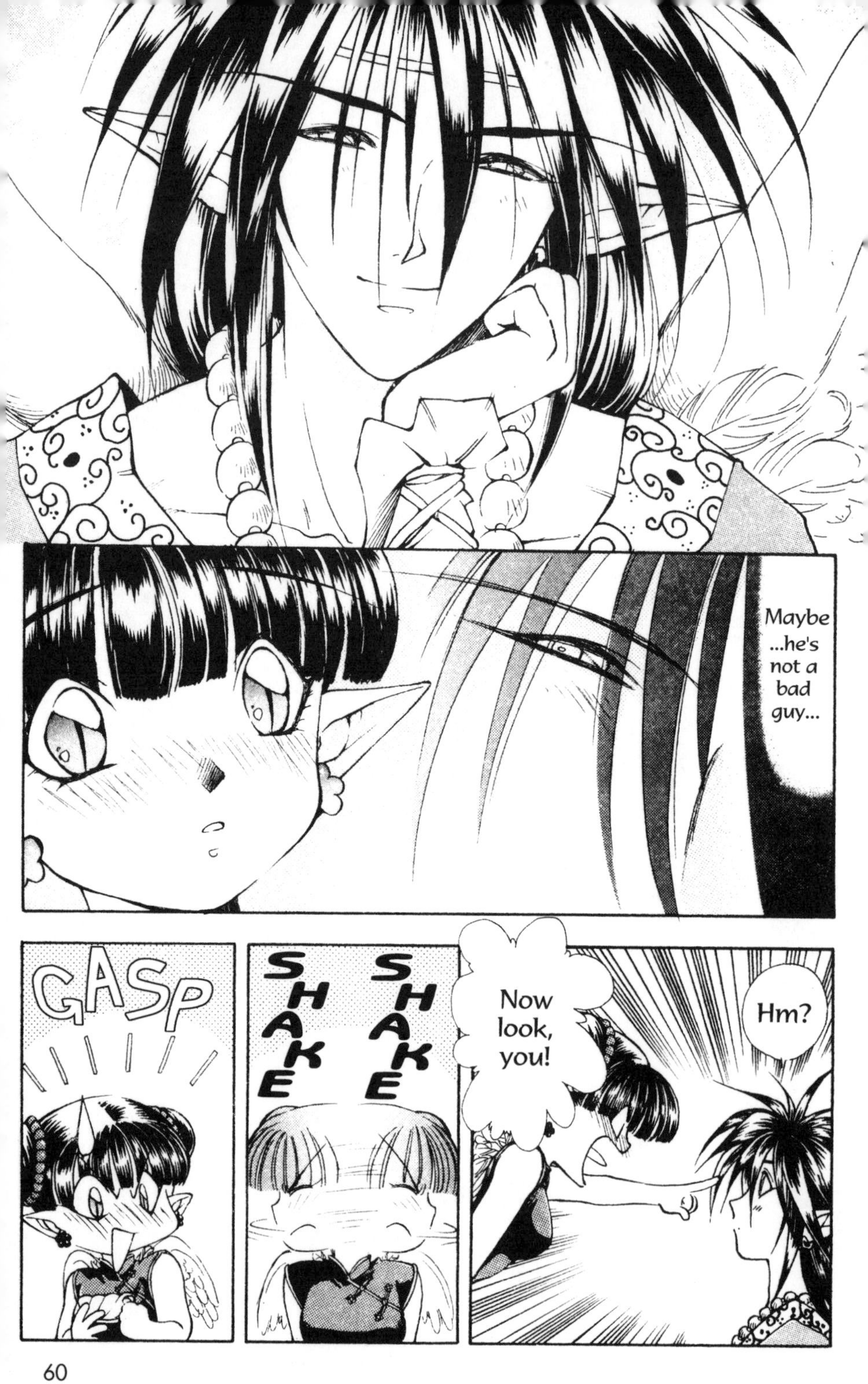
Maybe ...he's not a bad guy...
GASP
SHAKE SHAKE
Now look, you!
Hm?

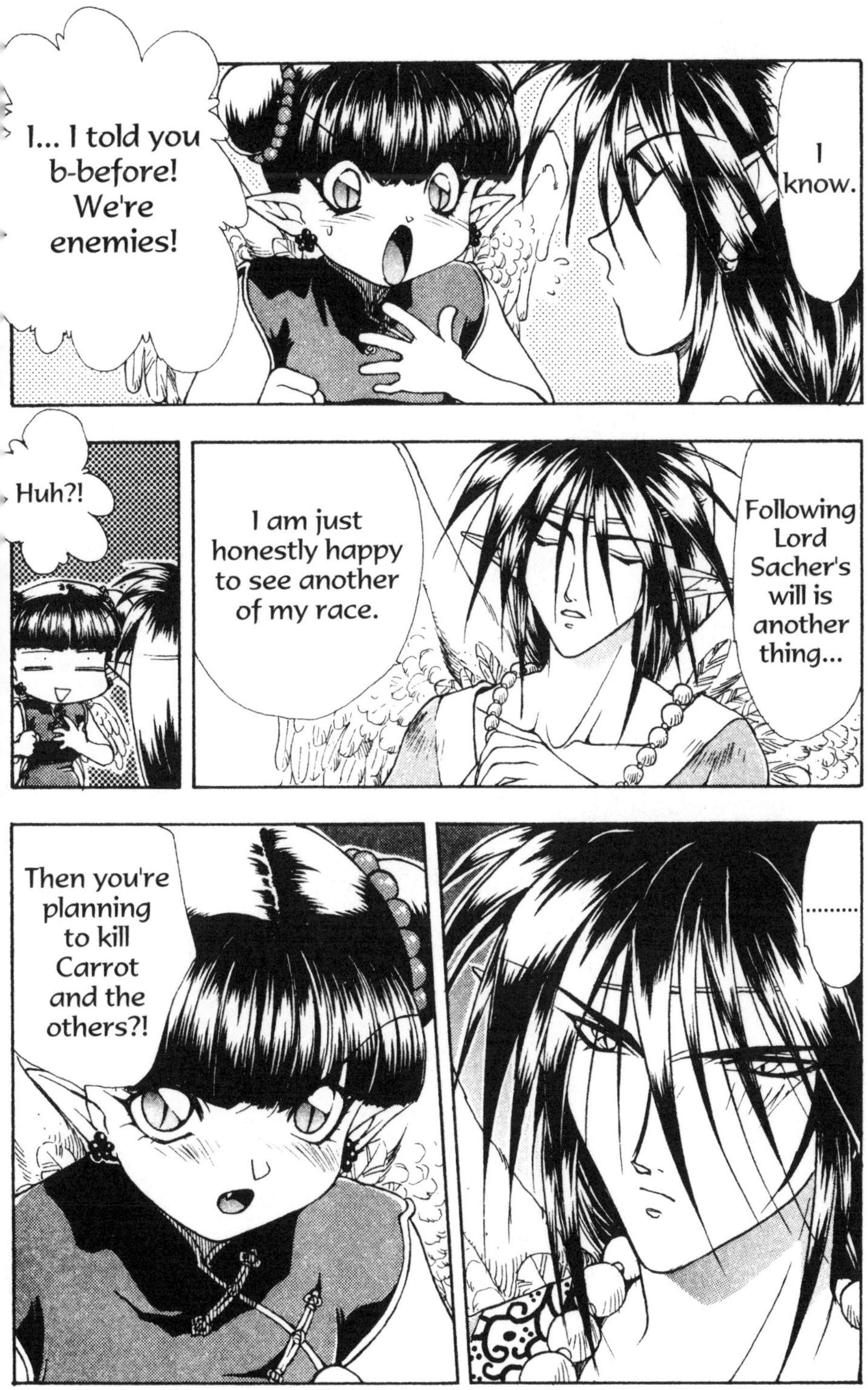
I... I told you b-before! We're enemies!
I know.
Huh?!
I am just honestly happy to see another of my race.
Following Lord Sacher's will is another thing...
Then you're planning to kill Carrot and the others?!
....

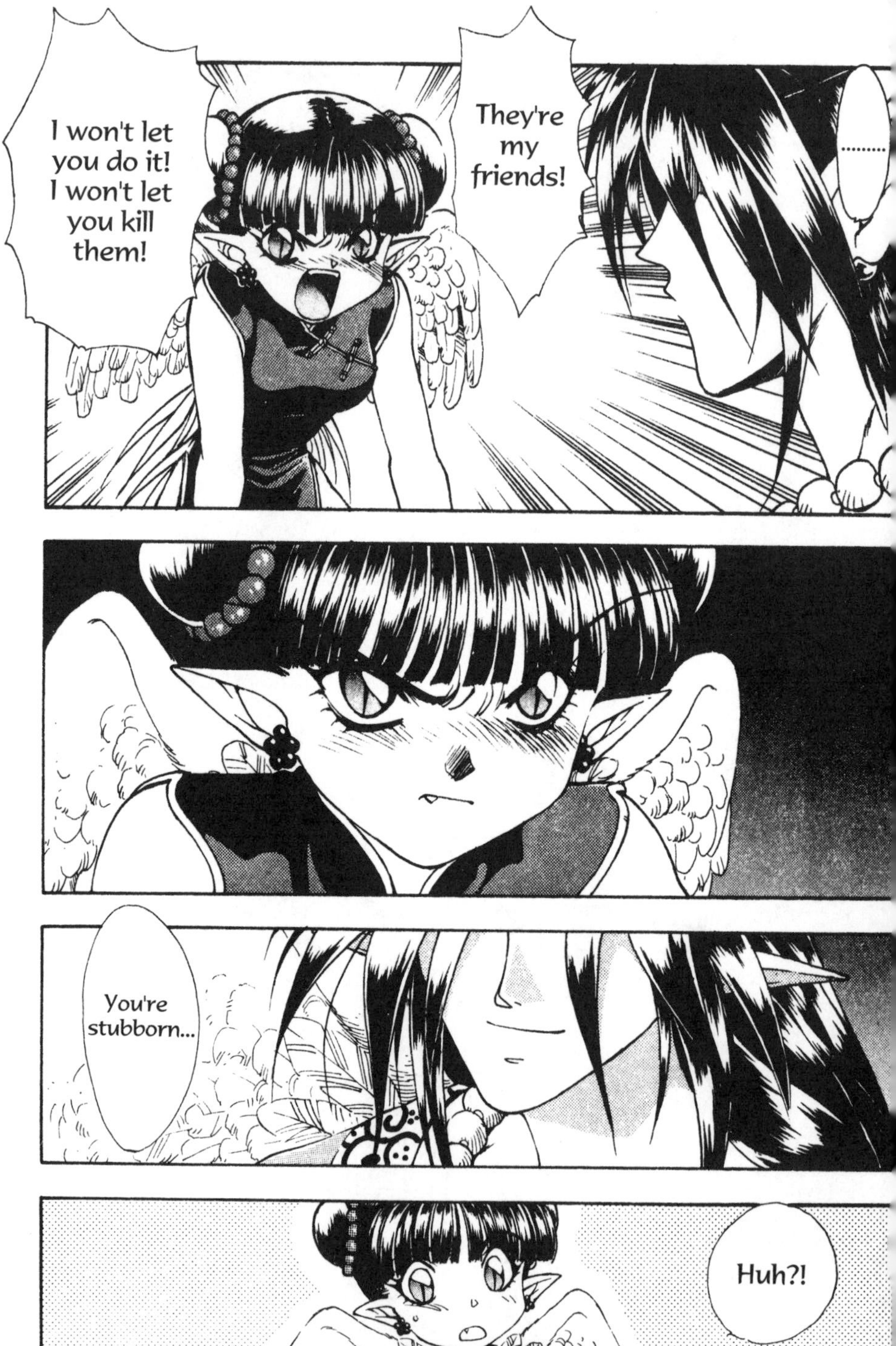
I won't let you do it! I won't let you kill them!
They're my friends!
....
You're stubborn...
Huh?!

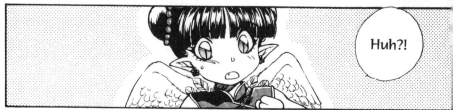

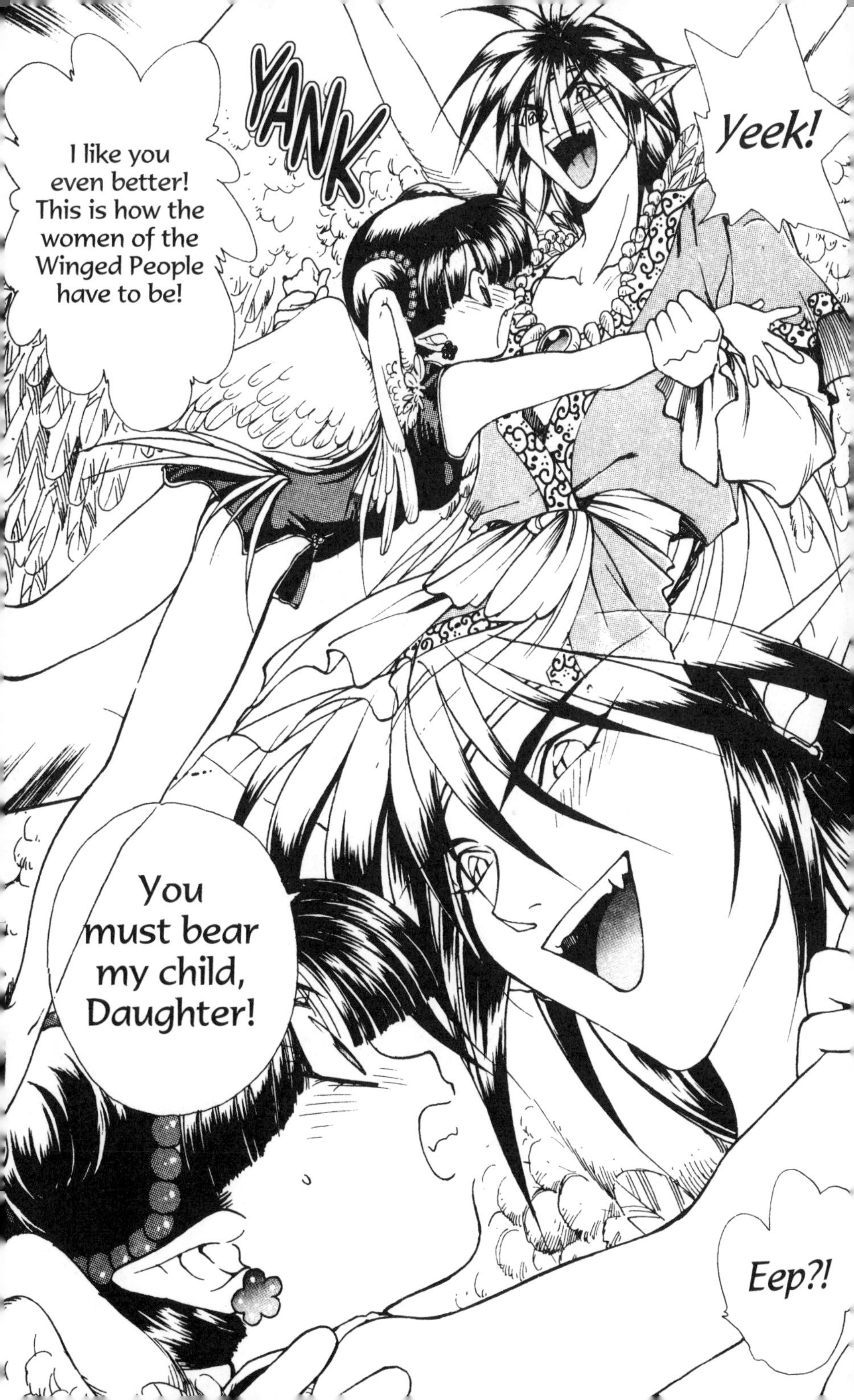
I like you even better! This is how the women of the Winged People have to be!
YANK
Yeek!
You must bear my child, Daughter!
Eep?!

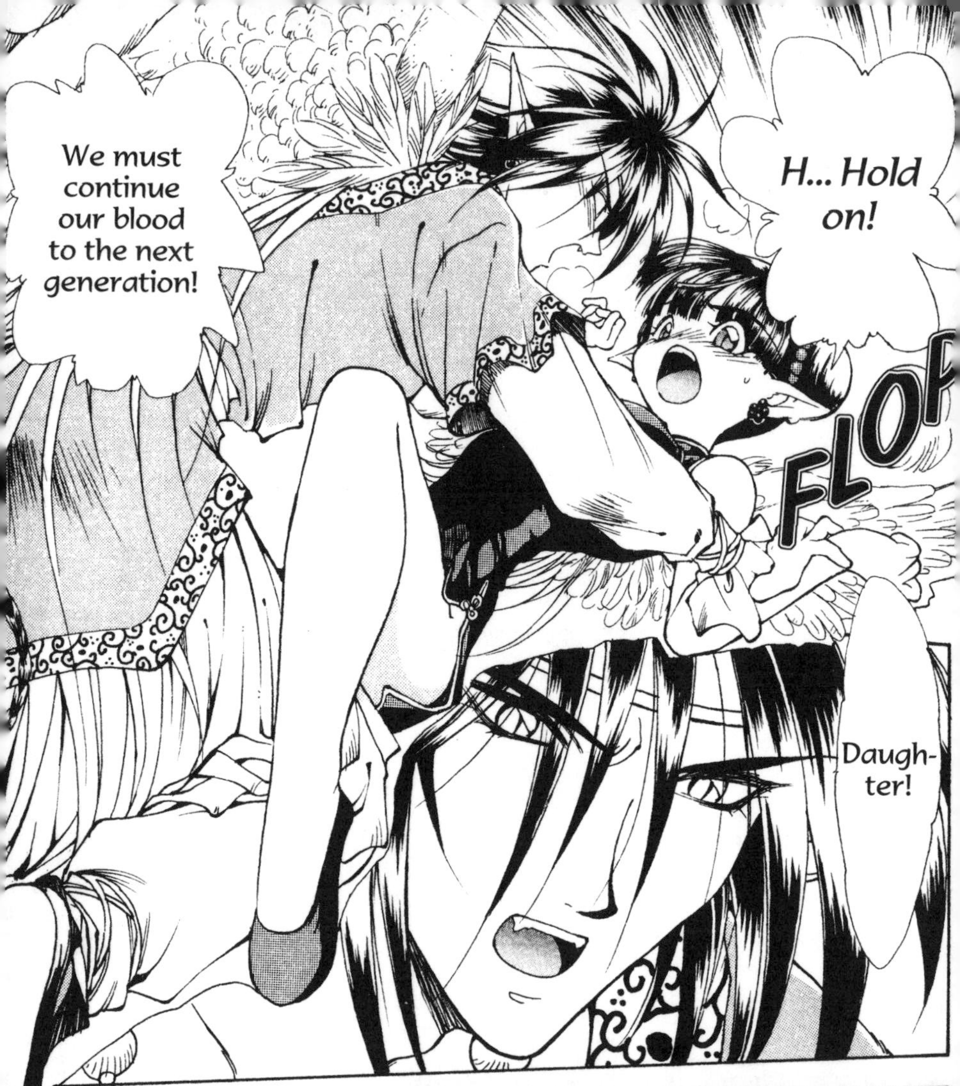
H... Hold on!
We must continue our blood to the next generation!
FLOP
Daughter!

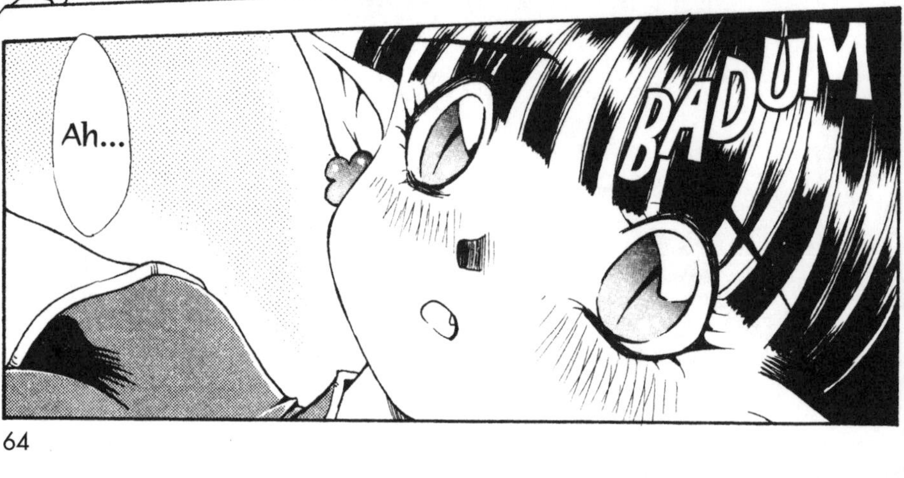
BADUM
Ah...

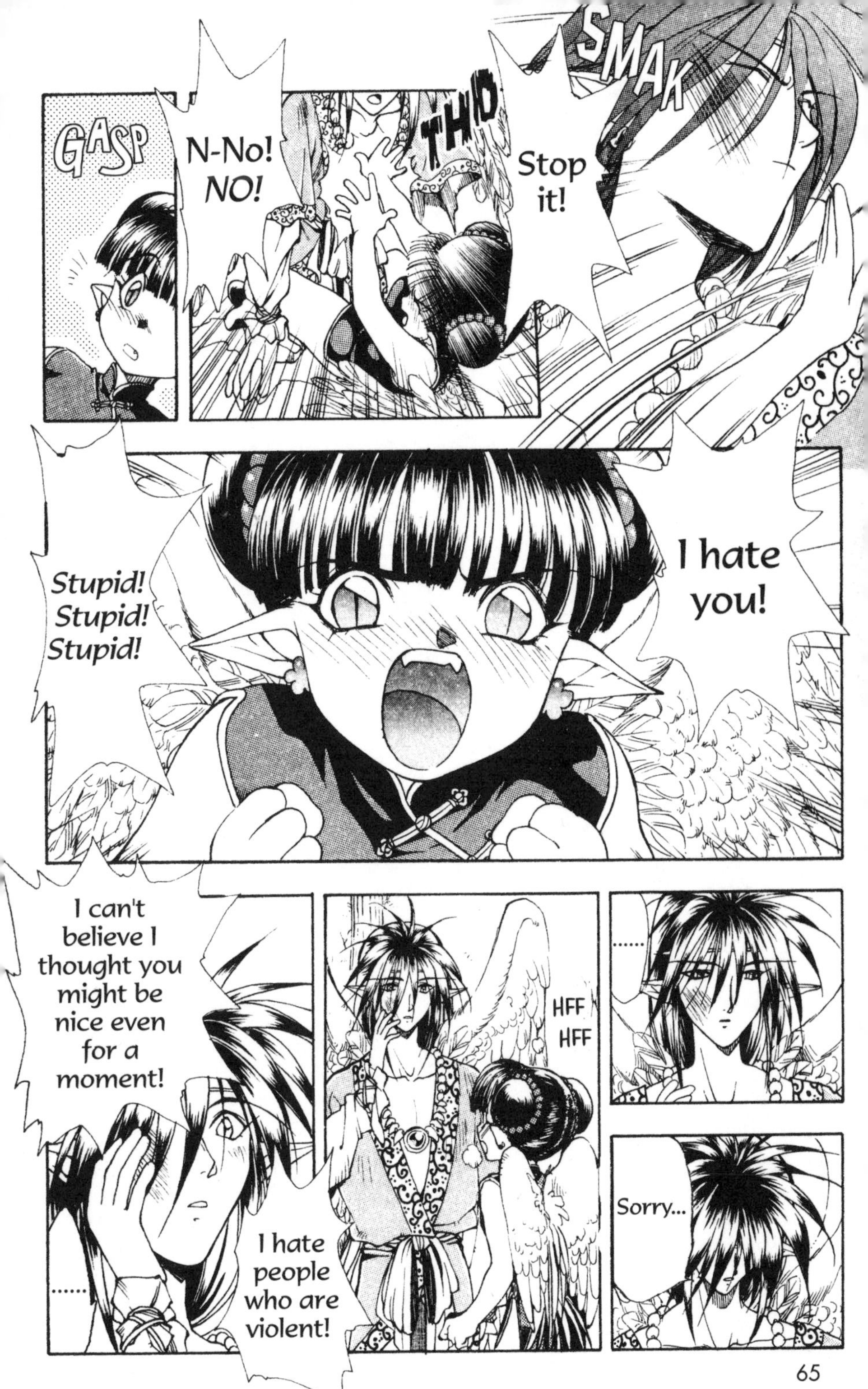
SMAK
Stop it!
THID
N-No! NO!
GASP
I hate you!
Stupid! Stupid! Stupid!
......
Sorry...
HFF HFF
I hate people who are violent!
I can't believe I thought you might be nice even for a moment!
......

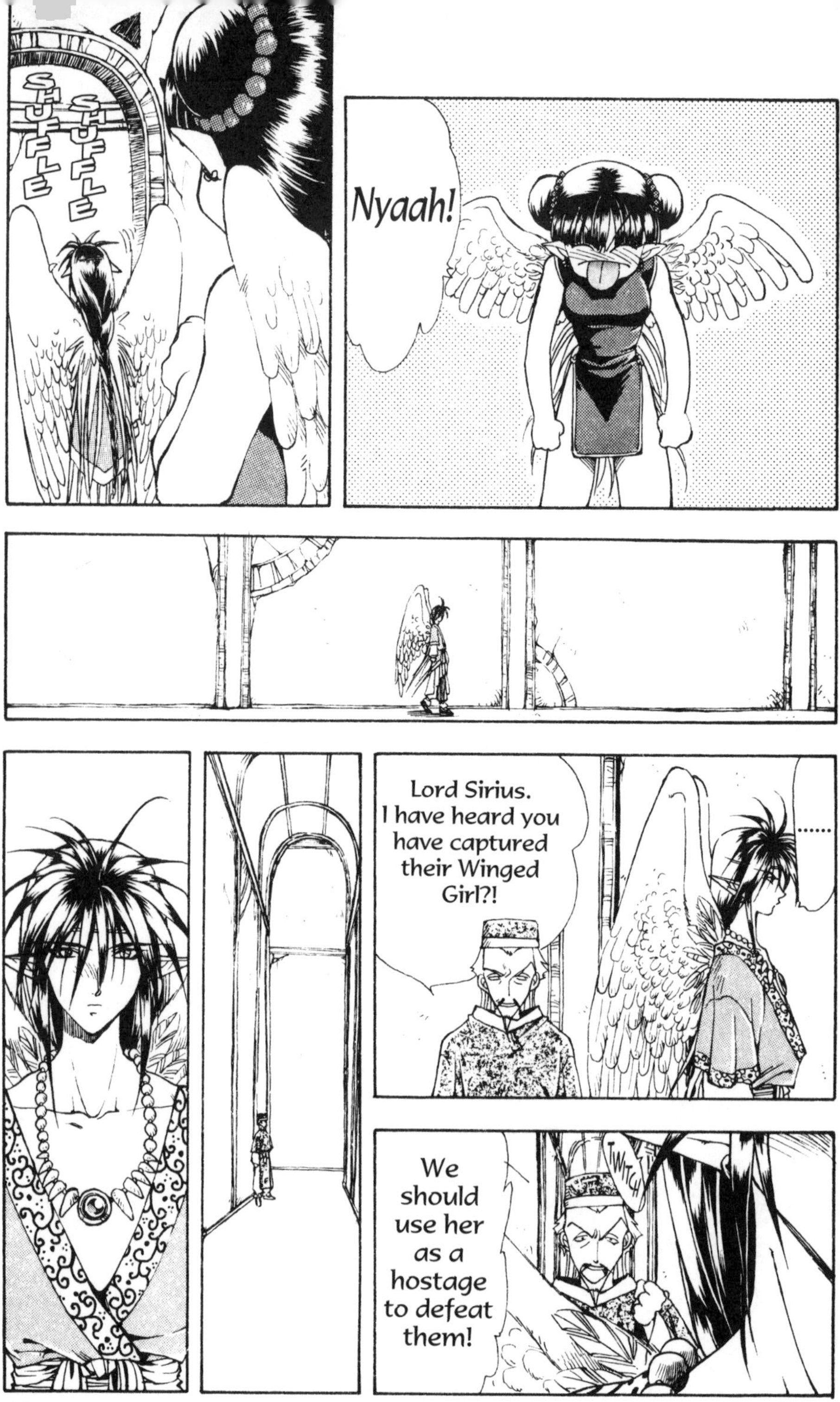
Nyaah!
SHUFFLE SHUFFLE
Lord Sirius. I have heard you have captured their Winged Girl?!
......
TWITCH
We should use her as a hostage to defeat them!

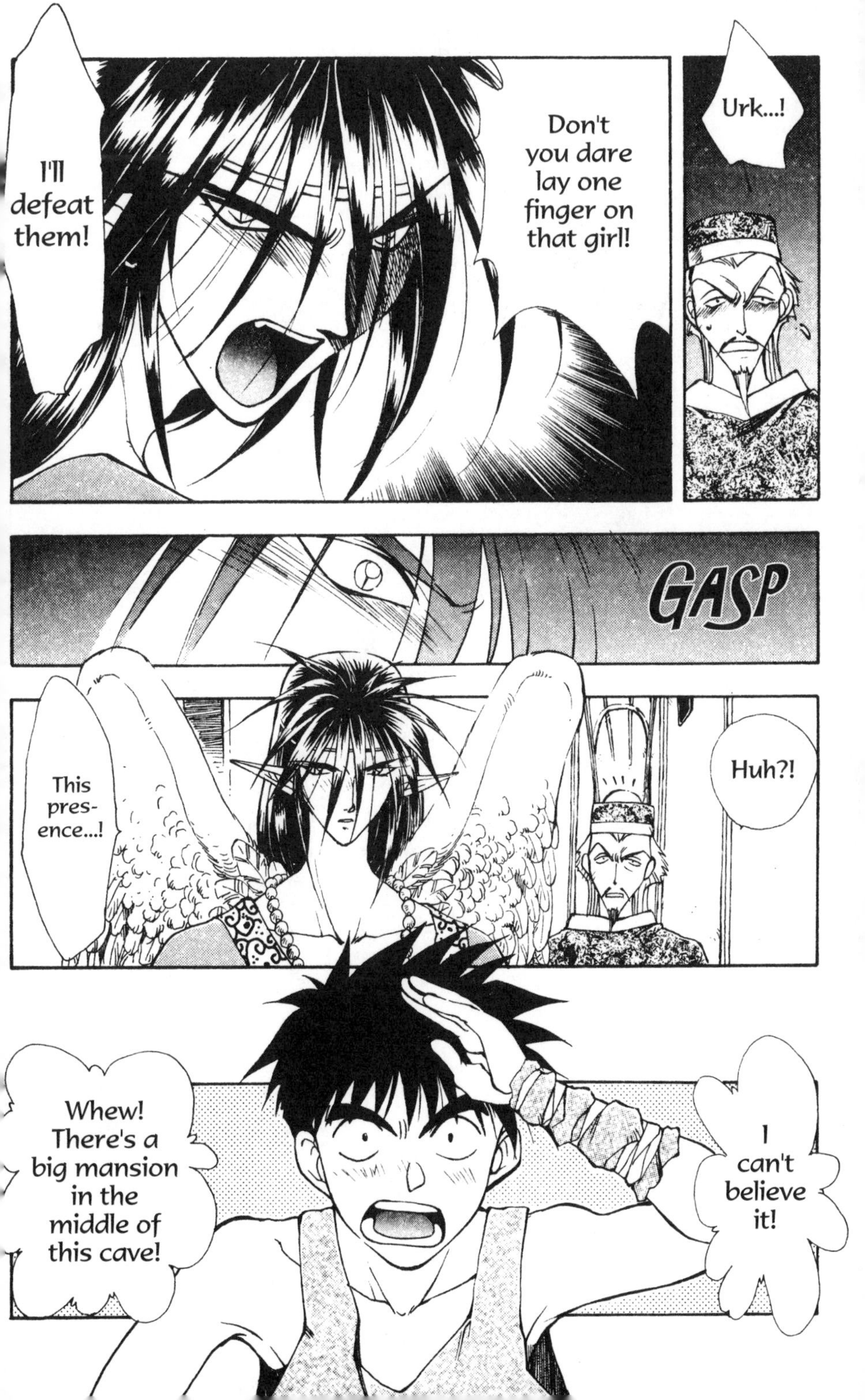
Urk...!
Don't you dare lay one finger on that girl!
I'll defeat them!
GASP
Huh?!
This presence...!
I can't believe it!
Whew! There's a big mansion in the middle of this cave!

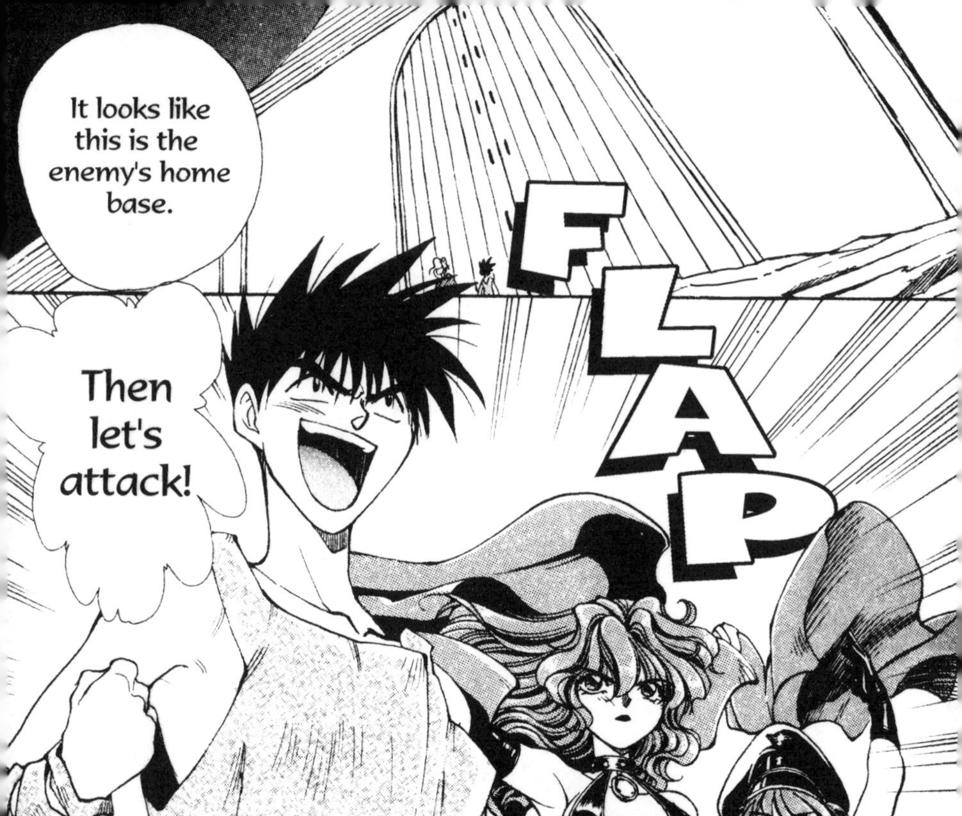
It looks like this is the enemy's home base.
Then let's attack!
FLAP

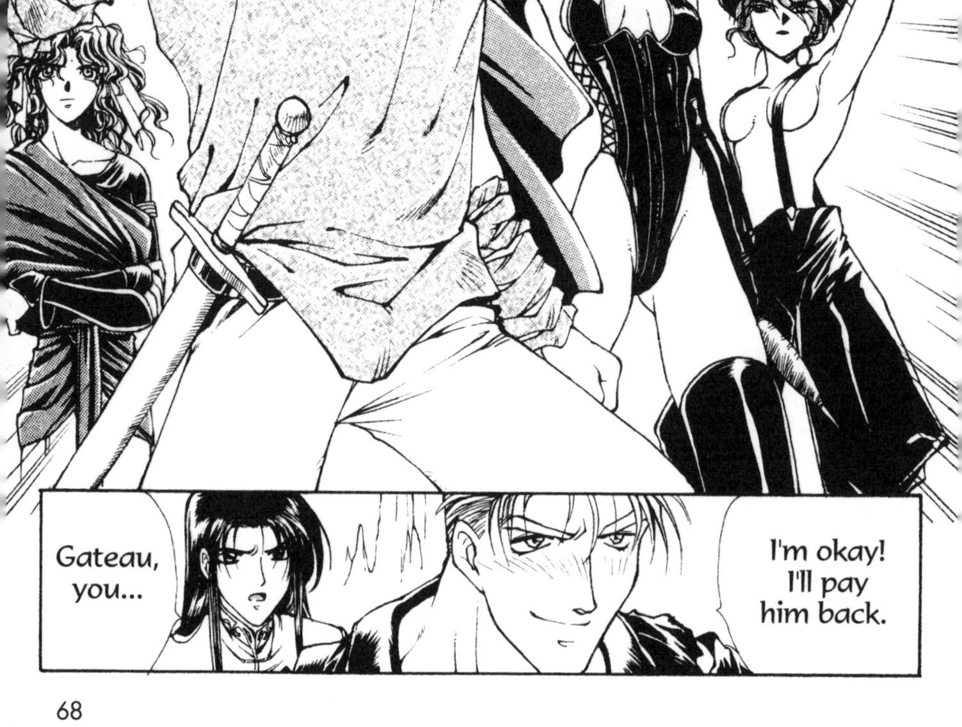
Gateau, you...
I'm okay! I'll pay him back.

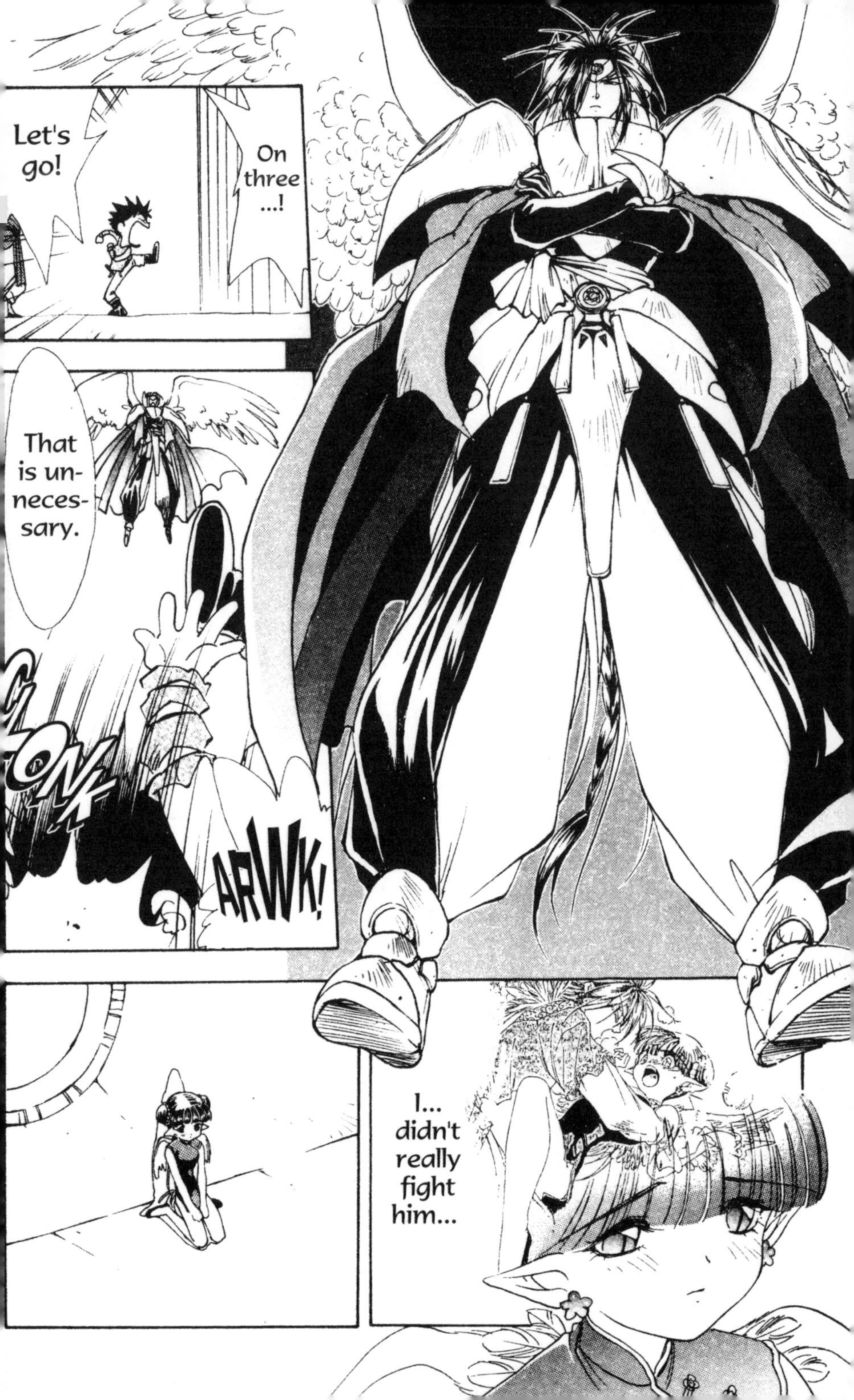
On three ...!
Let's go!
That is un-neces-sary.
CLONK
ARWK!
I... didn't really fight him...

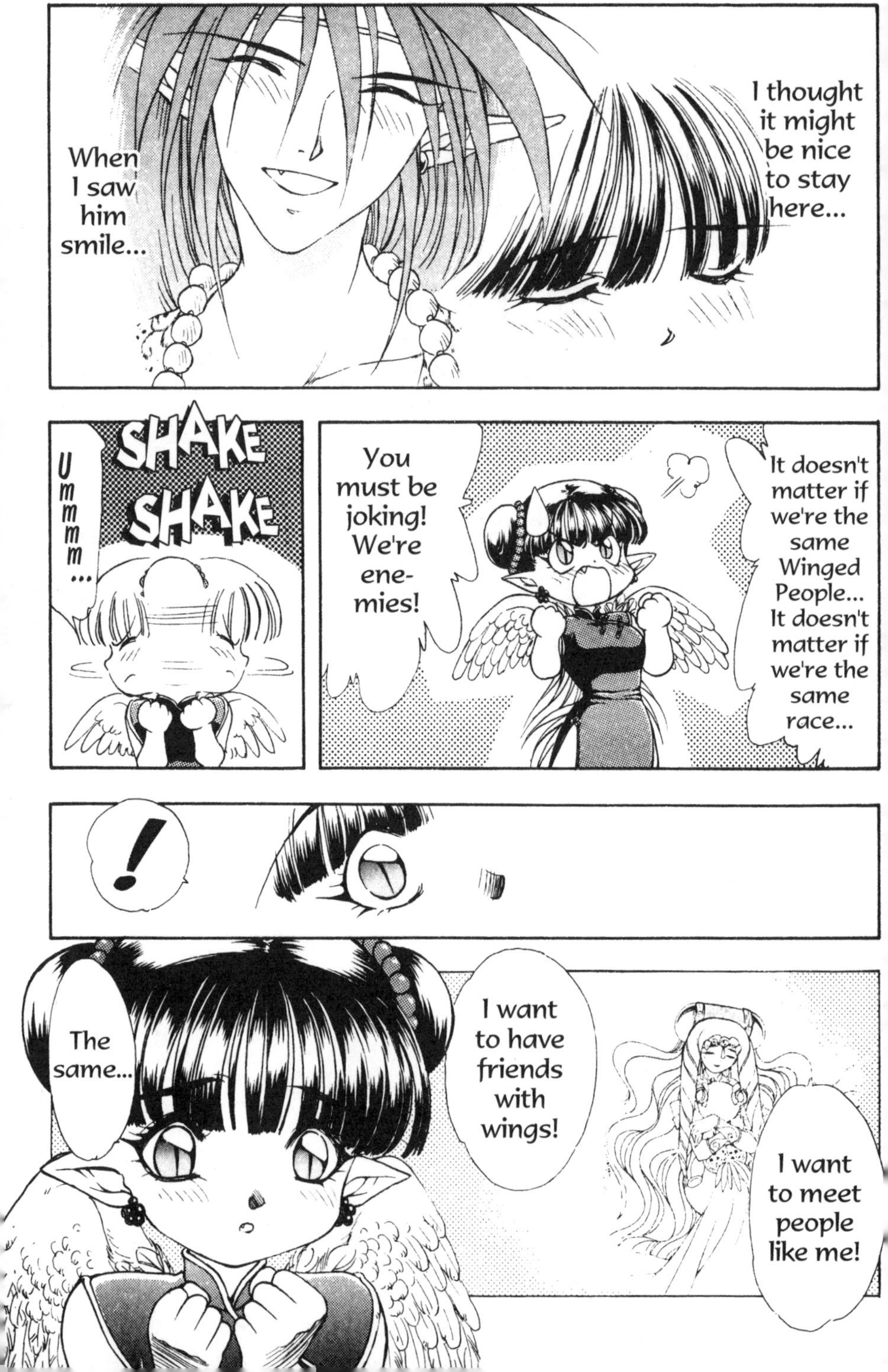
I thought it might be nice to stay here...
When I saw him smile...
It doesn't matter if we're the same Winged People... It doesn't matter if we're the same race...
You must be joking! We're ene-mies!
SHAKE SHAKE
Ummmm...
!
I want to have friends with wings!
I want to meet people like me!
The same...

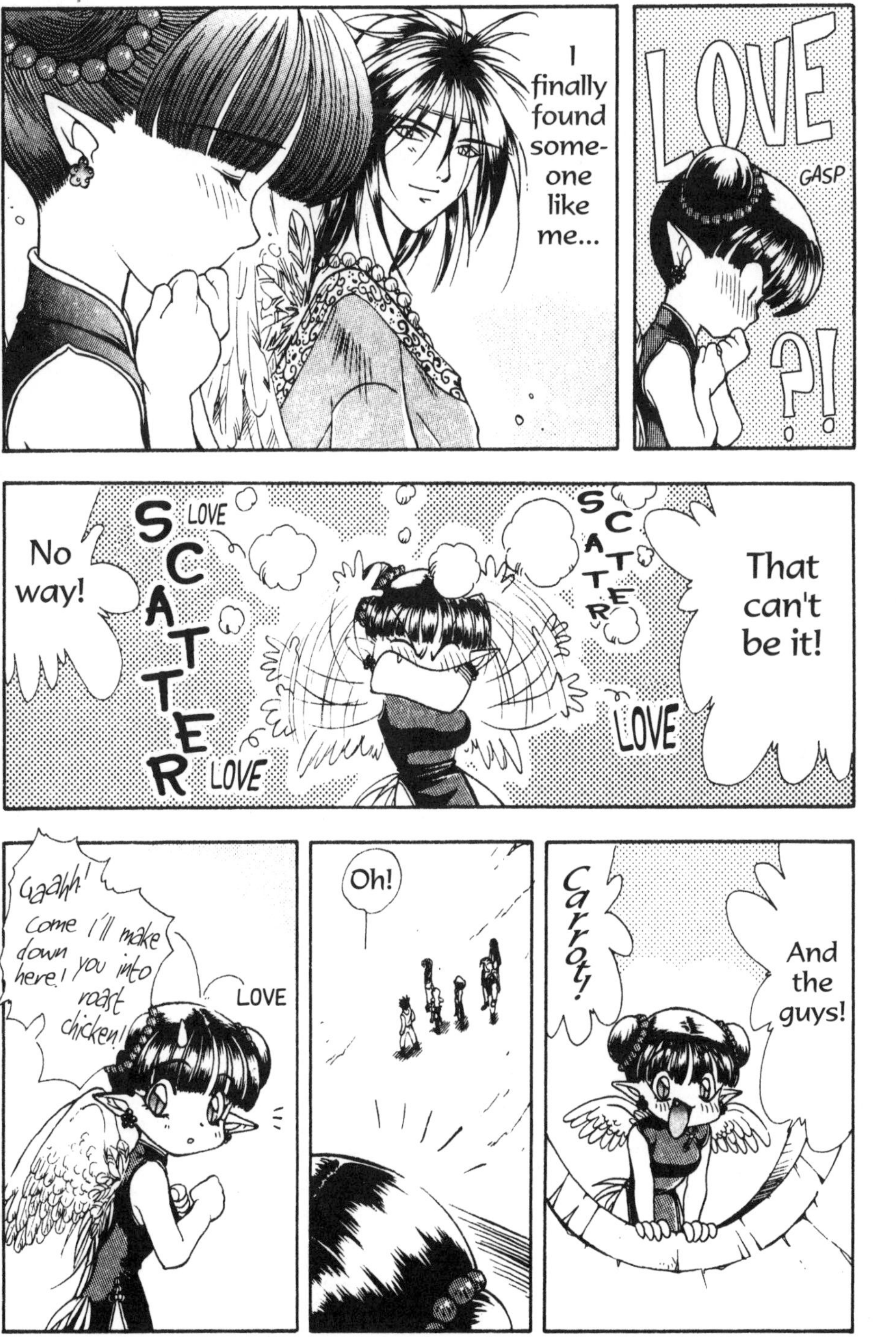
I finally found some-one like me...
LOVE
GASP
?!
No way!
SCATTER
LOVE
LOVE
SCATTER
LOVE
That can't be it!
Gaahh! Come down here! I'll make you into roast chicken!
LOVE
Oh!
Carrot!
And the guys!

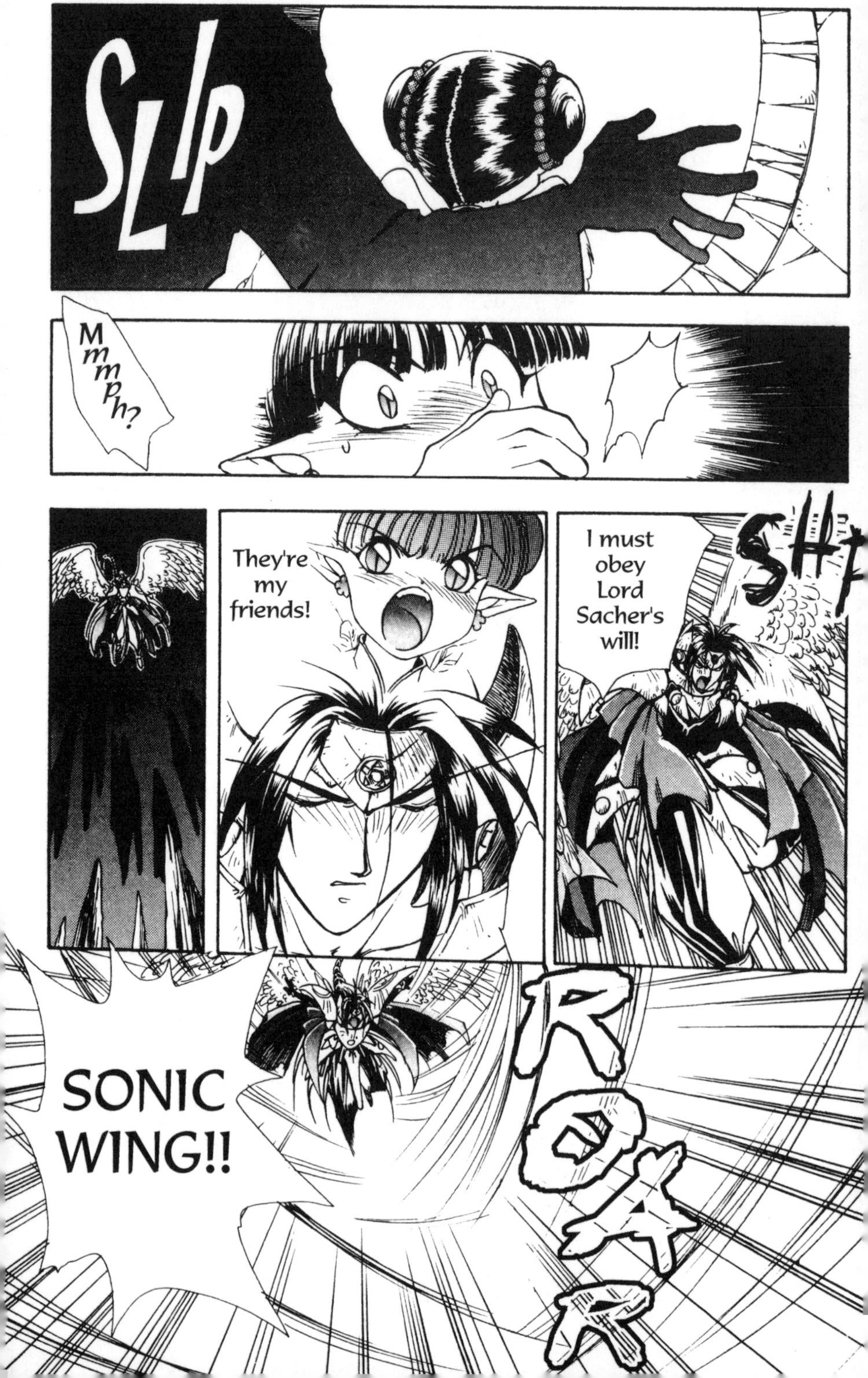
SLIP
Mmmph?
SHF
I must obey Lord Sacher's will!
They're my friends!
ROAR
SONIC WING!!

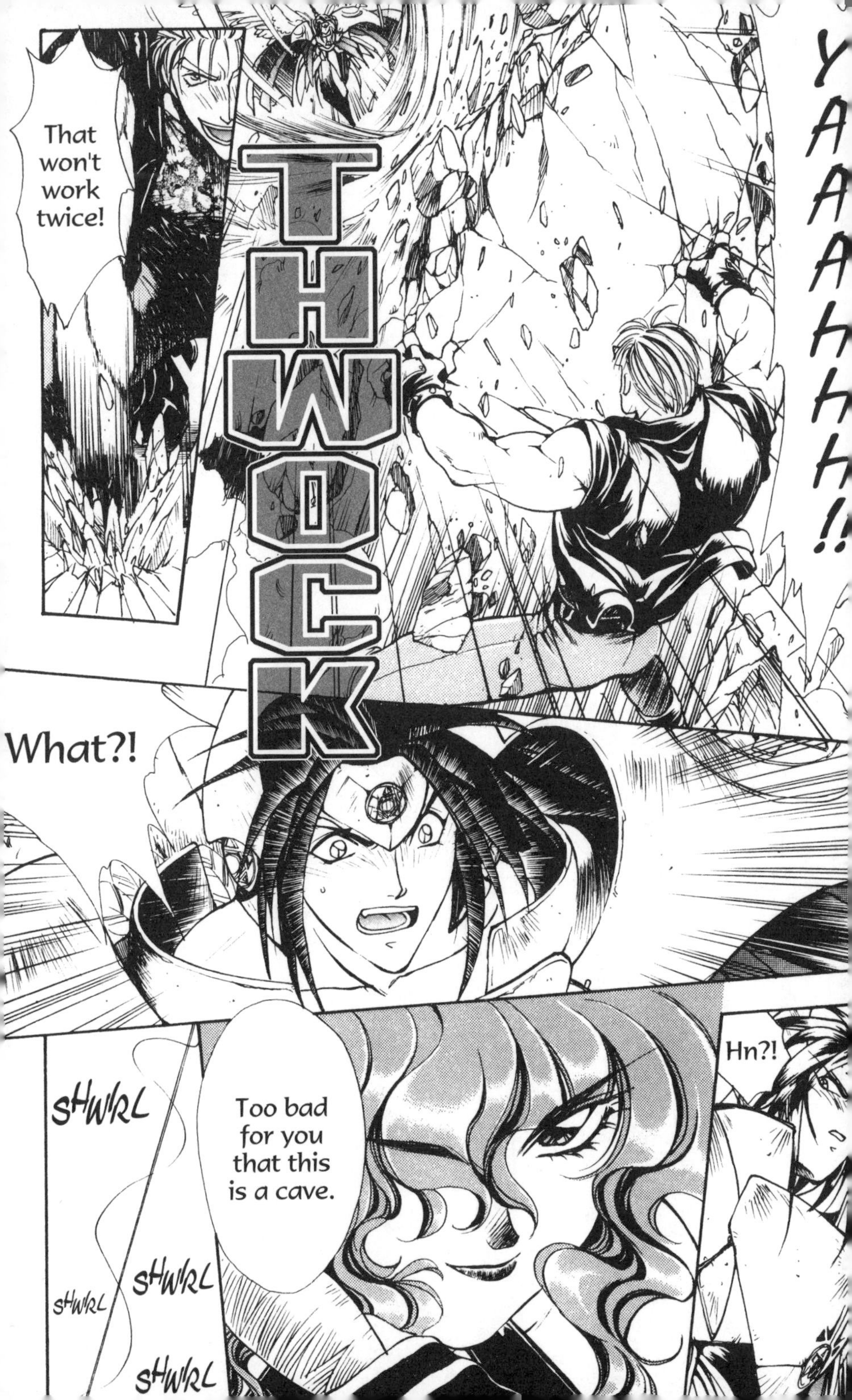
YAAAHHH!!
THWOCK
That won't work twice!
What?!
Hn?!
Too bad for you that this is a cave.
SHWIRL
SHWIRL
SHWIRL
SHWIRL

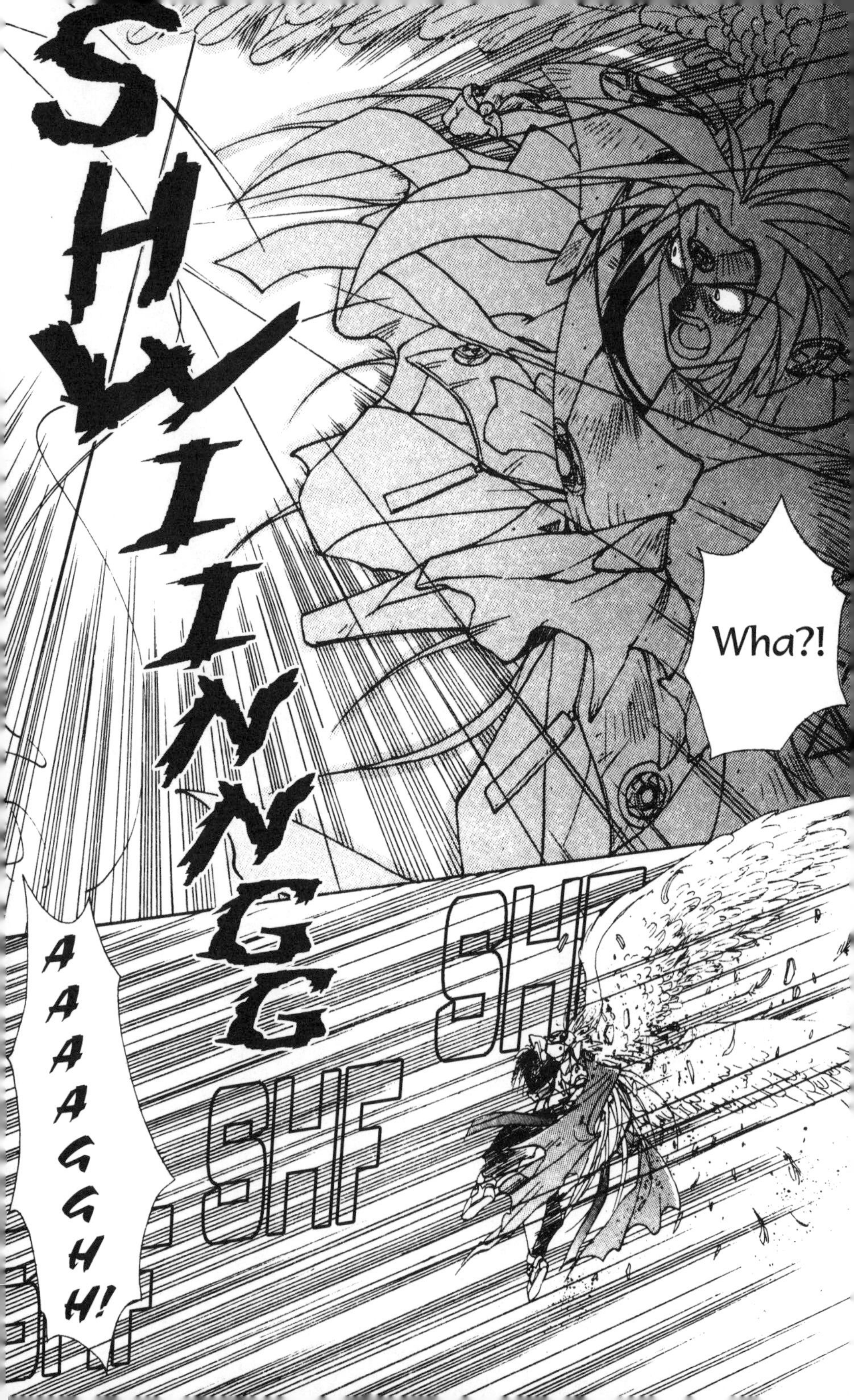
Wha?!
SHWIINNGG
SHF
SHF
AAAAAGGHH!

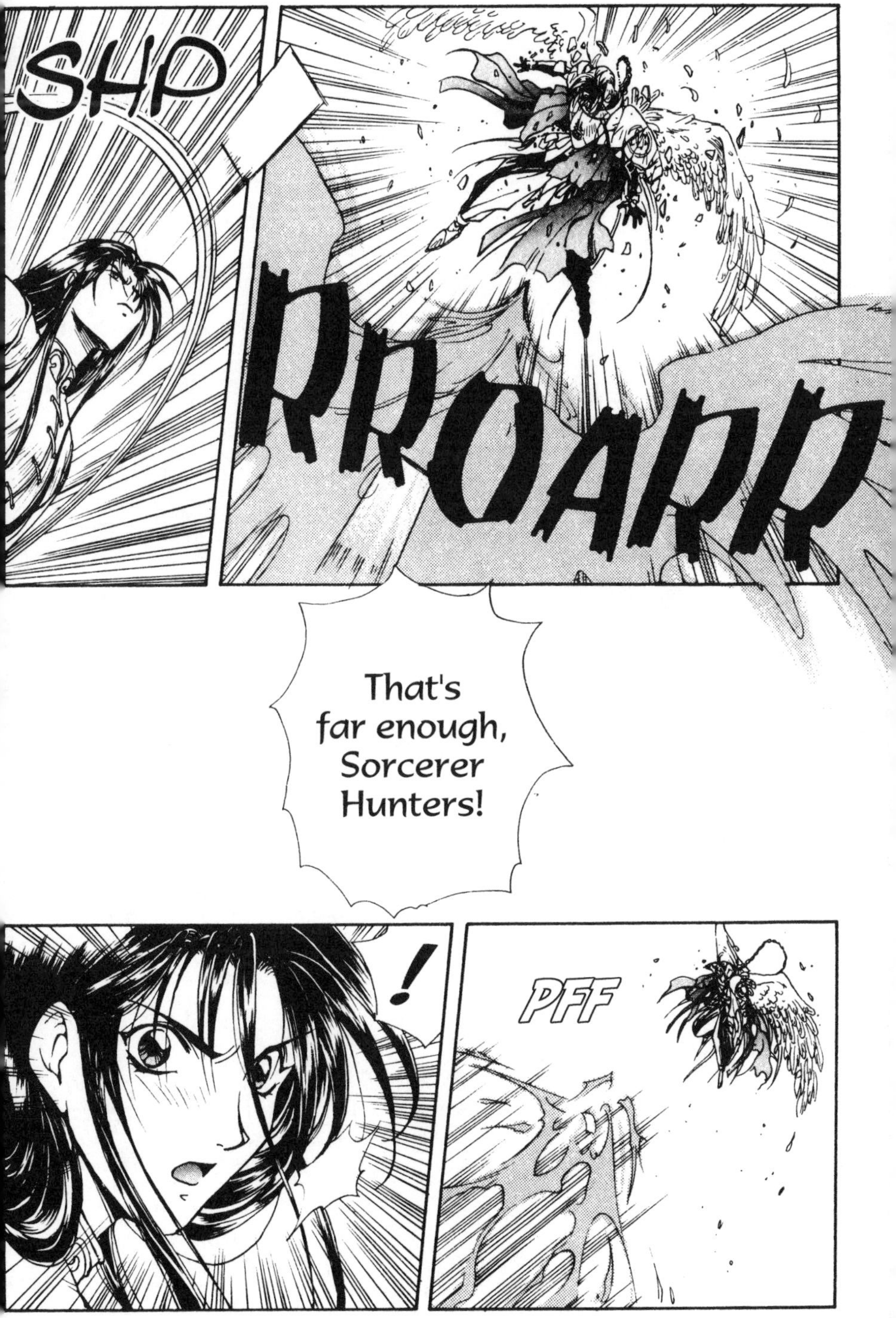
RROARR
SHP
That's far enough, Sorcerer Hunters!
PFF
!

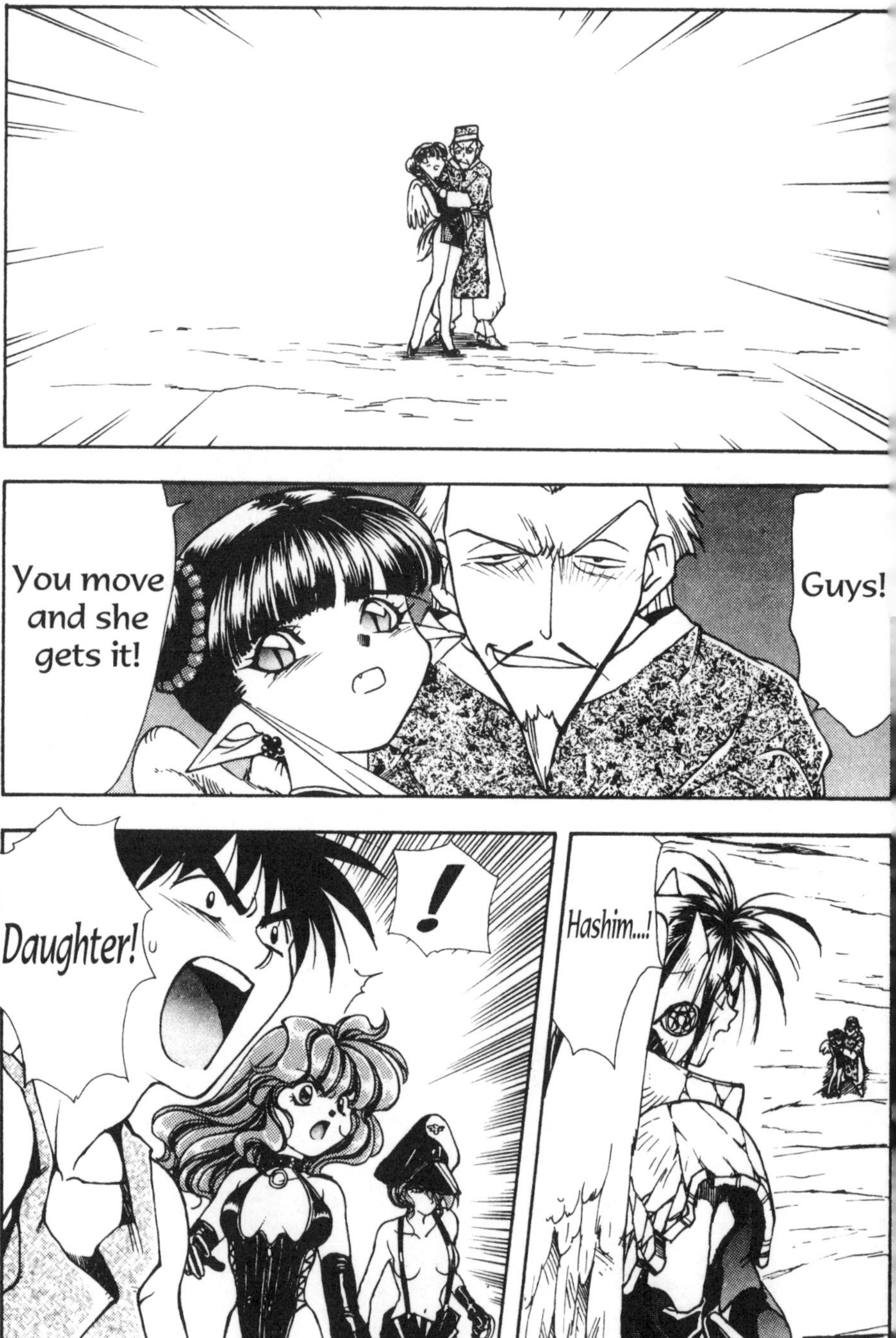
Guys!
You move and she gets it!
Hashim...!
!
Daughter!

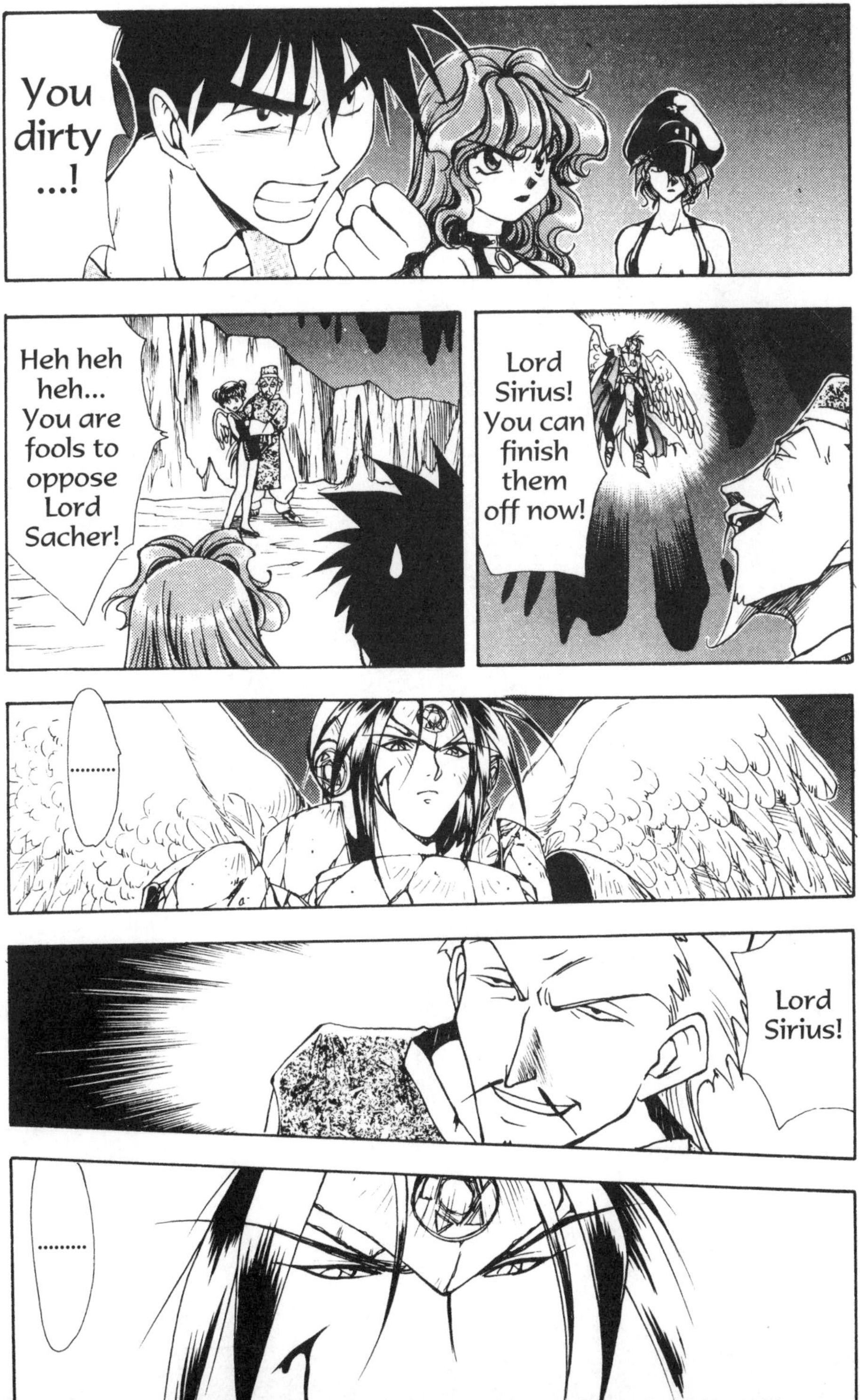
You dirty ...!
Lord Sirius! You can finish them off now!
Heh heh heh... You are fools to oppose Lord Sacher!
....
Lord Sirius!
....

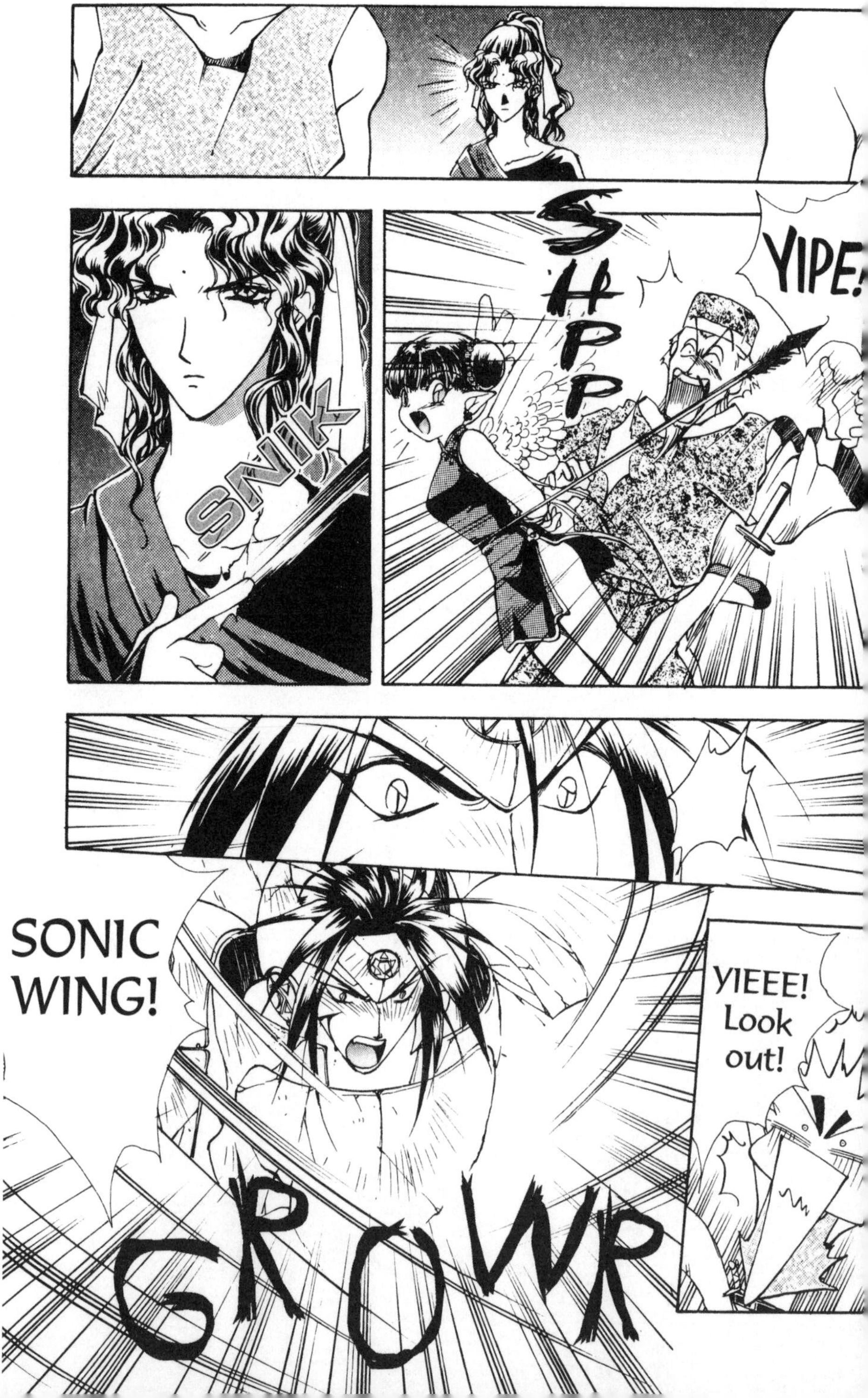
YIPE!
SHPP
SNIK
YIEEE! Look out!
SONIC WING!
GROWR

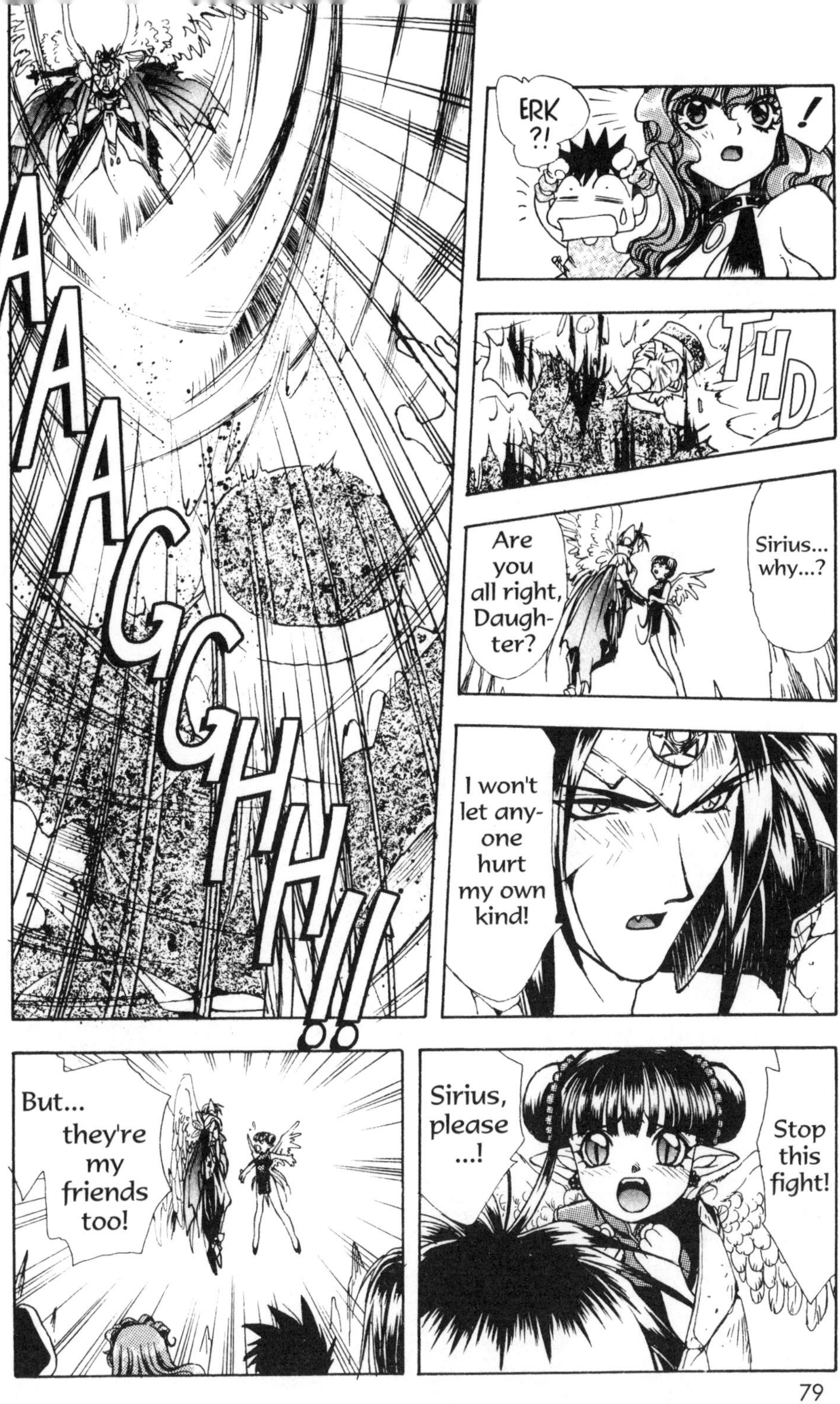
ERK ?!
!
THD
Sirius... why...?
Are you all right, Daughter?
I won't let anyone hurt my own kind!
AAAAGGHH!!
Stop this fight!
Sirius, please ...!
But... they're my friends too!

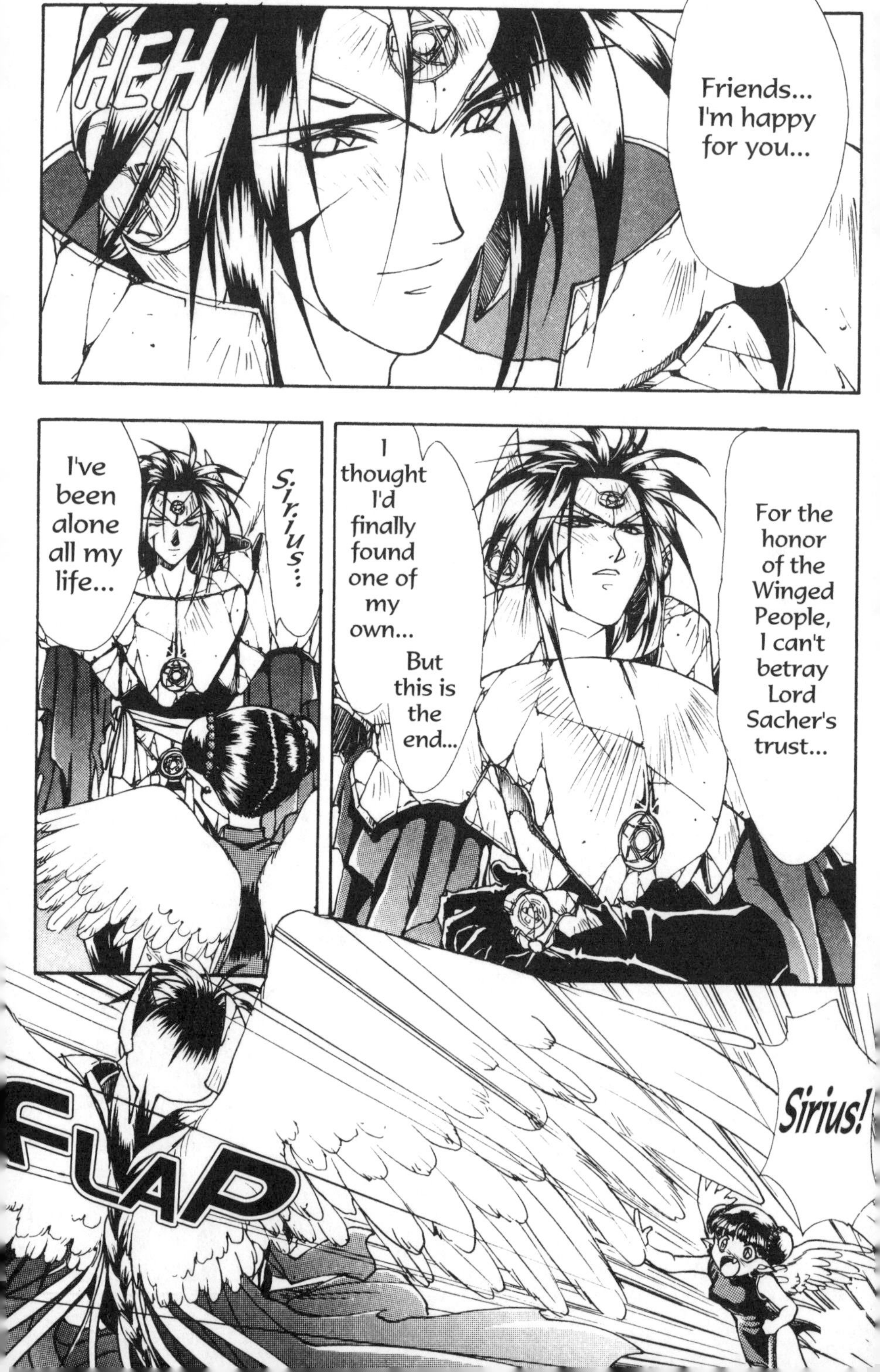
Friends... I'm happy for you...
HEH
For the honor of the Winged People, I can't betray Lord Sacher's trust...
I thought I'd finally found one of my own...
But this is the end...
Sirius...
I've been alone all my life...
Sirius!
FLAP

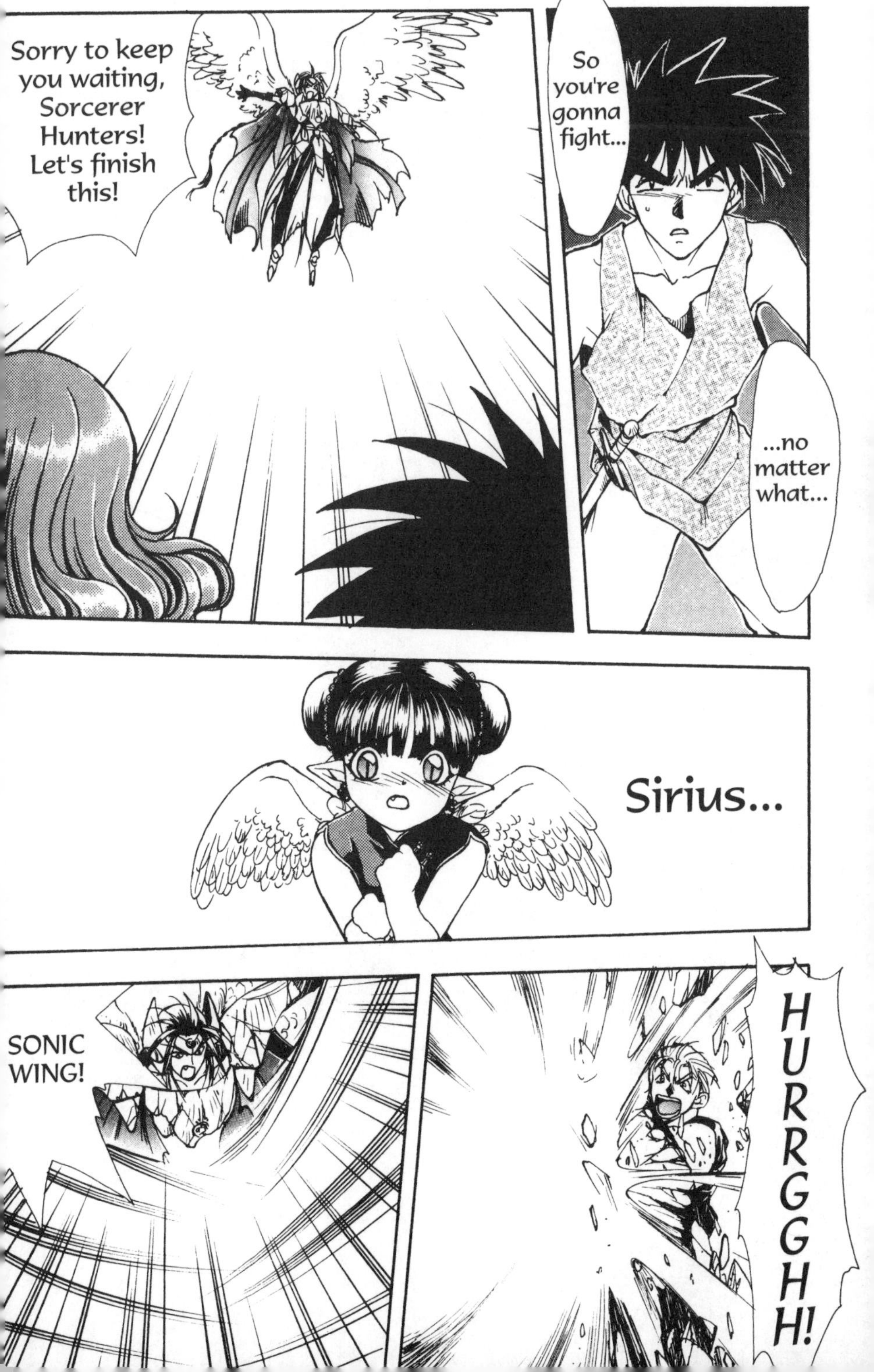
Sorry to keep you waiting, Sorcerer Hunters! Let's finish this!
So you're gonna fight...
...no matter what...
Sirius...
SONIC WING!
HURRGGH!

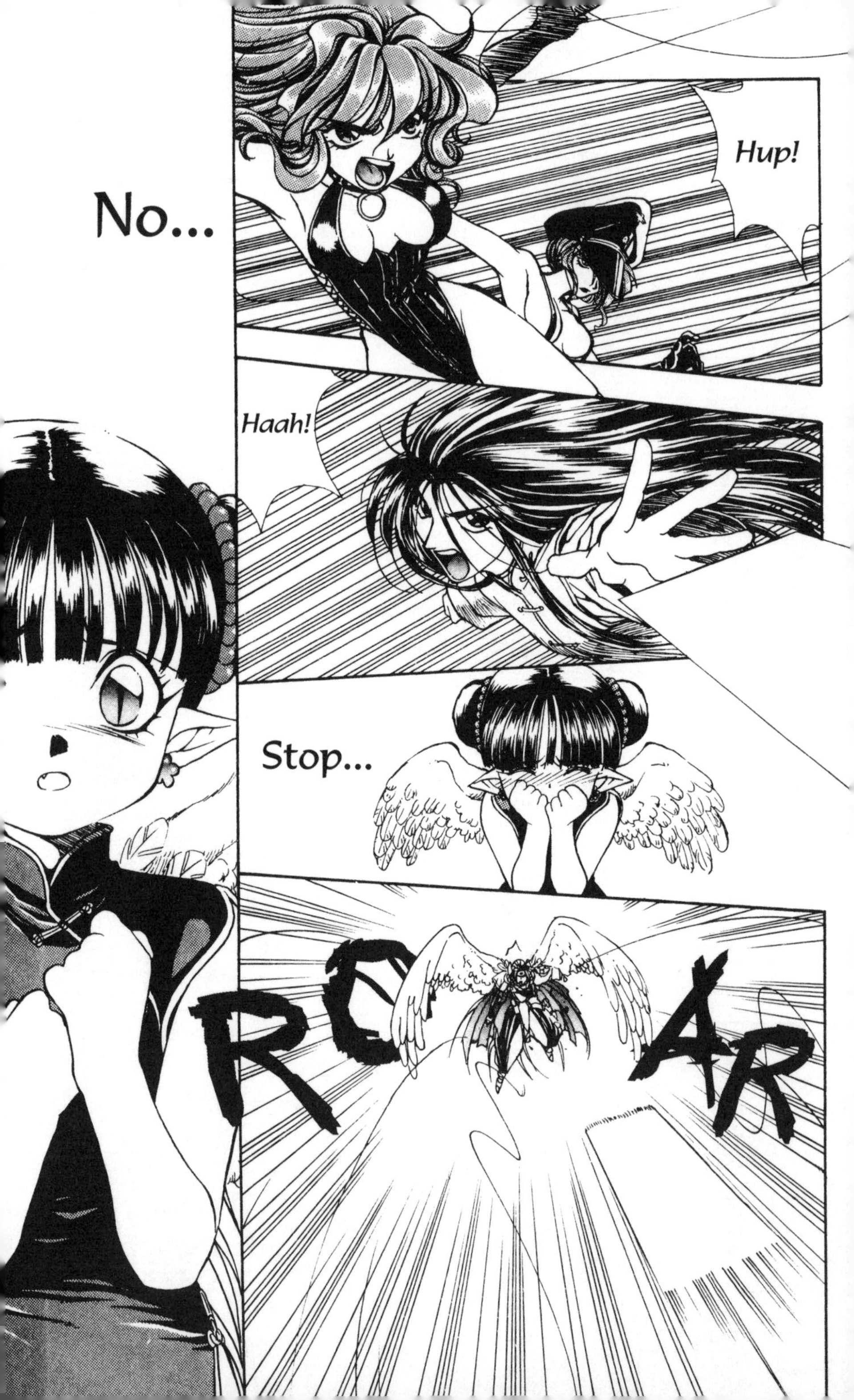
Hup!
No...
Haah!
Stop...
ROAR

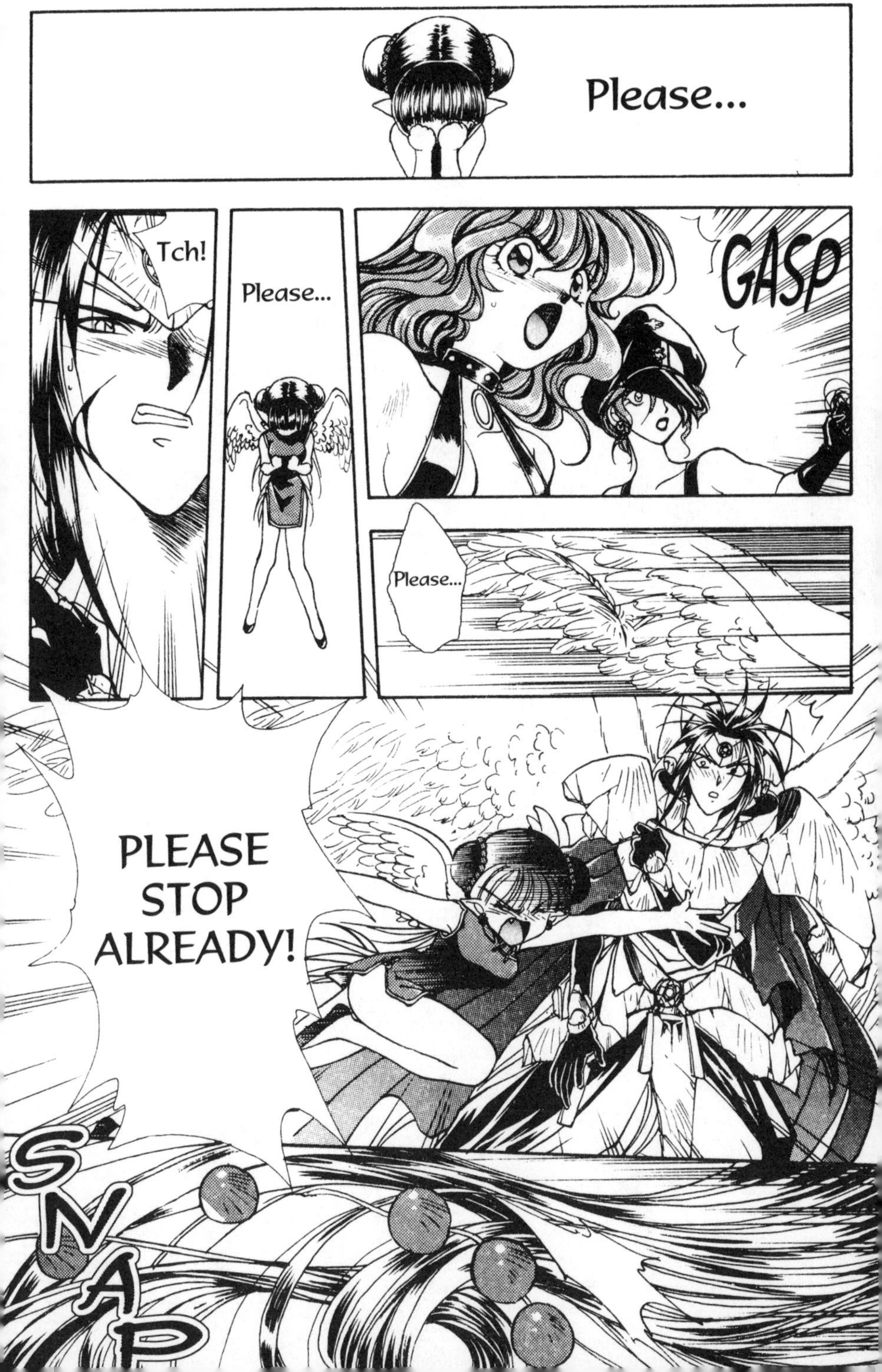
Please...
GASP
Please...
Please...
Tch!
PLEASE STOP ALREADY!
SNAP

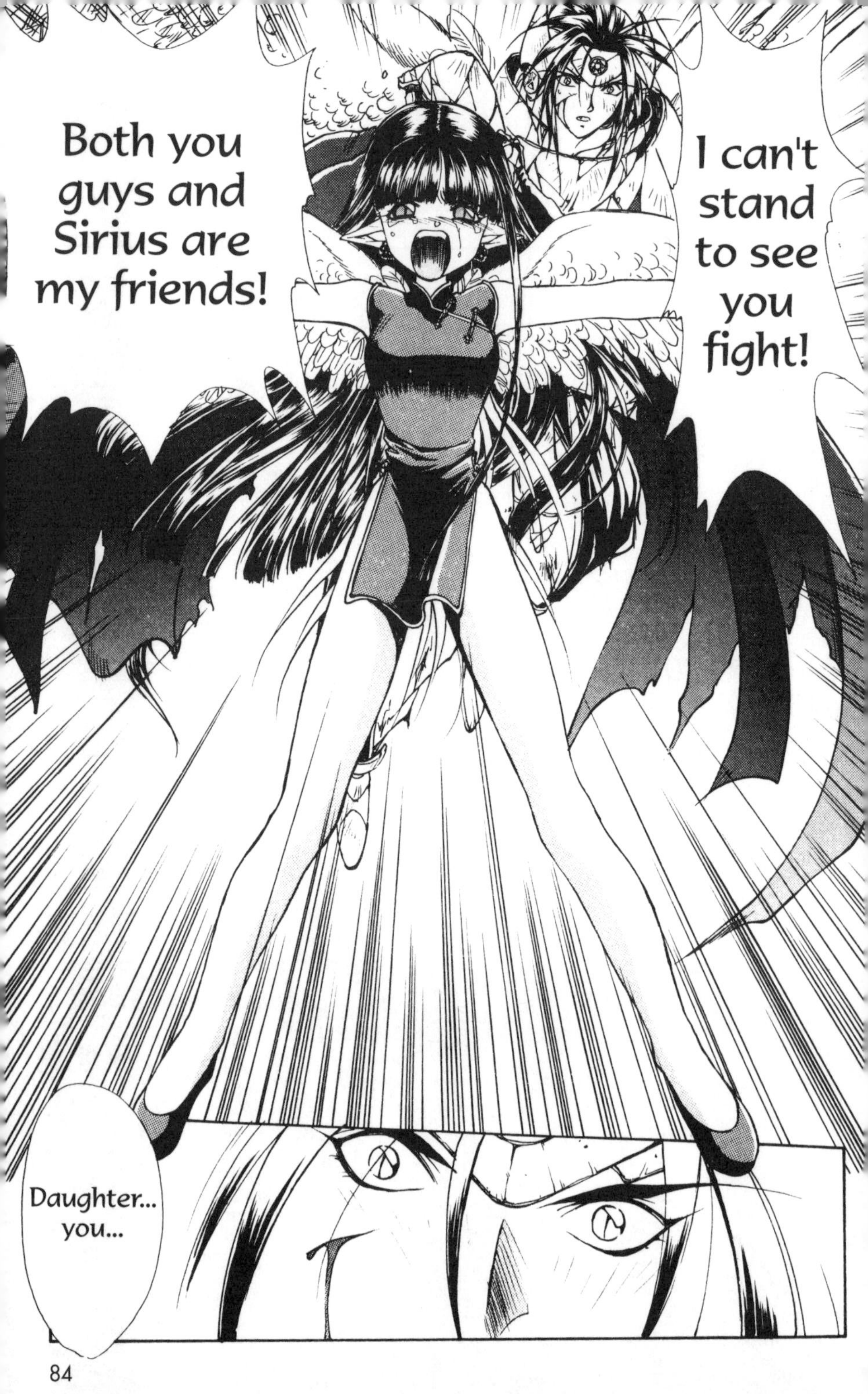
I can't stand to see you fight!
Both you guys and Sirius are my friends!
Daughter... you...

...aughter...

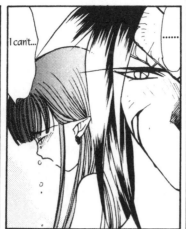

I can't...

......

Huh?

CLATTER

The Platina Stone is in there... Do what you will.

Sirius...

SNIK

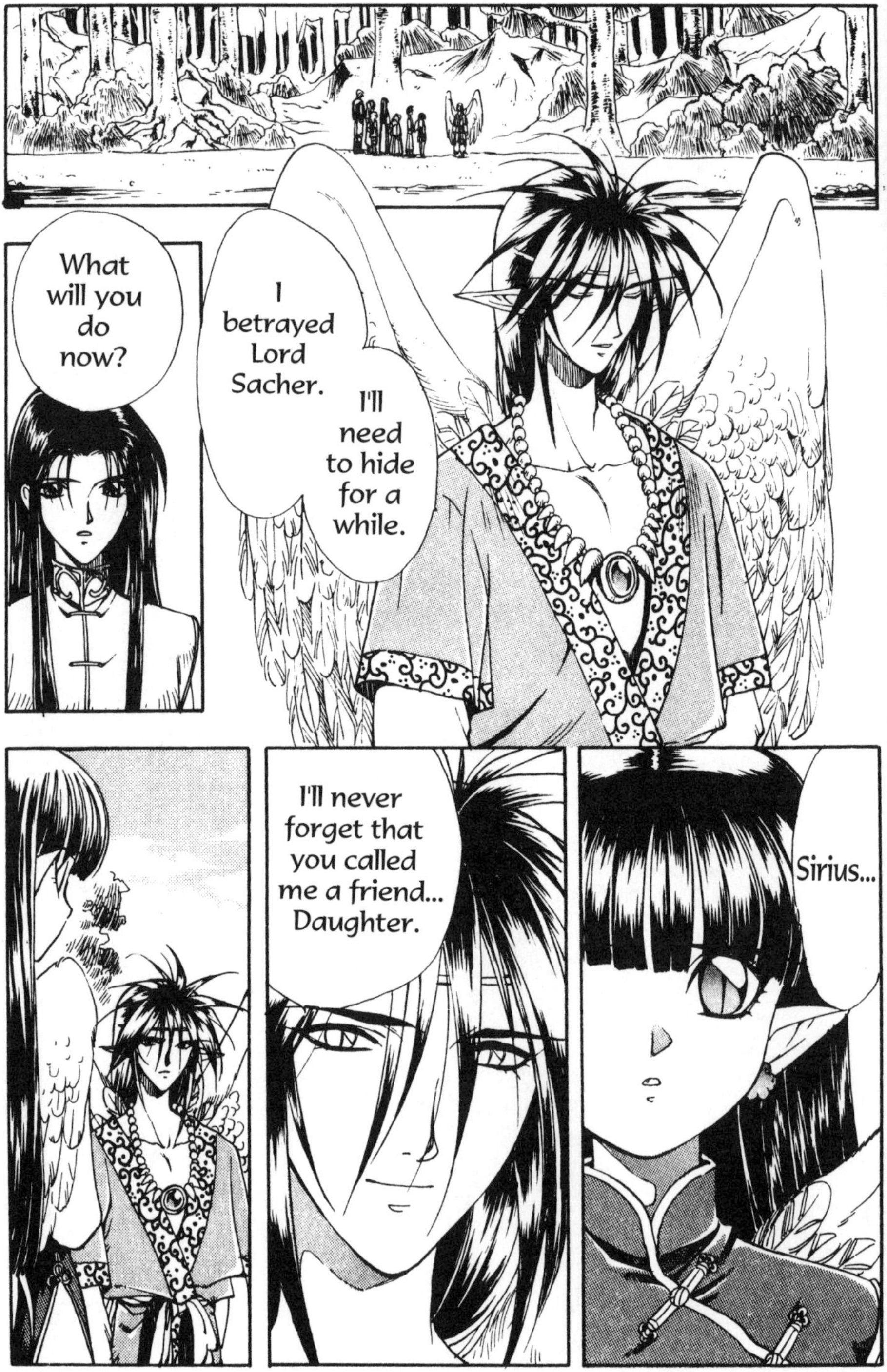
What will you do now?
I betrayed Lord Sacher.
I'll need to hide for a while.
I'll never forget that you called me a friend... Daughter.
Sirius...

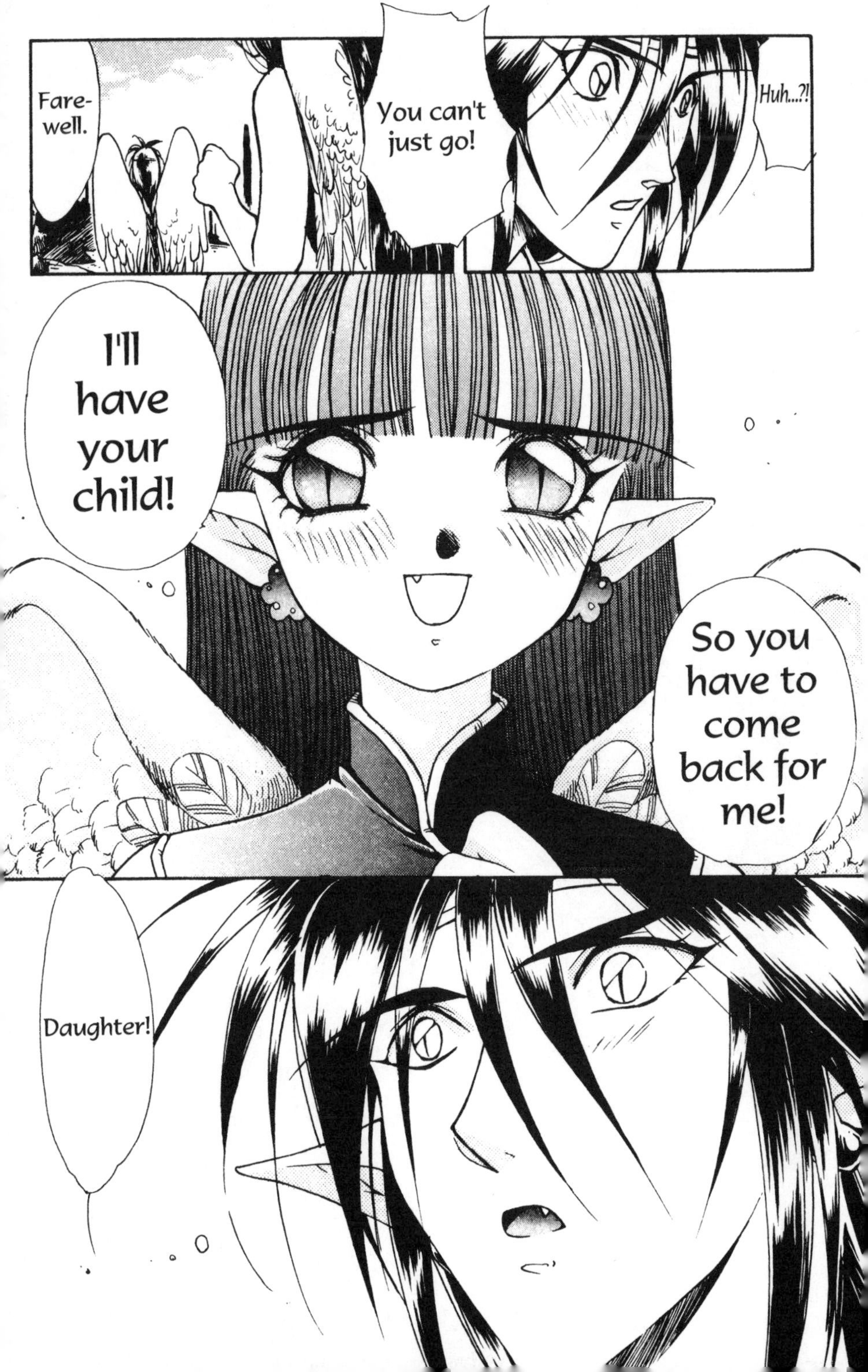
Huh...?!
You can't just go!
Fare-well.
So you have to come back for me!
I'll have your child!
Daughter!

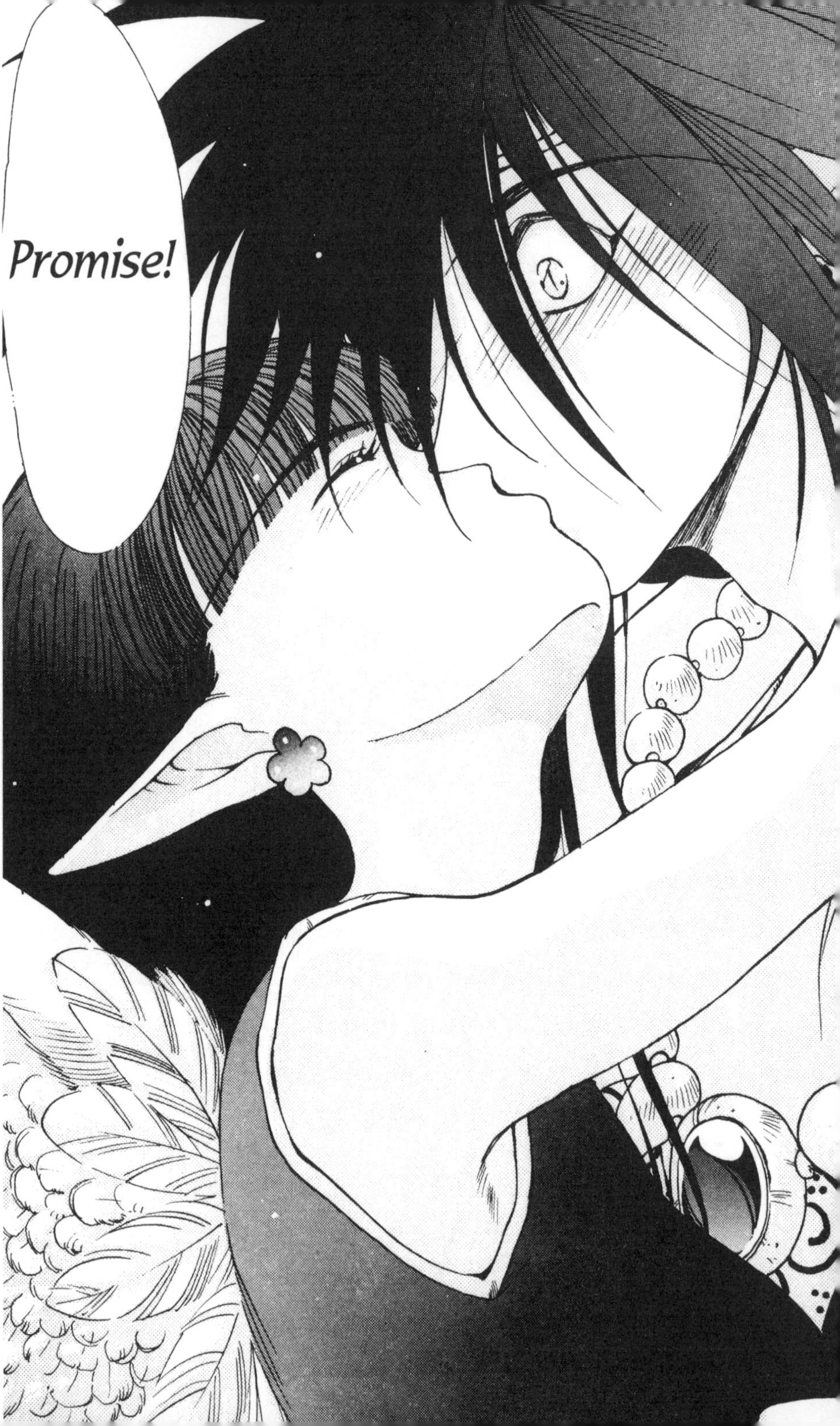
Promise!

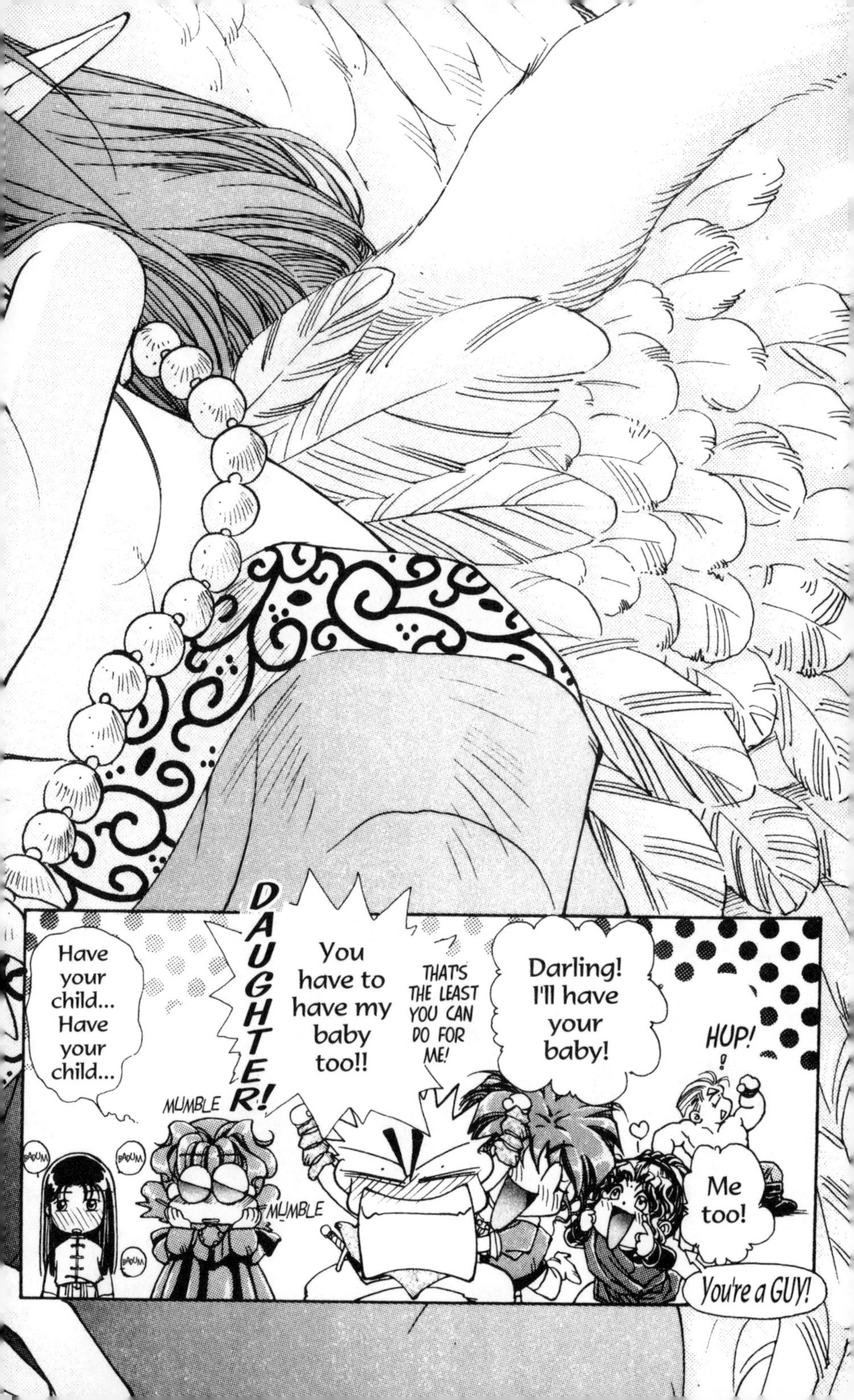
HUP!
Darling! I'll have your baby!
Me too!
You're a GUY!
THAT'S THE LEAST YOU CAN DO FOR ME!
You have to have my baby too!!
DAUGHTER!
Have your child... Have your child...
MUMBLE
MUMBLE
BADUM
BADUM
BADUM

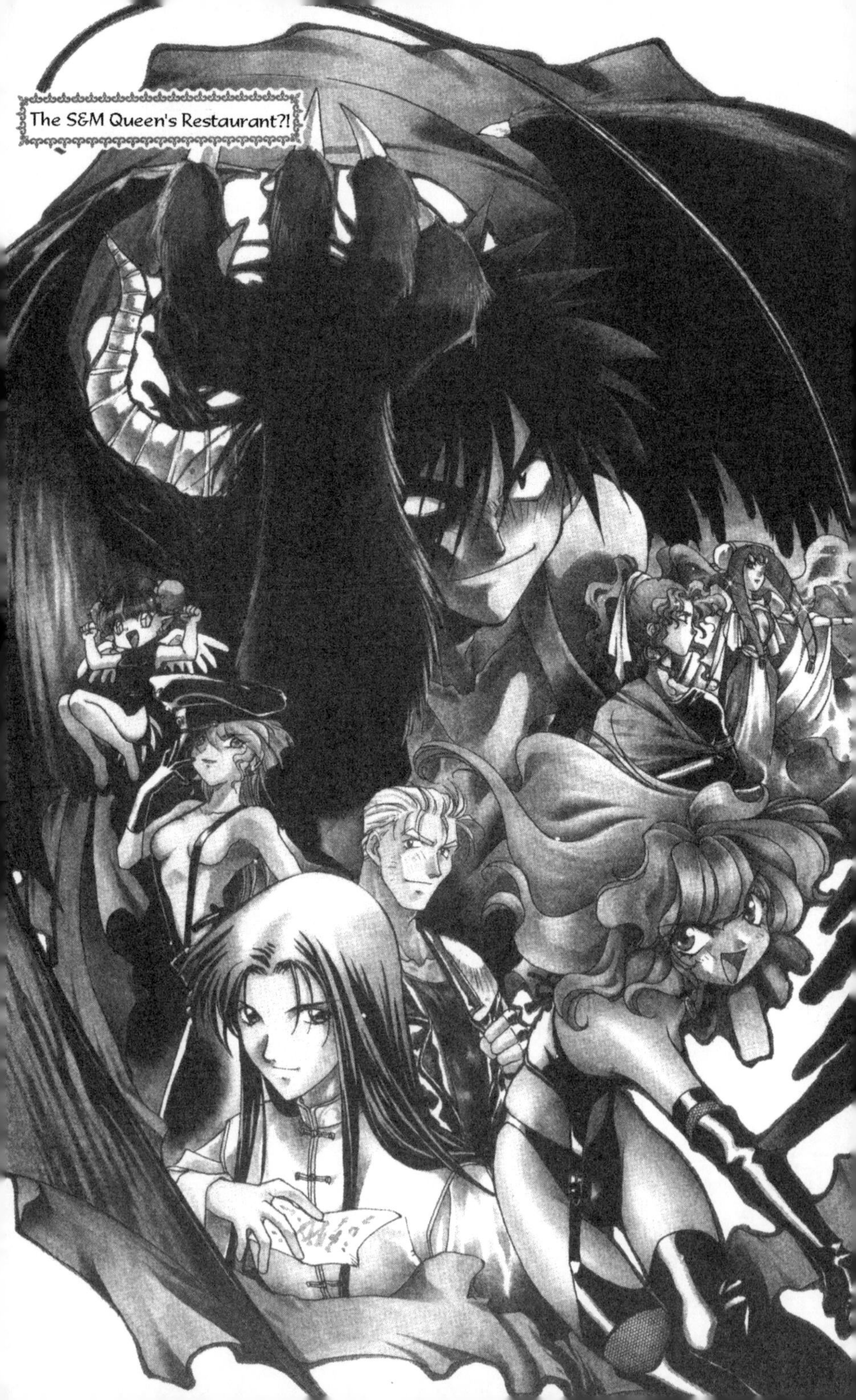
The S&M Queen's Restaurant?!

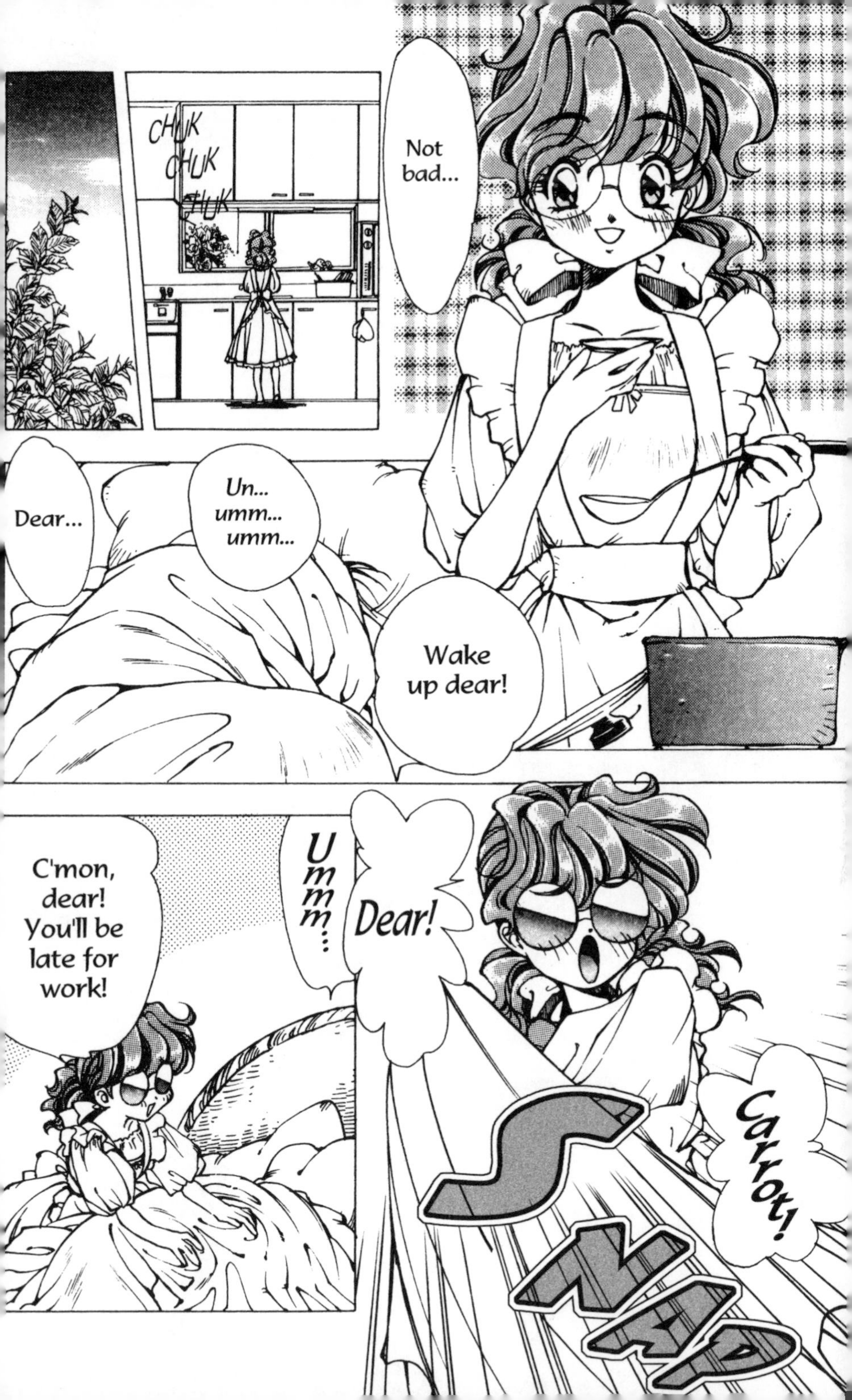
CHUK CHUK CHUK
Not bad...
Dear...
Un... umm... umm...
Wake up dear!
C'mon, dear! You'll be late for work!
Ummm...
Dear!
Carrot!
SNAP

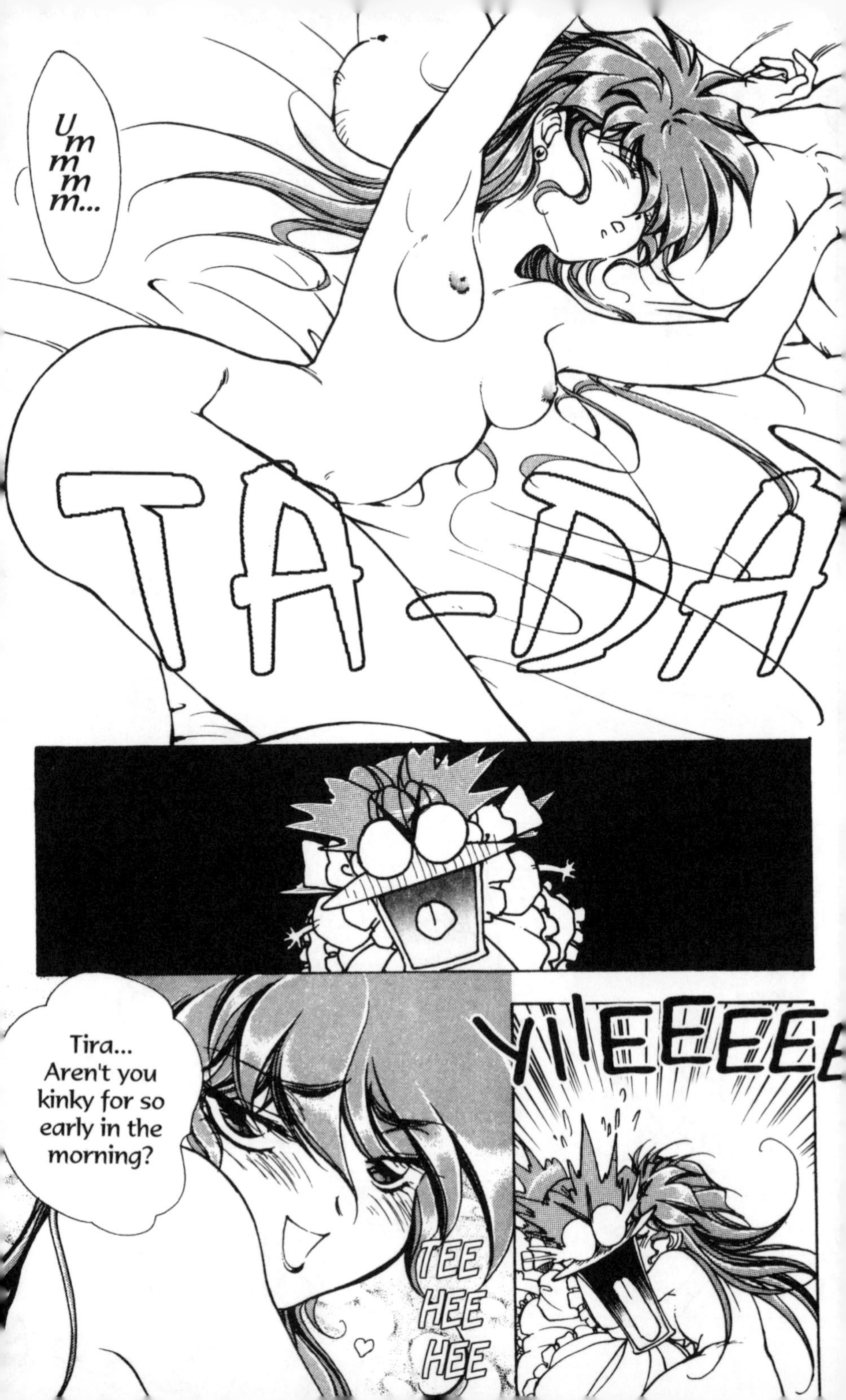
Ummmm...
TA-DA
Tira... Aren't you kinky for so early in the morning?
TEE HEE HEE
YIEEEEE

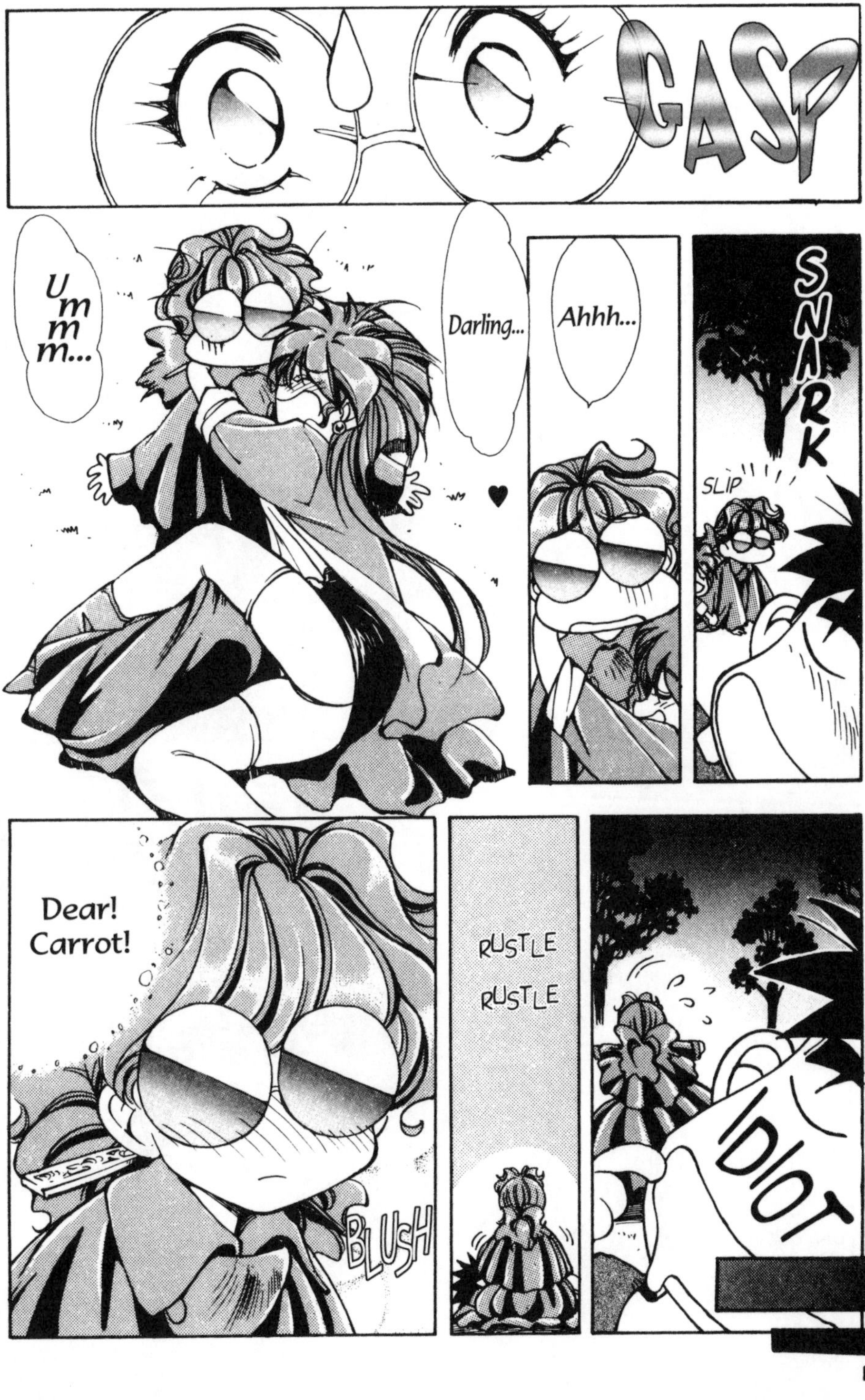
GASP
SNARK
SLIP
Ahhh...
Darling...
Ummmm...
IDIOT
RUSTLE
RUSTLE
Dear! Carrot!
BLUSH

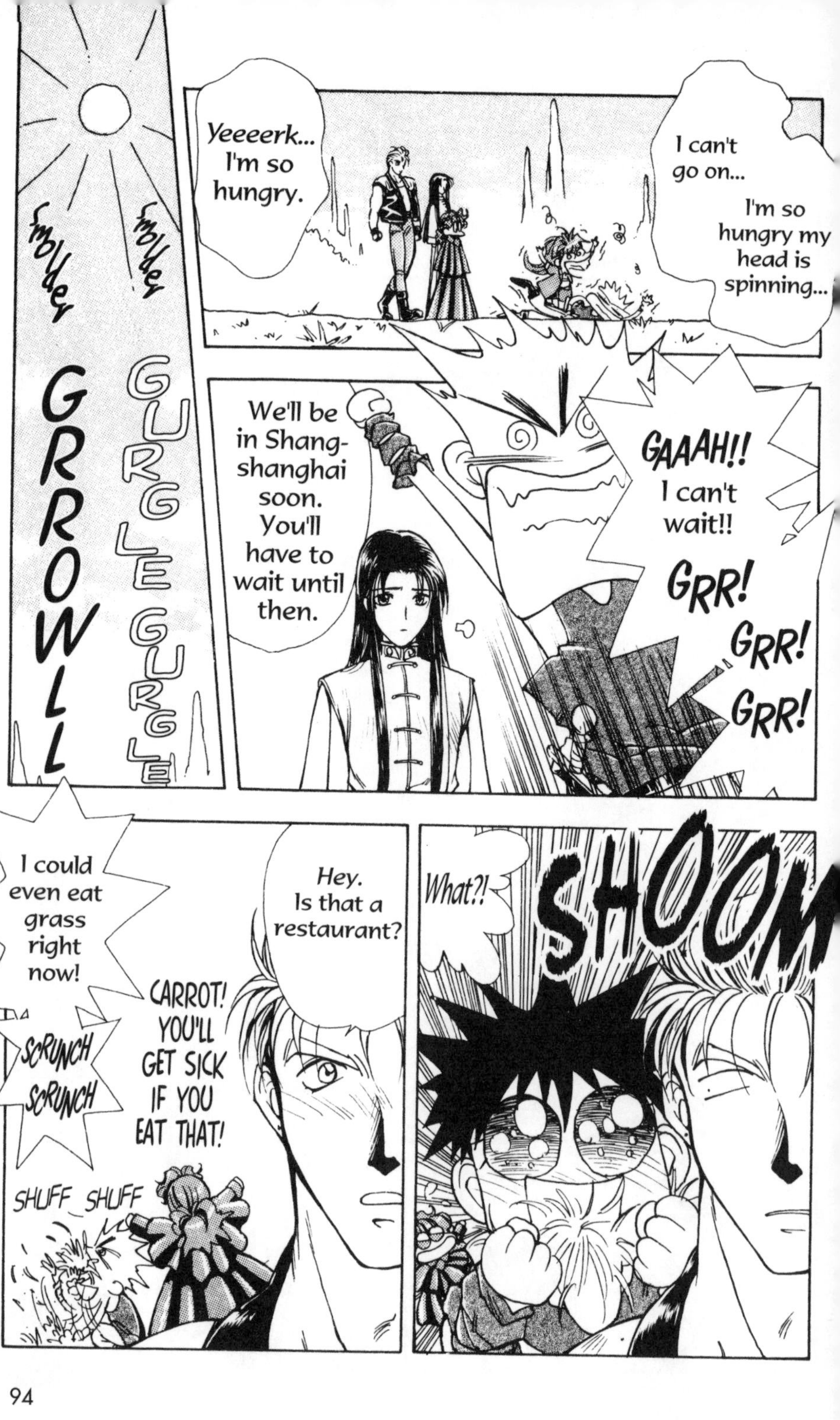
smolder smolder
GRROWLL
GURGLE GURGLE
Yeeeerk... I'm so hungry.
I can't go on...
I'm so hungry my head is spinning...
We'll be in Shang-shanghai soon. You'll have to wait until then.
GAAAH!! I can't wait!!
GRR! GRR! GRR!
I could even eat grass right now!
SCRUNCH SCRUNCH
CARROT! YOU'LL GET SICK IF YOU EAT THAT!
SHUFF SHUFF
Hey. Is that a restaurant?
What?!
SHOOM

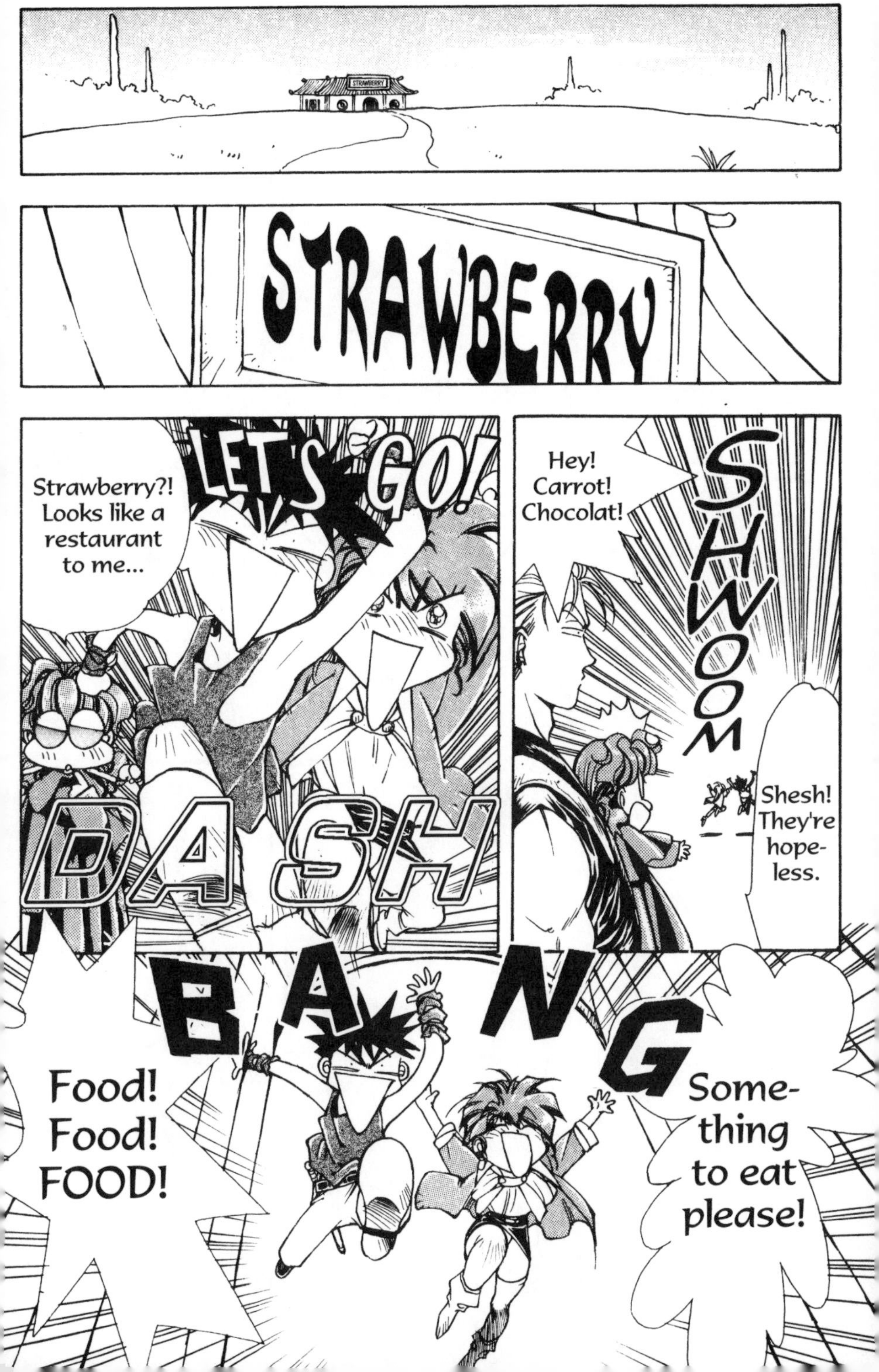
STRAWBERRY
STRAWBERRY
Strawberry?! Looks like a restaurant to me...
LET'S GO!
DASH
Hey! Carrot! Chocolat!
SHWOOM
Shesh! They're hope-less.
BANG
Food! Food! FOOD!
Some-thing to eat please!

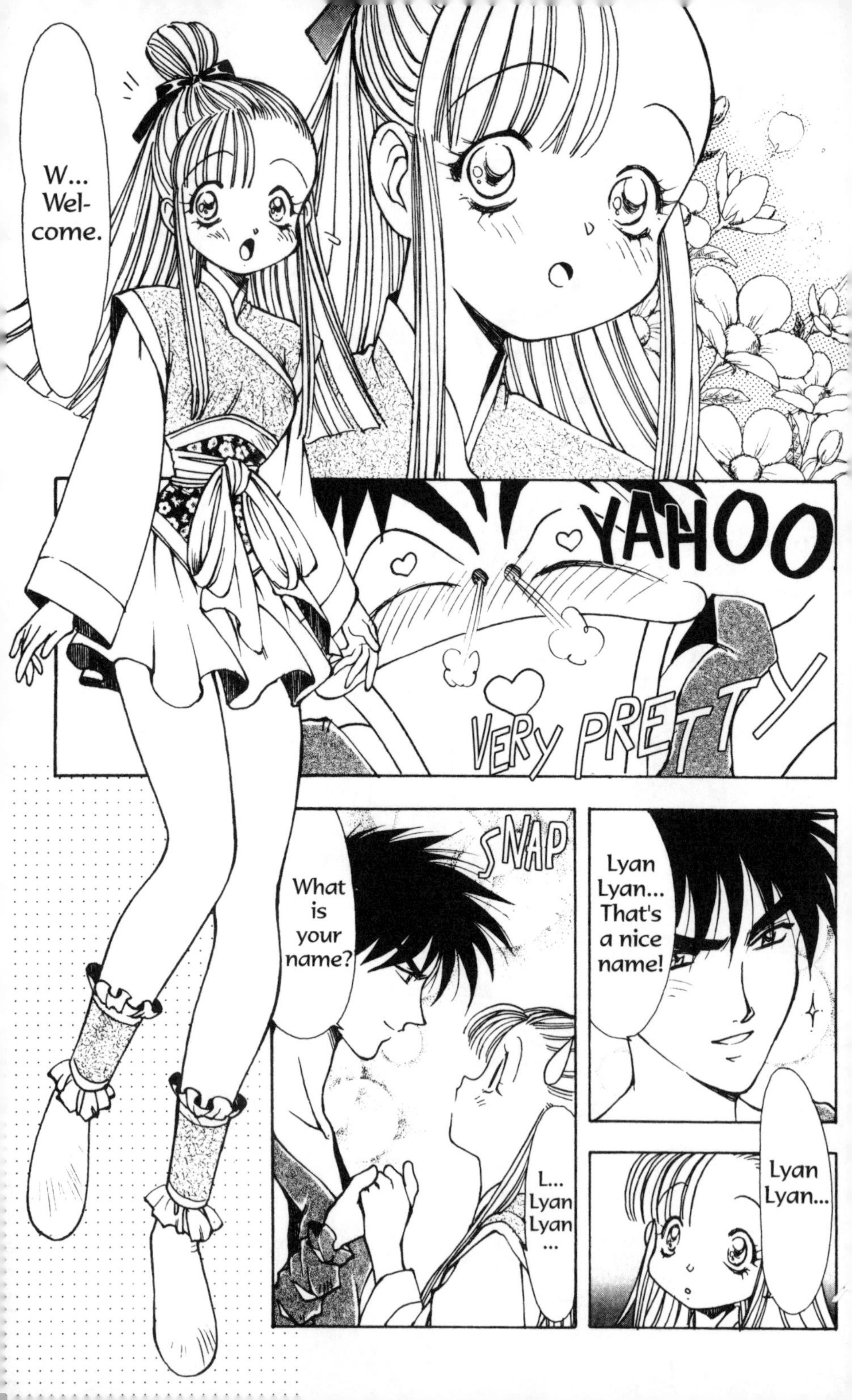
W... Wel-come.
YAHOO
VERY PRETTY
SNAP
What is your name?
L... Lyan Lyan ...
Lyan Lyan... That's a nice name!
Lyan Lyan...

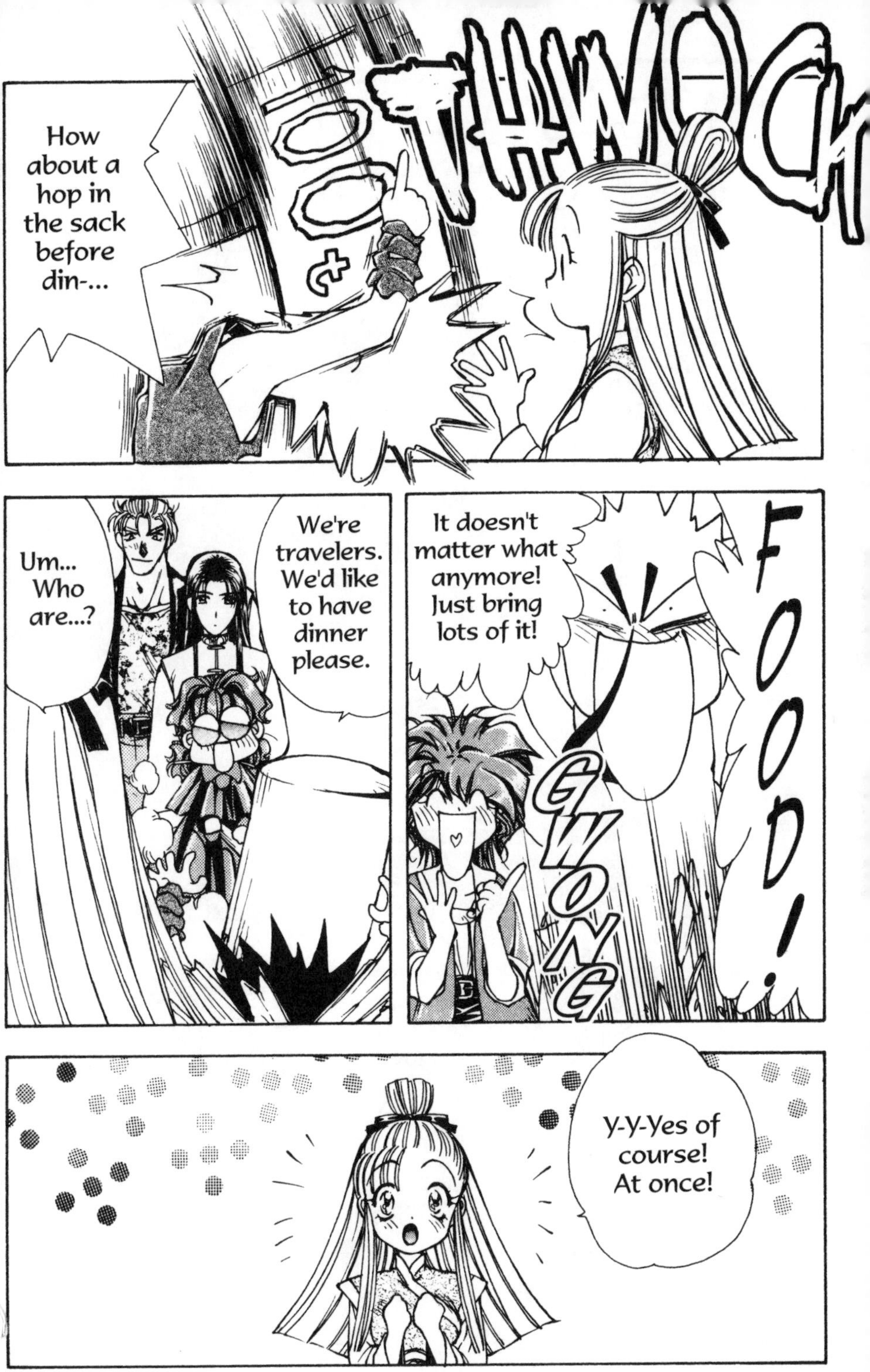
How about a hop in the sack before din-...
THWOCK
Um... Who are...?
We're travelers. We'd like to have dinner please.
It doesn't matter what anymore! Just bring lots of it!
GWONG
FOOD!
Y-Y-Yes of course! At once!

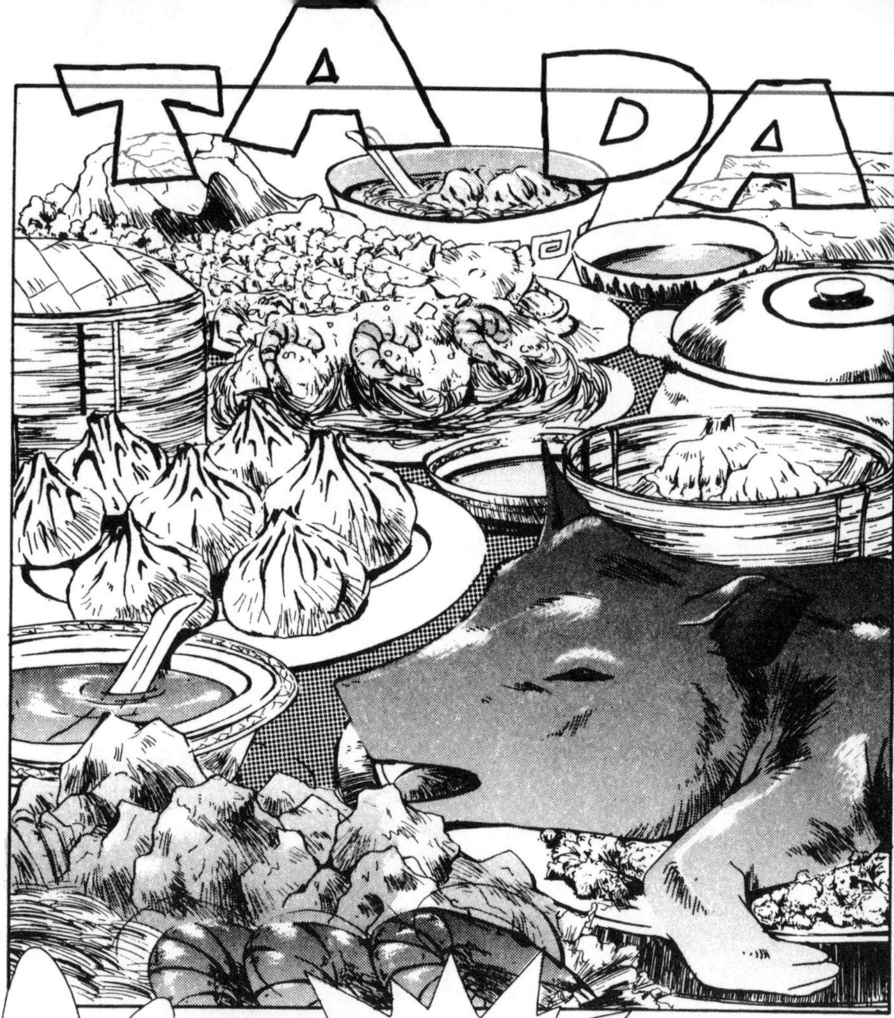
TA DA

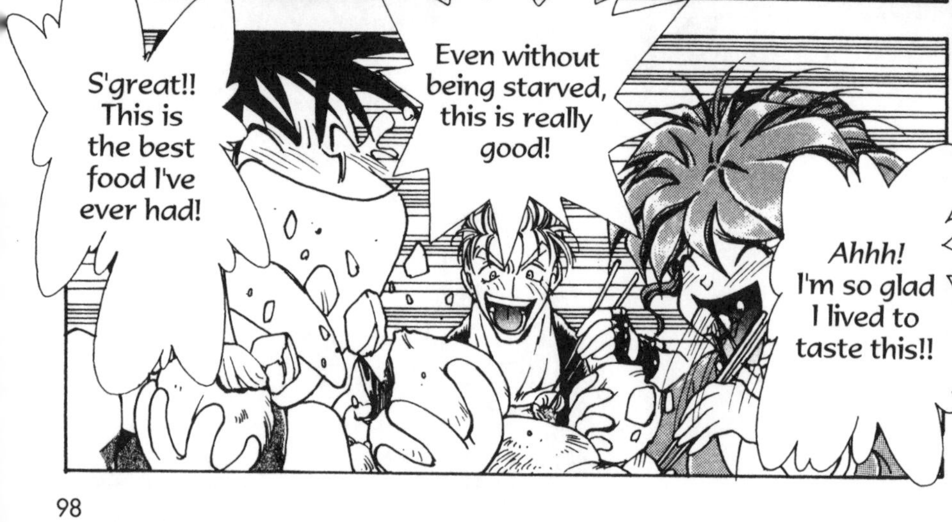
Ahhh! I'm so glad I lived to taste this!!
Even without being starved, this is really good!
S'great!! This is the best food I've ever had!

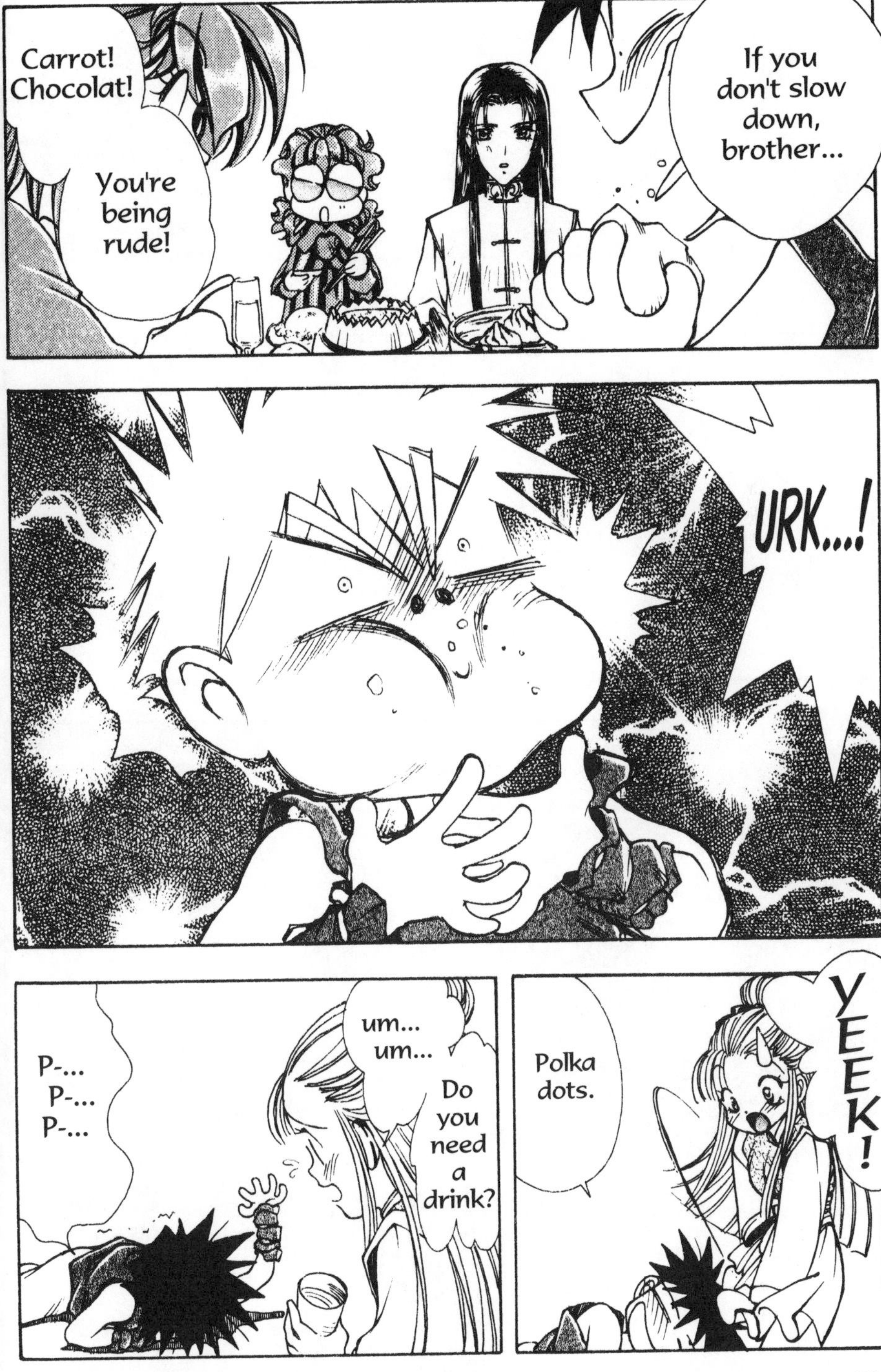
If you don't slow down, brother...
Carrot! Chocolat!
You're being rude!
URK...!
YEEK!
Polka dots.
um... um...
Do you need a drink?
P-... P-... P-...

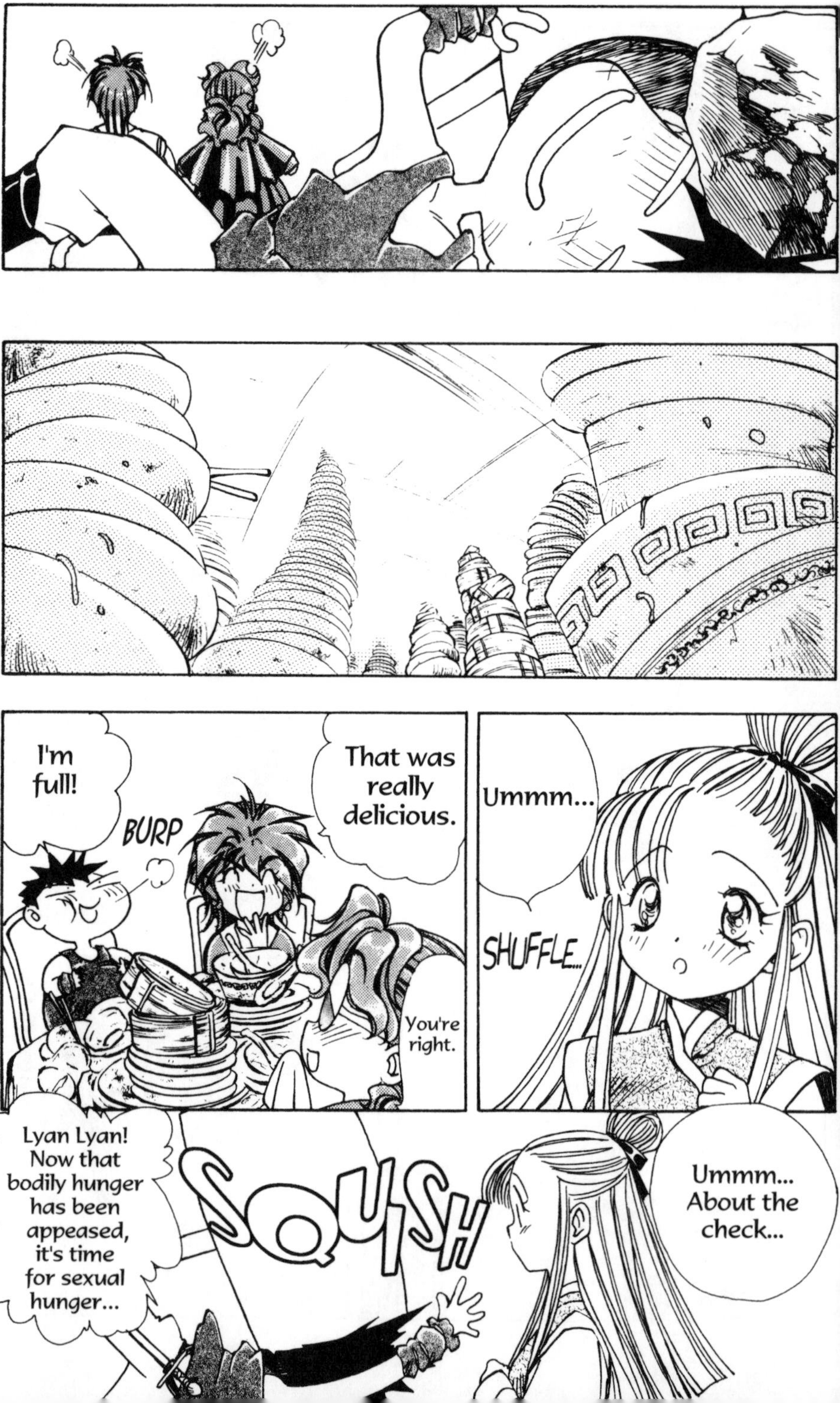
Ummm...
SHUFFLE...
That was really delicious.
I'm full!
BURP
You're right.
Ummm... About the check...
SQUISH
Lyan Lyan! Now that bodily hunger has been appeased, it's time for sexual hunger...

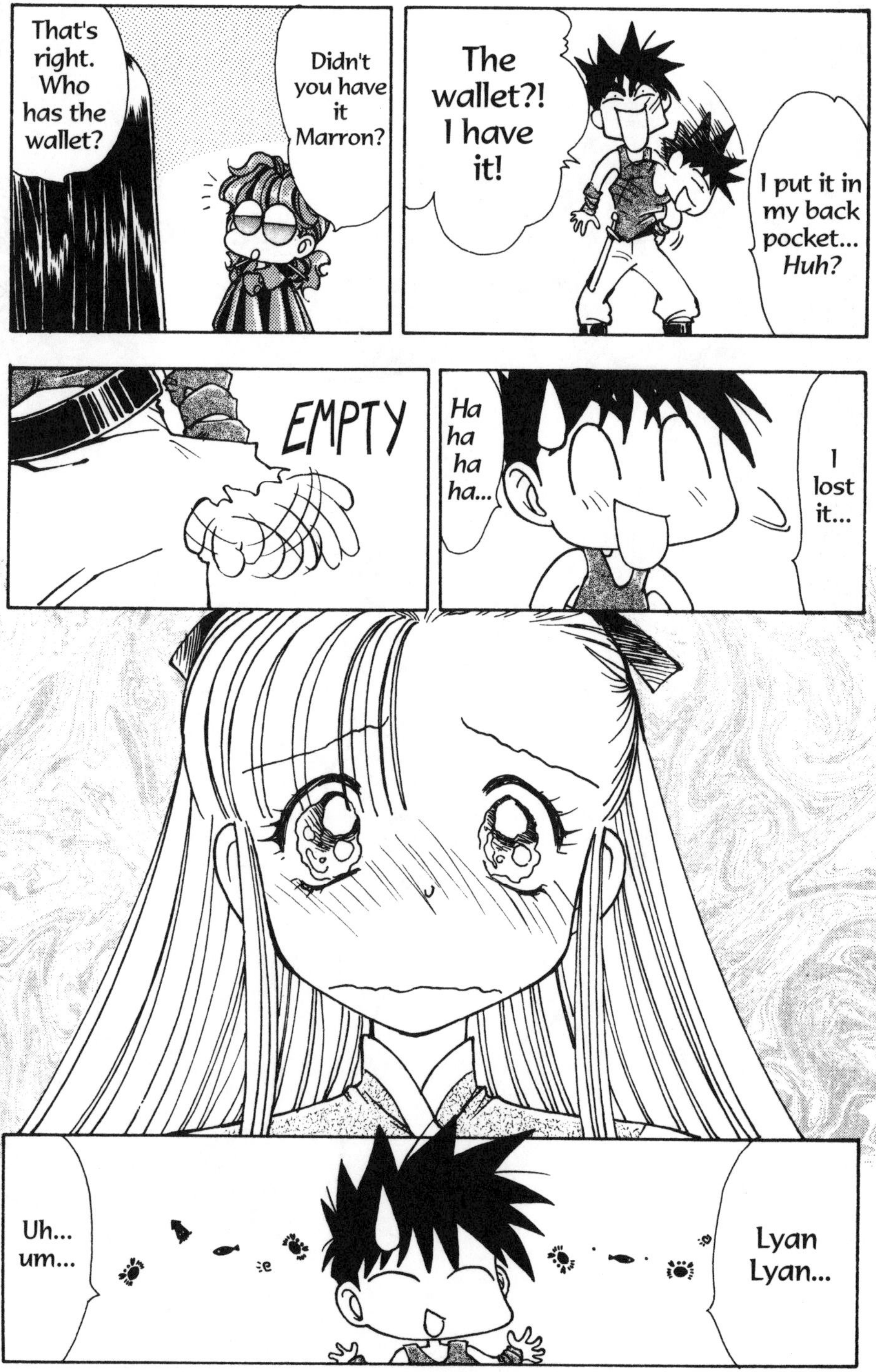
That's right. Who has the wallet?
Didn't you have it Marron?
The wallet?! I have it!
I put it in my back pocket... *Huh?*
EMPTY
Ha ha ha ha...
I lost it...
Uh... um...
Lyan Lyan...

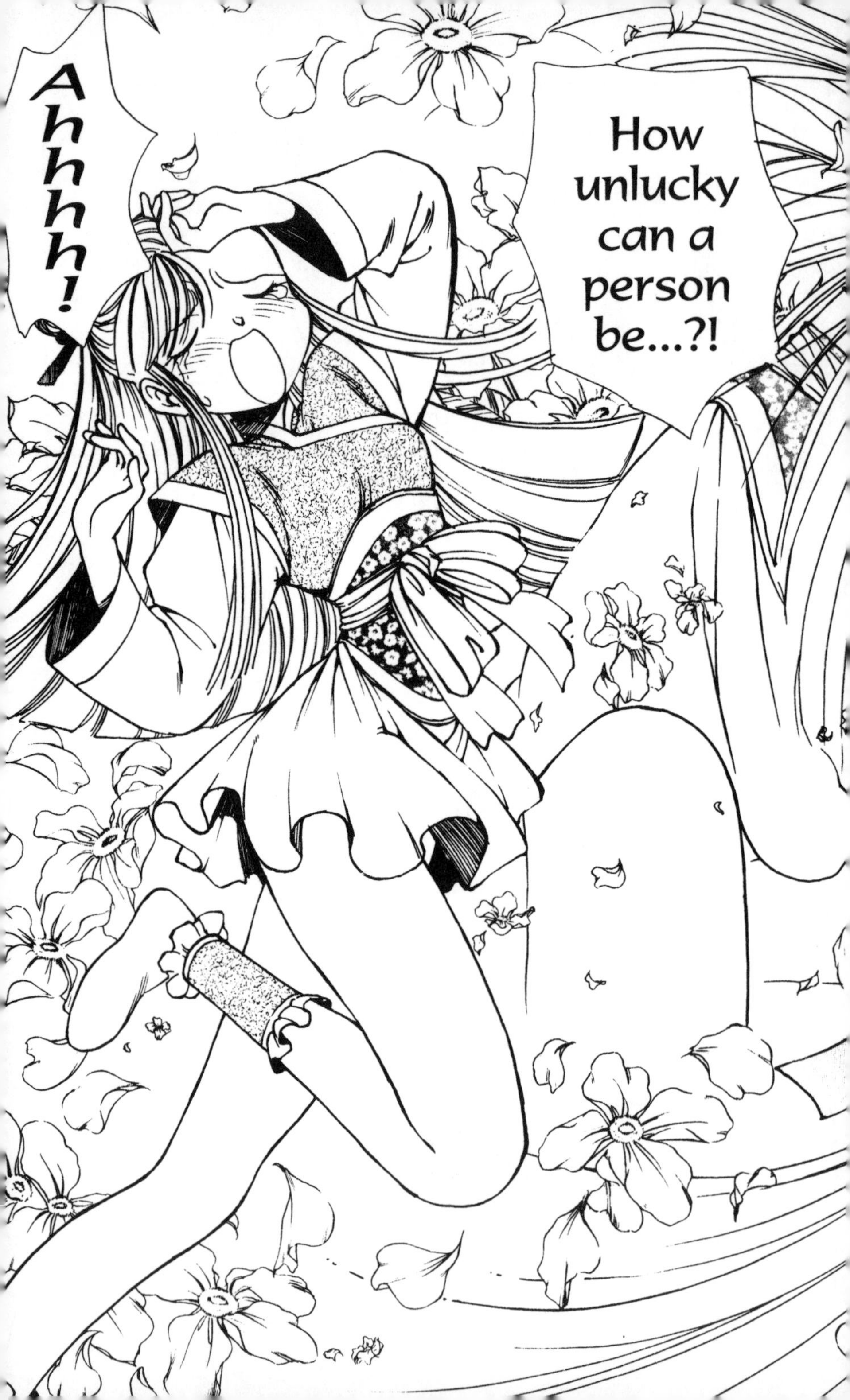
How unlucky can a person be...?!
Ahhhh!

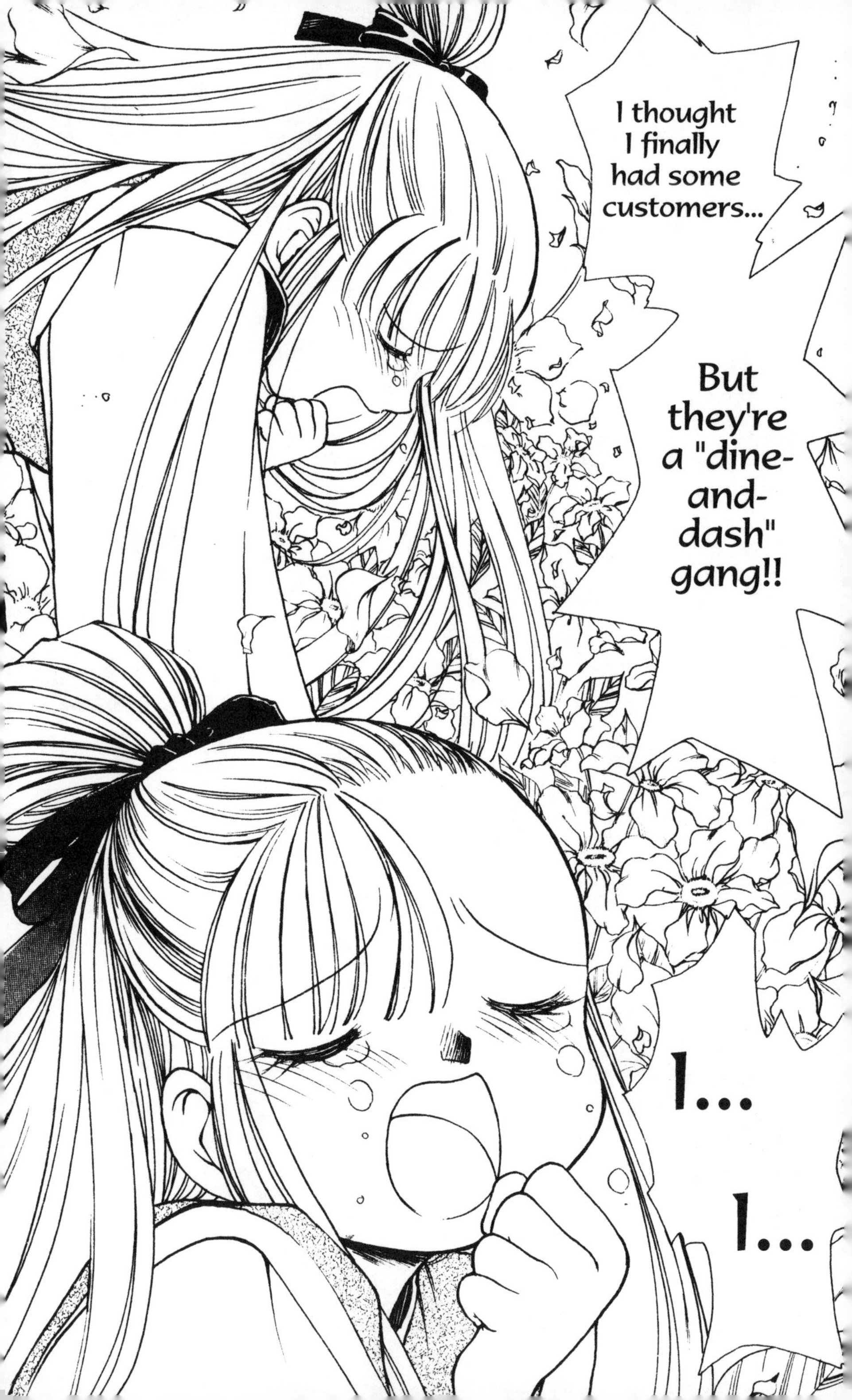
I thought I finally had some customers...
But they're a "dine-and-dash" gang!!
I...
I...

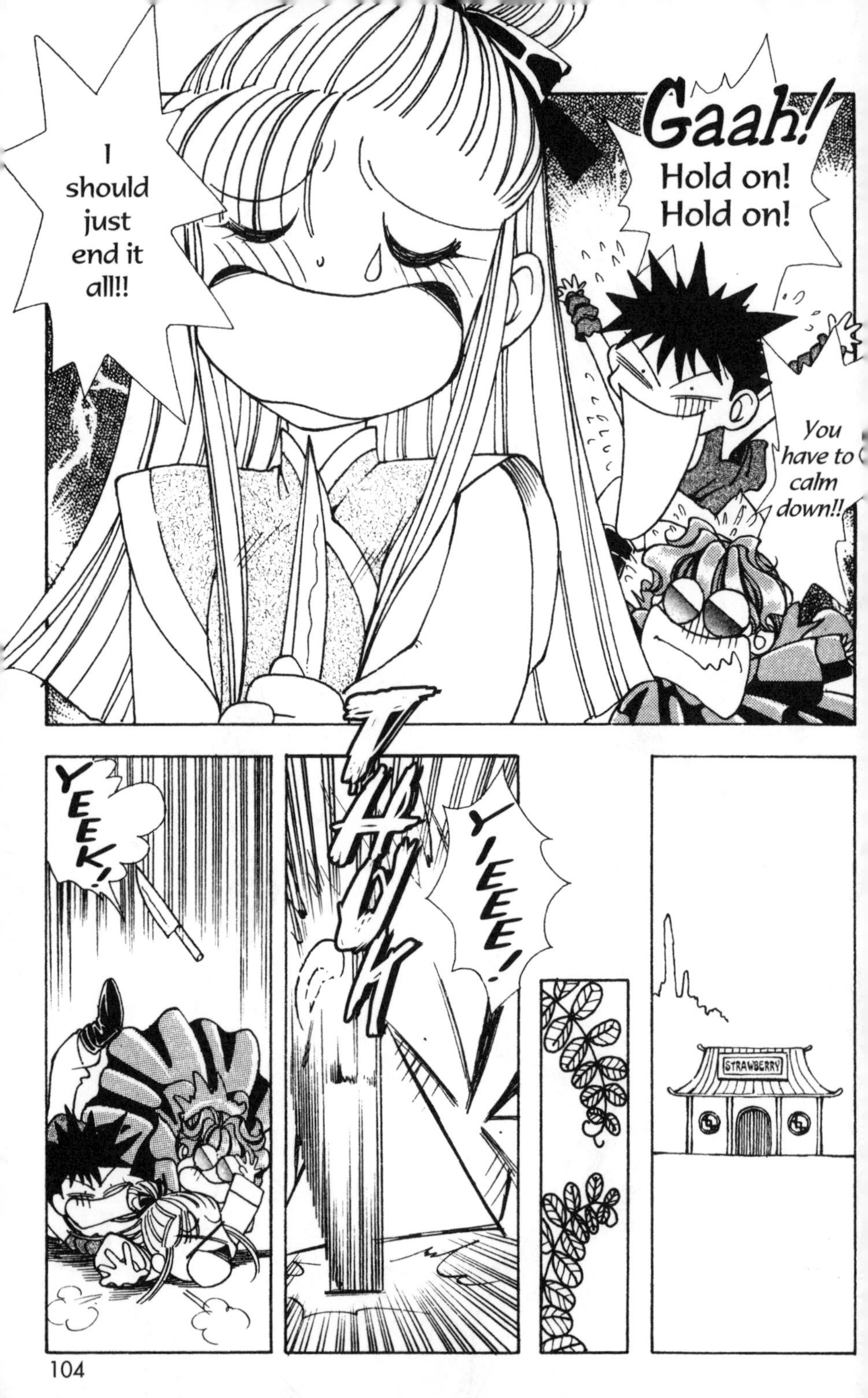
I should just end it all!!
Gaah! Hold on! Hold on!
You have to calm down!!
STRAWBERRY
YIEEEE!
THUNK
YEEK!

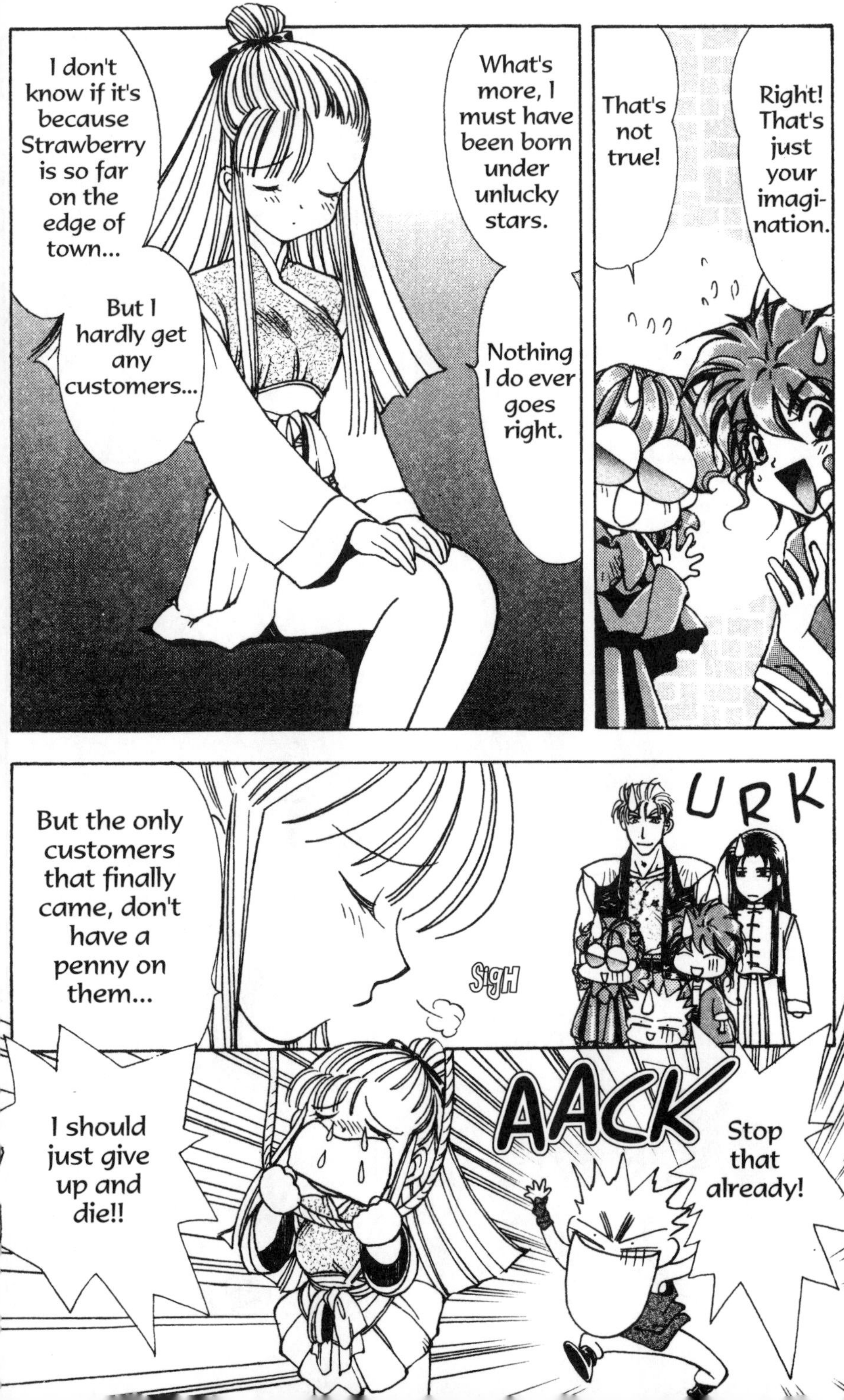
I don't know if it's because Strawberry is so far on the edge of town...
But I hardly get any customers...
What's more, I must have been born under unlucky stars.
Nothing I do ever goes right.
That's not true!
Right! That's just your imagination.
But the only customers that finally came, don't have a penny on them...
SIGH
URK
I should just give up and die!!
AACK
Stop that already!

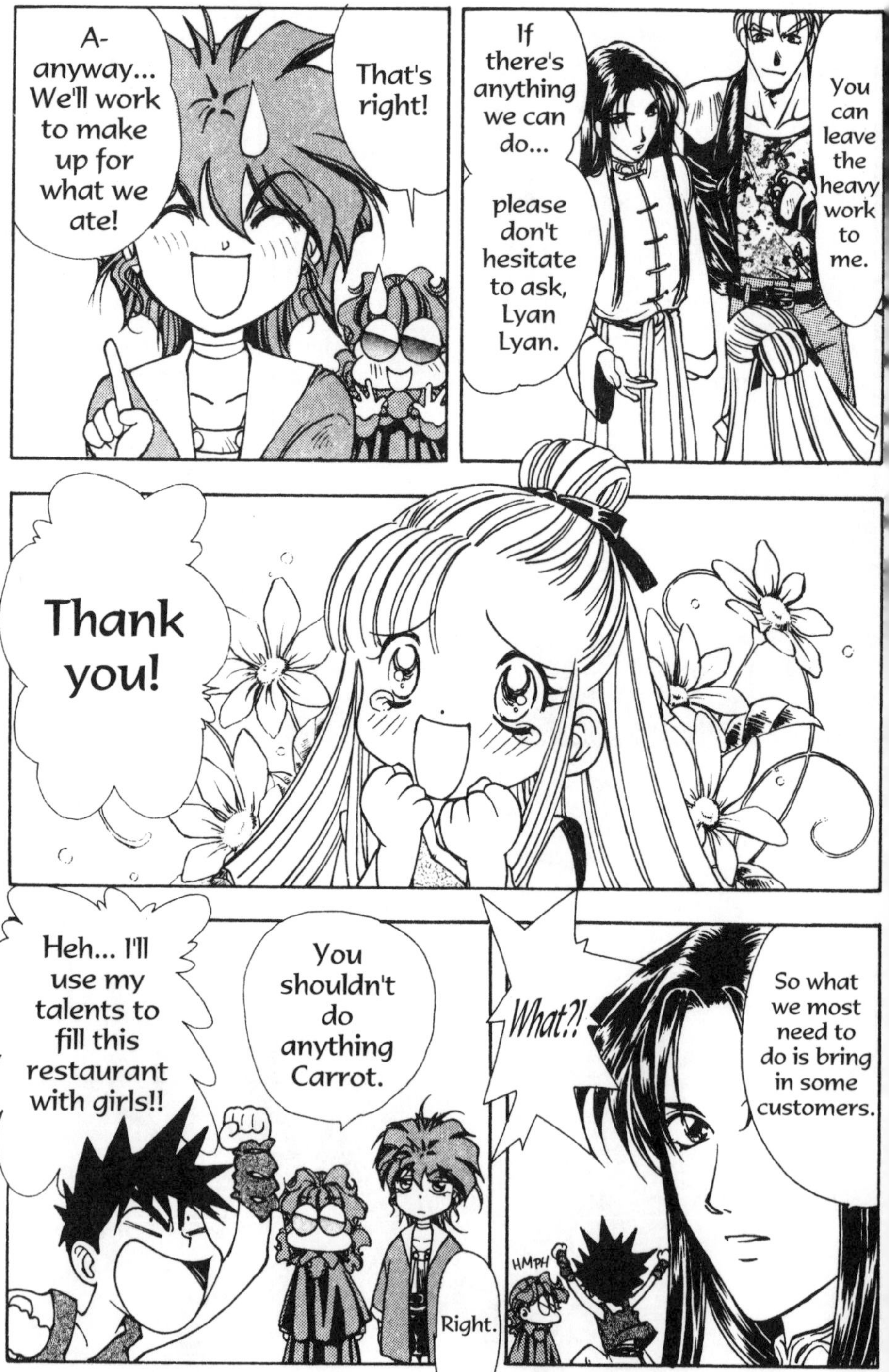
A- anyway... We'll work to make up for what we ate!
That's right!
If there's anything we can do...
please don't hesitate to ask, Lyan Lyan.
You can leave the heavy work to me.
Thank you!
Heh... I'll use my talents to fill this restaurant with girls!!
You shouldn't do anything Carrot.
Right.
What?!
HMPH
So what we most need to do is bring in some customers.

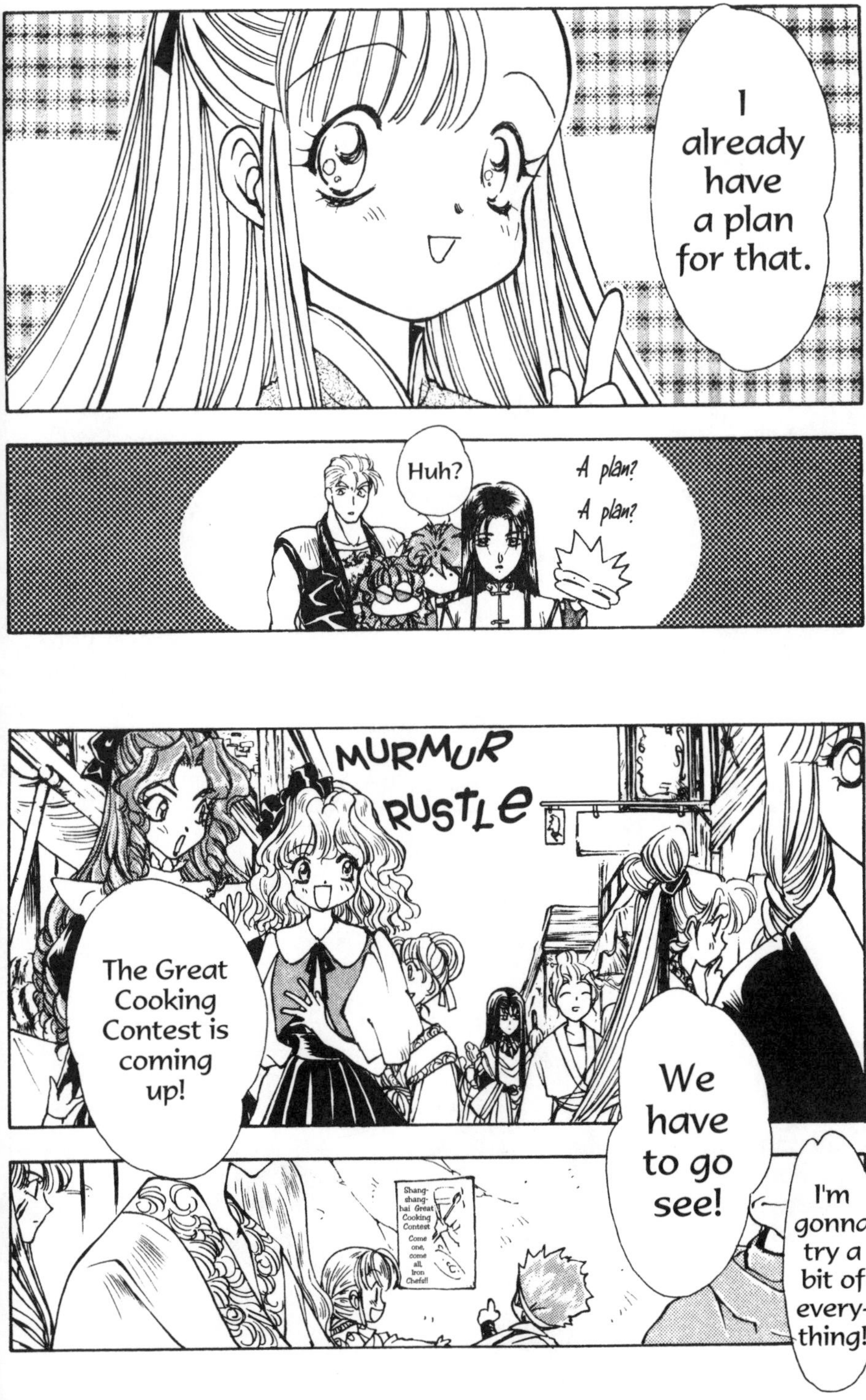
I already have a plan for that.
A plan?
A plan?
Huh?
MURMUR
RUSTLE
The Great Cooking Contest is coming up!
We have to go see!
I'm gonna try a bit of every-thing!
Shang-shang-hai Great Cooking Contest
Come one, come all, Iron Chefs!!

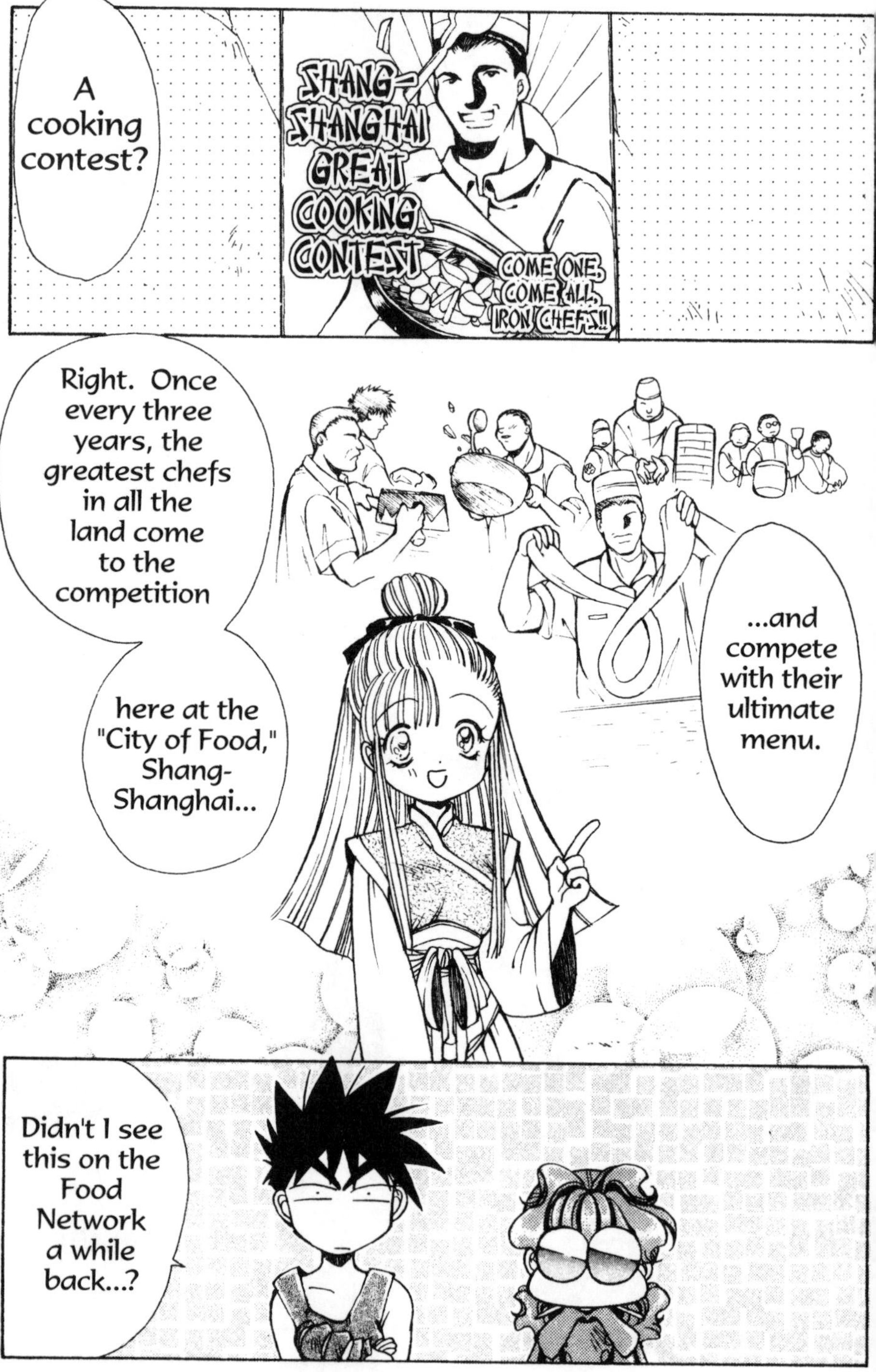
A cooking contest?
SHANG-SHANGHAI GREAT COOKING CONTEST
COME ONE, COME ALL, IRON CHEFS!!
Right. Once every three years, the greatest chefs in all the land come to the competition
here at the "City of Food," Shang-Shanghai...
...and compete with their ultimate menu.
Didn't I see this on the Food Network a while back...?

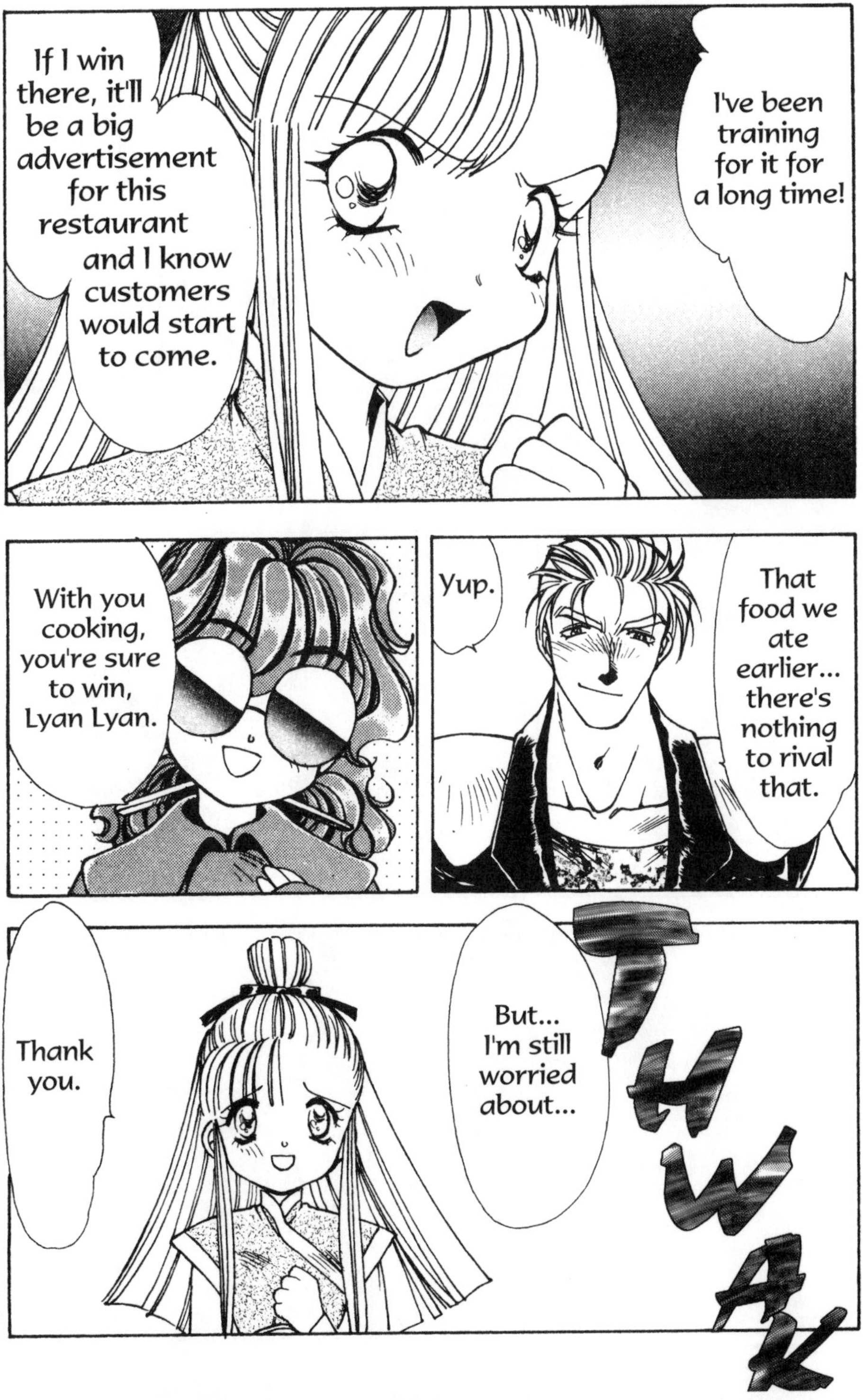
I've been training for it for a long time!
If I win there, it'll be a big advertisement for this restaurant and I know customers would start to come.
That food we ate earlier... there's nothing to rival that.
Yup.
With you cooking, you're sure to win, Lyan Lyan.
Thank you.
But... I'm still worried about...
THWAK

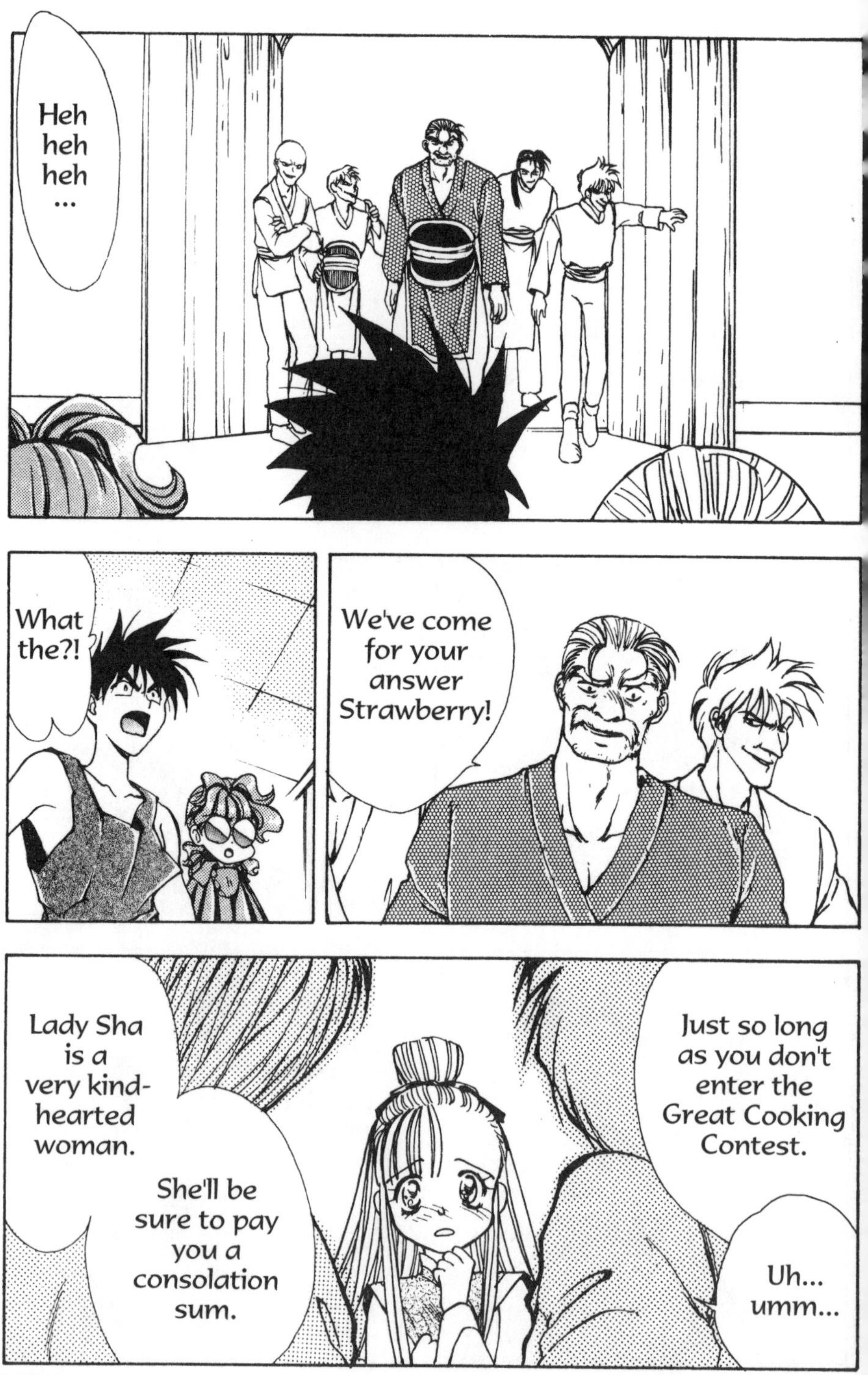
Heh heh heh ...
We've come for your answer Strawberry!
What the?!
Just so long as you don't enter the Great Cooking Contest.
Lady Sha is a very kind-hearted woman.
She'll be sure to pay you a consolation sum.
Uh... umm...

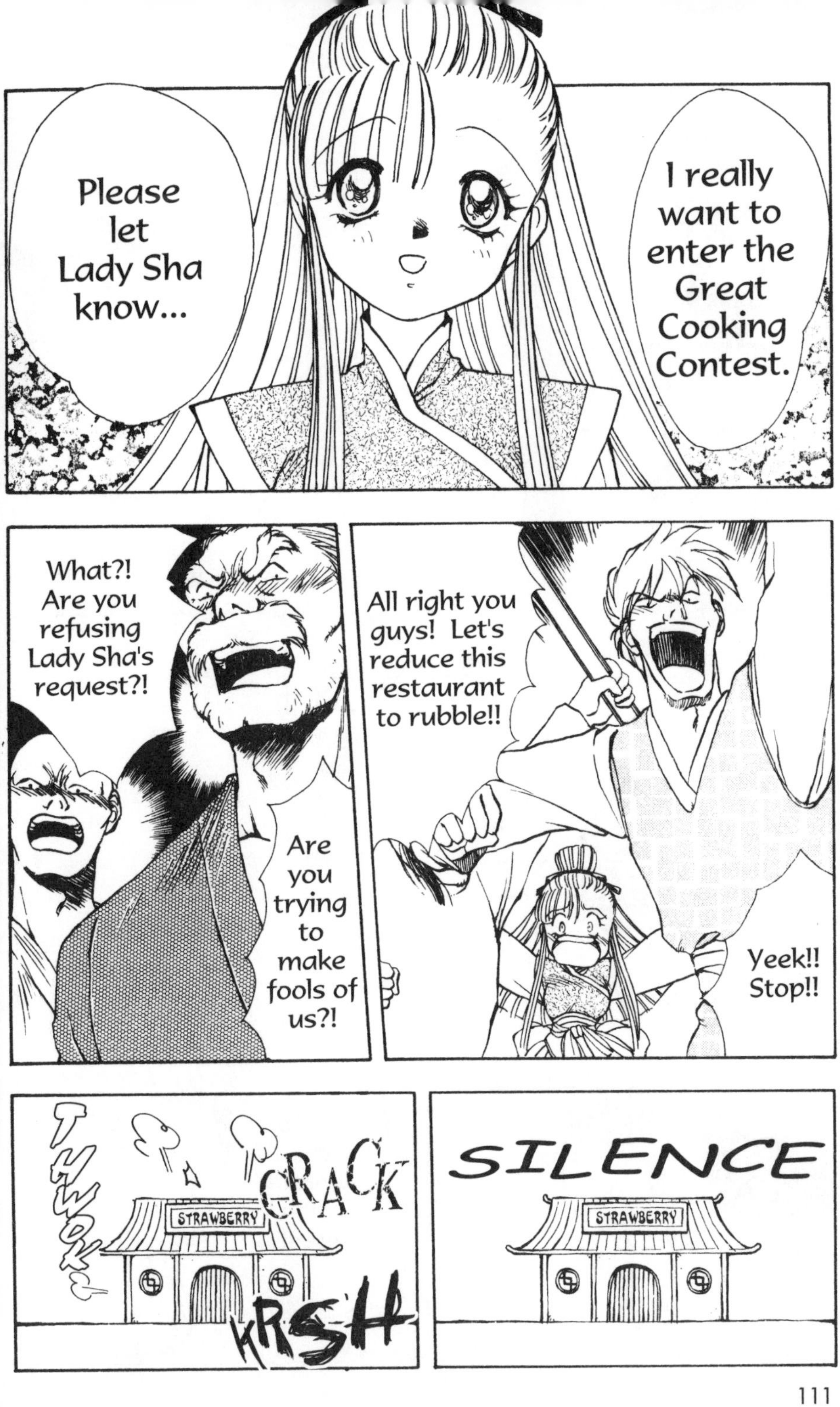
Please let Lady Sha know...
I really want to enter the Great Cooking Contest.
What?! Are you refusing Lady Sha's request?!
Are you trying to make fools of us?!
All right you guys! Let's reduce this restaurant to rubble!!
Yeek!! Stop!!
THWOK
CRACK
KRSH
STRAWBERRY
SILENCE
STRAWBERRY

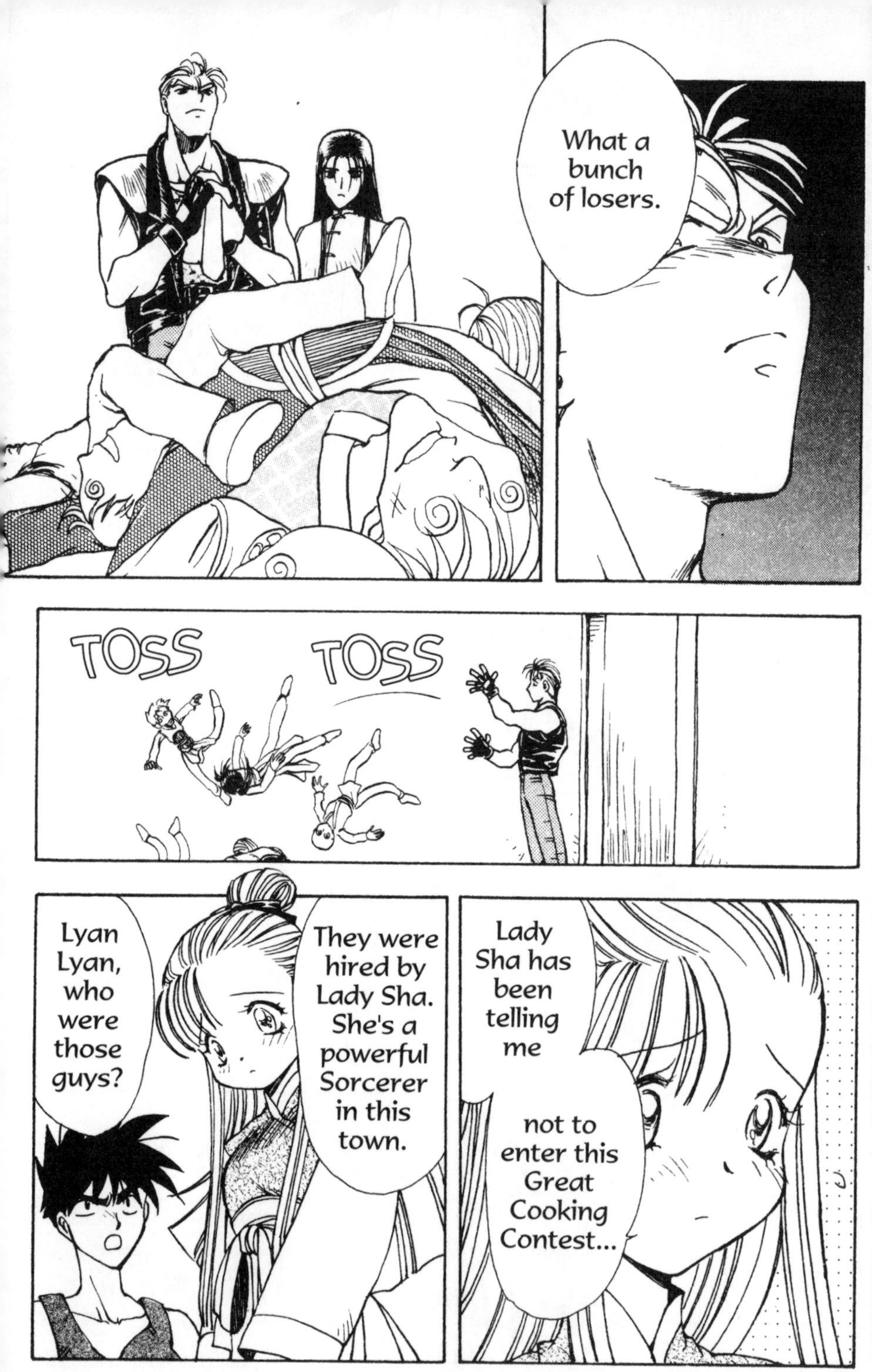
What a bunch of losers.
TOSS
TOSS
Lyan Lyan, who were those guys?
They were hired by Lady Sha. She's a powerful Sorcerer in this town.
Lady Sha has been telling me
not to enter this Great Cooking Contest...

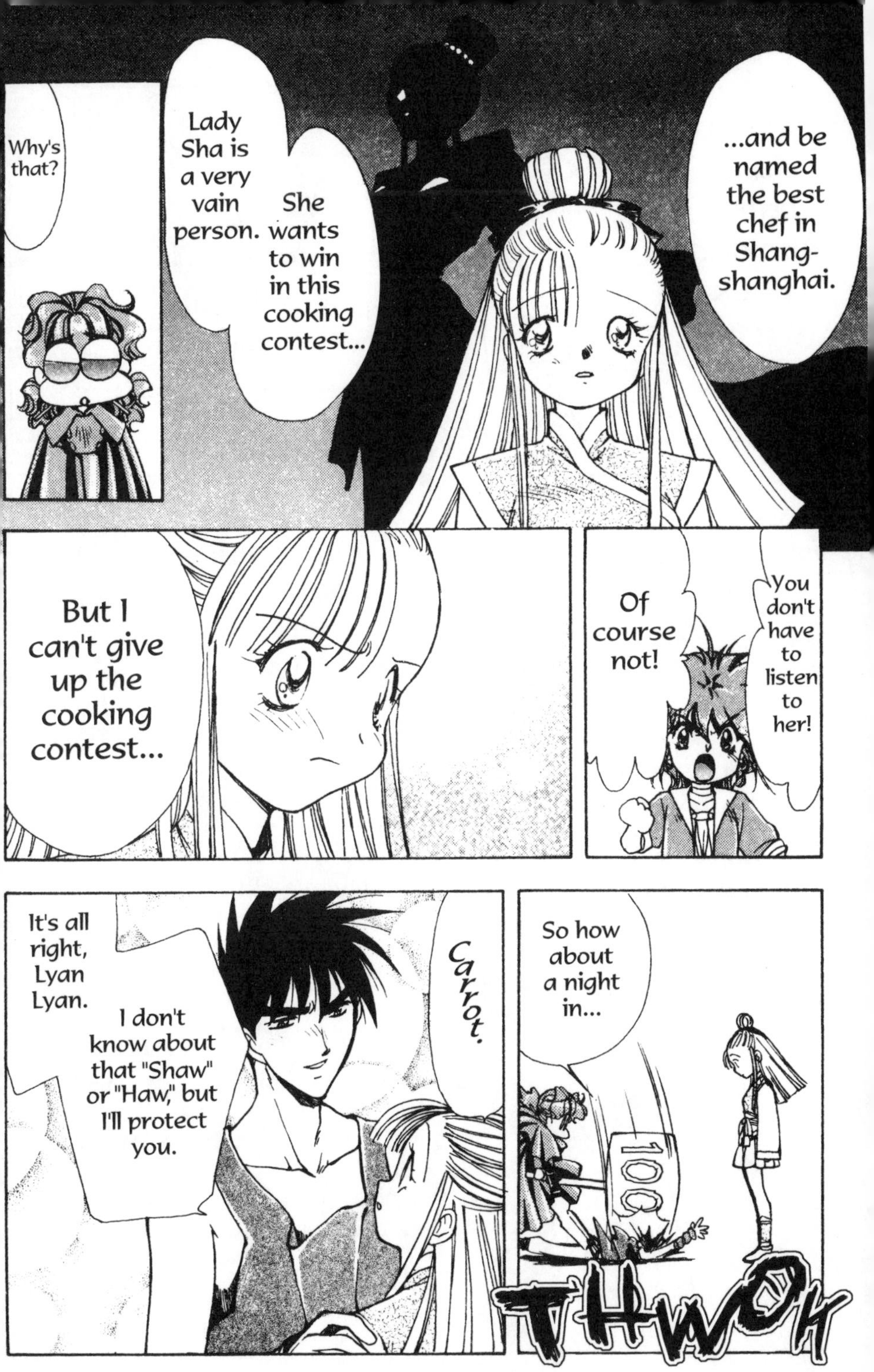
Why's that?
Lady Sha is a very vain person.
She wants to win in this cooking contest...
...and be named the best chef in Shang-shanghai.
But I can't give up the cooking contest...
Of course not!
You don't have to listen to her!
It's all right, Lyan Lyan.
I don't know about that "Shaw" or "Haw," but I'll protect you.
Carrot.
So how about a night in...
100
THWOK

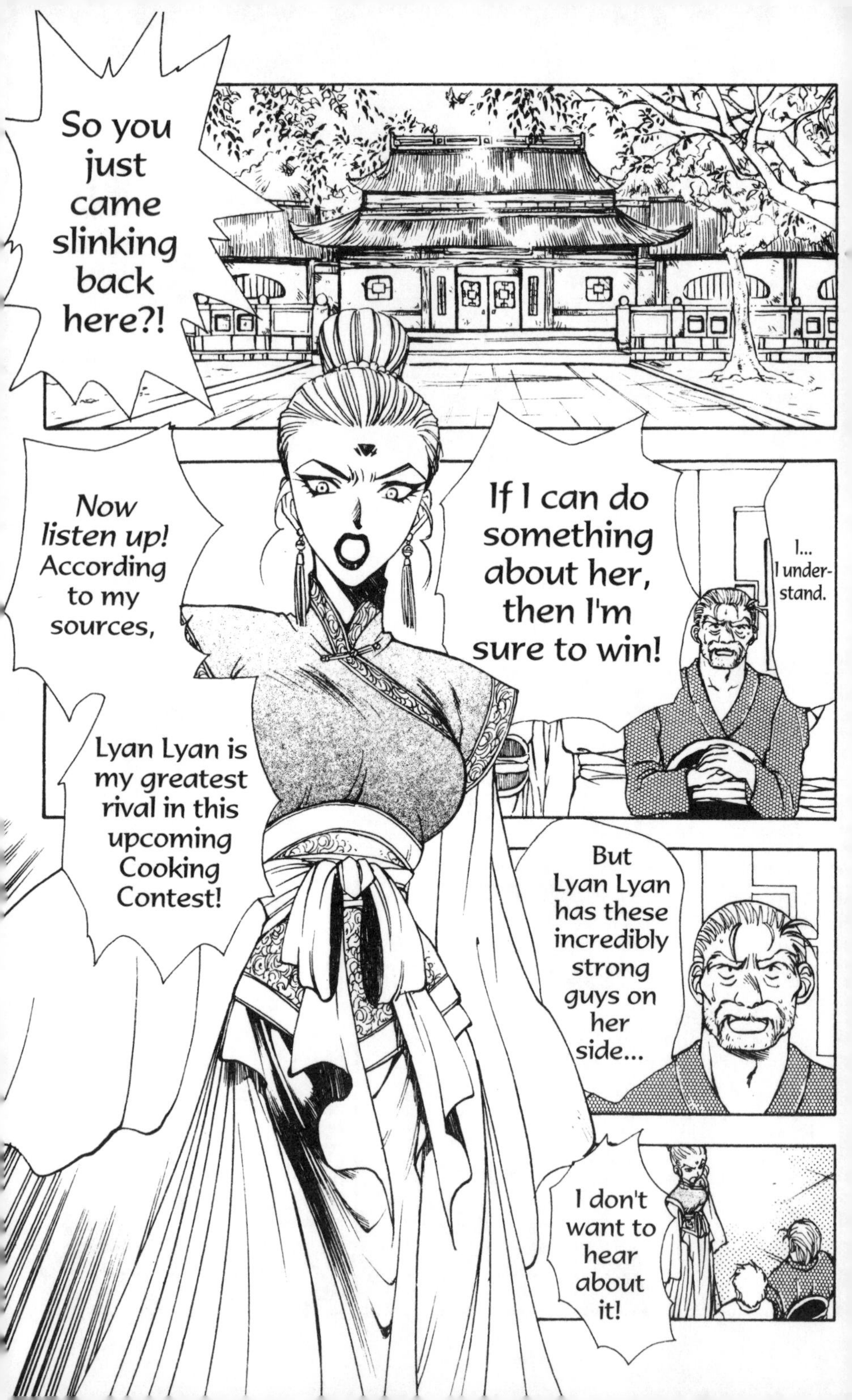
So you just came slinking back here?!
Now listen up! According to my sources,
Lyan Lyan is my greatest rival in this upcoming Cooking Contest!
If I can do something about her, then I'm sure to win!
I... I understand.
But Lyan Lyan has these incredibly strong guys on her side...
I don't want to hear about it!

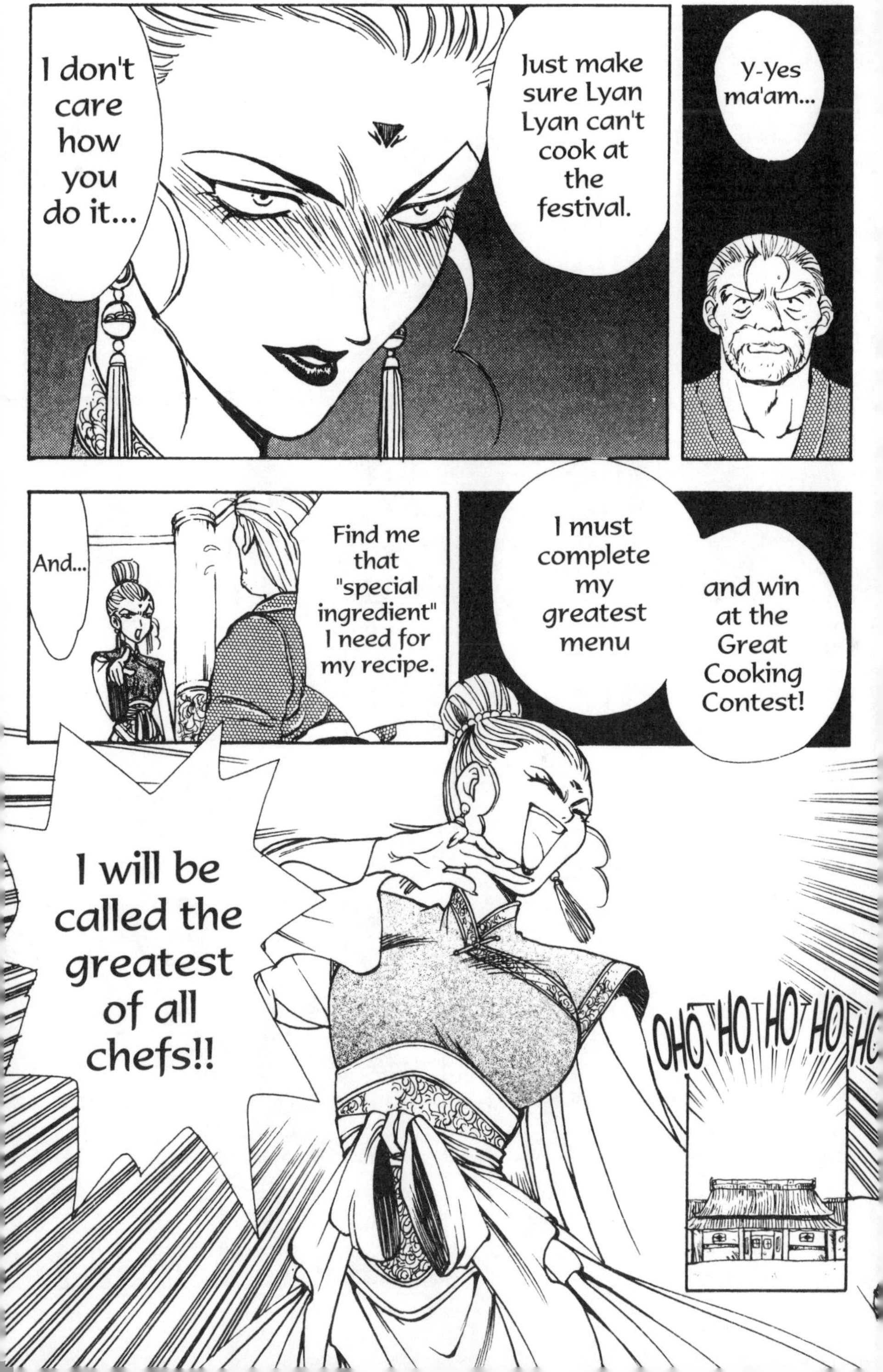
I don't care how you do it...
Just make sure Lyan Lyan can't cook at the festival.
Y-Yes ma'am...
And...
Find me that "special ingredient" I need for my recipe.
I must complete my greatest menu
and win at the Great Cooking Contest!
I will be called the greatest of all chefs!!
OHO HO HO HO HO

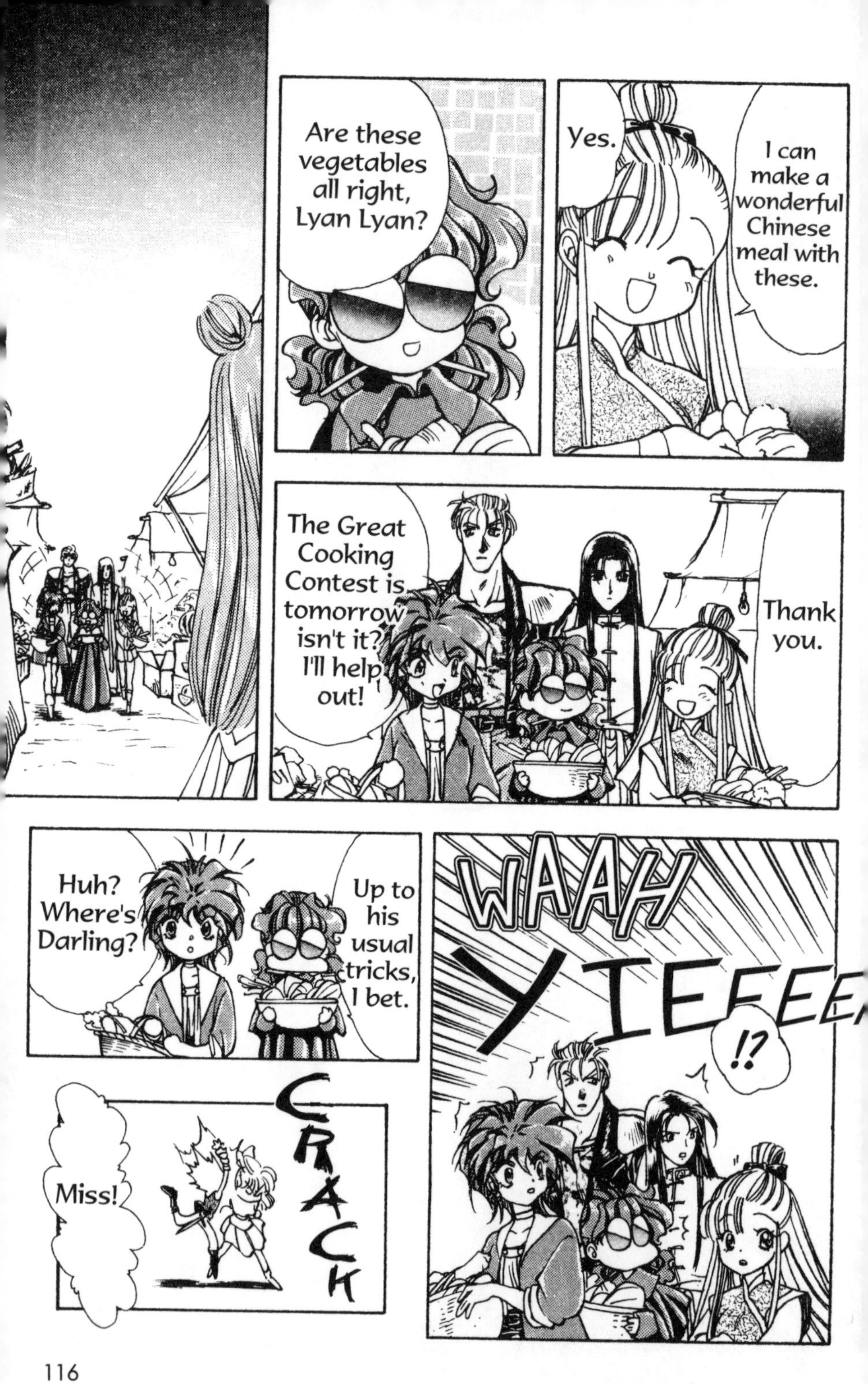
Are these vegetables all right, Lyan Lyan?
Yes.
I can make a wonderful Chinese meal with these.
The Great Cooking Contest is tomorrow isn't it? I'll help out!
Thank you.
Huh? Where's Darling?
Up to his usual tricks, I bet.
Miss!
CRACK
WAAH
YIEEE
!?

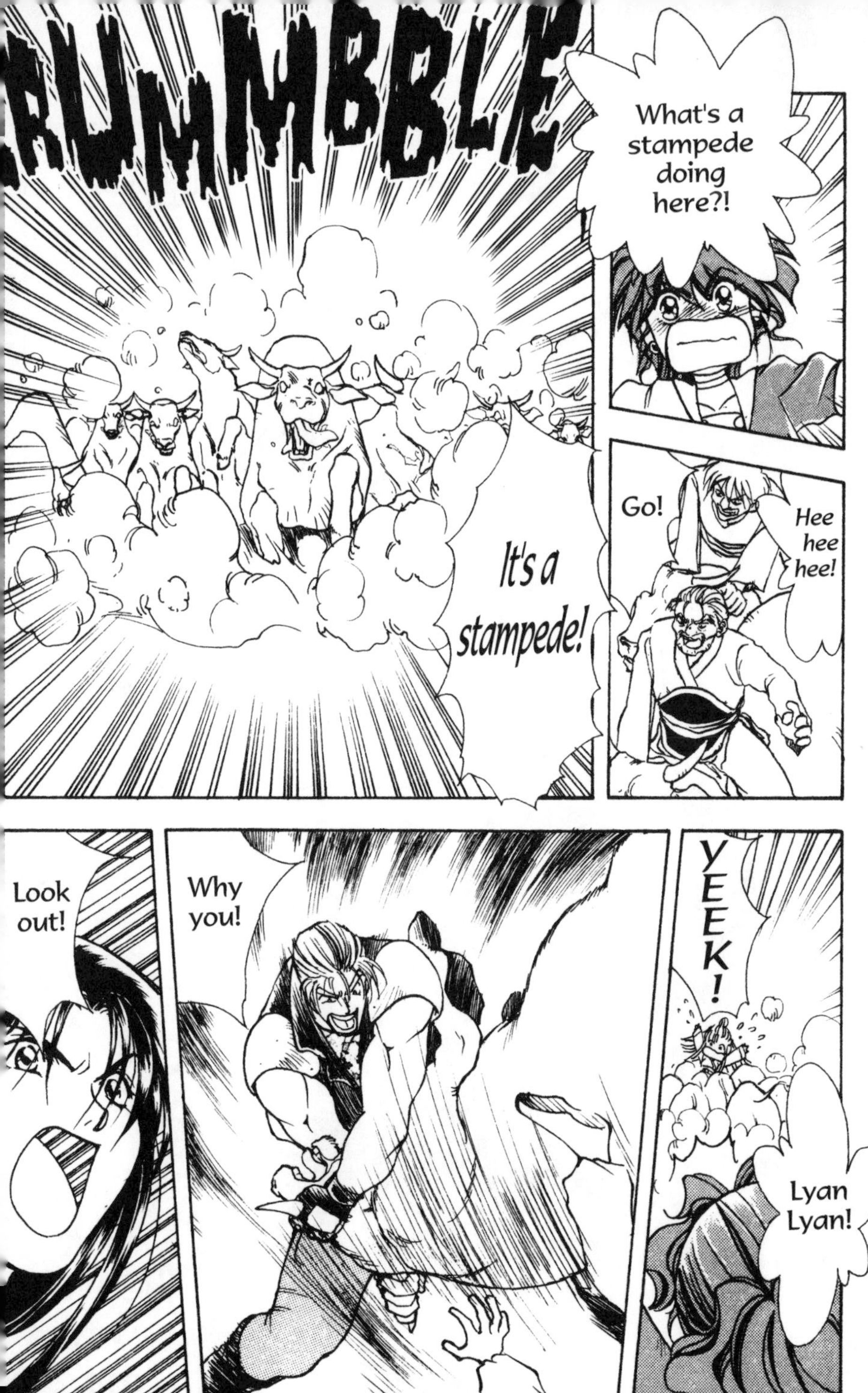
What's a stampede doing here?!
Hee hee hee!
Go!
RUMMBBLE
It's a stampede!
YEEK!
Lyan Lyan!
Why you!
Look out!

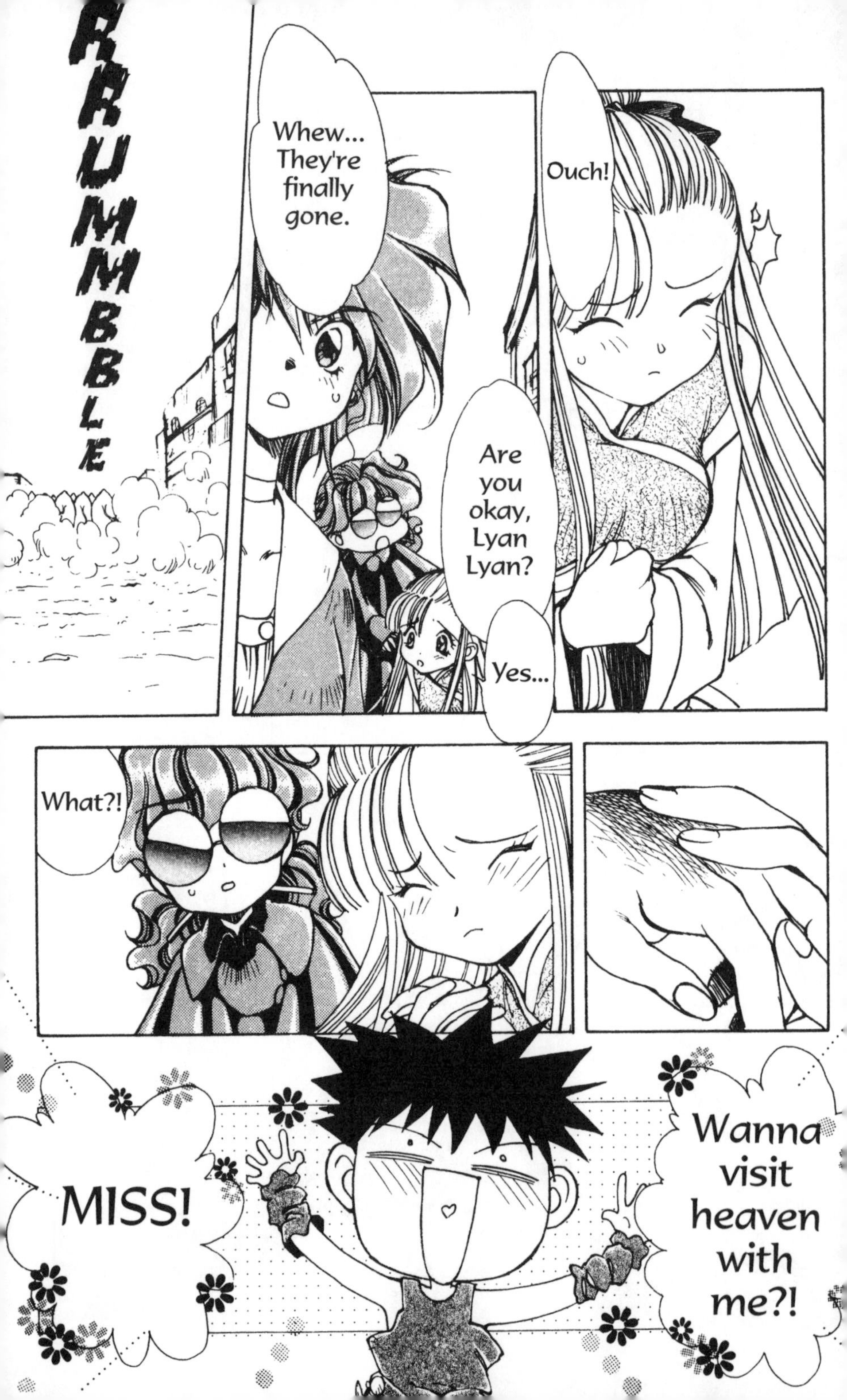
Ouch!
Whew... They're finally gone.
Are you okay, Lyan Lyan?
Yes...
RRUMMBBLE
What?!
MISS!
Wanna visit heaven with me?!

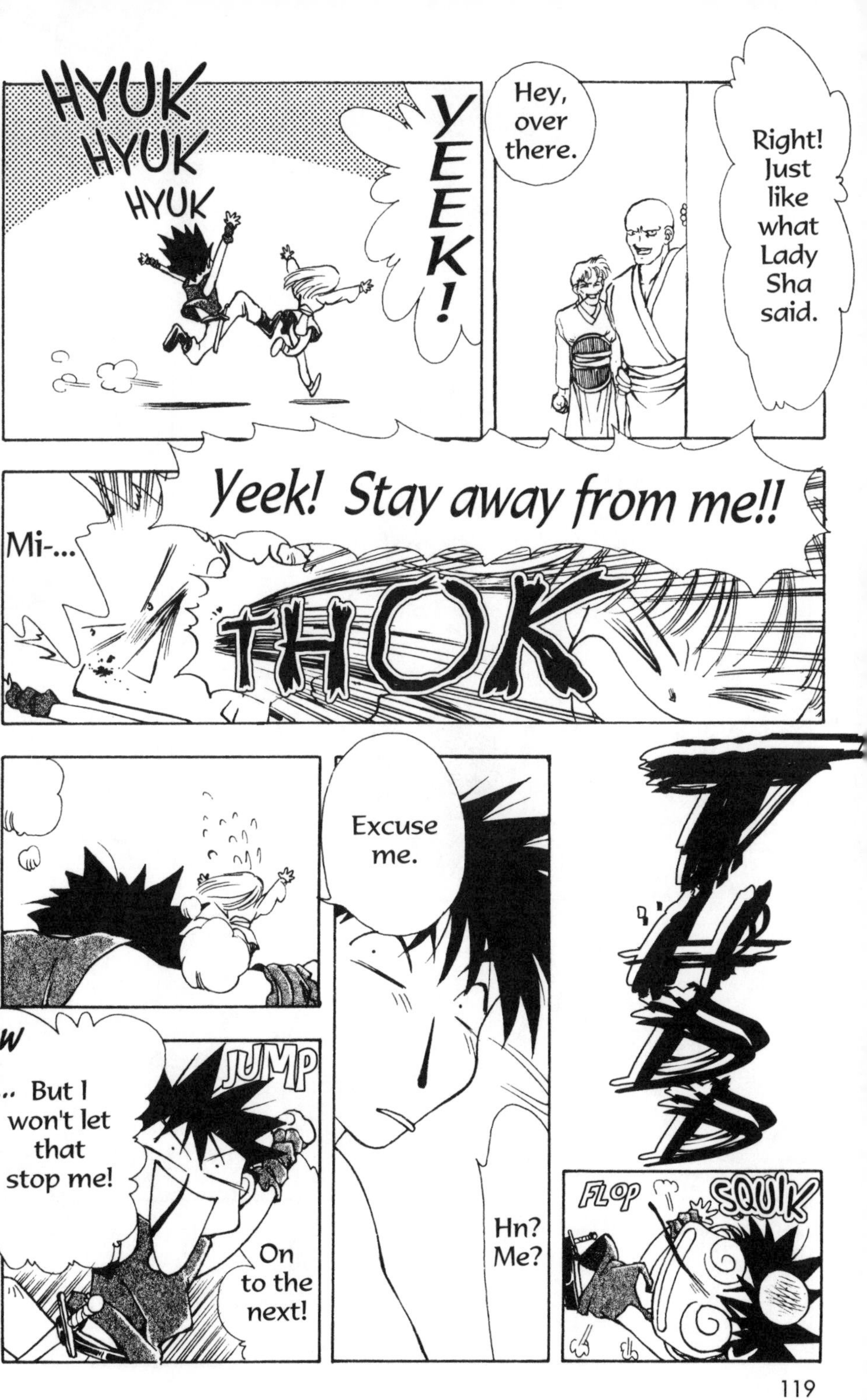
Right! Just like what Lady Sha said.
Hey, over there.
YEEK!
HYUK HYUK HYUK
Yeek! Stay away from me!!
THOK
Mi-...
SQUIK
FLOP
Excuse me.
Hn? Me?
JUMP
... But I won't let that stop me!
On to the next!

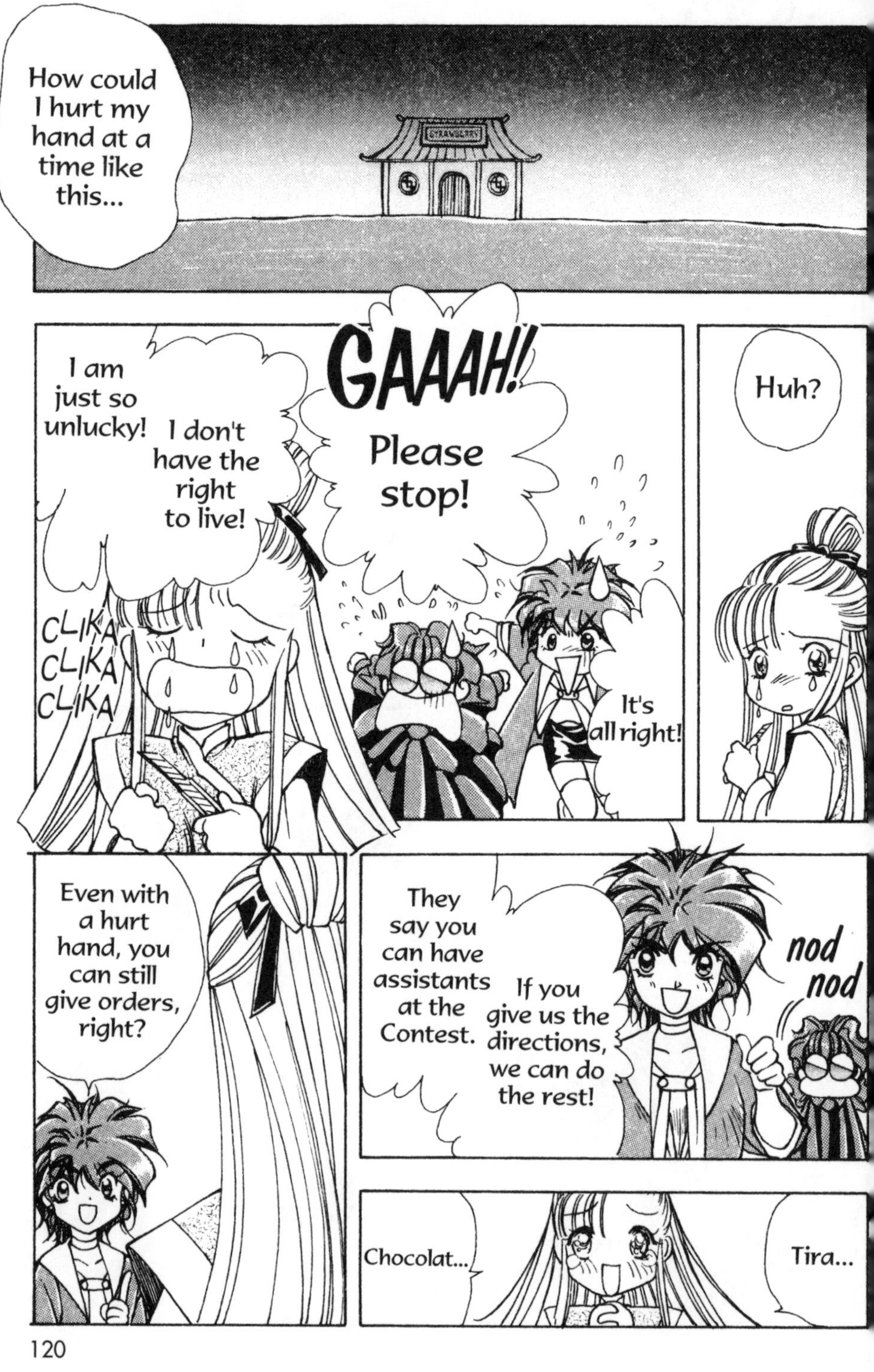
How could I hurt my hand at a time like this...
I am just so unlucky!
I don't have the right to live!
GAAAH!
Please stop!
It's all right!
Huh?
CLIKA CLIKA CLIKA
Even with a hurt hand, you can still give orders, right?
They say you can have assistants at the Contest.
If you give us the directions, we can do the rest!
nod nod
Chocolat...
Tira...

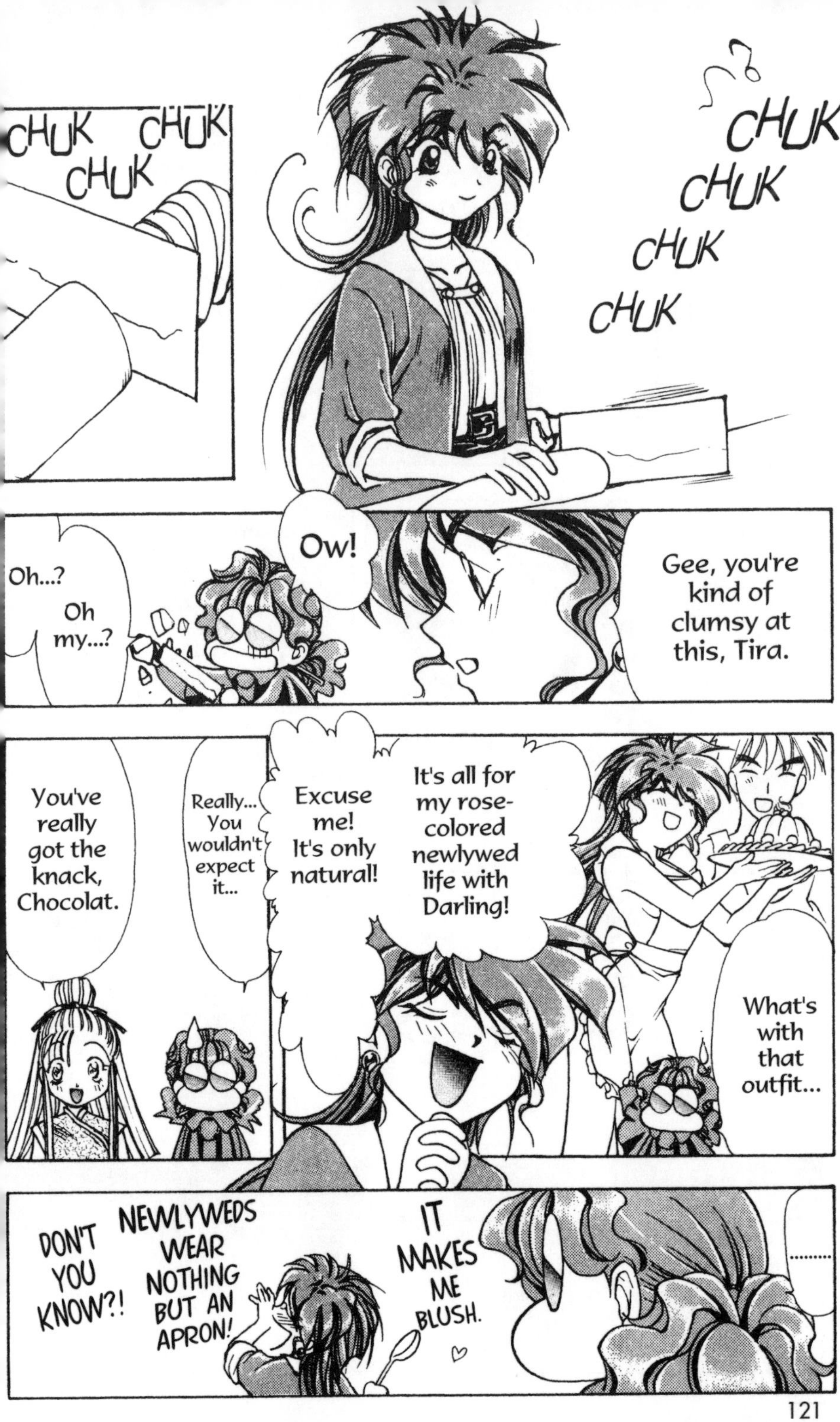
CHUK
CHUK
CHUK
CHUK
CHUK CHUK
CHUK
Gee, you're kind of clumsy at this, Tira.
Ow!
Oh...?
Oh my...?
What's with that outfit...
Excuse me! It's only natural!
It's all for my rose-colored newlywed life with Darling!
You've really got the knack, Chocolat.
Really... You wouldn't expect it...
....
DON'T YOU KNOW?!
NEWLYWEDS WEAR NOTHING BUT AN APRON!
IT MAKES ME BLUSH.

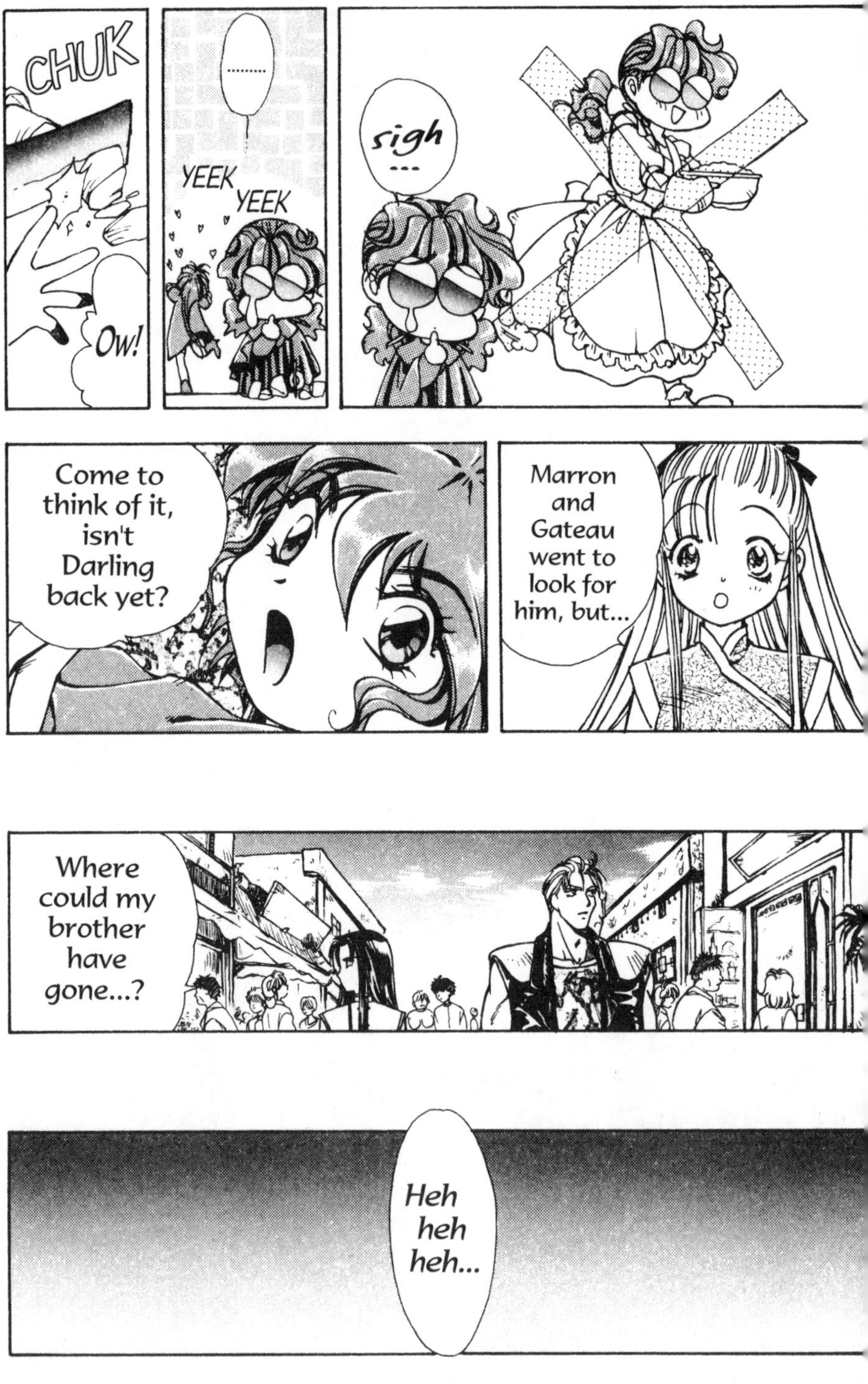
CHUK
Ow!
....
YEEK YEEK
sigh ---
Come to think of it, isn't Darling back yet?
Marron and Gateau went to look for him, but...
Where could my brother have gone...?
Heh heh heh...

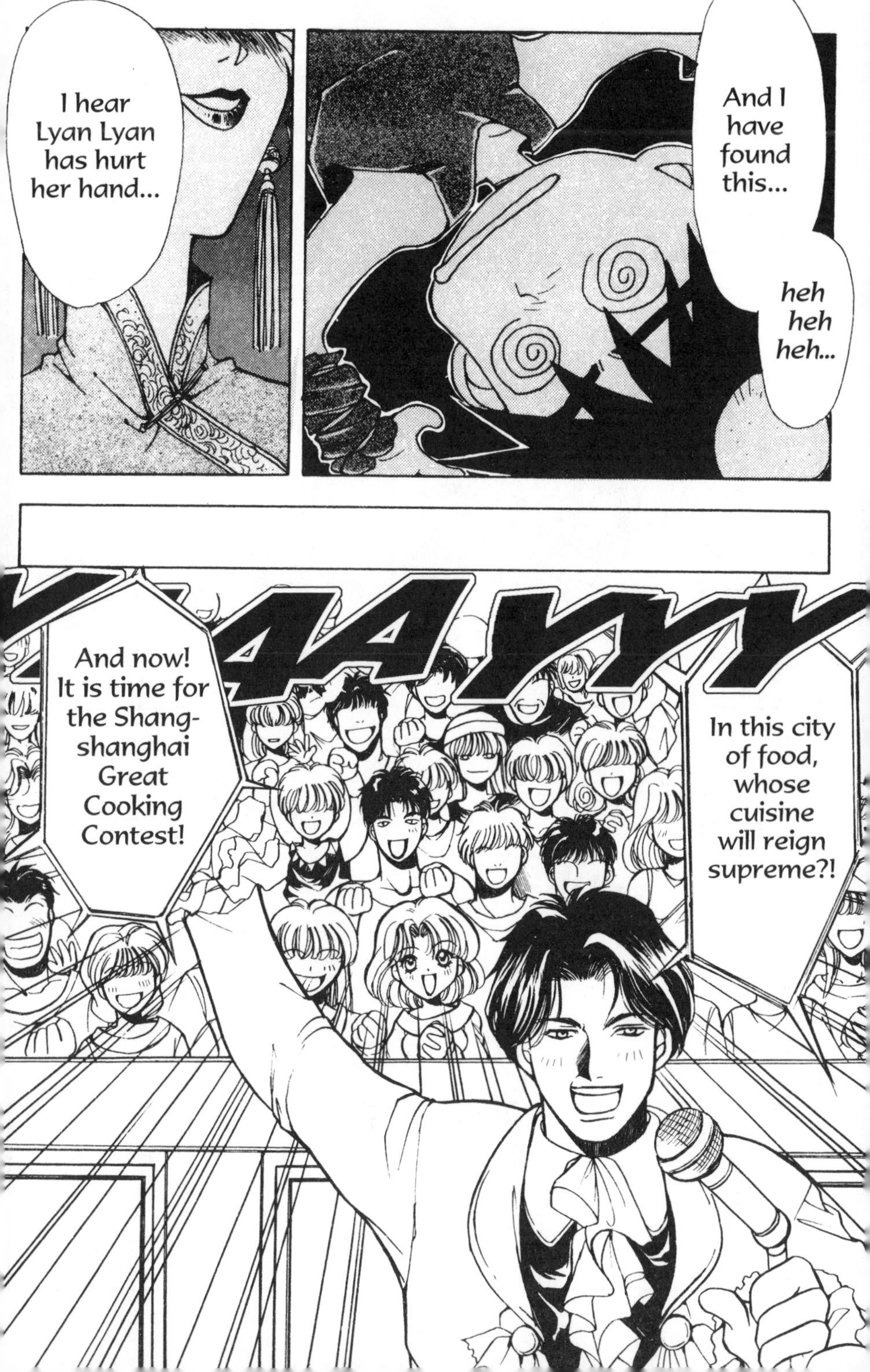
I hear Lyan Lyan has hurt her hand...
And I have found this...
heh heh heh...
And now! It is time for the Shang-shanghai Great Cooking Contest!
In this city of food, whose cuisine will reign supreme?!

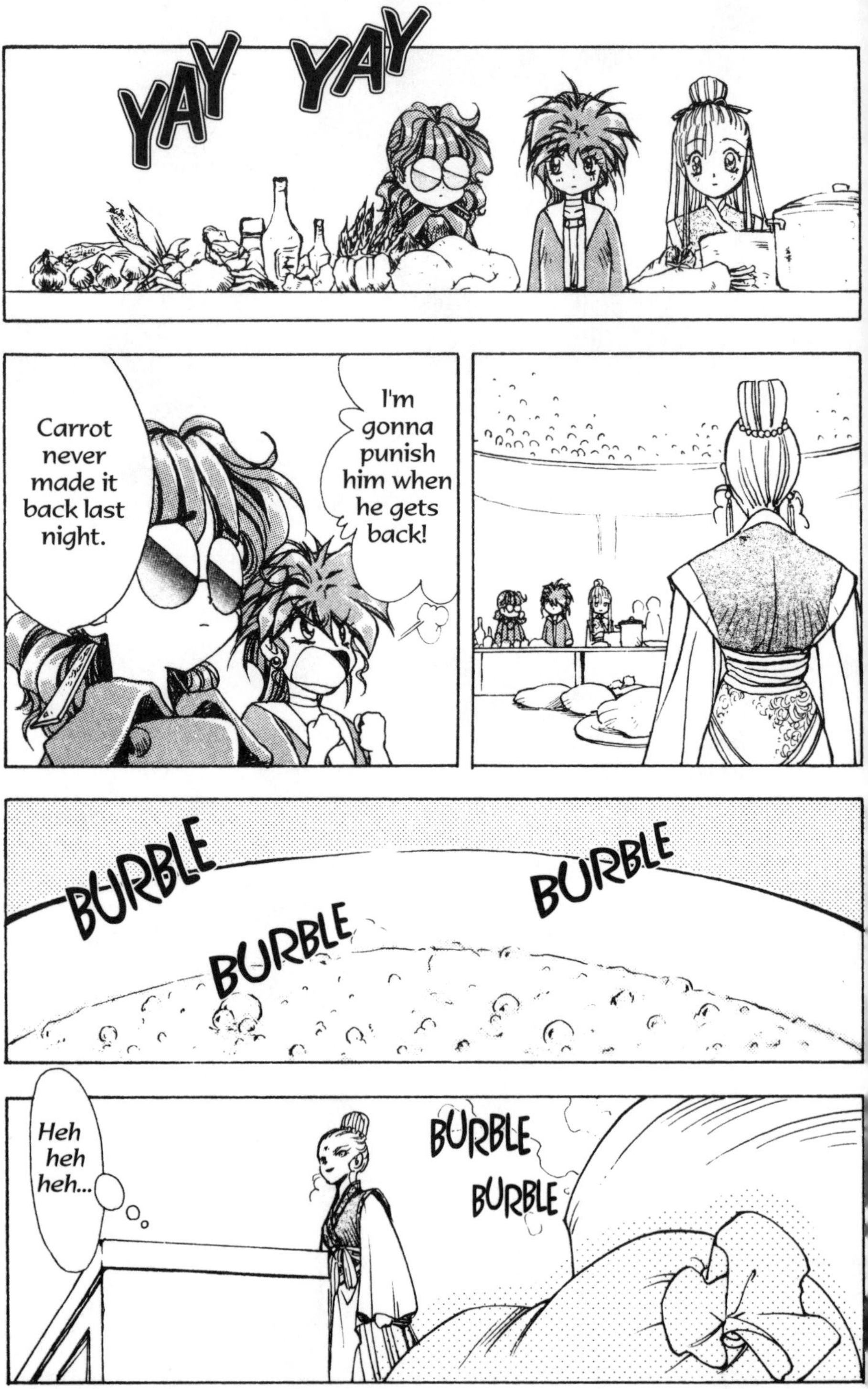
YAY YAY
Carrot never made it back last night.
I'm gonna punish him when he gets back!
BURBLE
BURBLE
BURBLE
Heh heh heh...
BURBLE
BURBLE

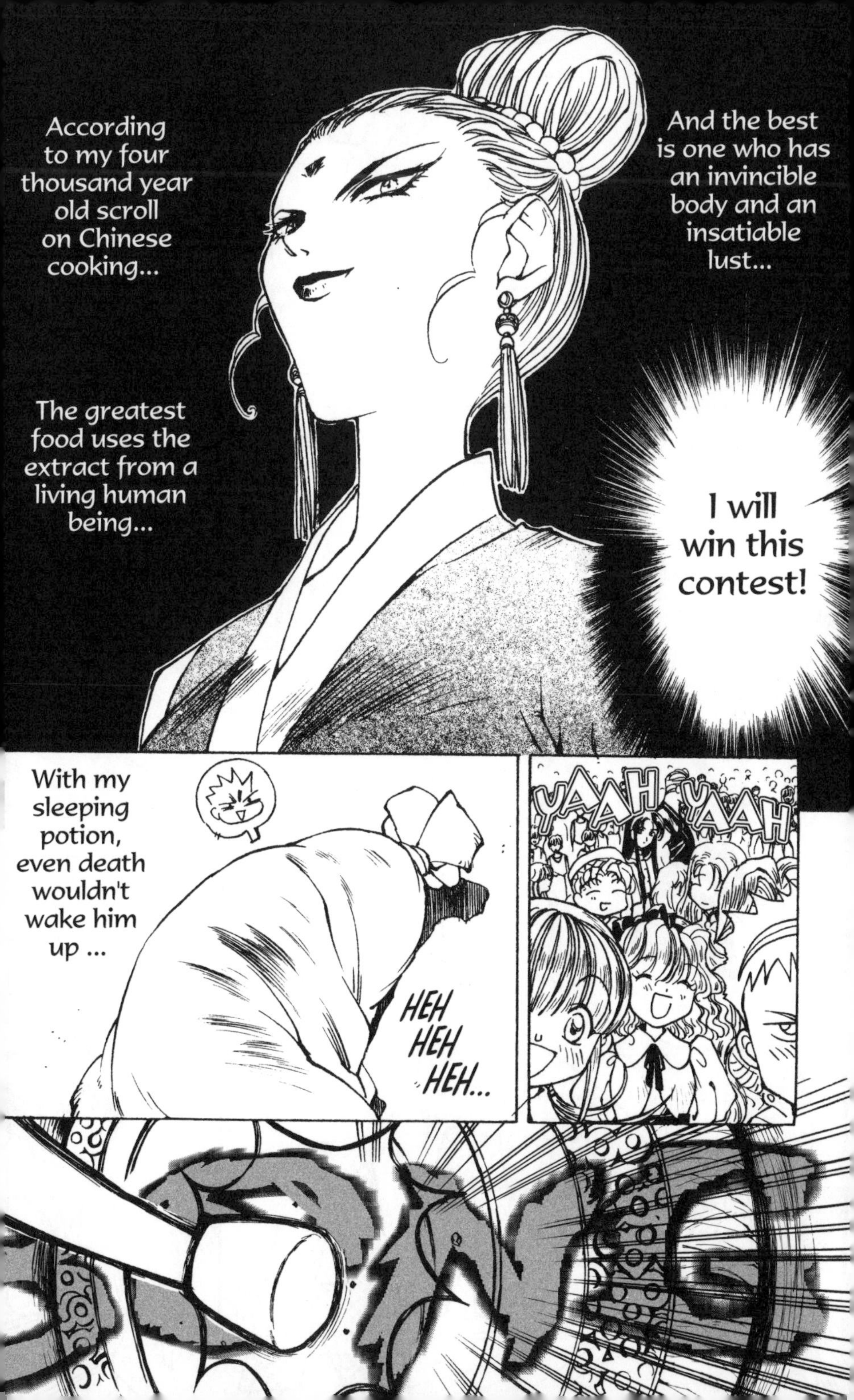
According to my four thousand year old scroll on Chinese cooking...
The greatest food uses the extract from a living human being...
And the best is one who has an invincible body and an insatiable lust...
I will win this contest!
With my sleeping potion, even death wouldn't wake him up ...
HEH HEH HEH...
YAAH YAAH

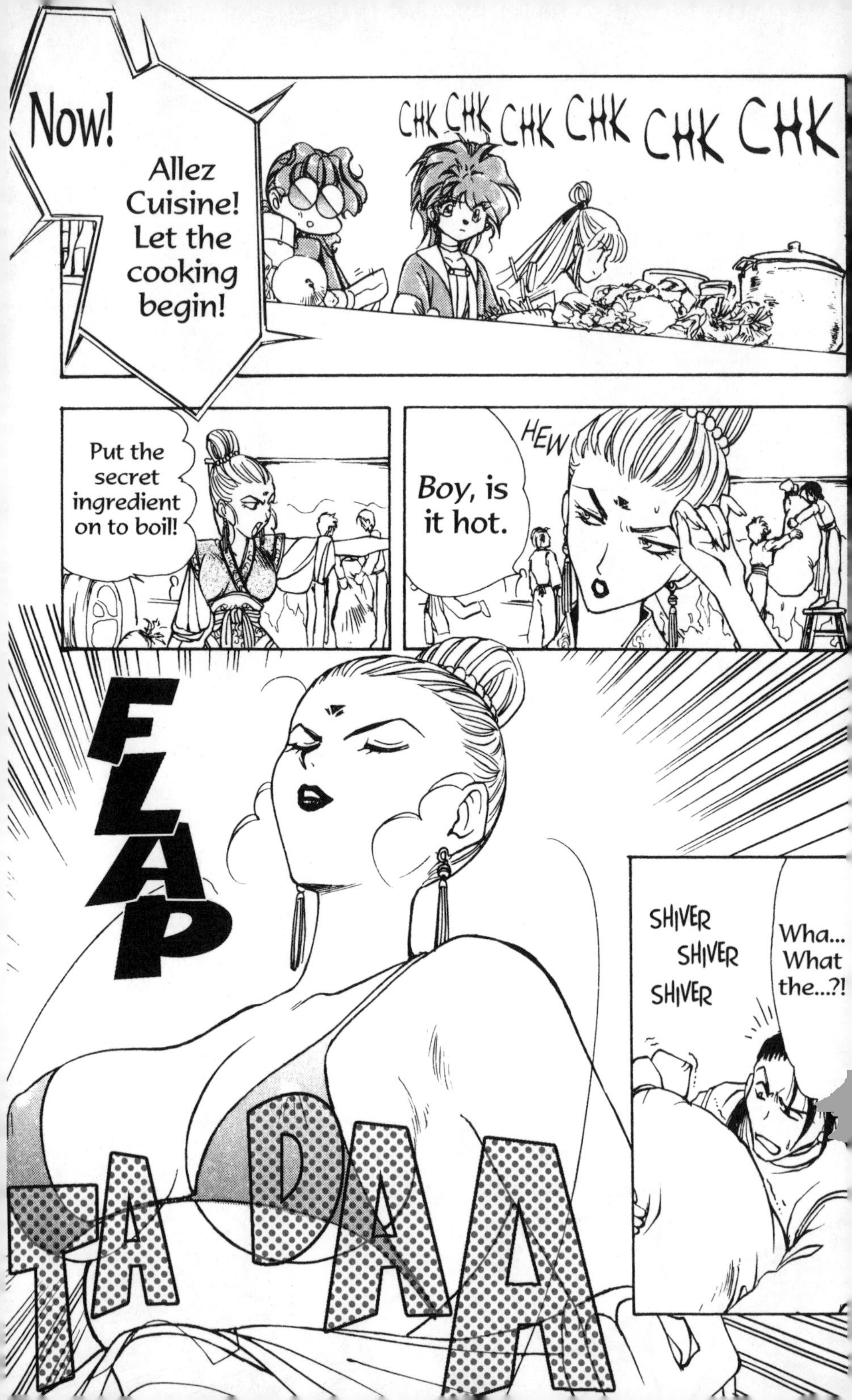
Now!
Allez Cuisine! Let the cooking begin!
CHK CHK CHK CHK CHK CHK
Put the secret ingredient on to boil!
HEW
Boy, is it hot.
FLAP
TA DAA
SHIVER SHIVER SHIVER
Wha... What the...?!

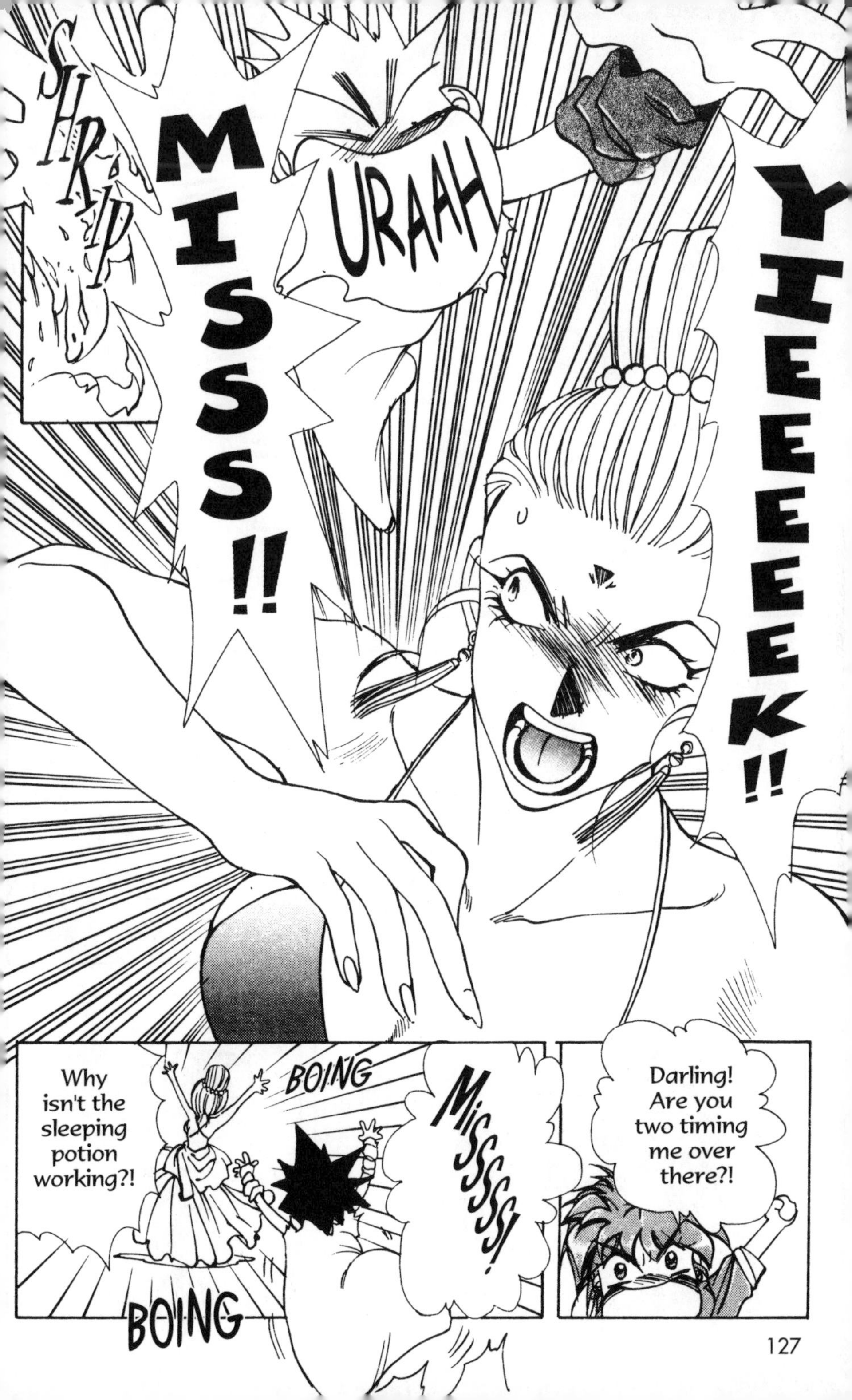
YIEEEEK!!
URAAH
MISS!!
SHRIP
Darling! Are you two timing me over there?!
BOING
MISSSSS!
Why isn't the sleeping potion working?!
BOING

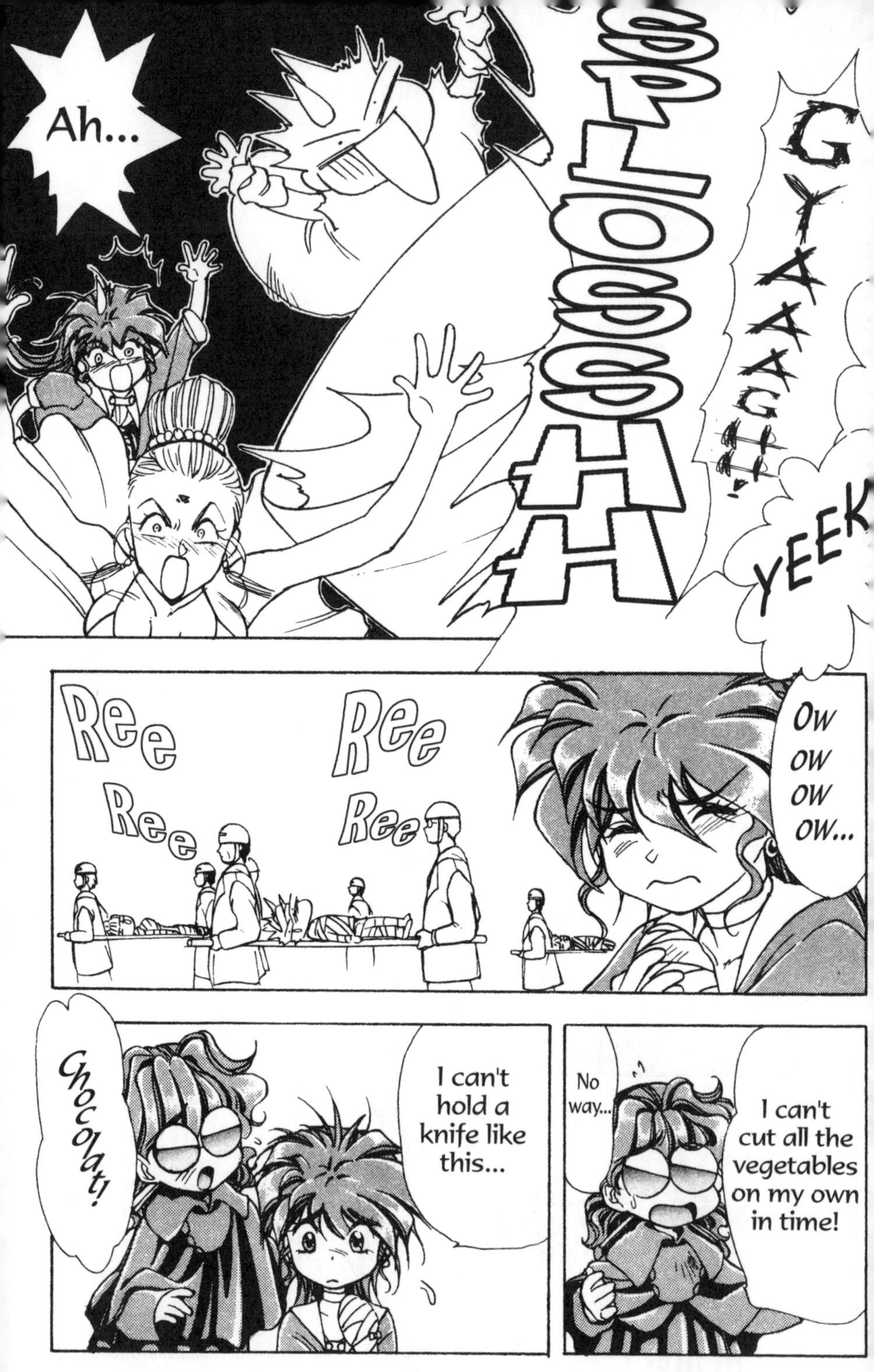
YEEK
GYAAAGH!!
SPLOSSHHH
Ah...
Ow ow ow ow...
Ree Ree
Ree Ree
I can't cut all the vegetables on my own in time!
No way...
I can't hold a knife like this...
Chocolat!

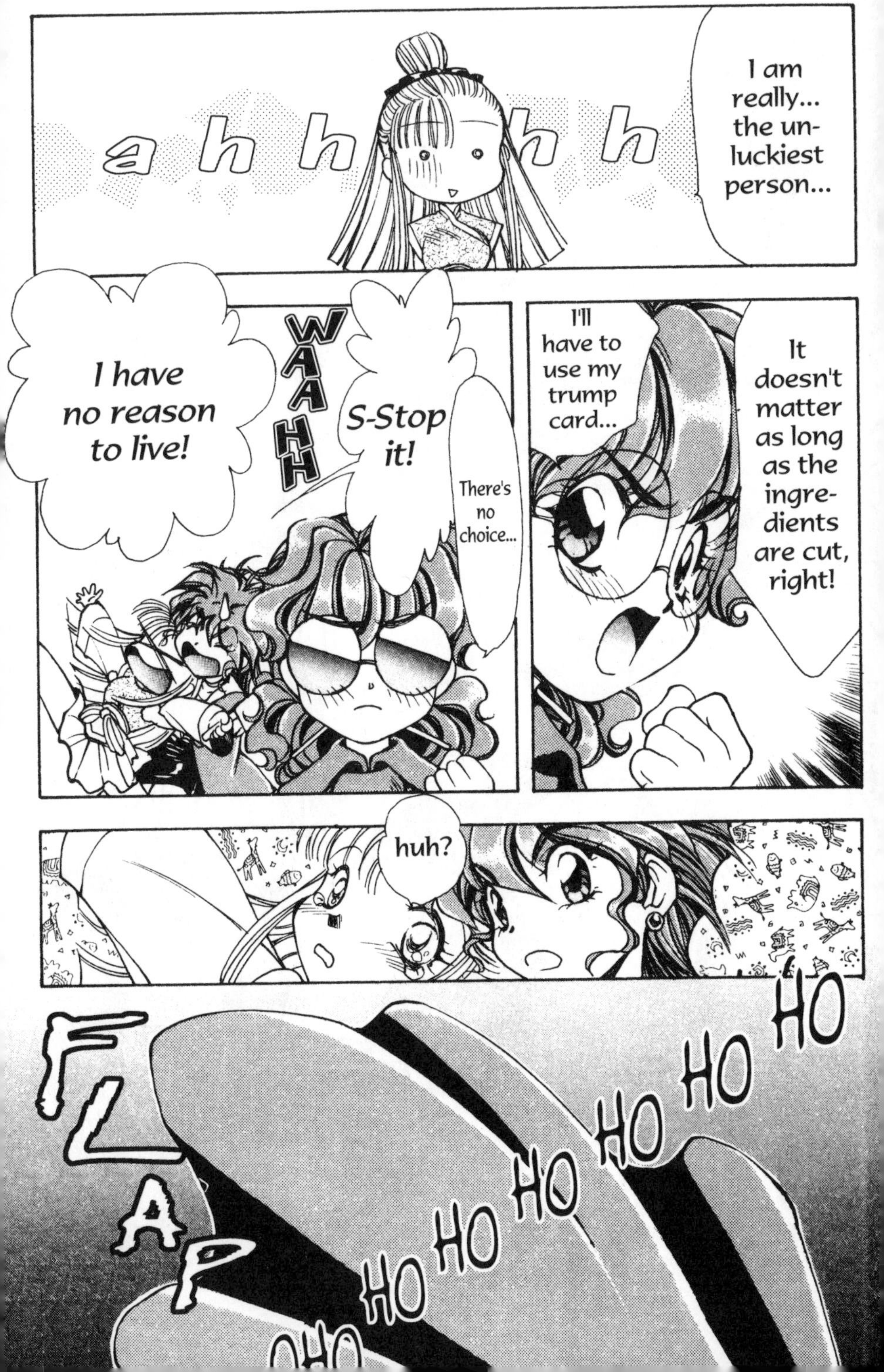
I am really... the un-luckiest person...
a h h h h h
It doesn't matter as long as the ingre-dients are cut, right!
I'll have to use my trump card...
There's no choice...
S-Stop it!
WAAHHH
I have no reason to live!
huh?
HO HO HO HO HO HO HO HO
FLAP

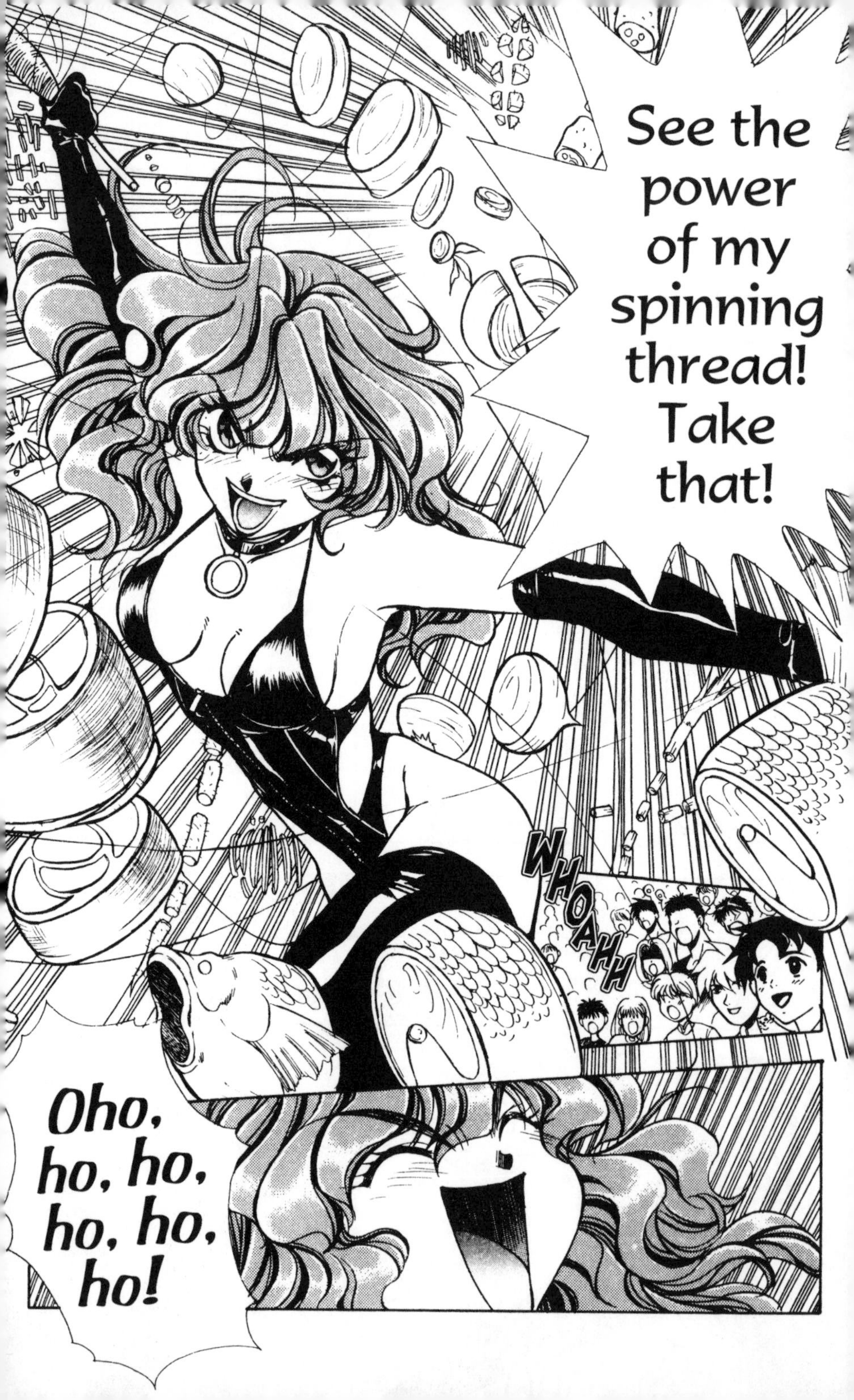
See the power of my spinning thread! Take that!
WHOAHH
Oho, ho, ho, ho, ho, ho!

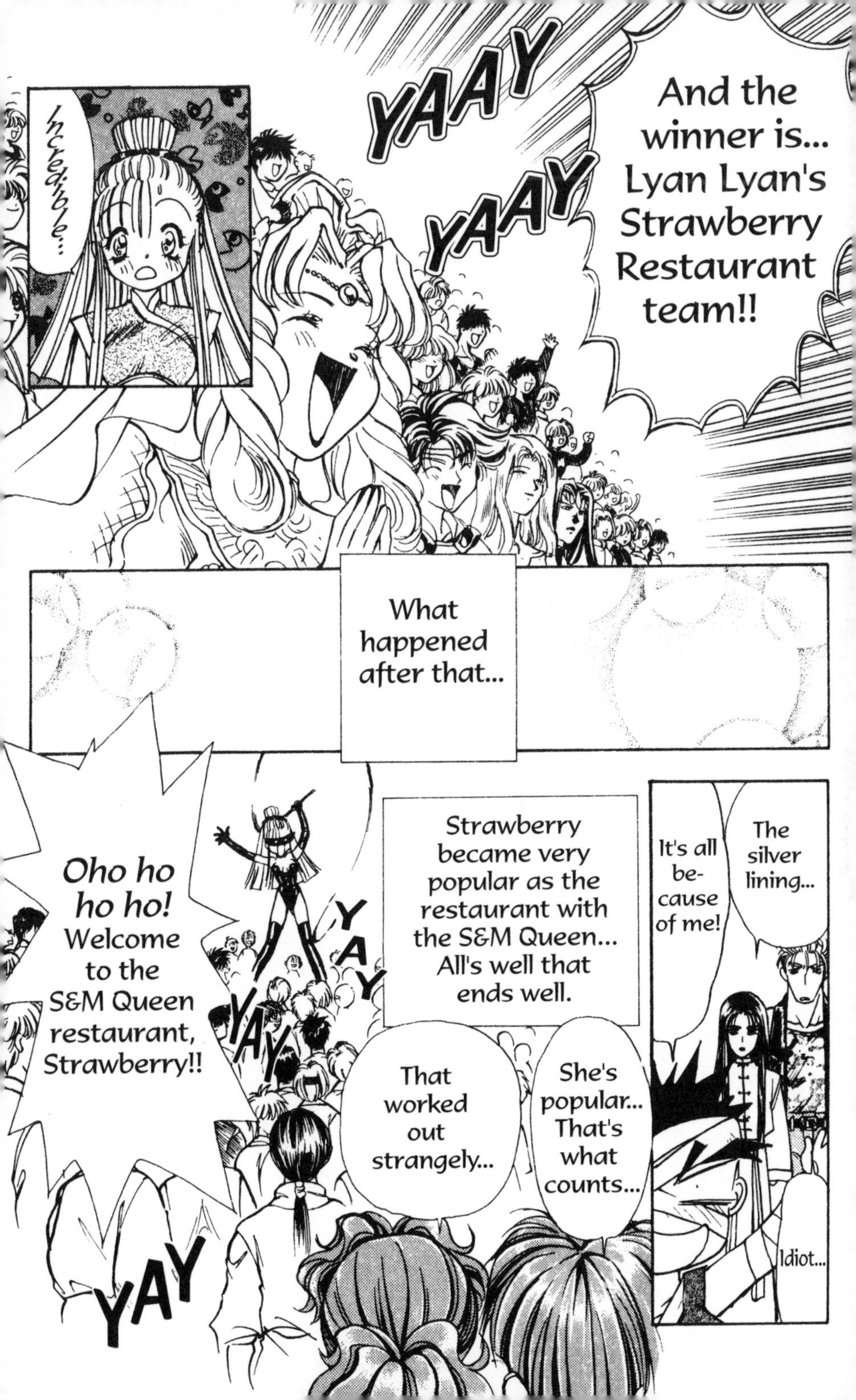
YAAY
YAAY
And the winner is... Lyan Lyan's Strawberry Restaurant team!!
Incredible...
What happened after that...
The silver lining...
It's all be-cause of me!
Idiot...
Strawberry became very popular as the restaurant with the S&M Queen... All's well that ends well.
YAY
YAY
Oho ho ho ho! Welcome to the S&M Queen restaurant, Strawberry!!
She's popular... That's what counts...
That worked out strangely...
YAY

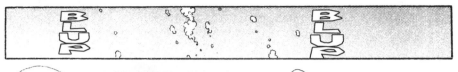

BLUP
BLUP
They are now heading east.
......
BADUM
Already, three of the Platina Stones have been destroyed...
I have no excuse...
BADUM
heh
To Kengyu...
BLUP
Kengyu is strong...
Lord Sacher?!

The Samurai of Doom! (Part 1)

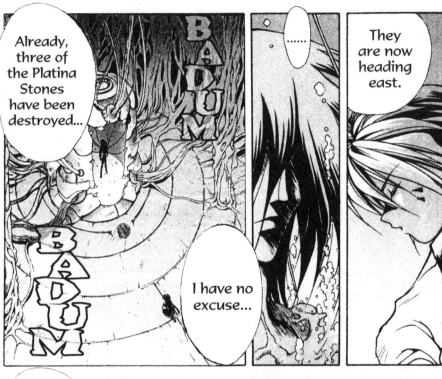

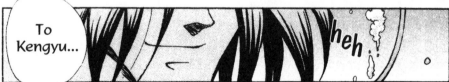

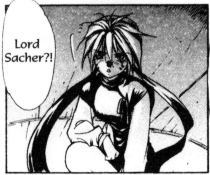

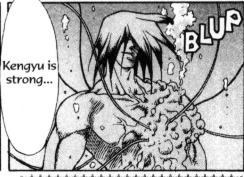

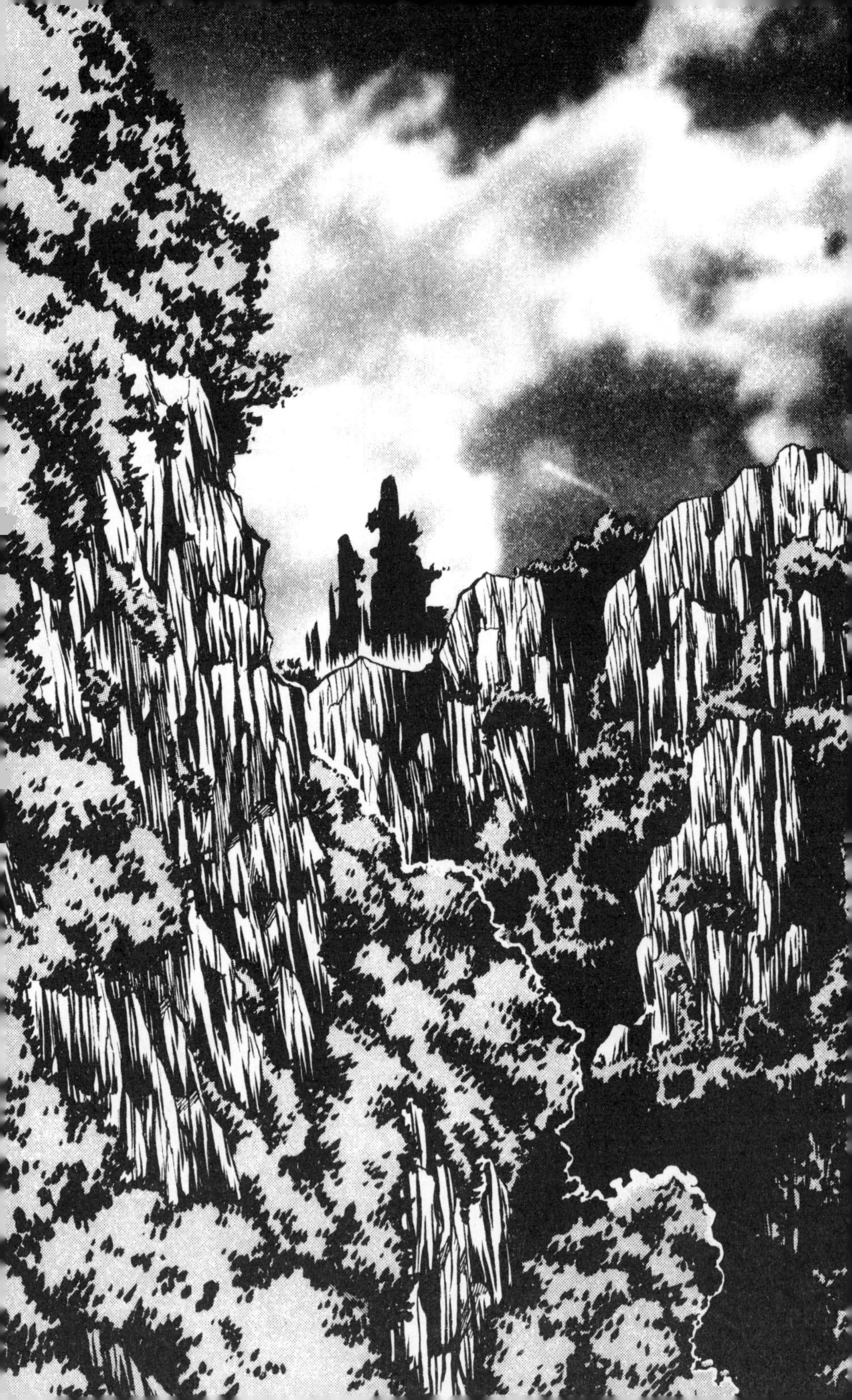

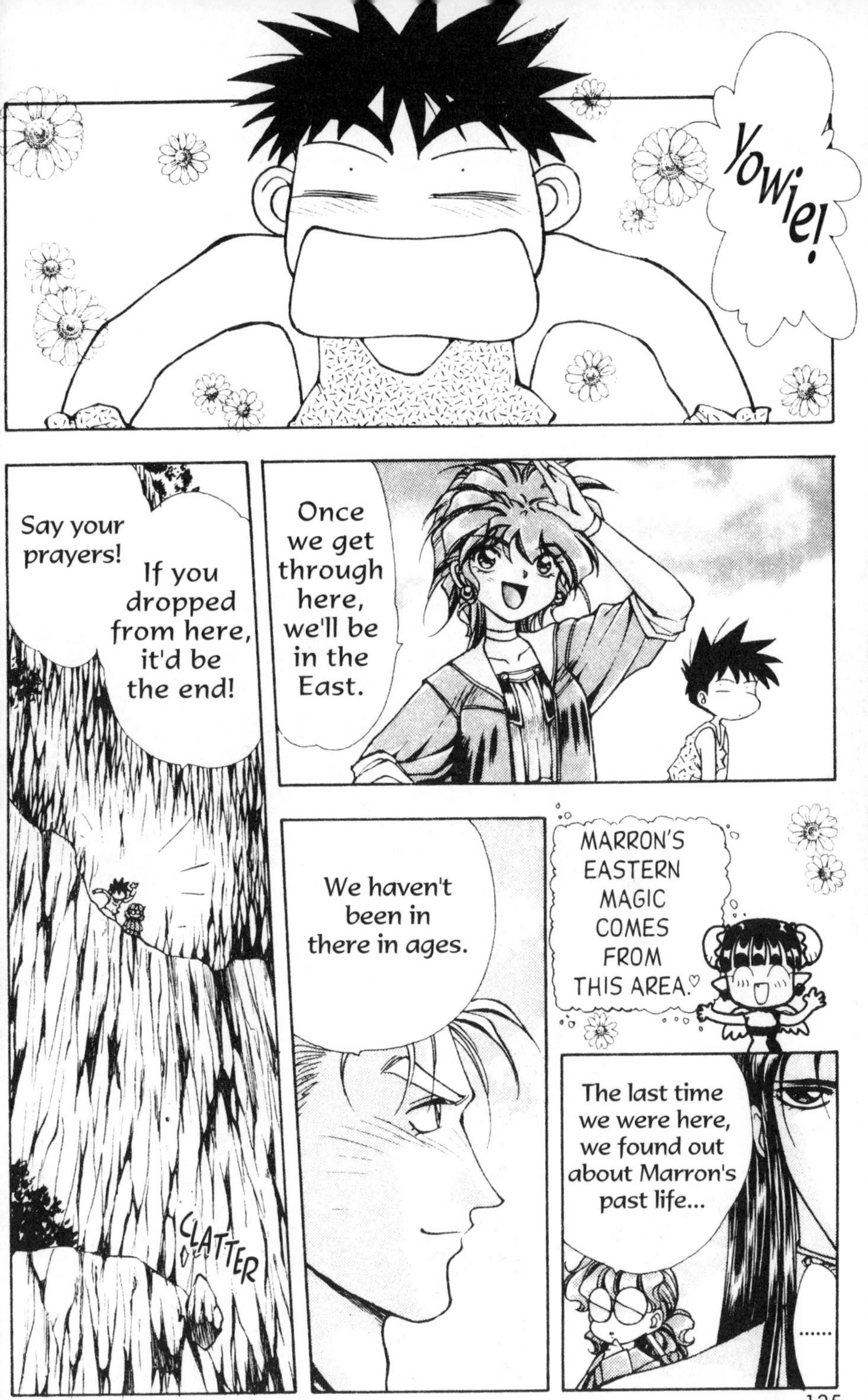
Yowie!
Say your prayers!
If you dropped from here, it'd be the end!
CLATTER
Once we get through here, we'll be in the East.
We haven't been in there in ages.
MARRON'S EASTERN MAGIC COMES FROM THIS AREA.♡
The last time we were here, we found out about Marron's past life...
......

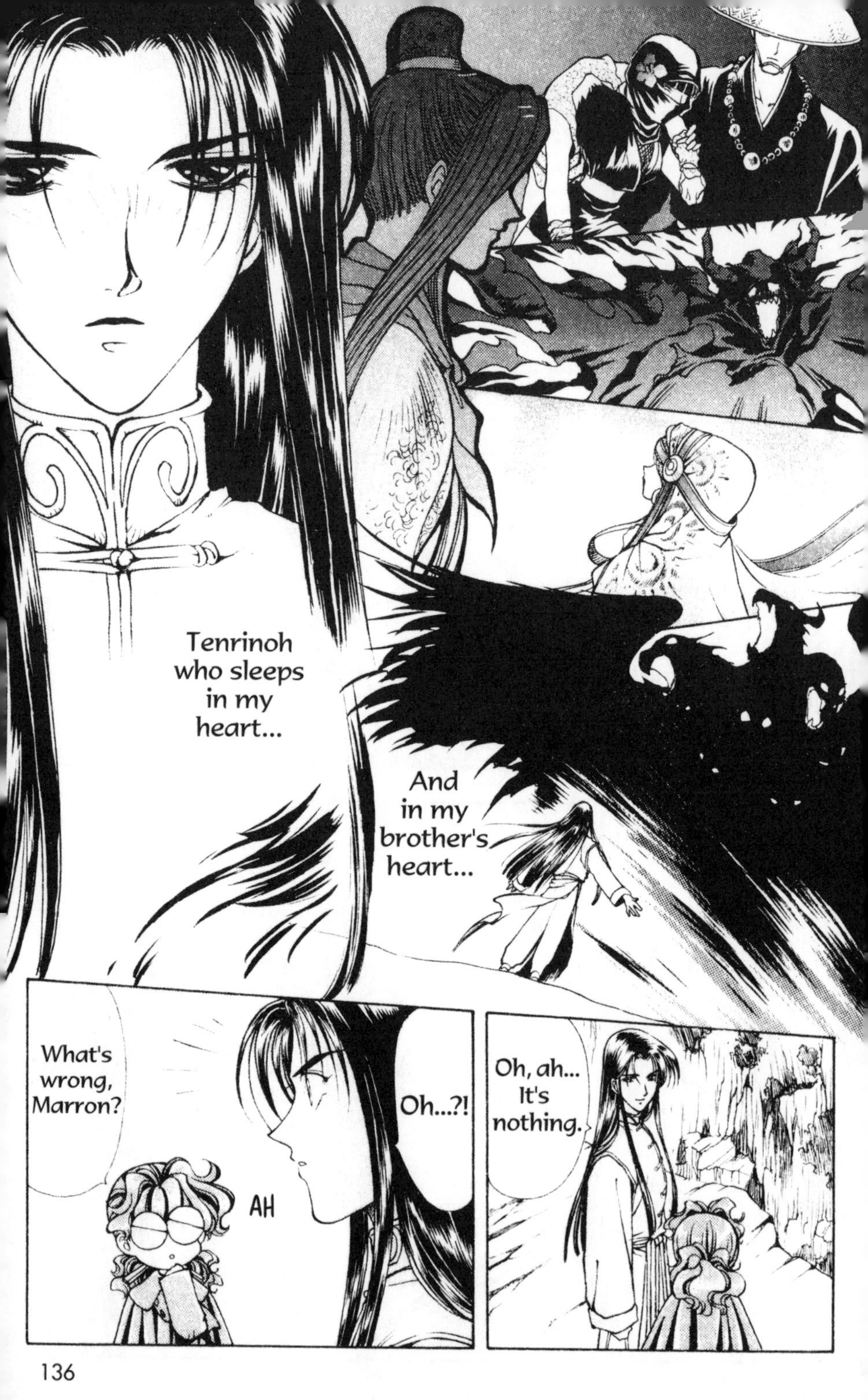
Tenrinoh who sleeps in my heart...
And in my brother's heart...
Oh, ah... It's nothing.
What's wrong, Marron?
Oh...?!
AH

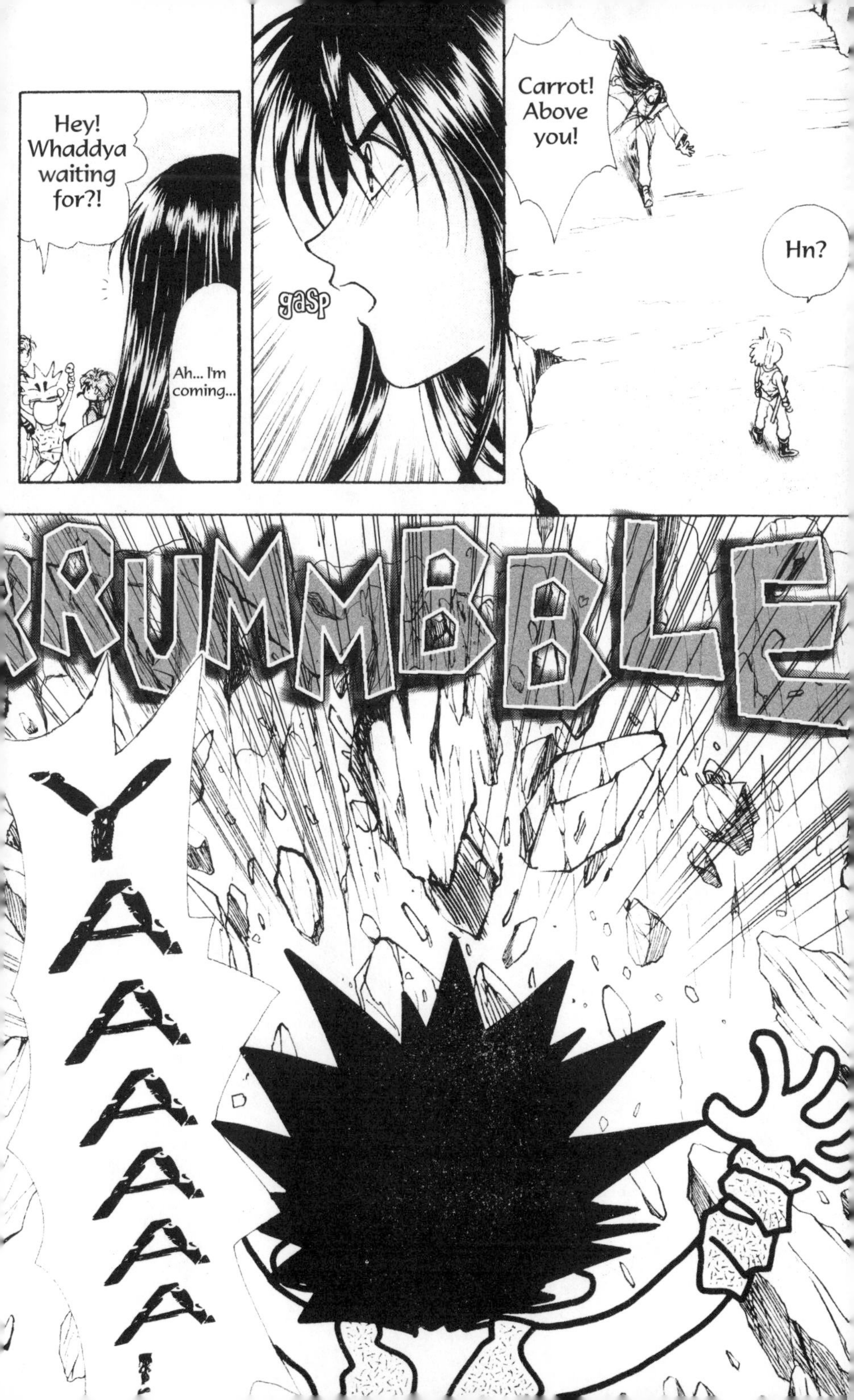
Carrot! Above you!
Hn?
gasp
Hey! Whaddya waiting for?!
Ah... I'm coming...
RRUMMBBLE
YAAAAAA!

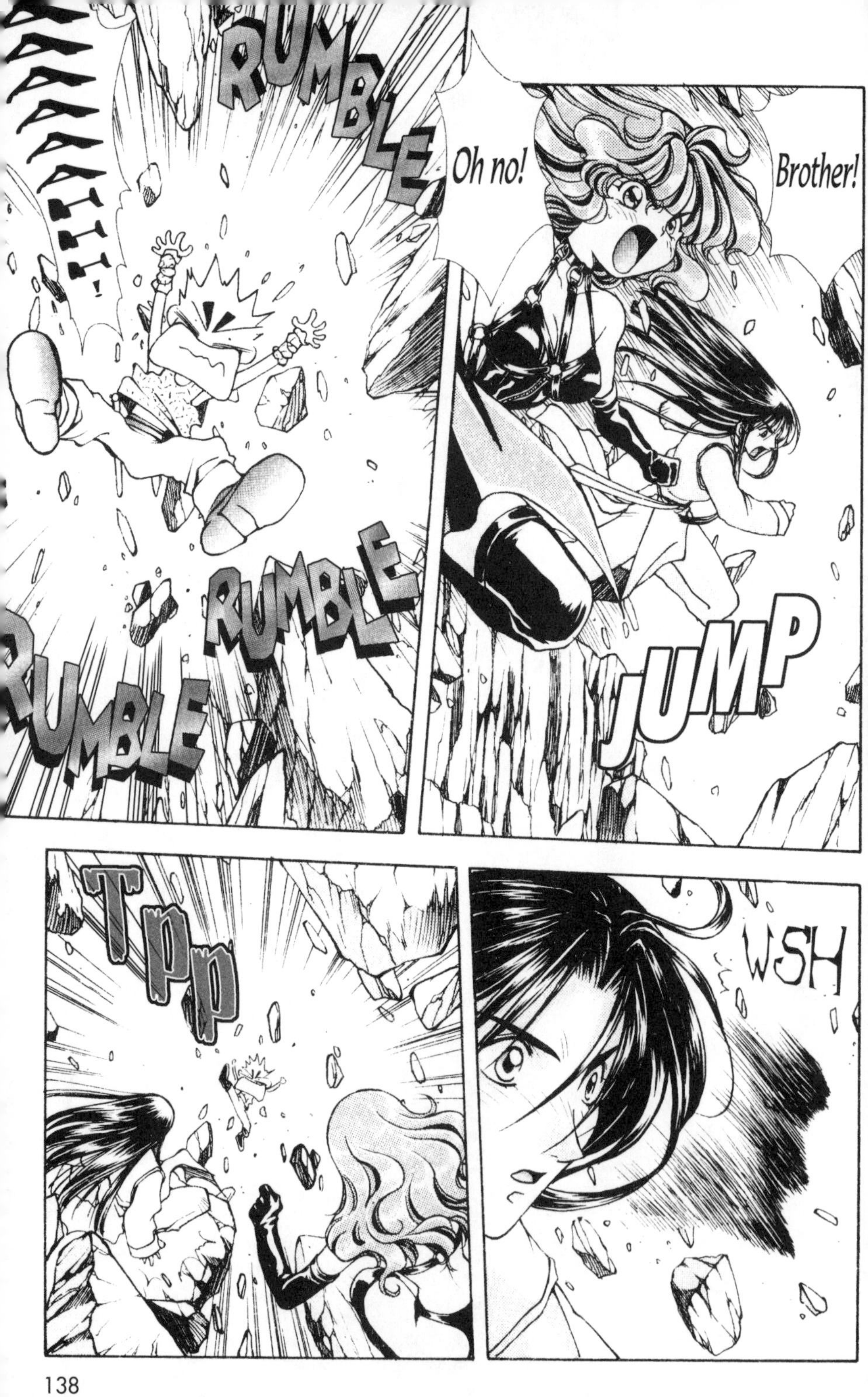
Oh no!
Brother!
JUMP
AAAAAAIII!
RUMBLE
RUMBLE
RUMBLE
WSH
Tpp

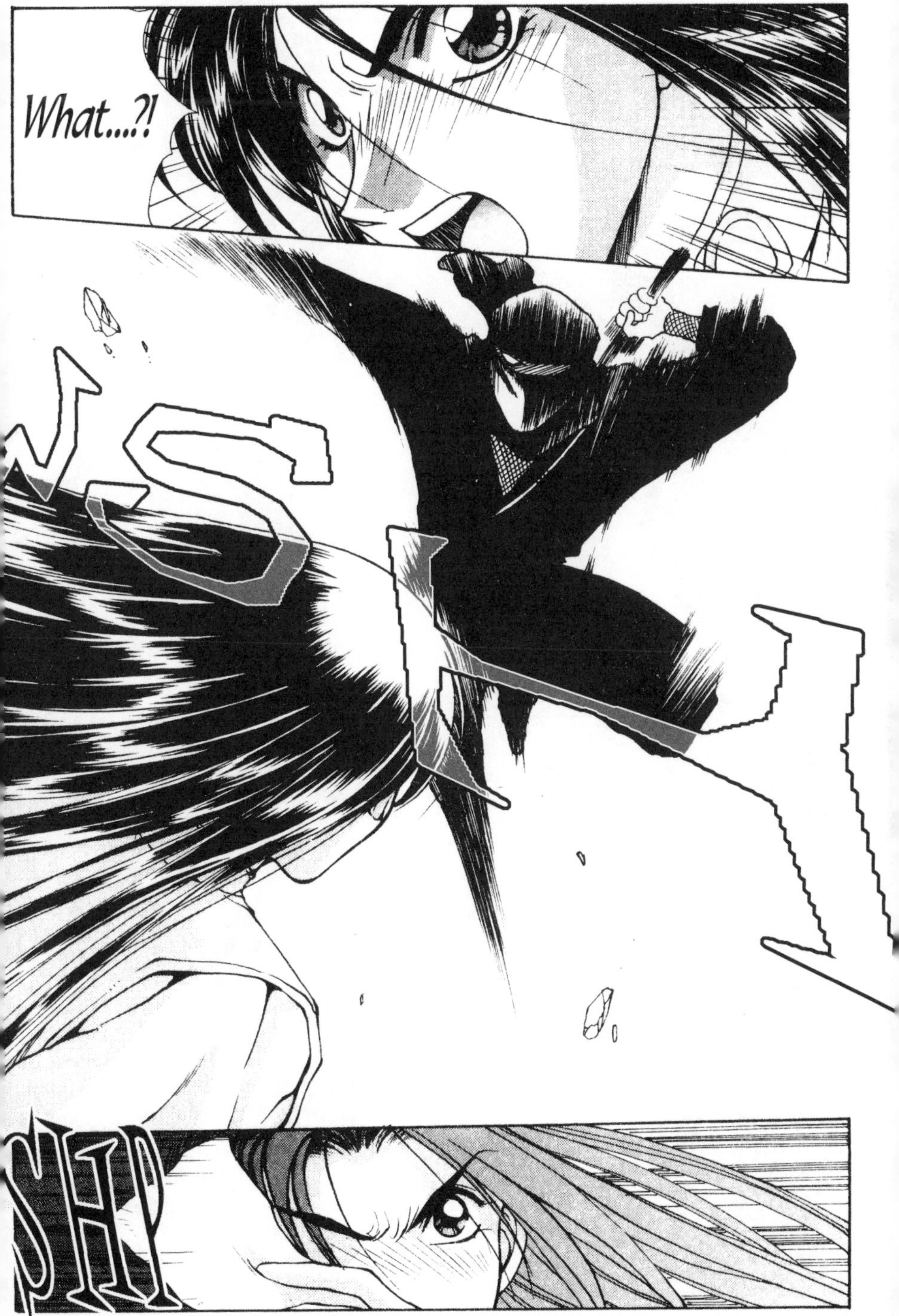
What...?!

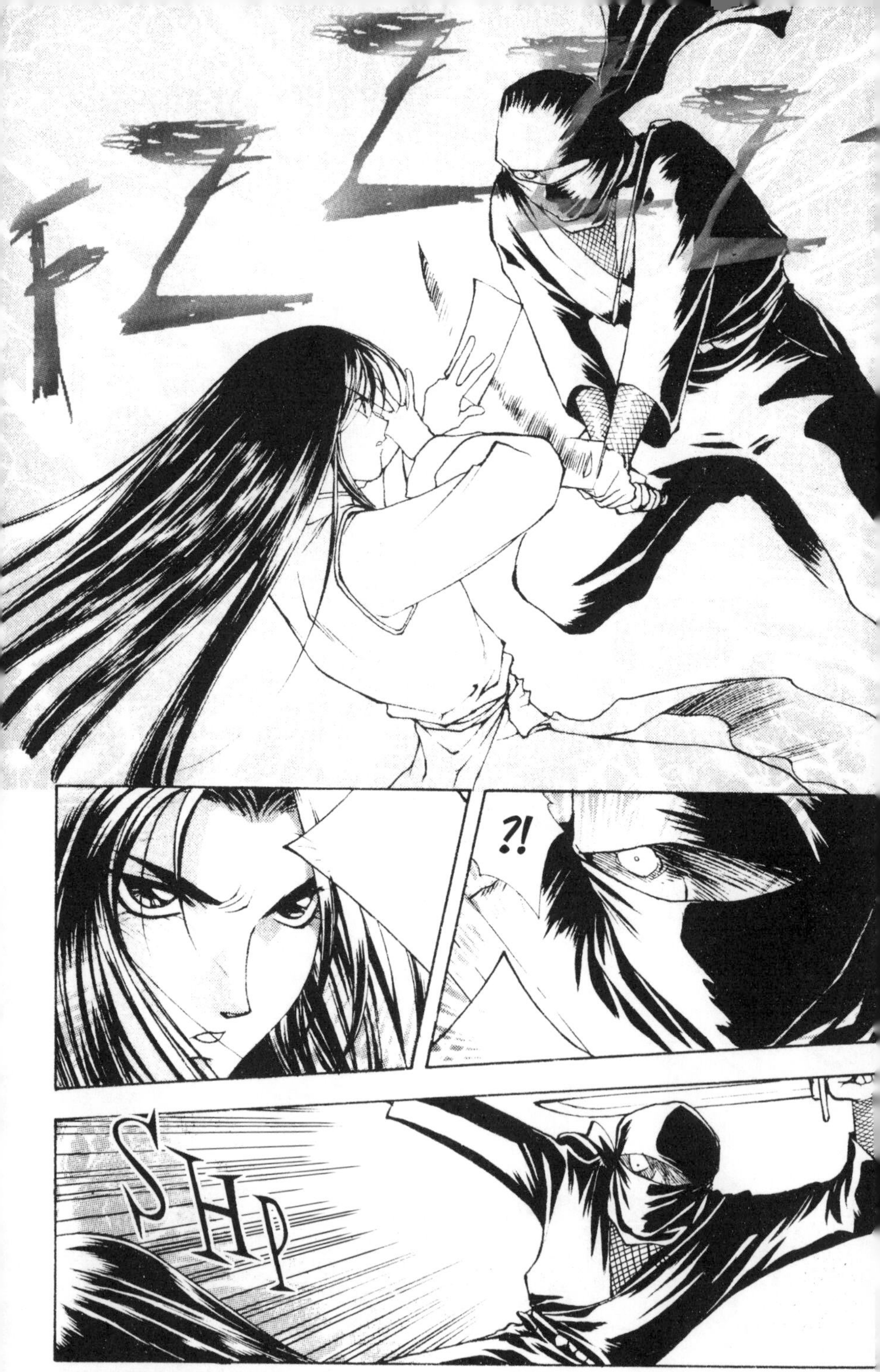
FZZZZ
?!
SHP

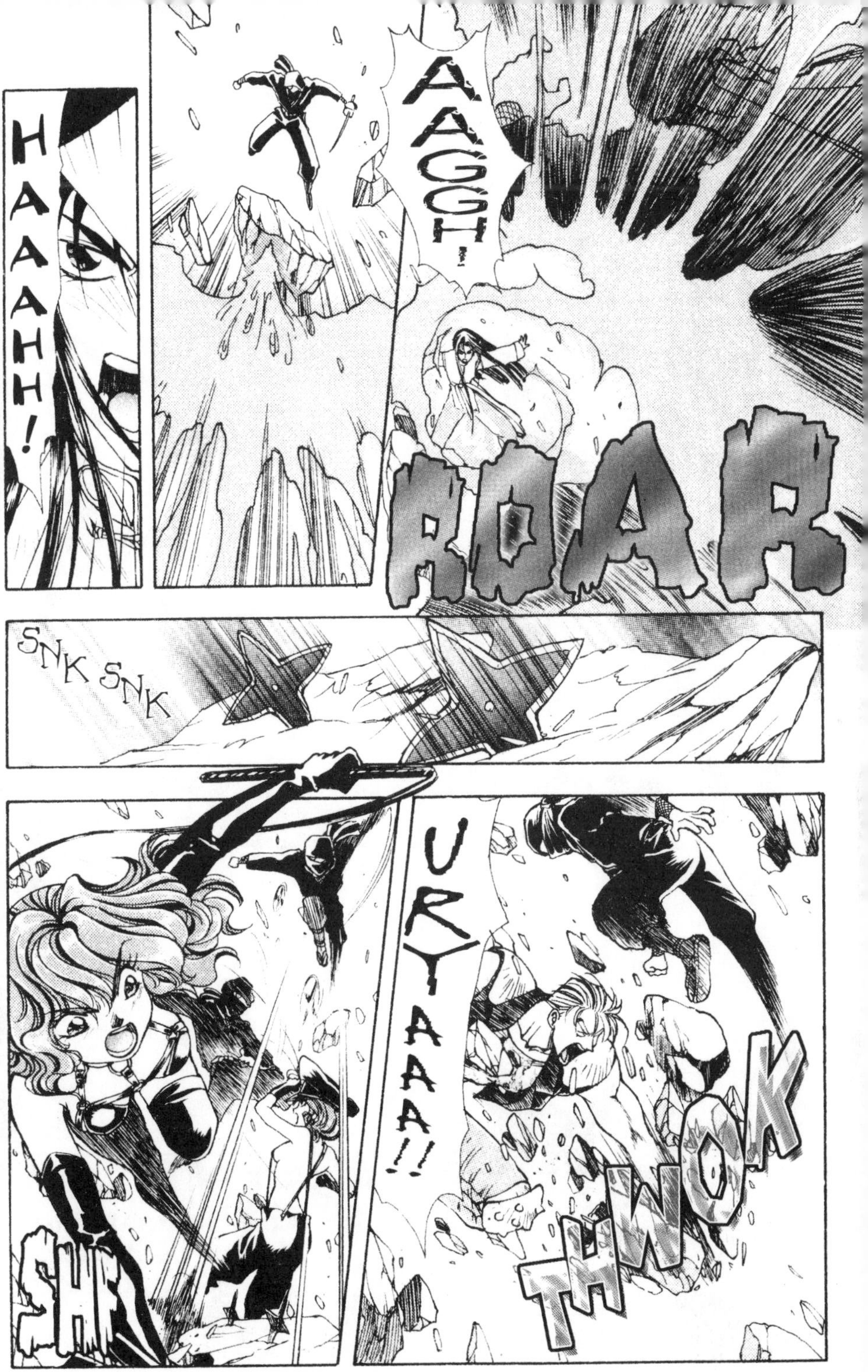
AAGH!
ROAR
HAAAAHH!
SNK SNK
URYAAAA!!
THWOK
SHF

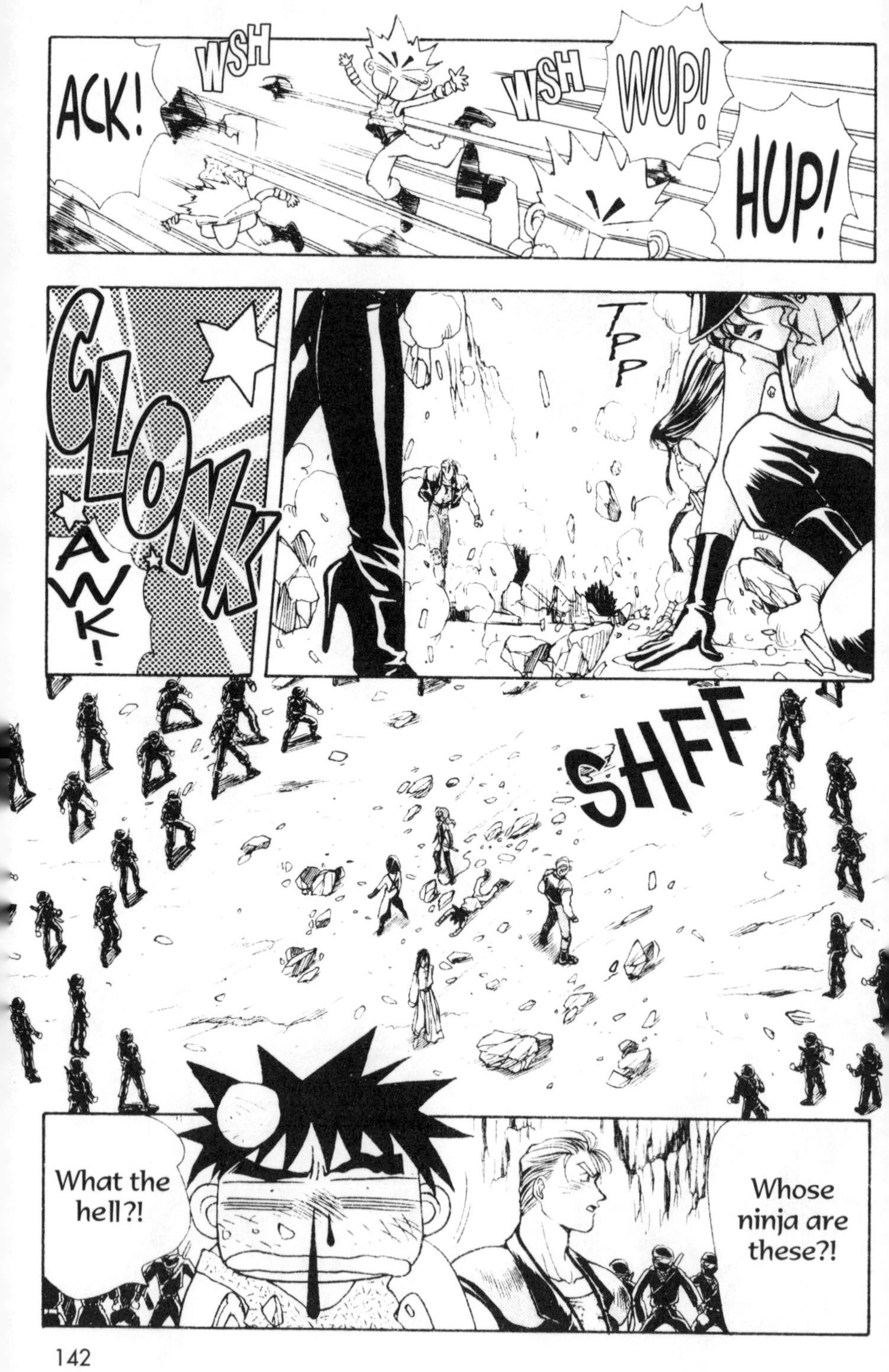
WUP!
HUP!
WSH
WSH
ACK!
TPP
CLONK
AWK!
SHFF
Whose ninja are these?!
What the hell?!

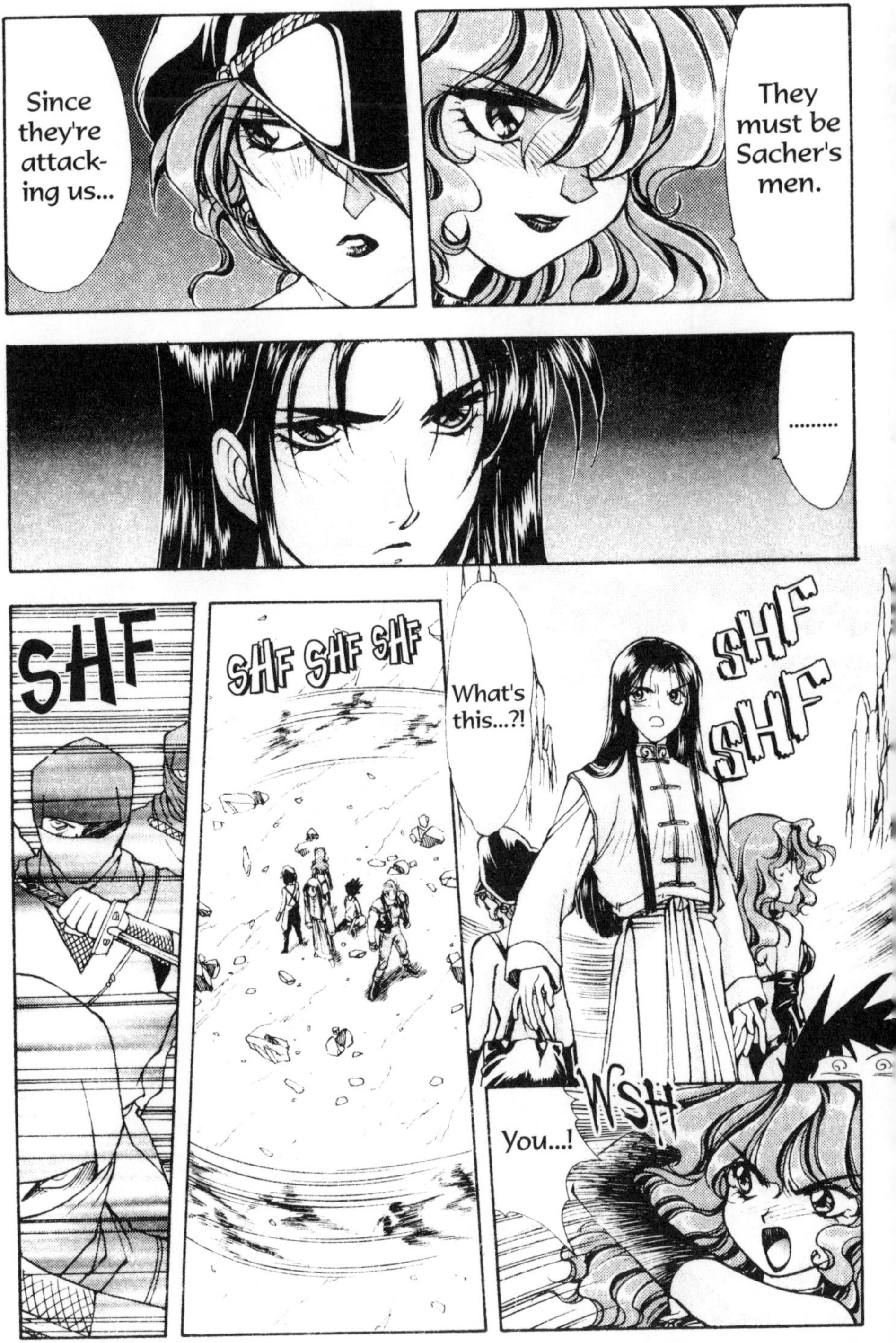
They must be Sacher's men.
Since they're attack-ing us...
....
What's this...?!
SHF SHF
WSH
You...!
SHF SHF SHF
SHF

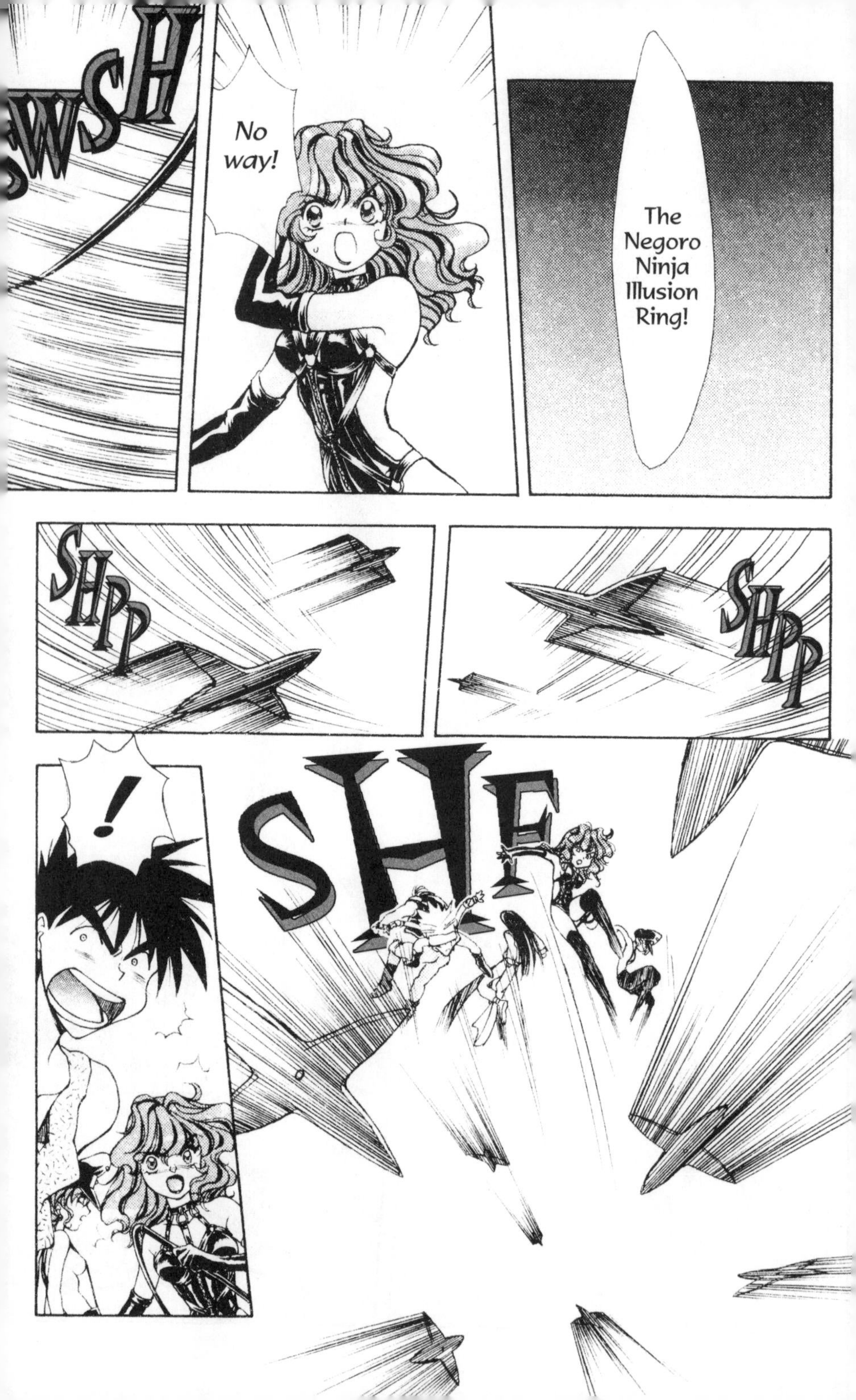
The Negoro Ninja Illusion Ring!
No way!
SWSH
SHPP
SHPP
SHF
!

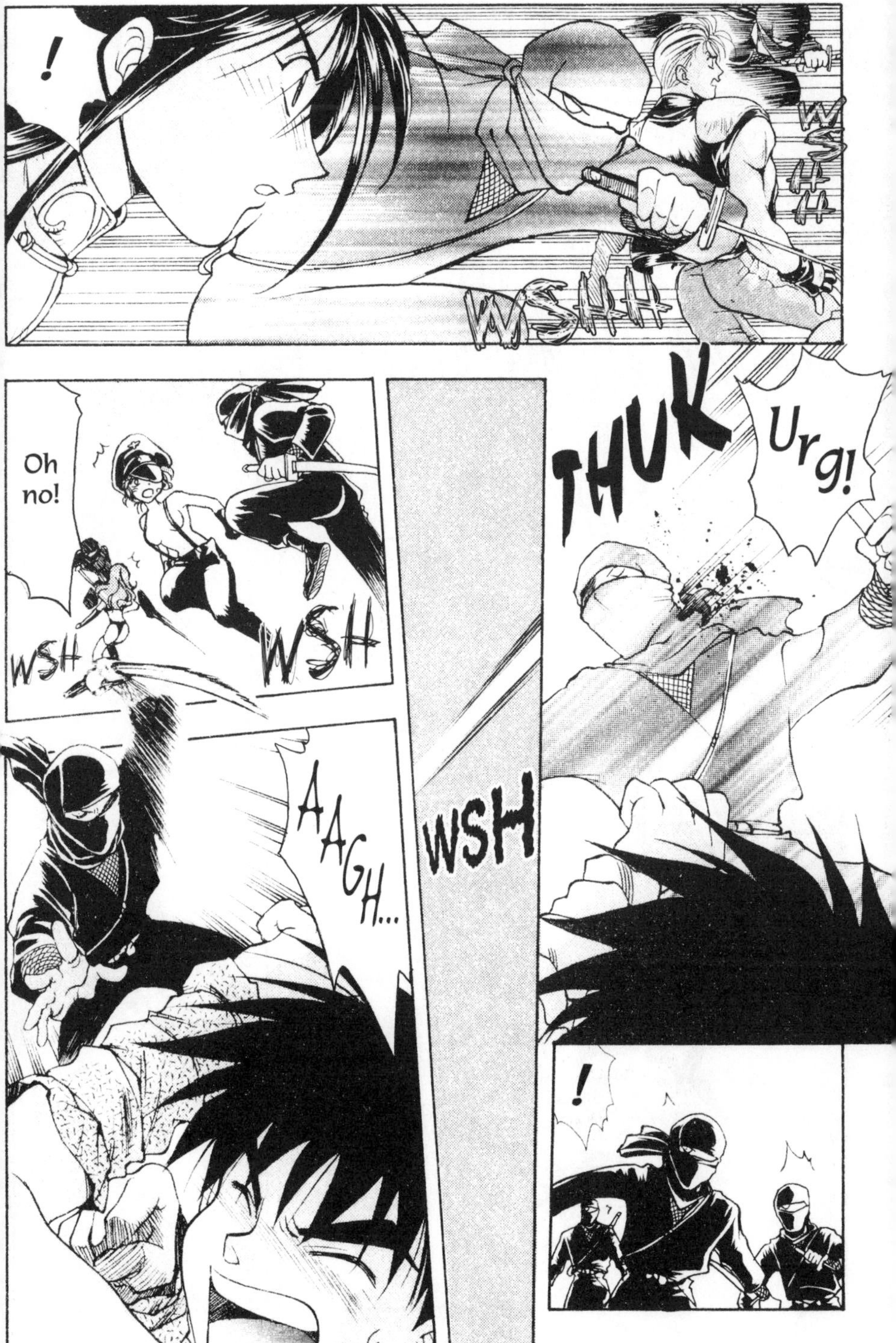
!
WSHH
WSHH
Urg!
THUK
WSH
Oh no!
WSH
WSH
AAGH...
!

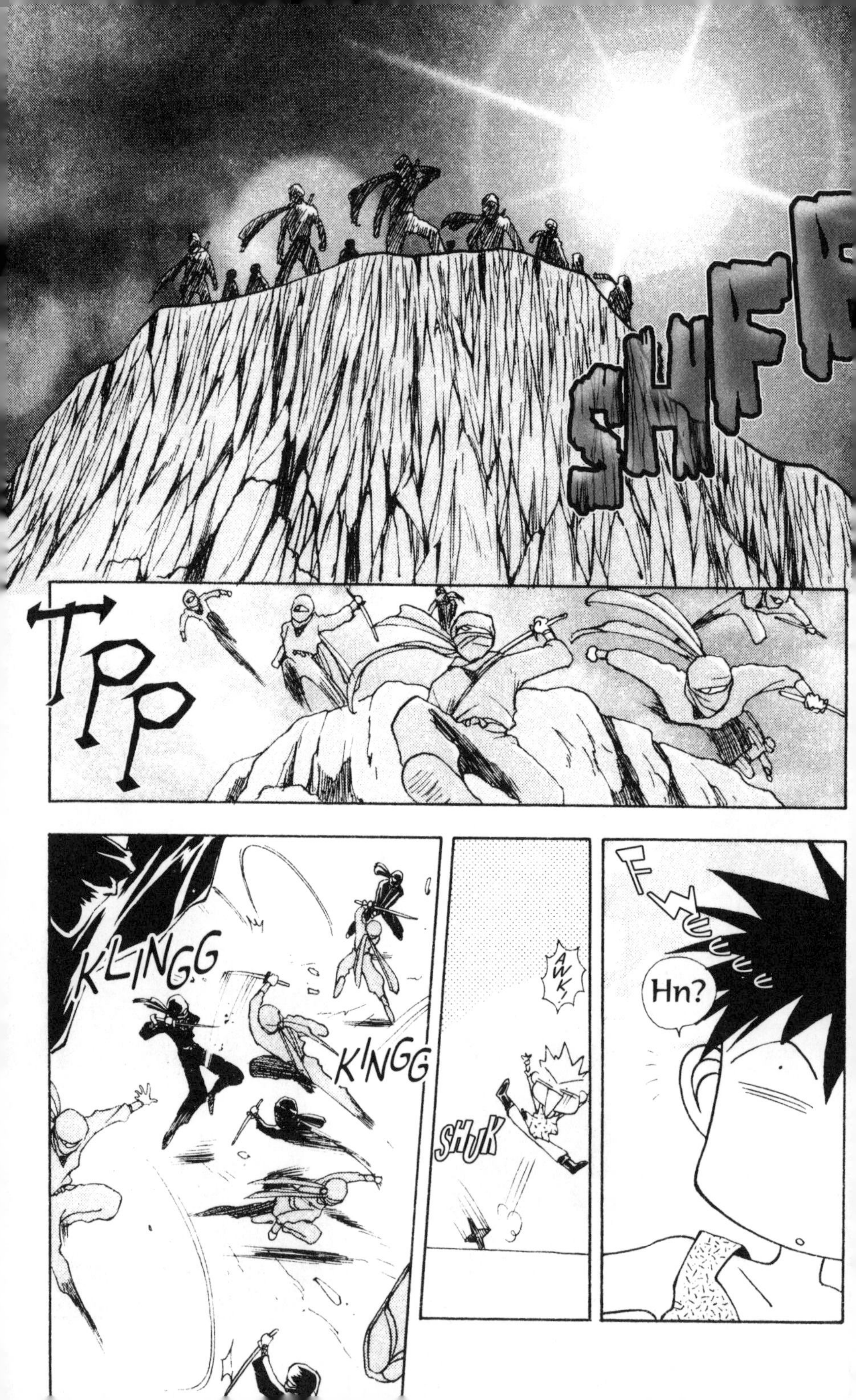
SHUFF
TPP
FWEEEEE
Hn?
AWK!
SHUK
KLINGG
KINGG

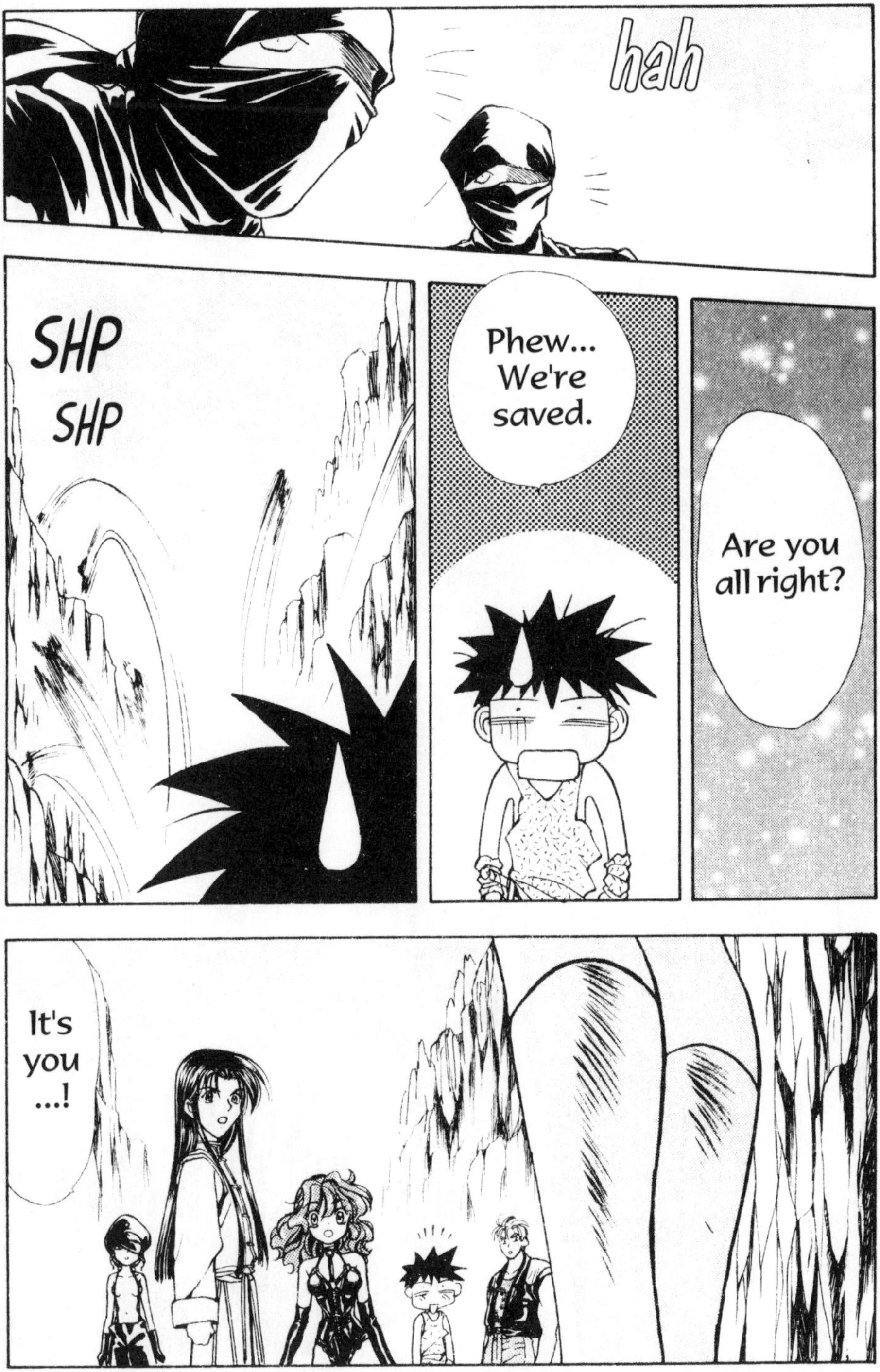
hah
Are you all right?
Phew... We're saved.
SHP SHP
It's you ...!

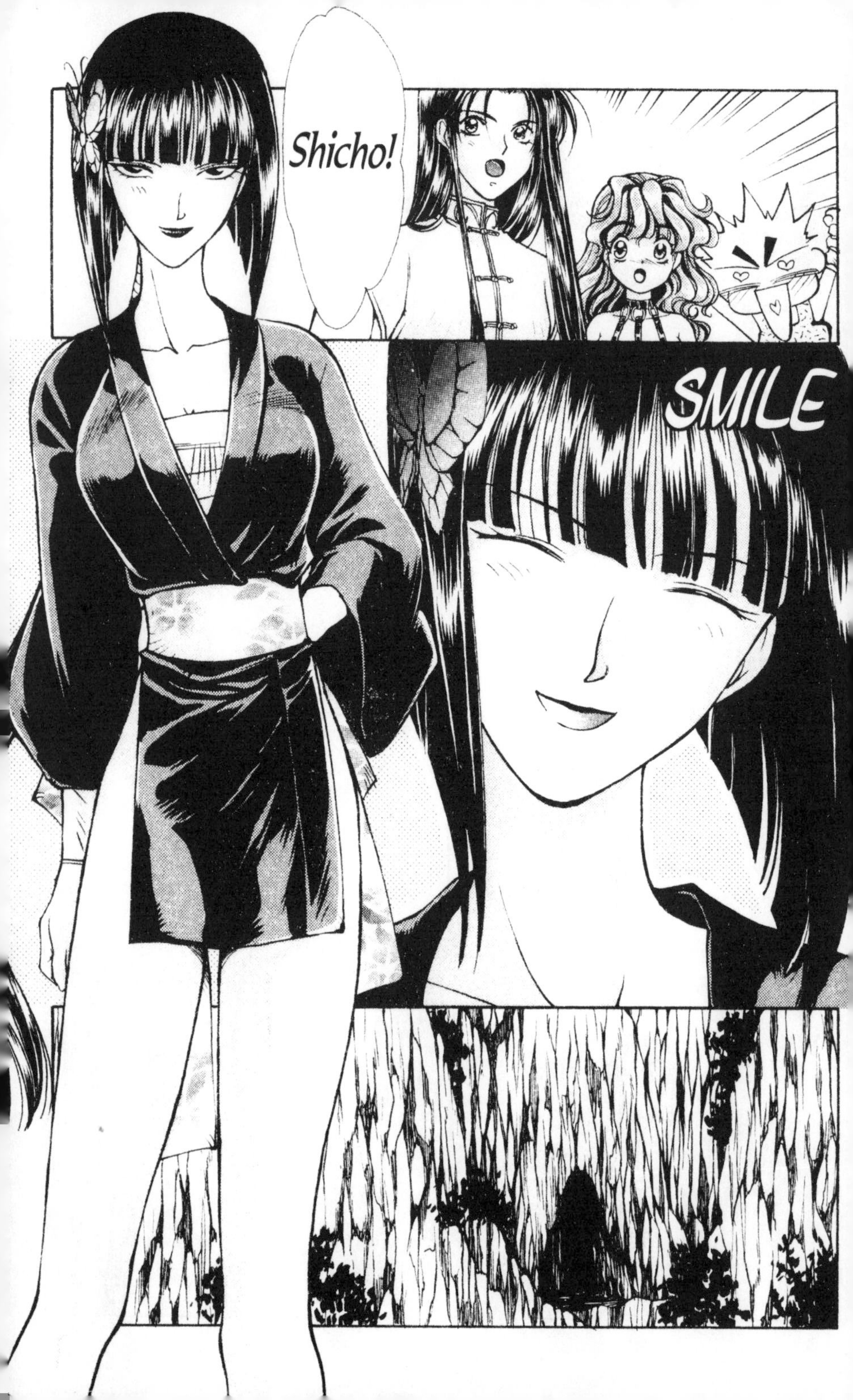
Shicho!
SMILE

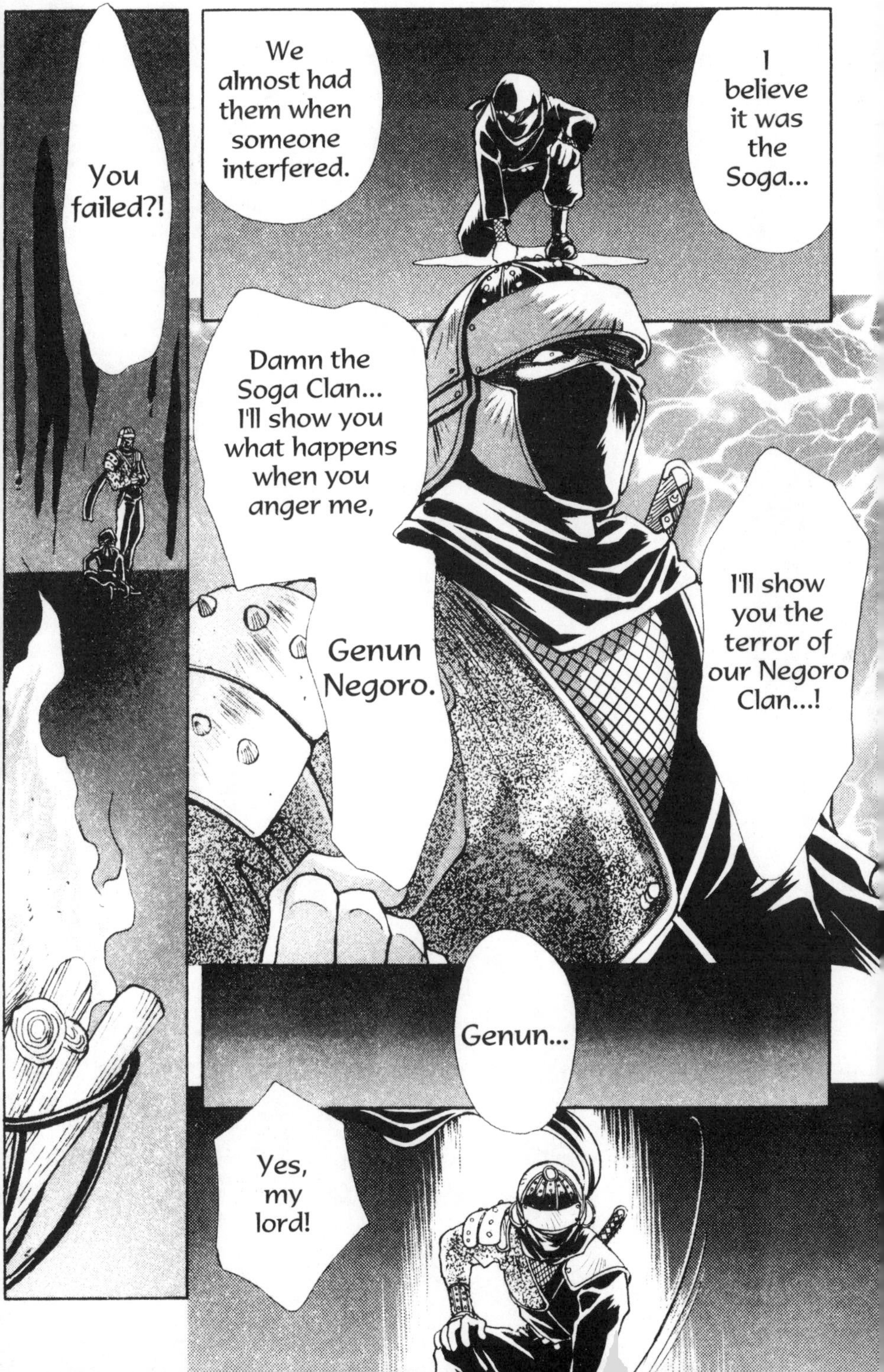
You failed?!
We almost had them when someone interfered.
I believe it was the Soga...
Damn the Soga Clan... I'll show you what happens when you anger me,
Genun Negoro.
I'll show you the terror of our Negoro Clan...!
Genun...
Yes, my lord!

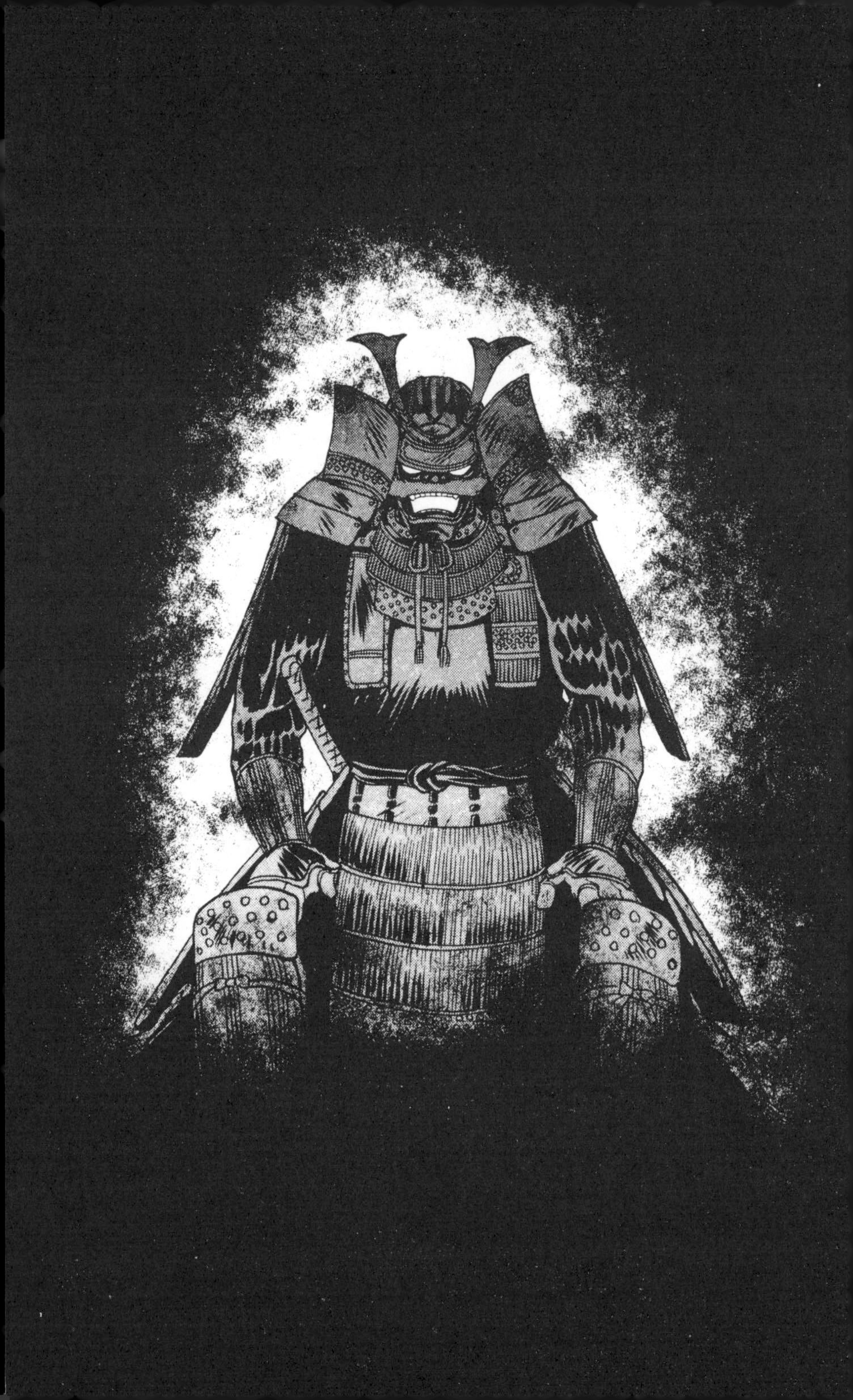

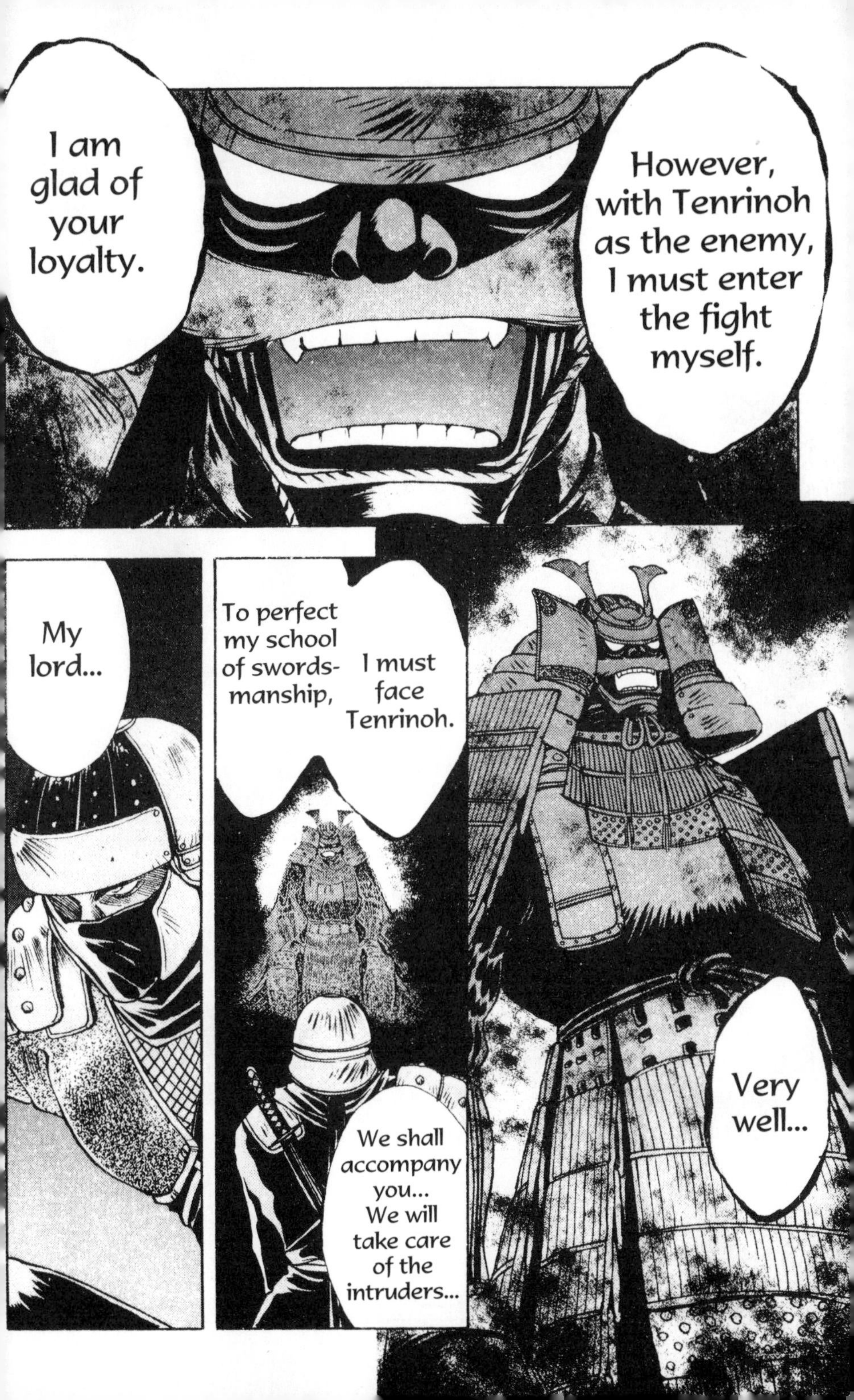
I am glad of your loyalty.
However, with Tenrinoh as the enemy, I must enter the fight myself.
My lord...
To perfect my school of swords-manship,
I must face Tenrinoh.
We shall accompany you... We will take care of the intruders...
Very well...

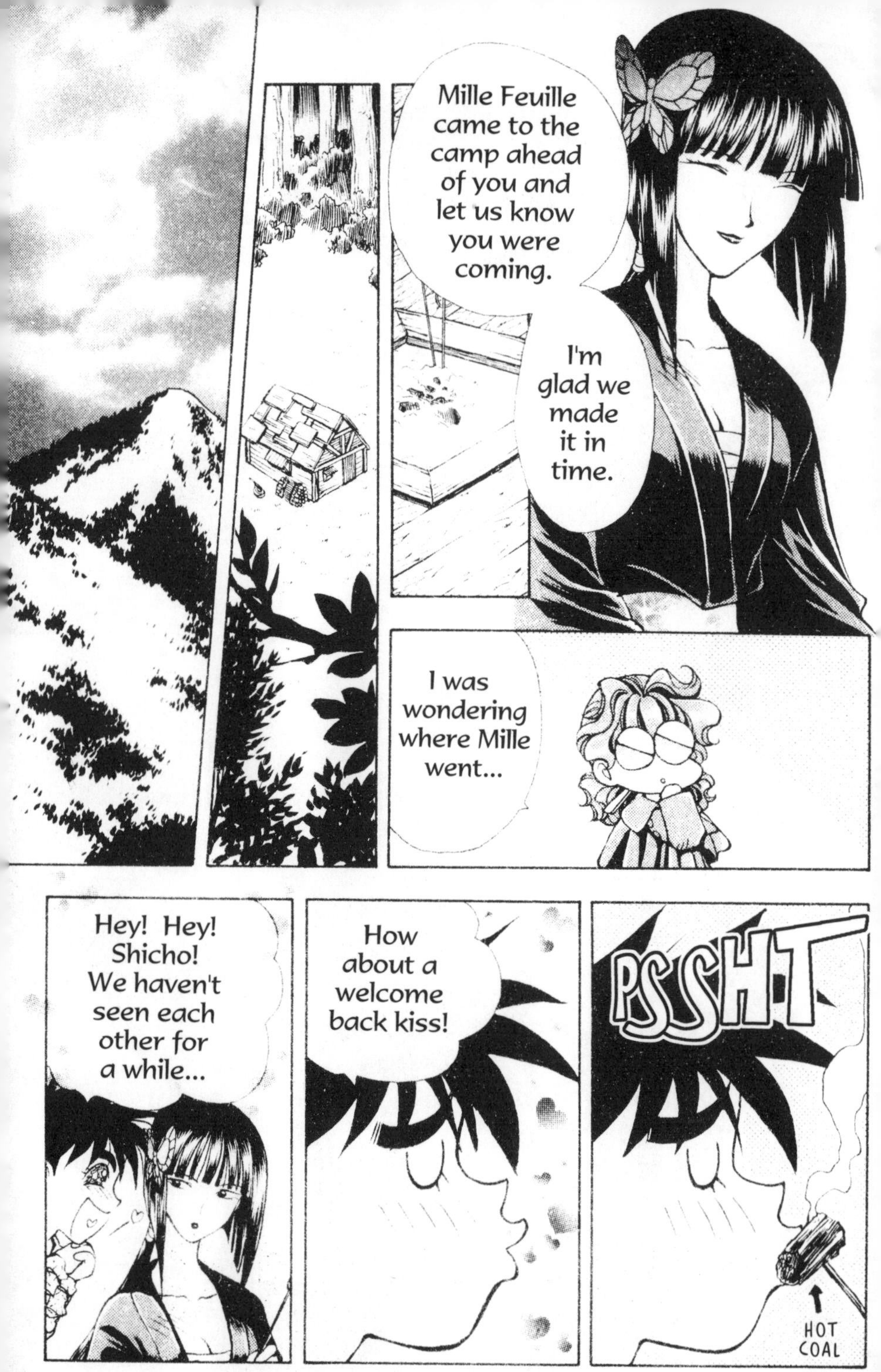
Mille Feuille came to the camp ahead of you and let us know you were coming.
I'm glad we made it in time.
I was wondering where Mille went...
Hey! Hey! Shicho! We haven't seen each other for a while...
How about a welcome back kiss!
PSSHT
HOT COAL

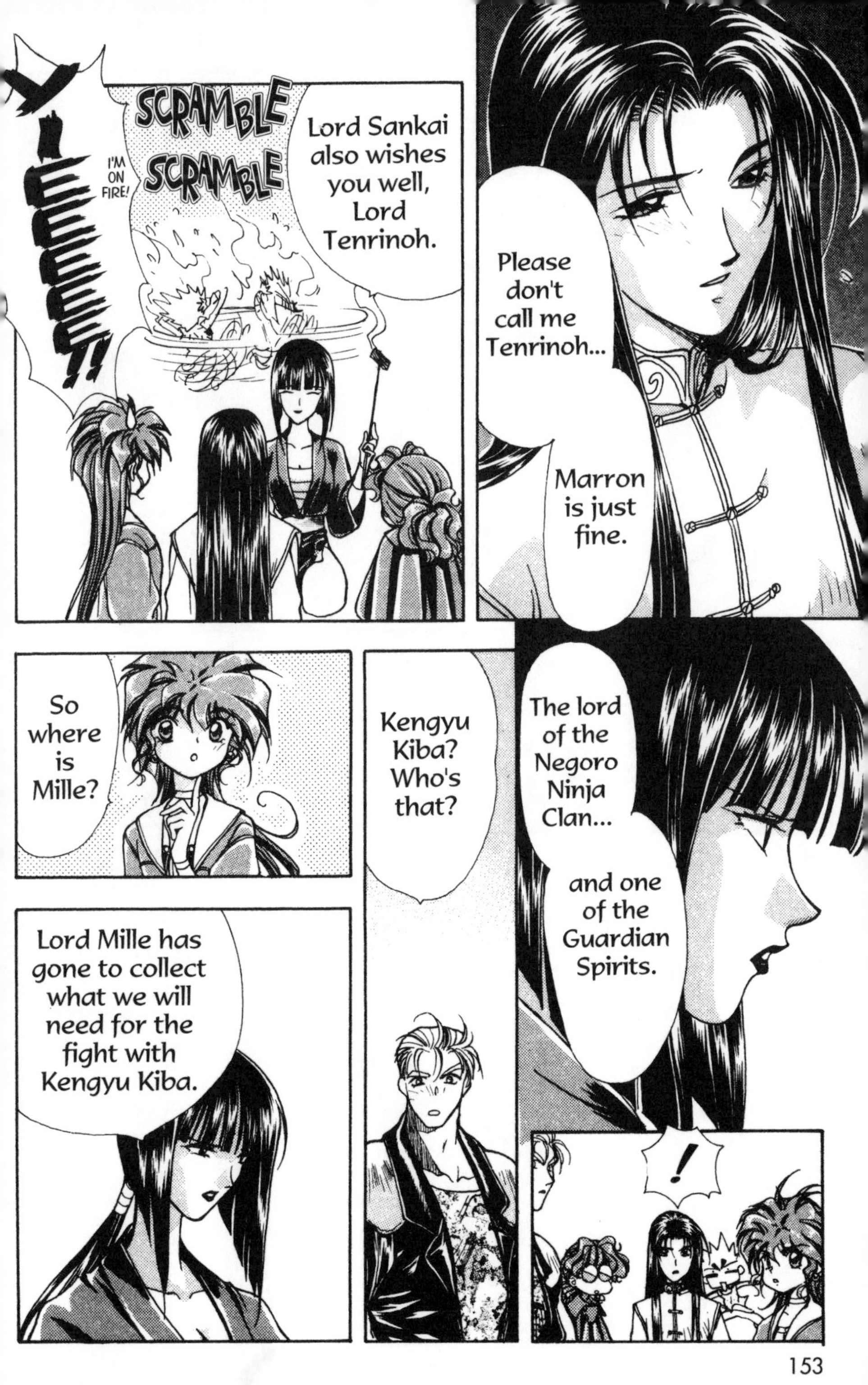
SCRAMBLE
SCRAMBLE
I'M ON FIRE!
Lord Sankai also wishes you well, Lord Tenrinoh.
Please don't call me Tenrinoh...
Marron is just fine.
So where is Mille?
Lord Mille has gone to collect what we will need for the fight with Kengyu Kiba.
Kengyu Kiba? Who's that?
The lord of the Negoro Ninja Clan...
and one of the Guardian Spirits.
!

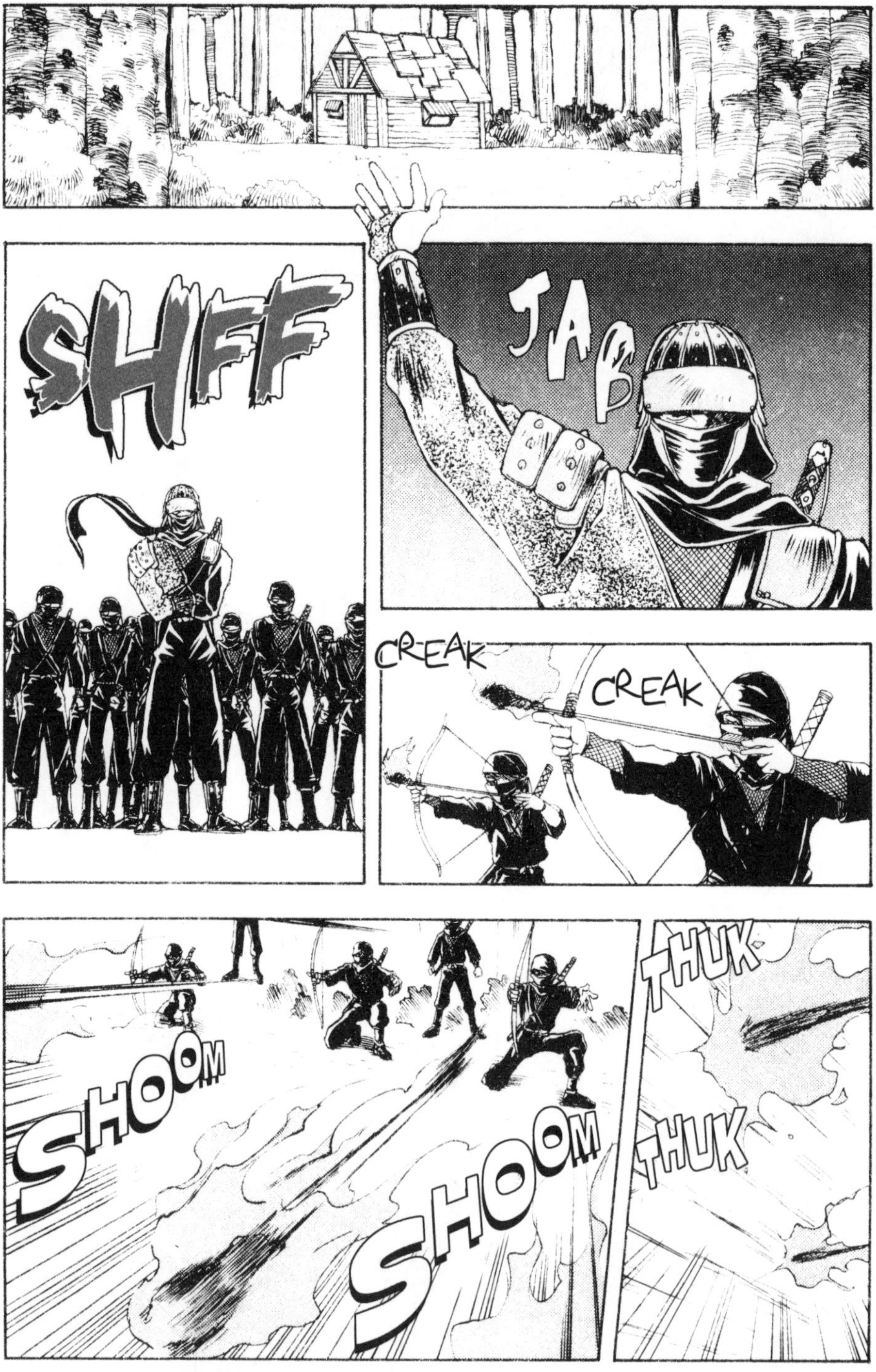
SHFF
JAB
CREAK
CREAK
SHOOM
SHOOM
THUK
THUK

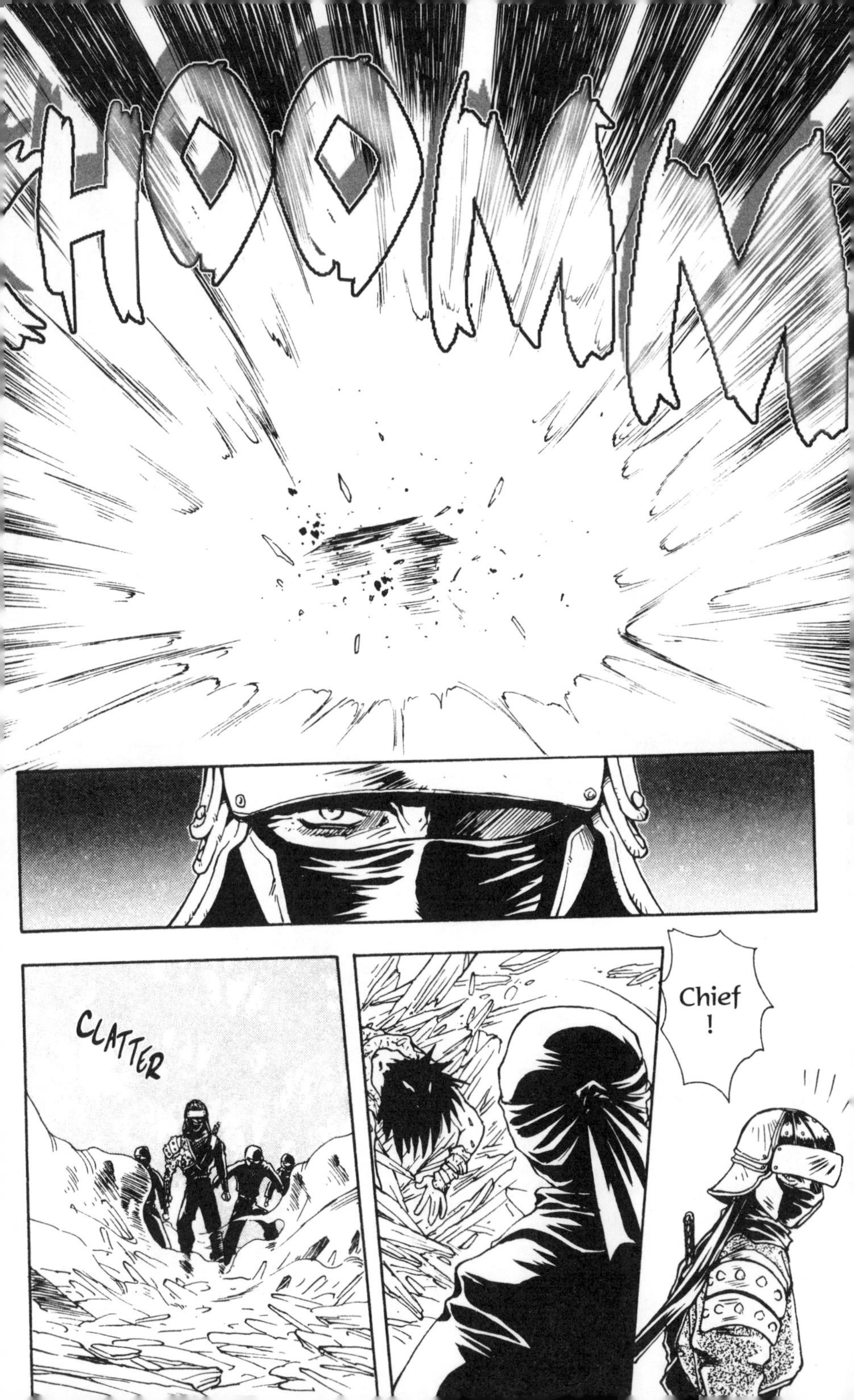
Chief !
CLATTER

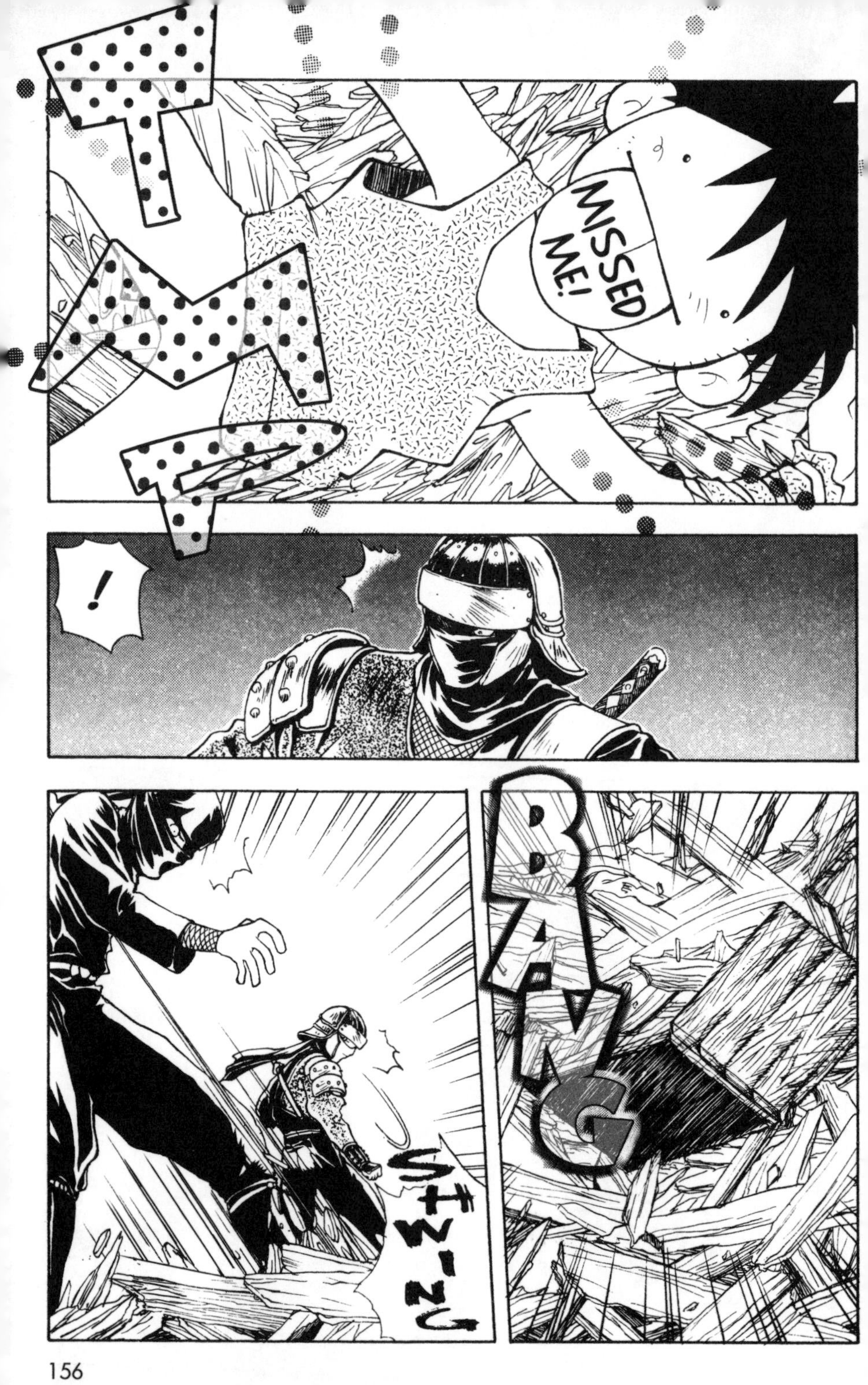
MISSED ME!
!
BANG
SHWING

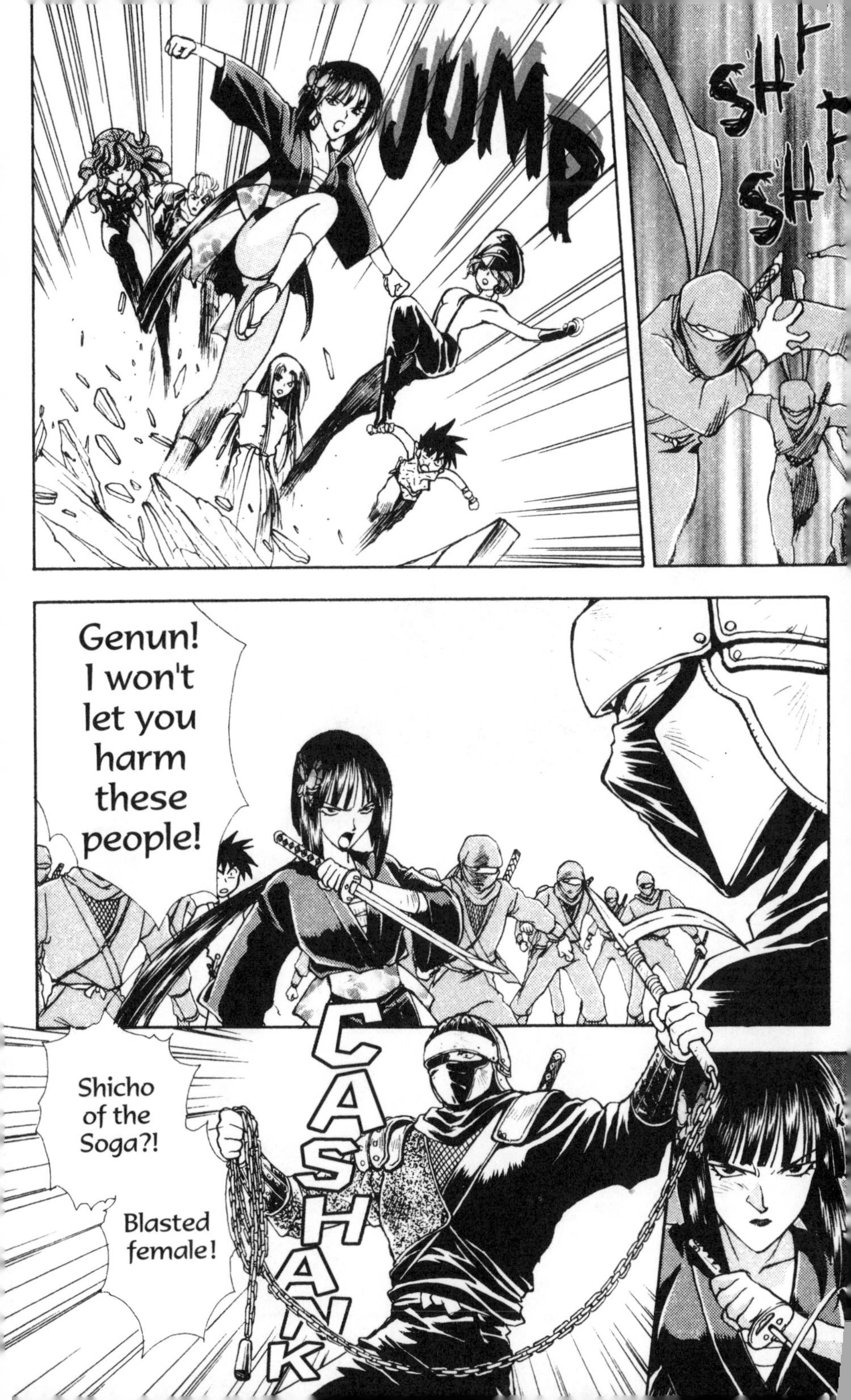

SHF SHF
JUMP
Genun! I won't let you harm these people!
CASHANK
Shicho of the Soga?!
Blasted female!

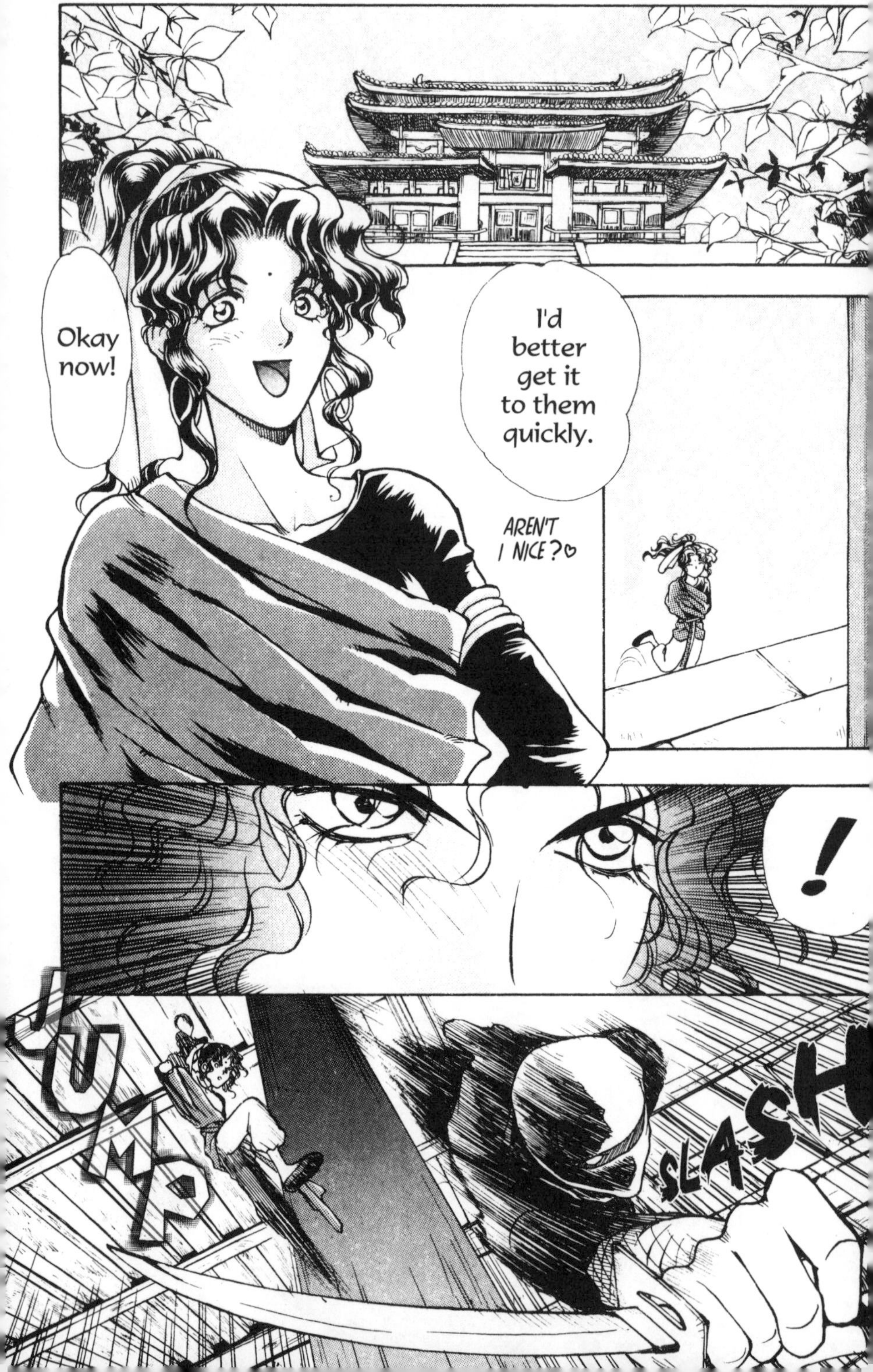
I'd better get it to them quickly.
AREN'T I NICE?♡
Okay now!
!
SLASH
JUMP

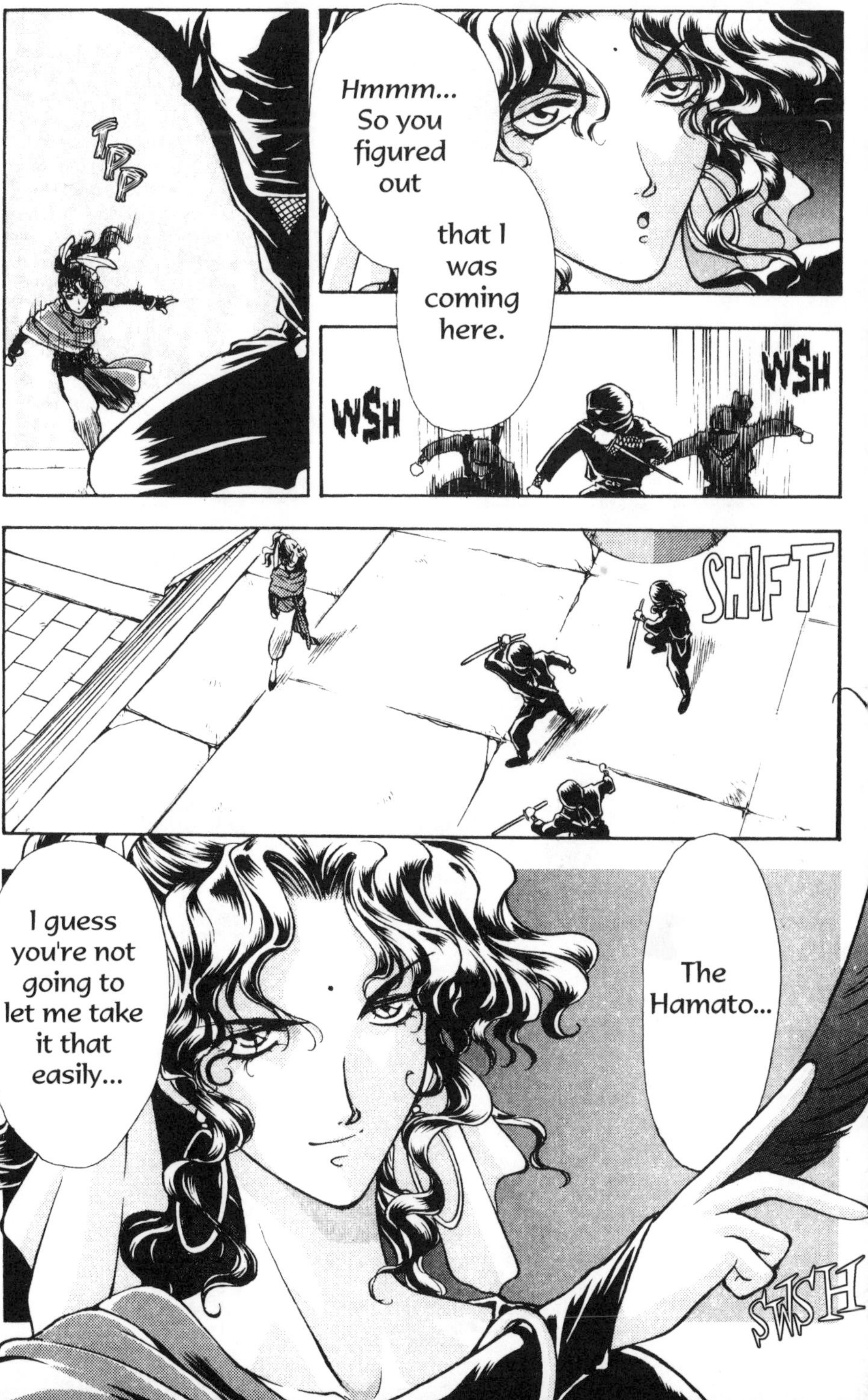
Hmmm... So you figured out that I was coming here.
WSH
WSH
TPP
SHIFT
The Hamato...
I guess you're not going to let me take it that easily...
SWSH

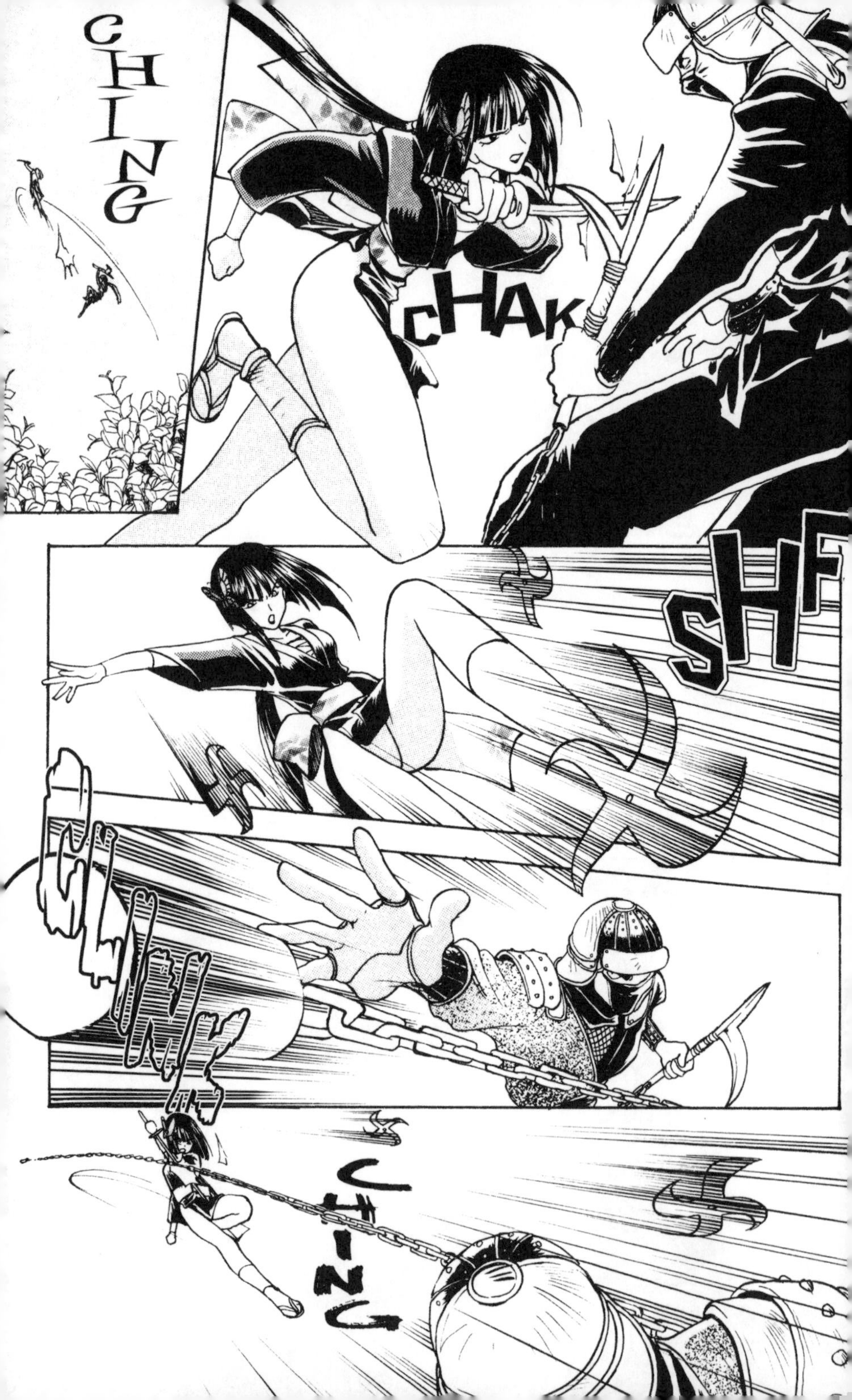
CHAK
CHING
SHF
CHING

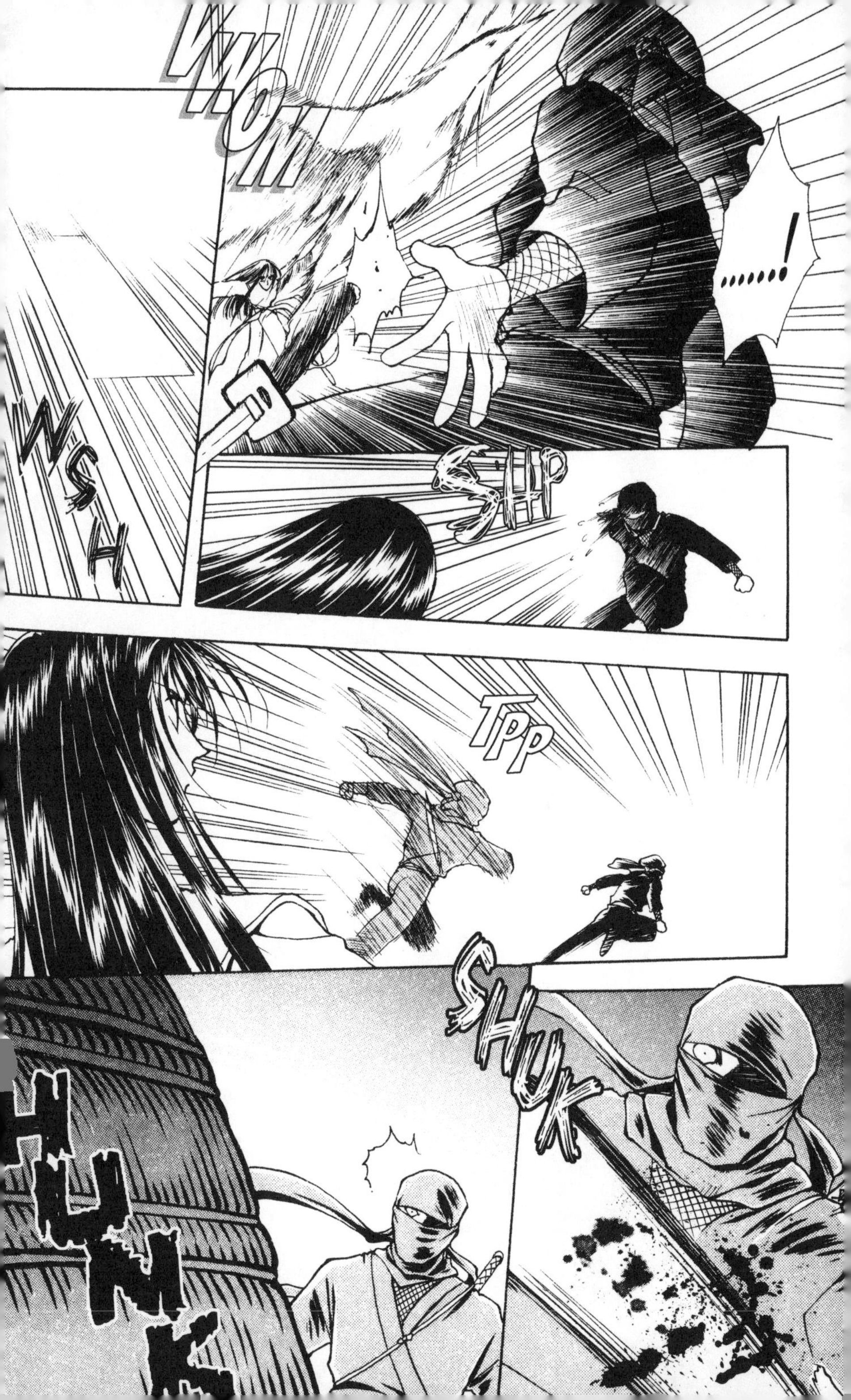
WHOM
......!
WSH
SHIP
TPP
SHUK

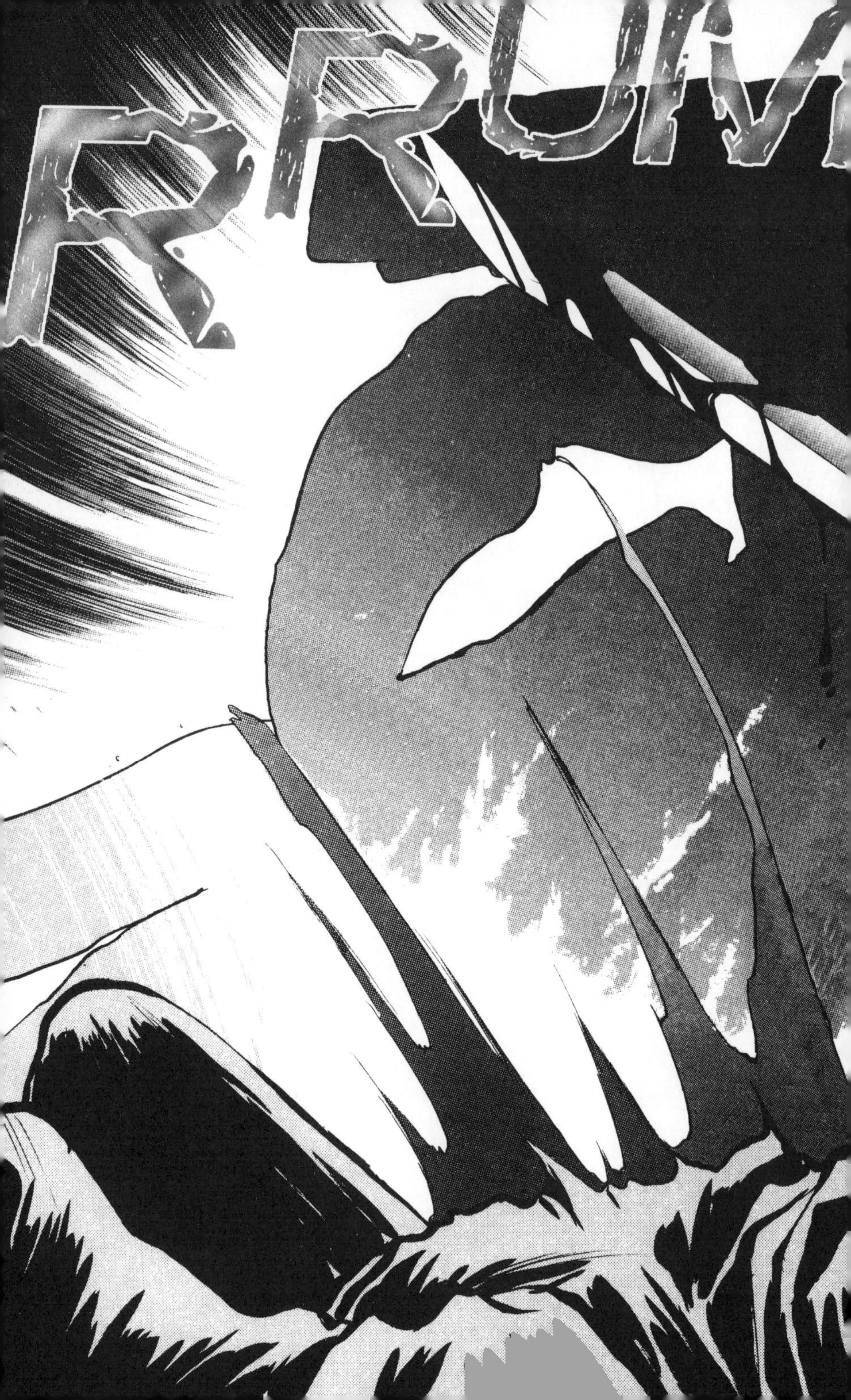
FRUM

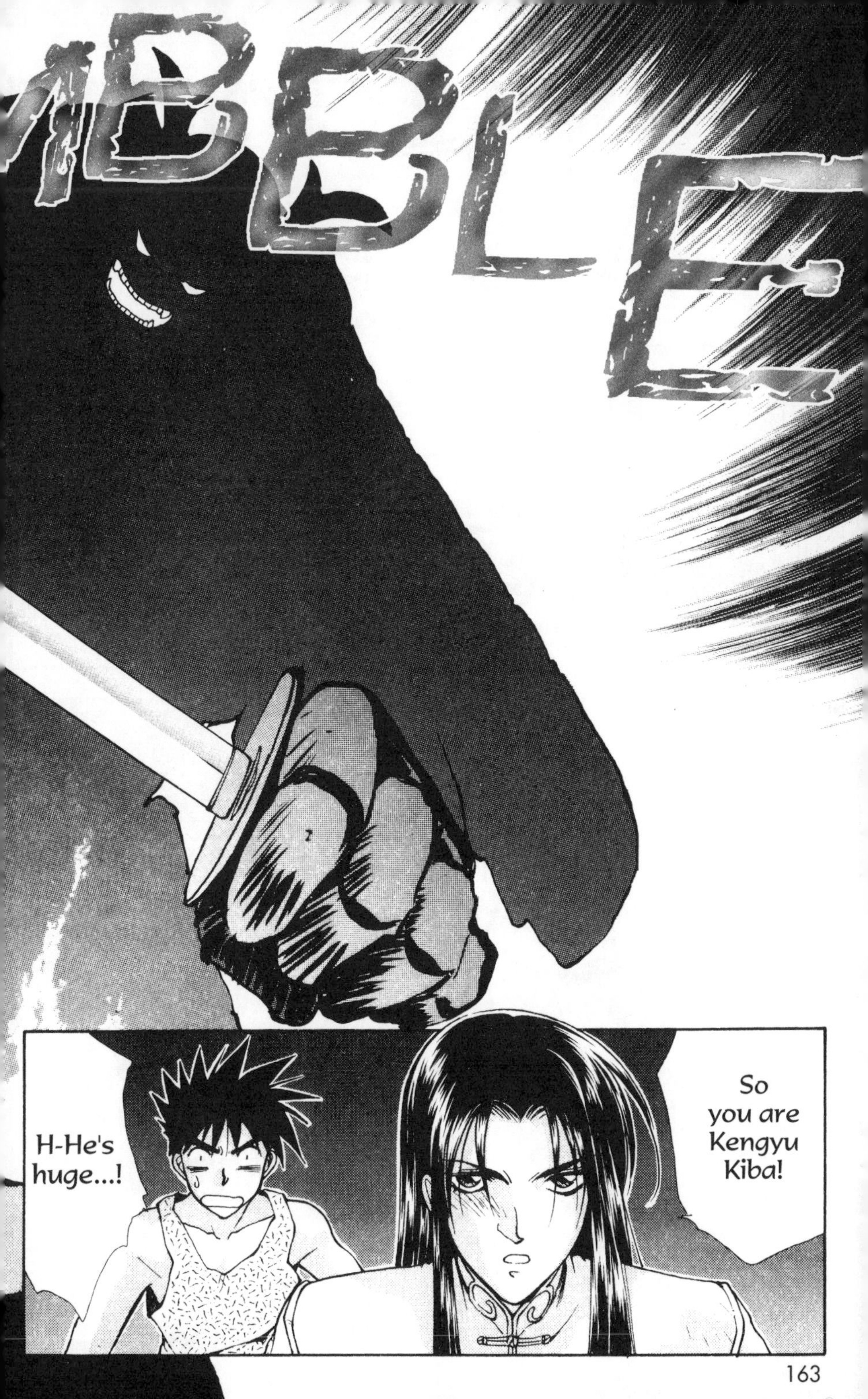
So you are Kengyu Kiba!
H-He's huge...!

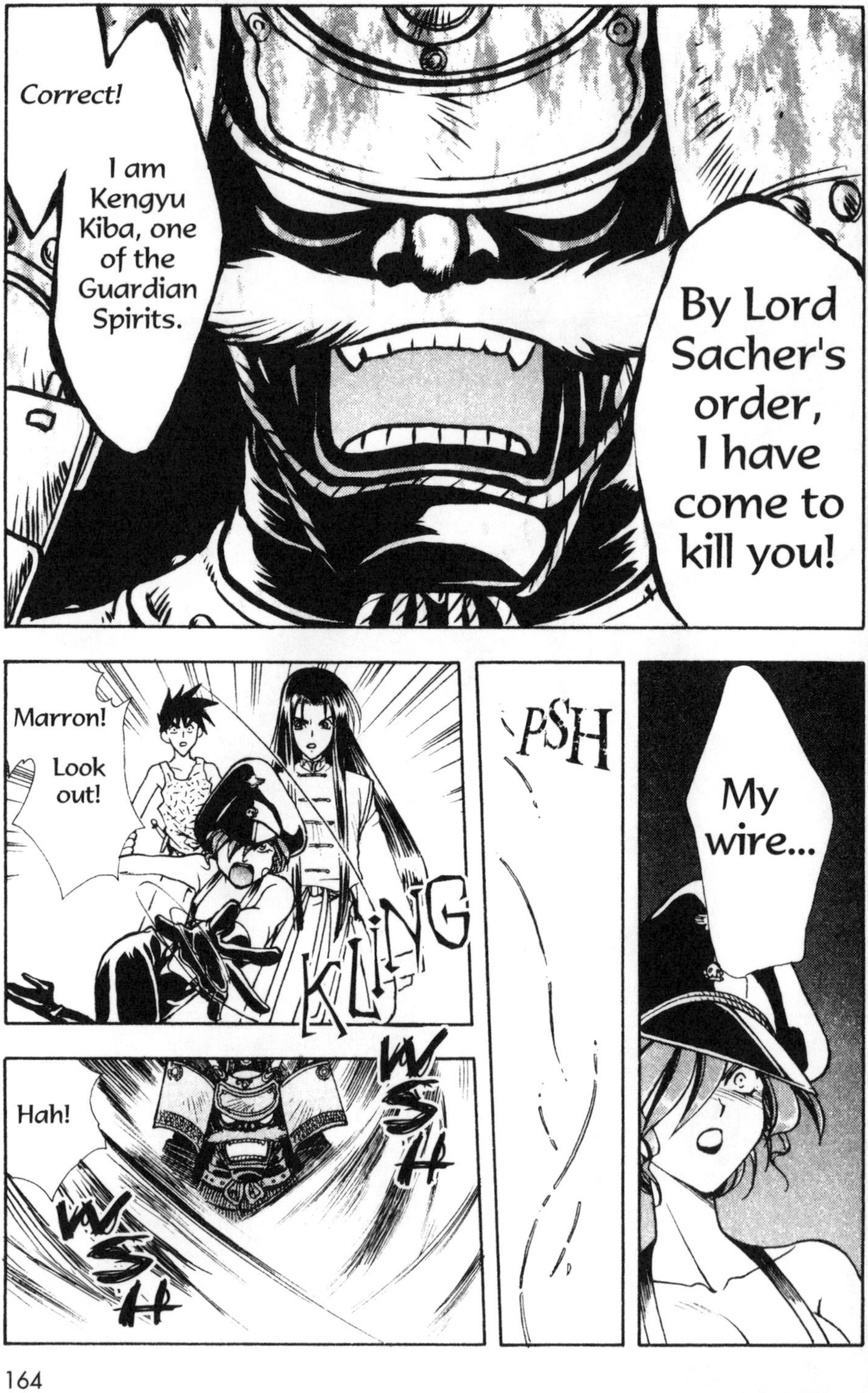
Correct!
I am Kengyu Kiba, one of the Guardian Spirits.
By Lord Sacher's order, I have come to kill you!
My wire...
PSH
Marron!
Look out!
KLING
Hah!
WSH
WSH

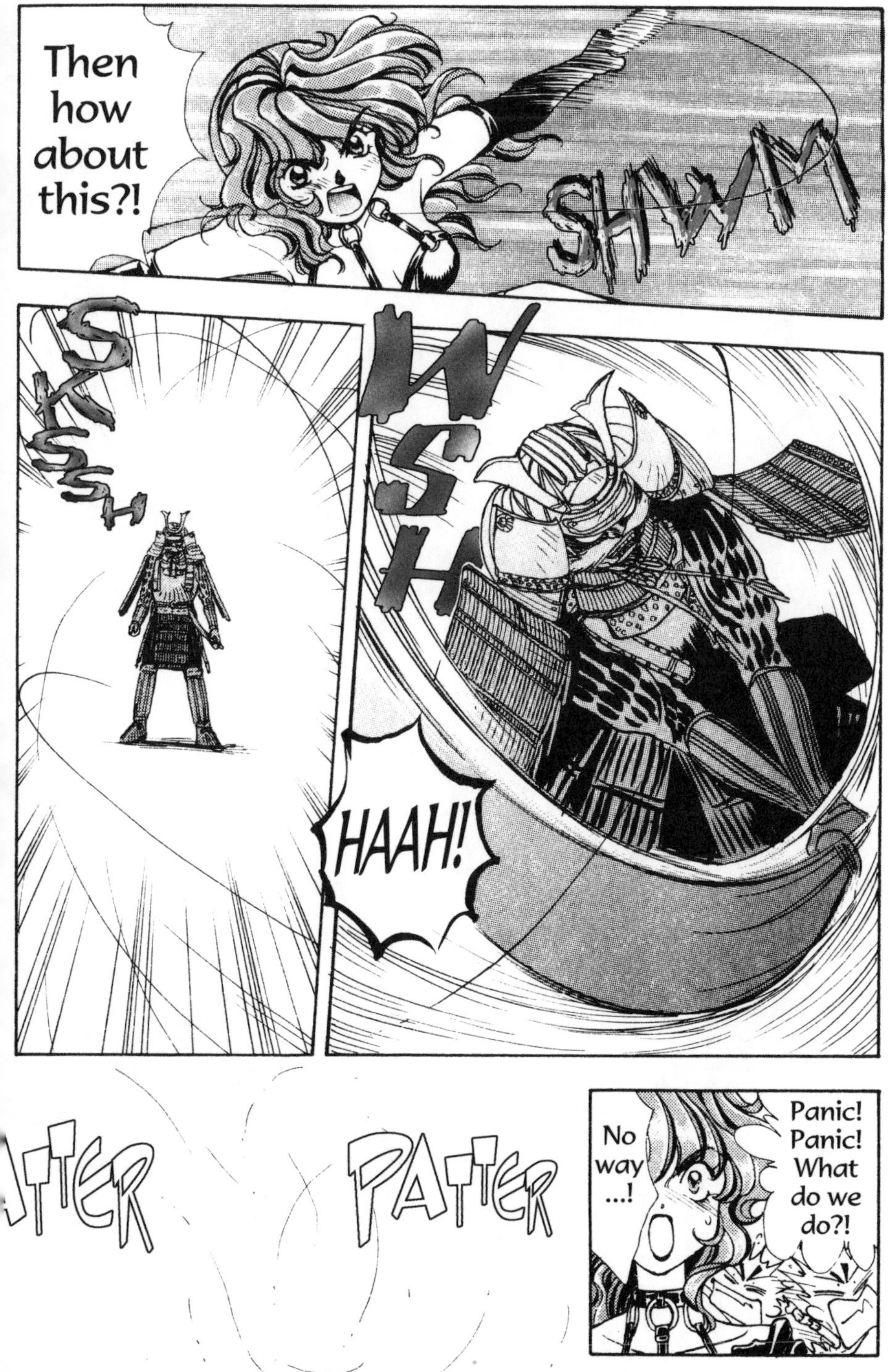
Then how about this?!
SHWM
WSSH
HAAH!
SKSSSH
Panic! Panic! What do we do?!
No way ...!
PATTER

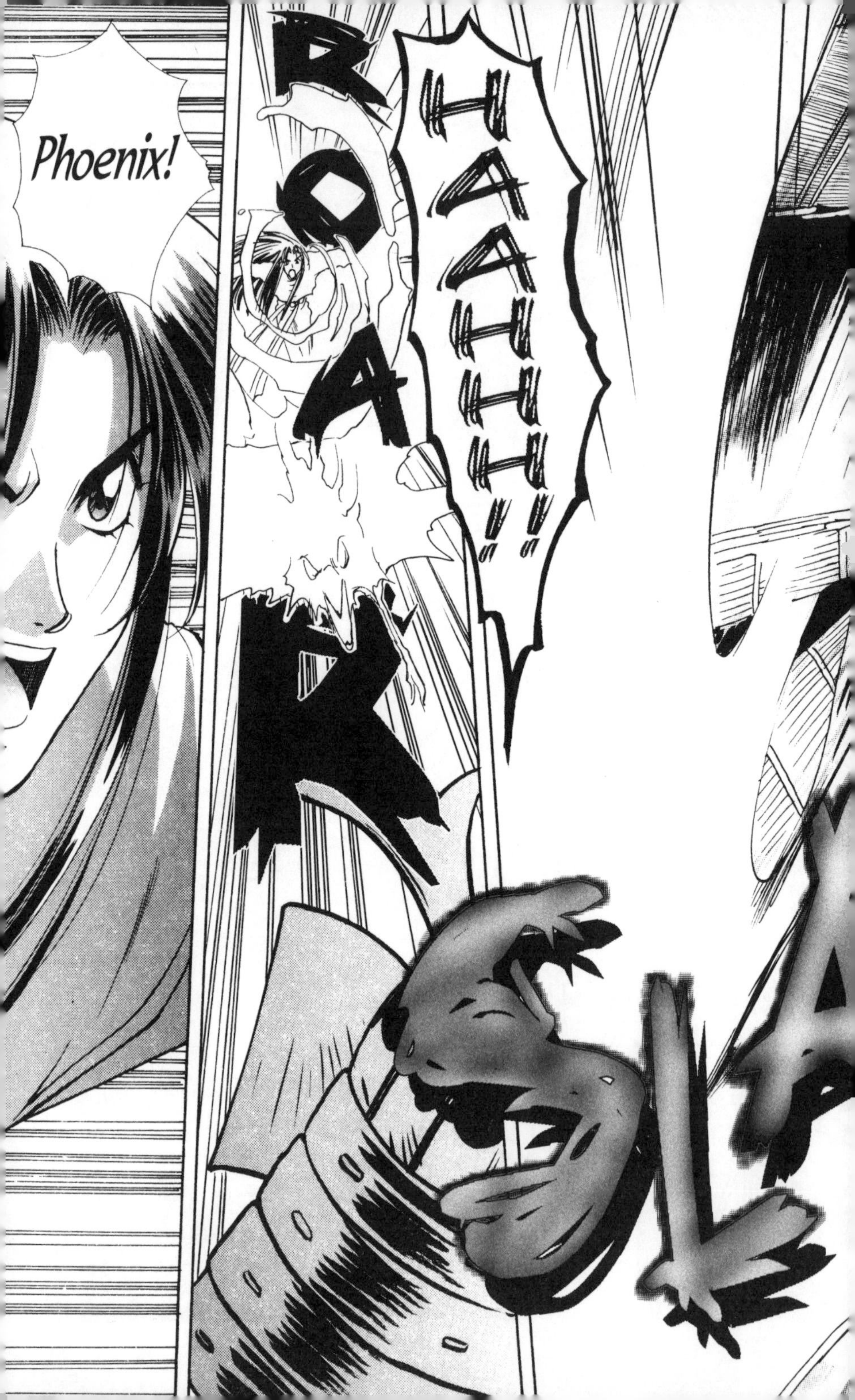
HAAHHH!!
ROAR
Phoenix!

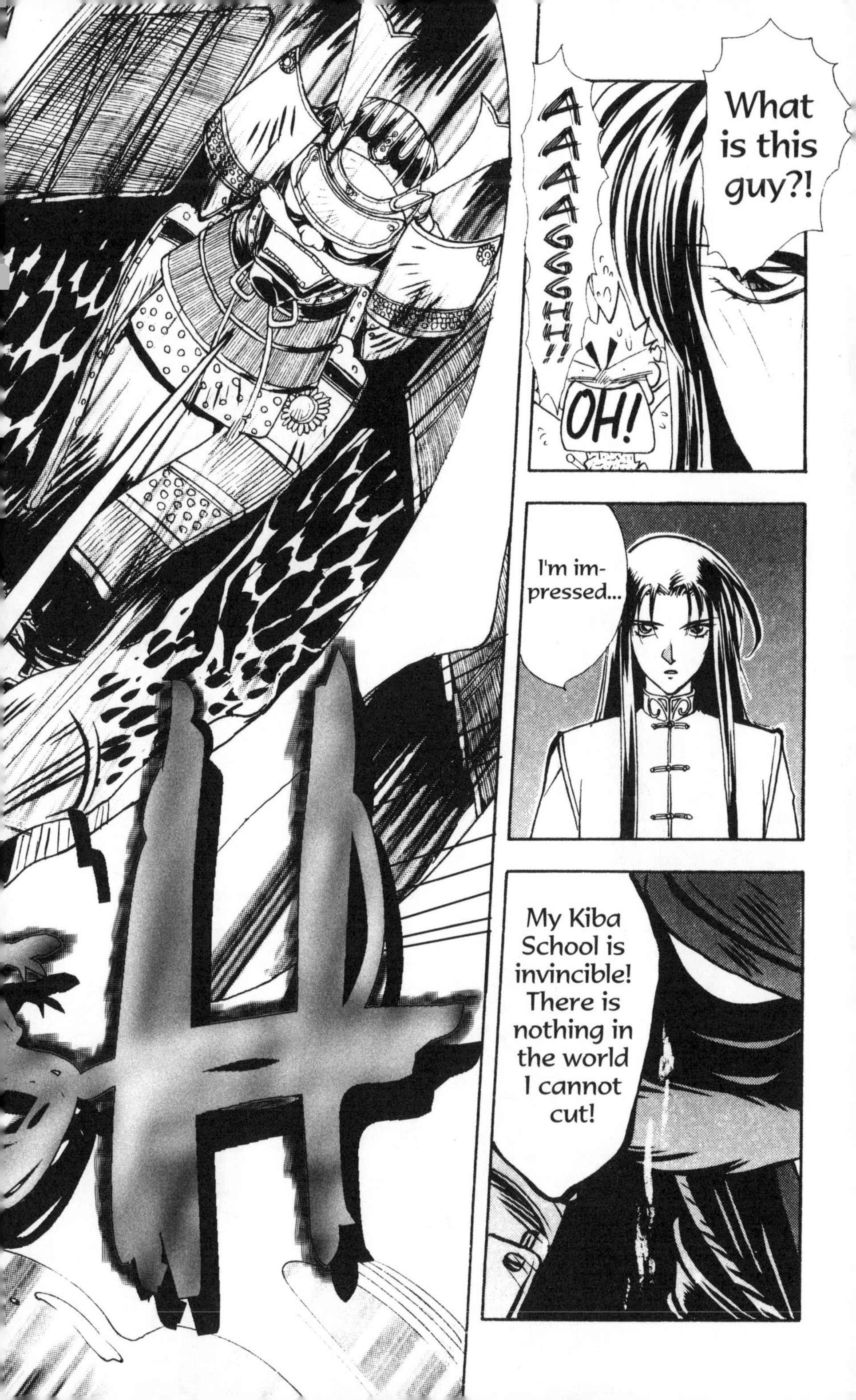
What is this guy?!
AAAAAAGGGIII!!
OH!
I'm im-pressed...
My Kiba School is invincible! There is nothing in the world I cannot cut!

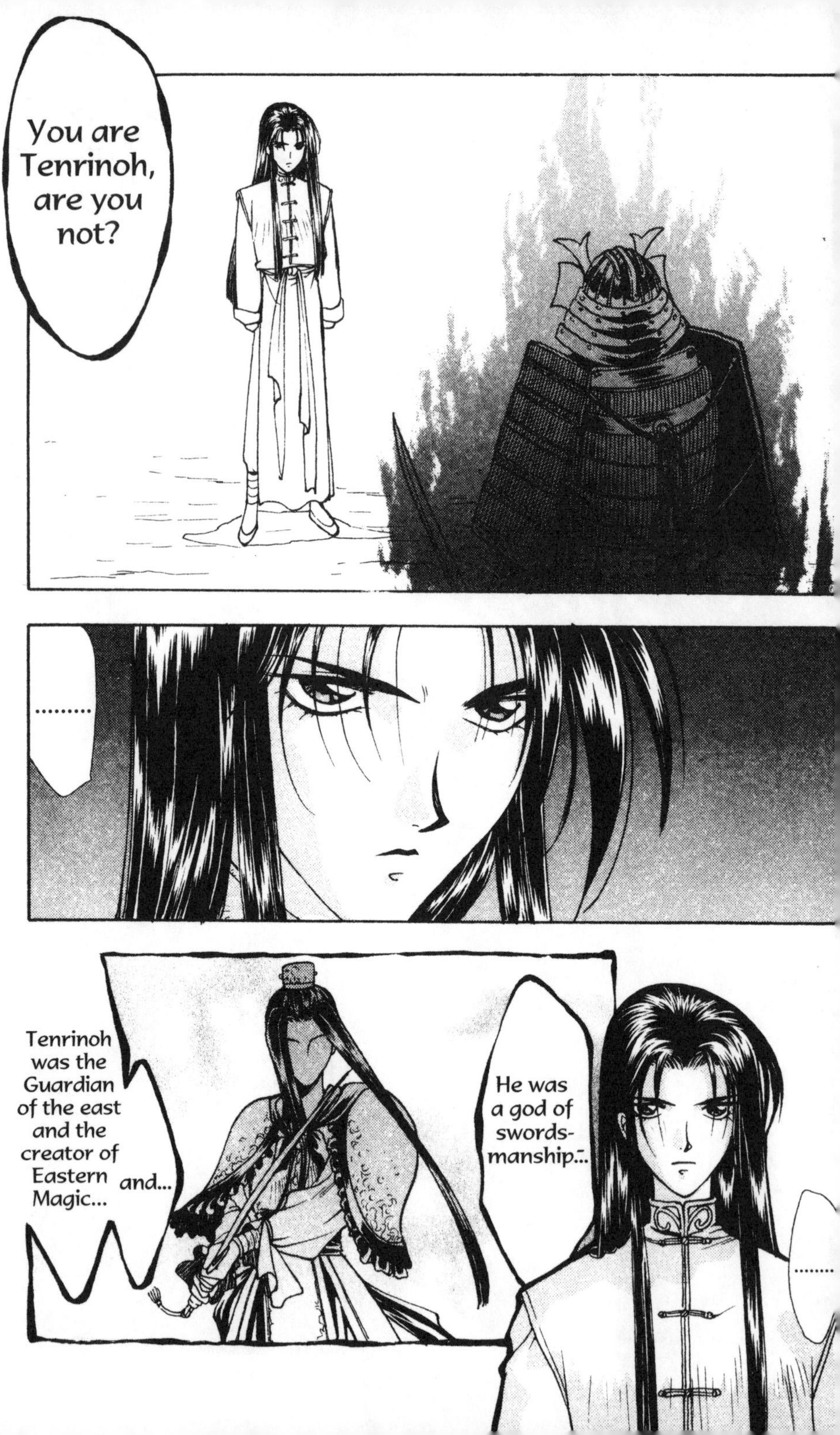
You are Tenrinoh, are you not?
....
Tenrinoh was the Guardian of the east and the creator of Eastern Magic...
and...
He was a god of swords-manship...
....

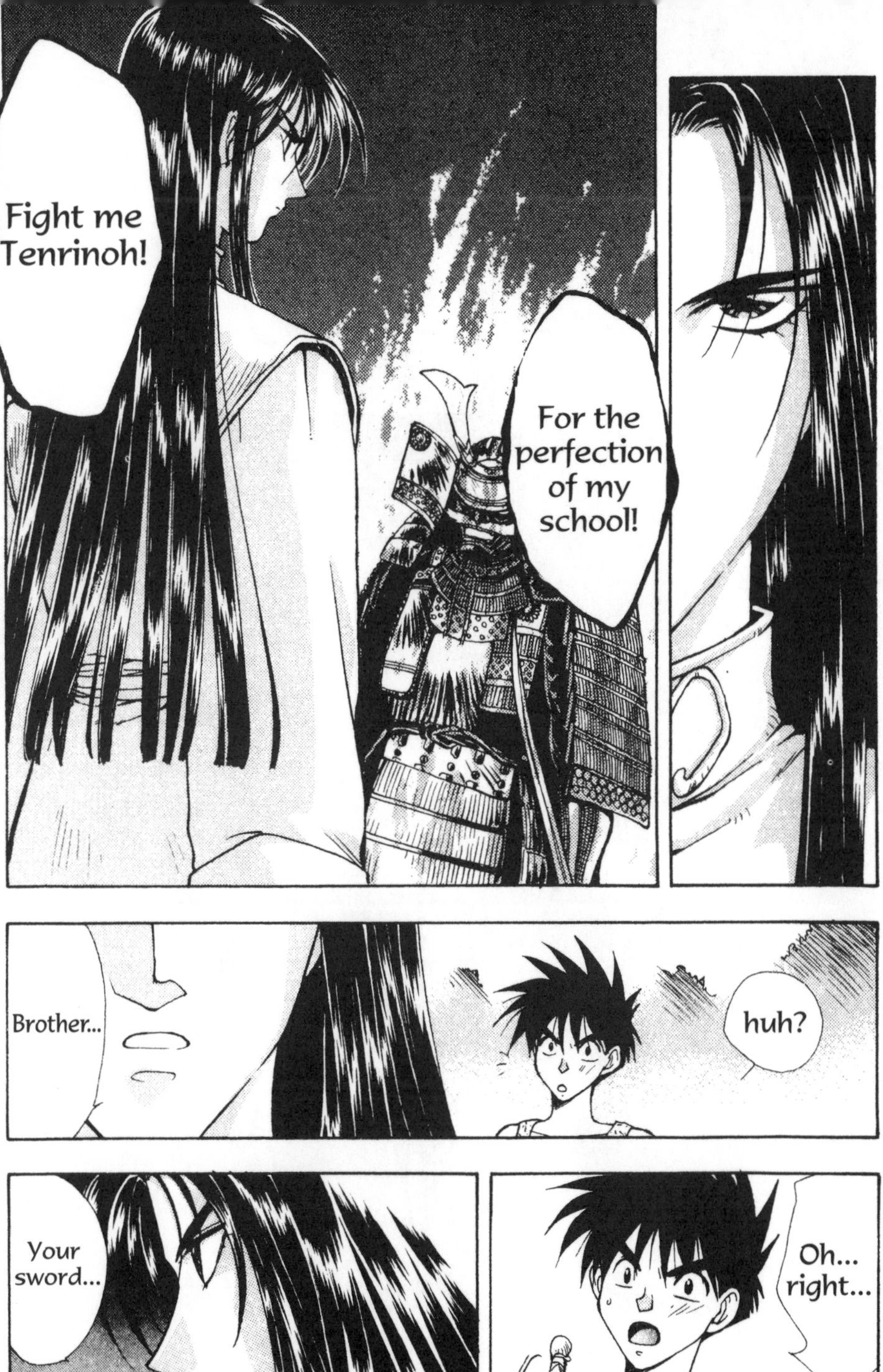
Fight me Tenrinoh!
For the perfection of my school!
Brother...
huh?
Your sword...
Oh... right...

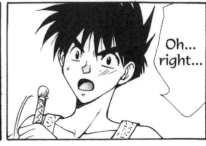

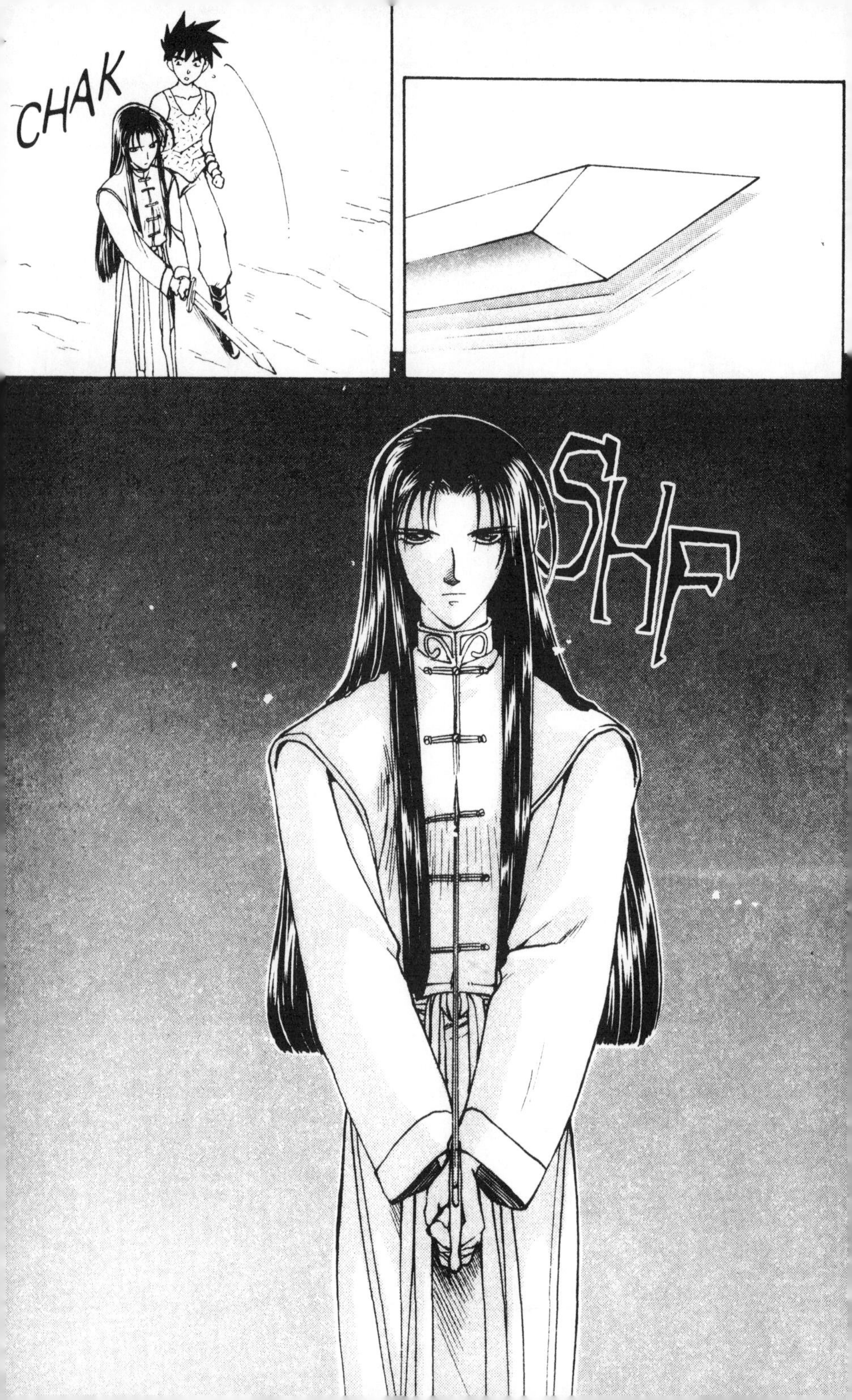
CHAK
SHF

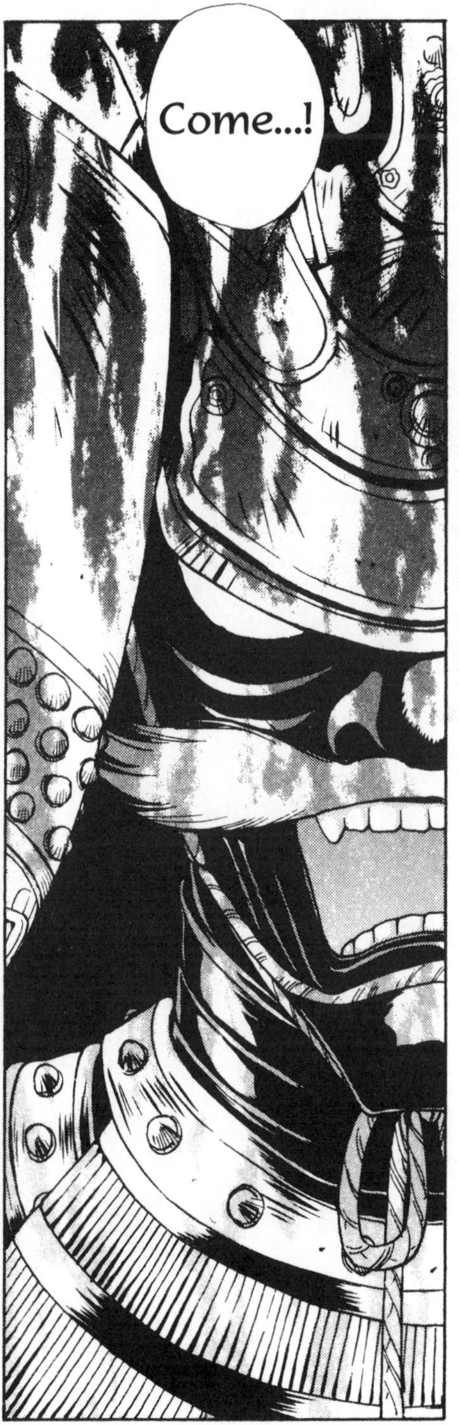
Come...!

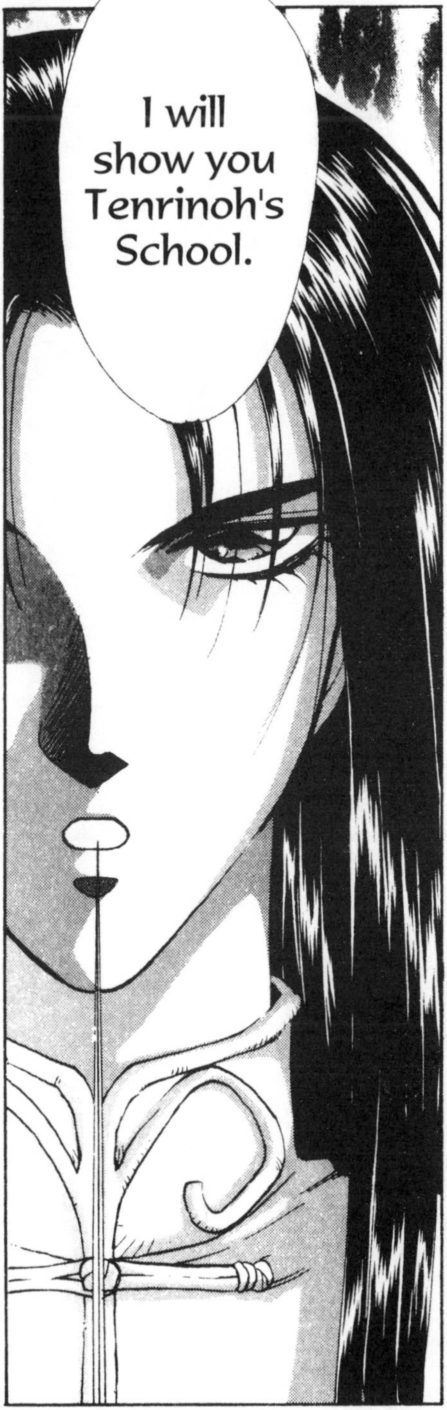
I will show you Tenrinoh's School.

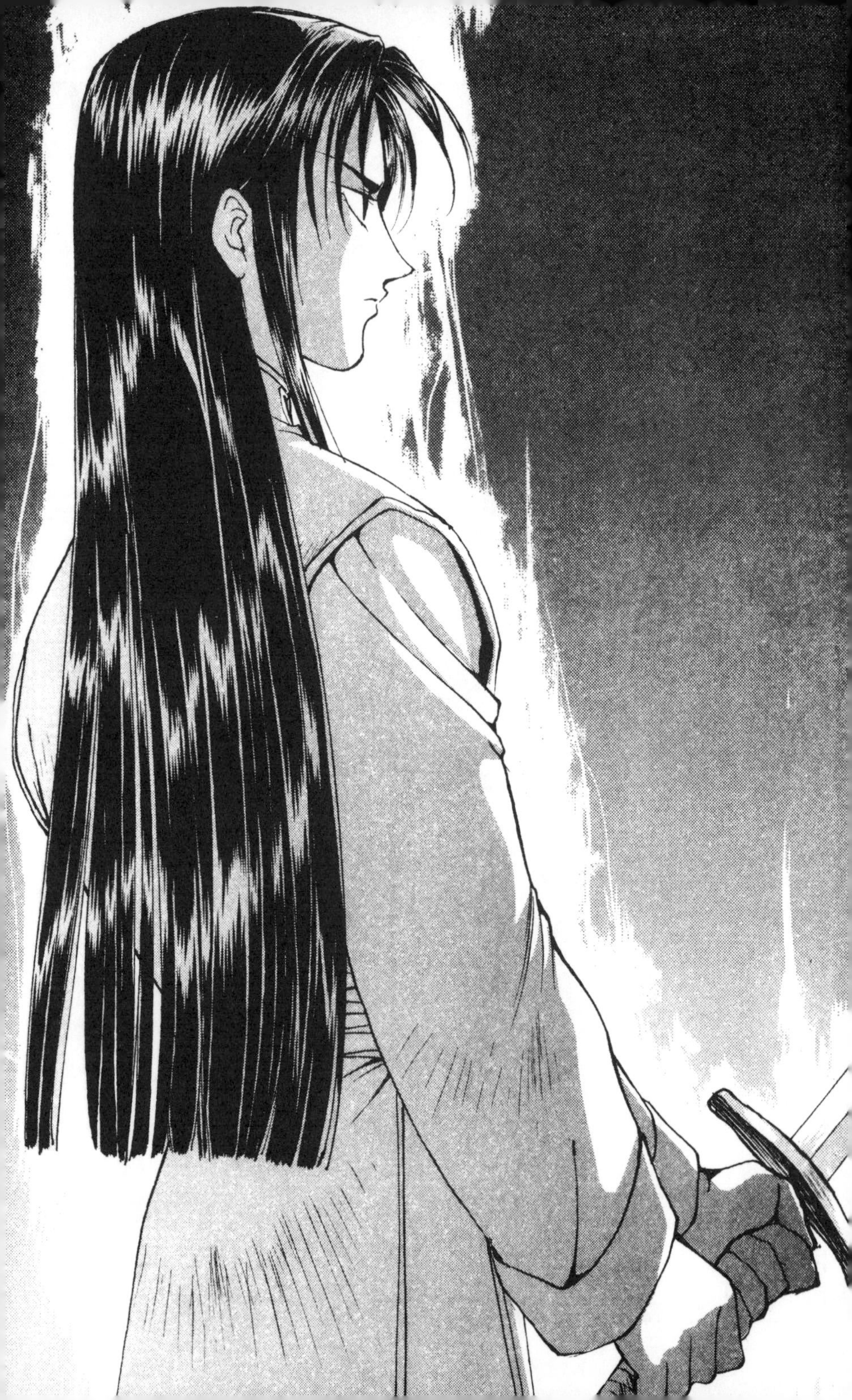

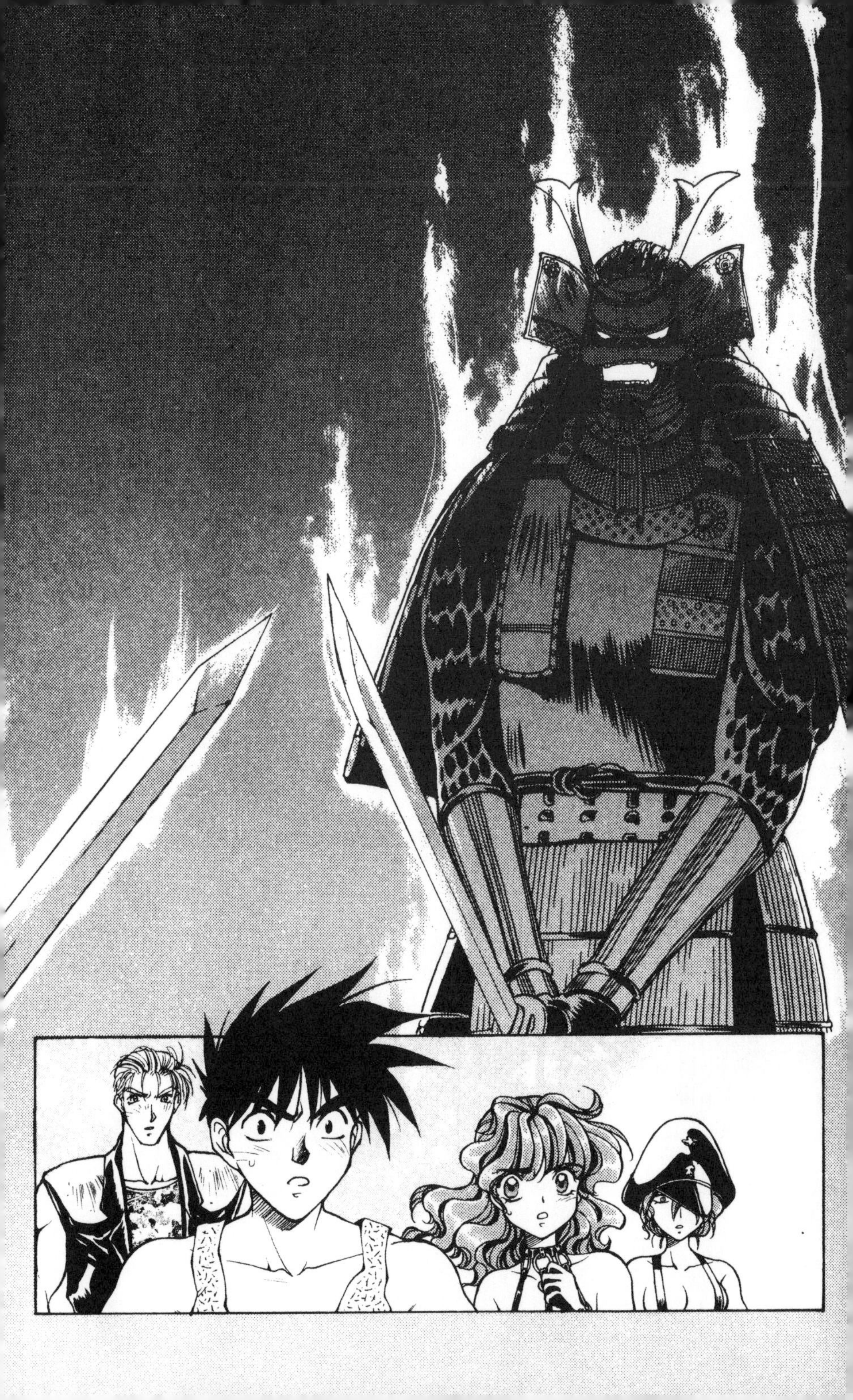

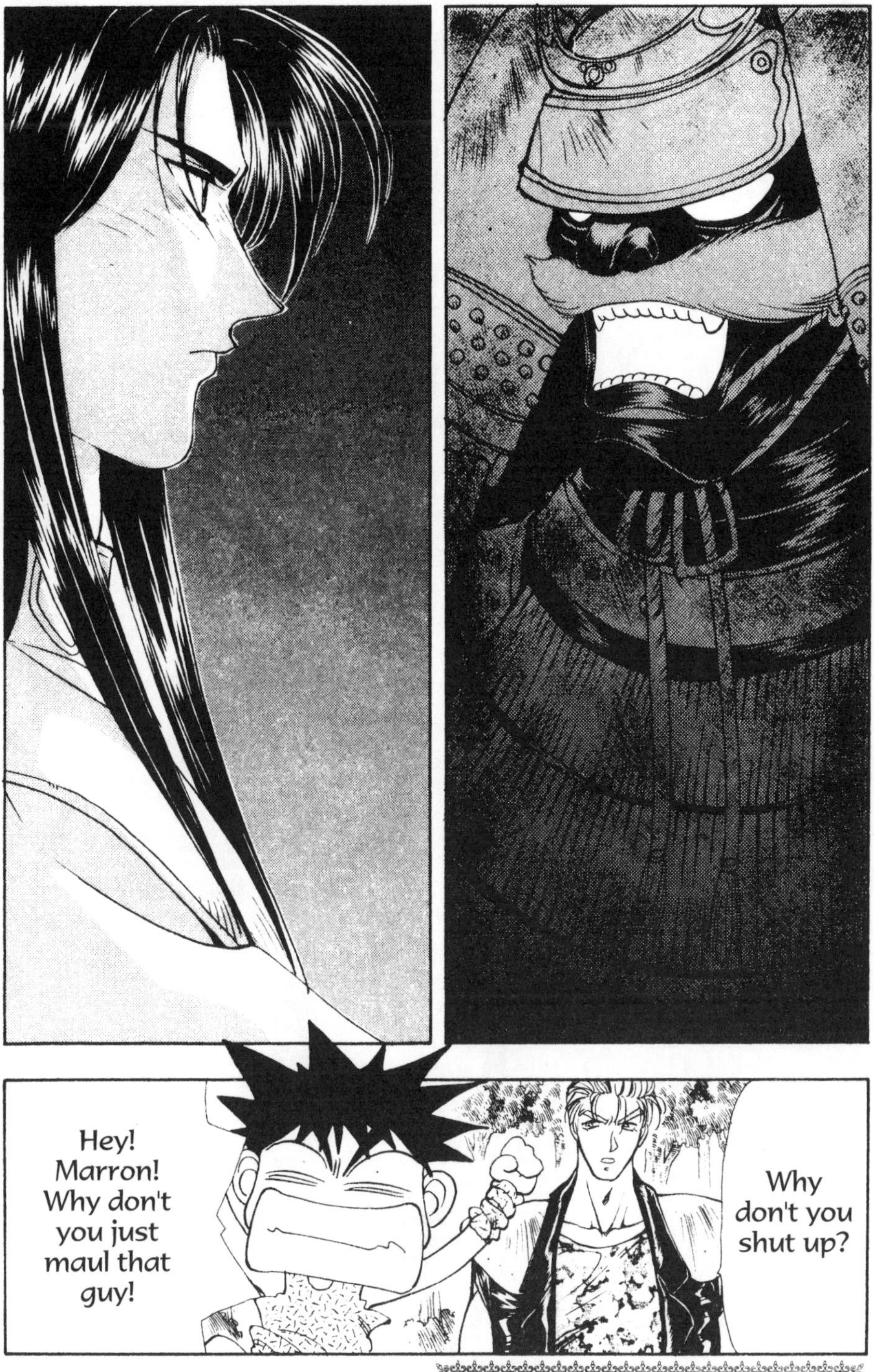
Hey! Marron! Why don't you just maul that guy!
Why don't you shut up?

The Samurai of Doom (Part 2)

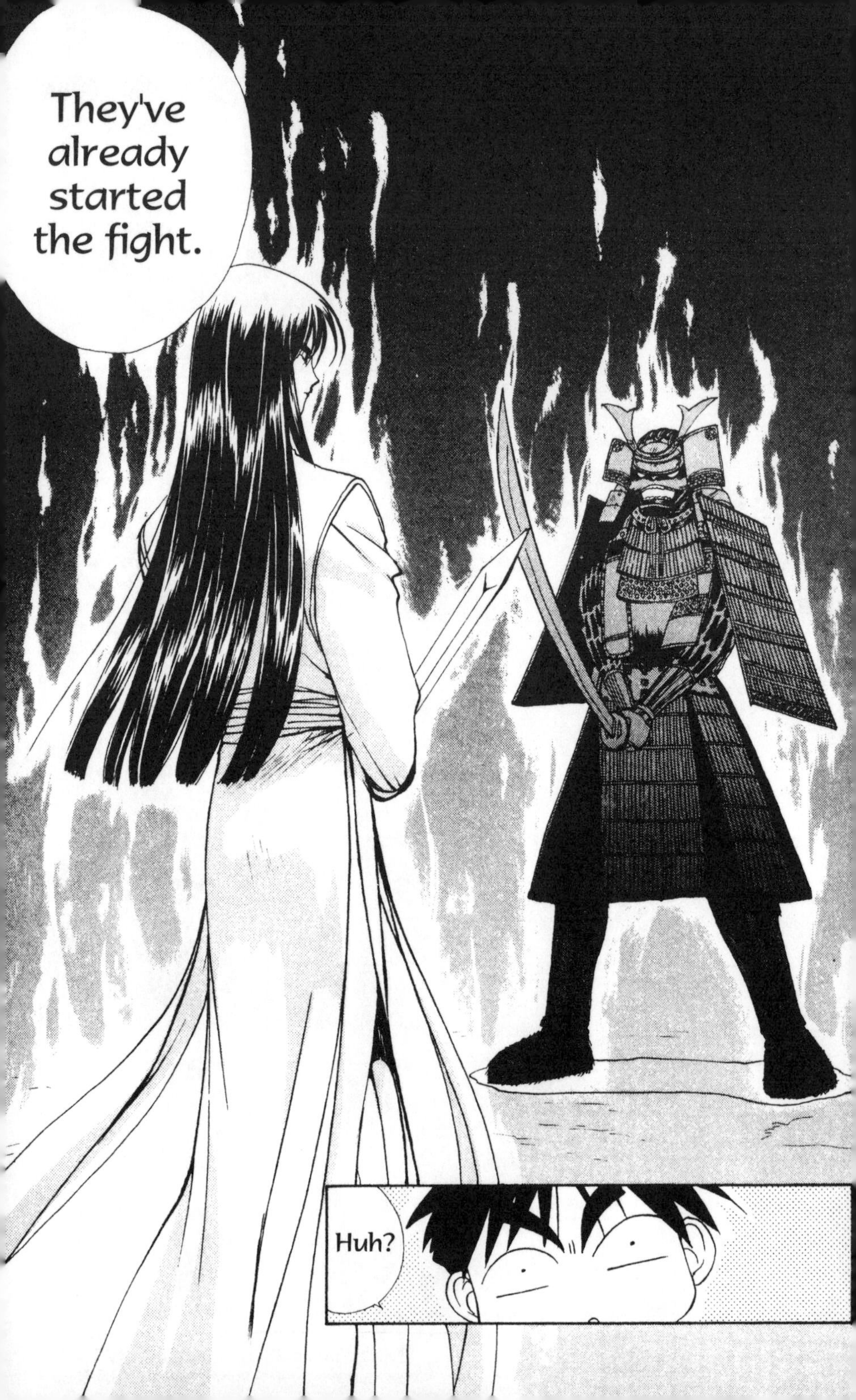
They've already started the fight.
Huh?

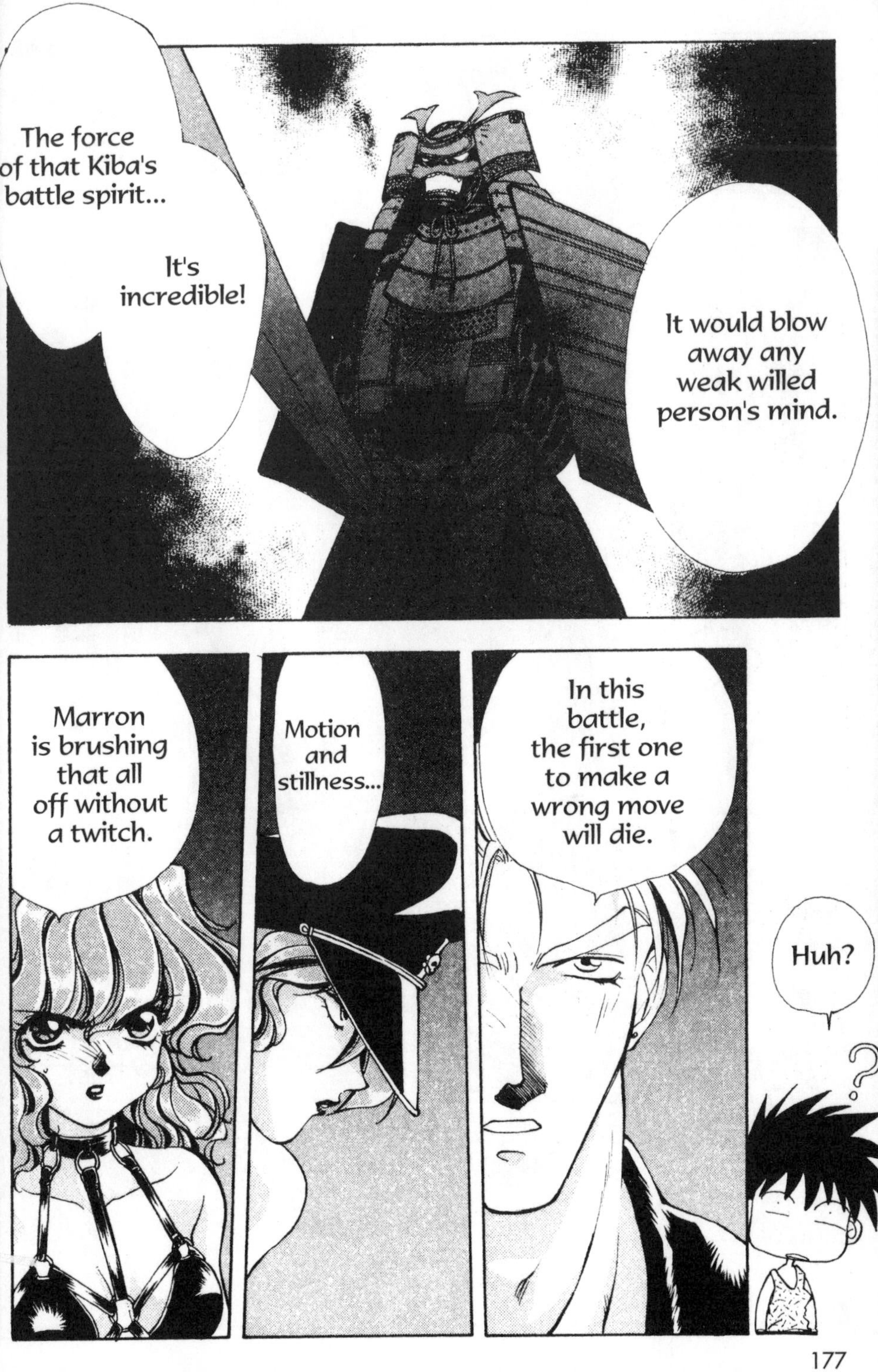
The force of that Kiba's battle spirit...
It's incredible!
It would blow away any weak willed person's mind.
Marron is brushing that all off without a twitch.
Motion and stillness...
In this battle, the first one to make a wrong move will die.
Huh?

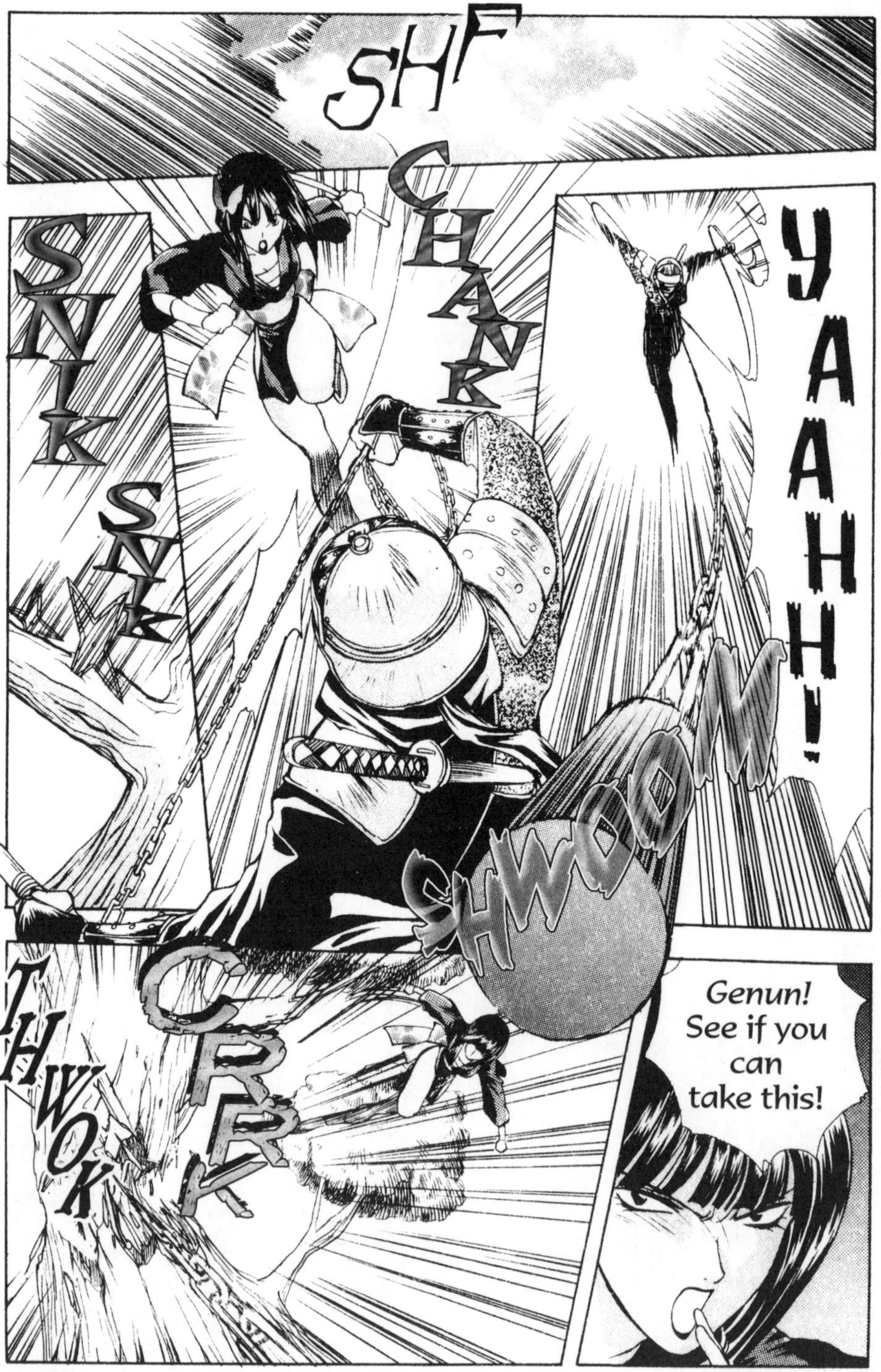
SHF
YAAHH!
CHANK
SNIK
SNIK
SHWOOM
Genun! See if you can take this!
CRRK
THWOK

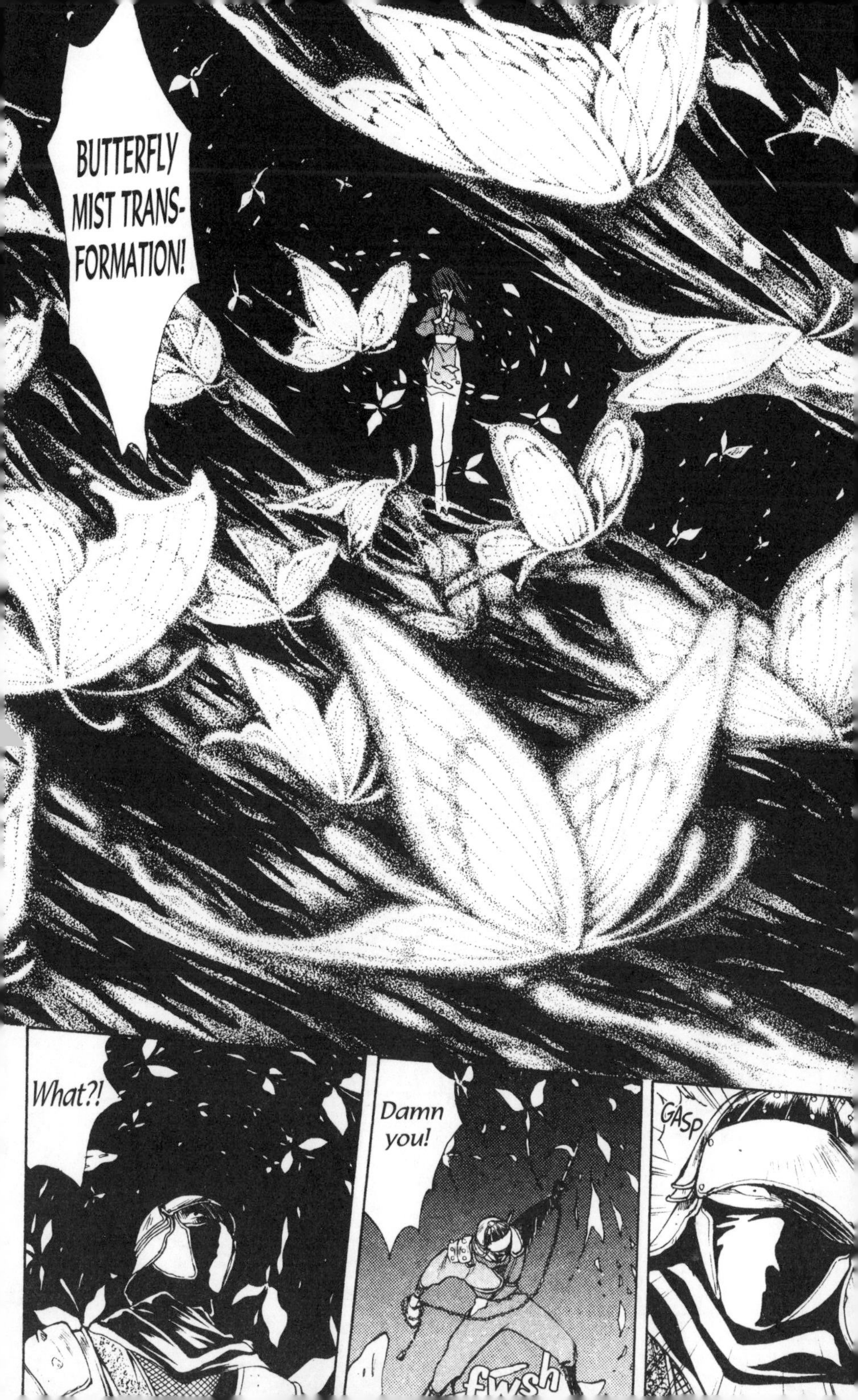
BUTTERFLY MIST TRANS-FORMATION!
What?!
Damn you!
fwsh
GASP

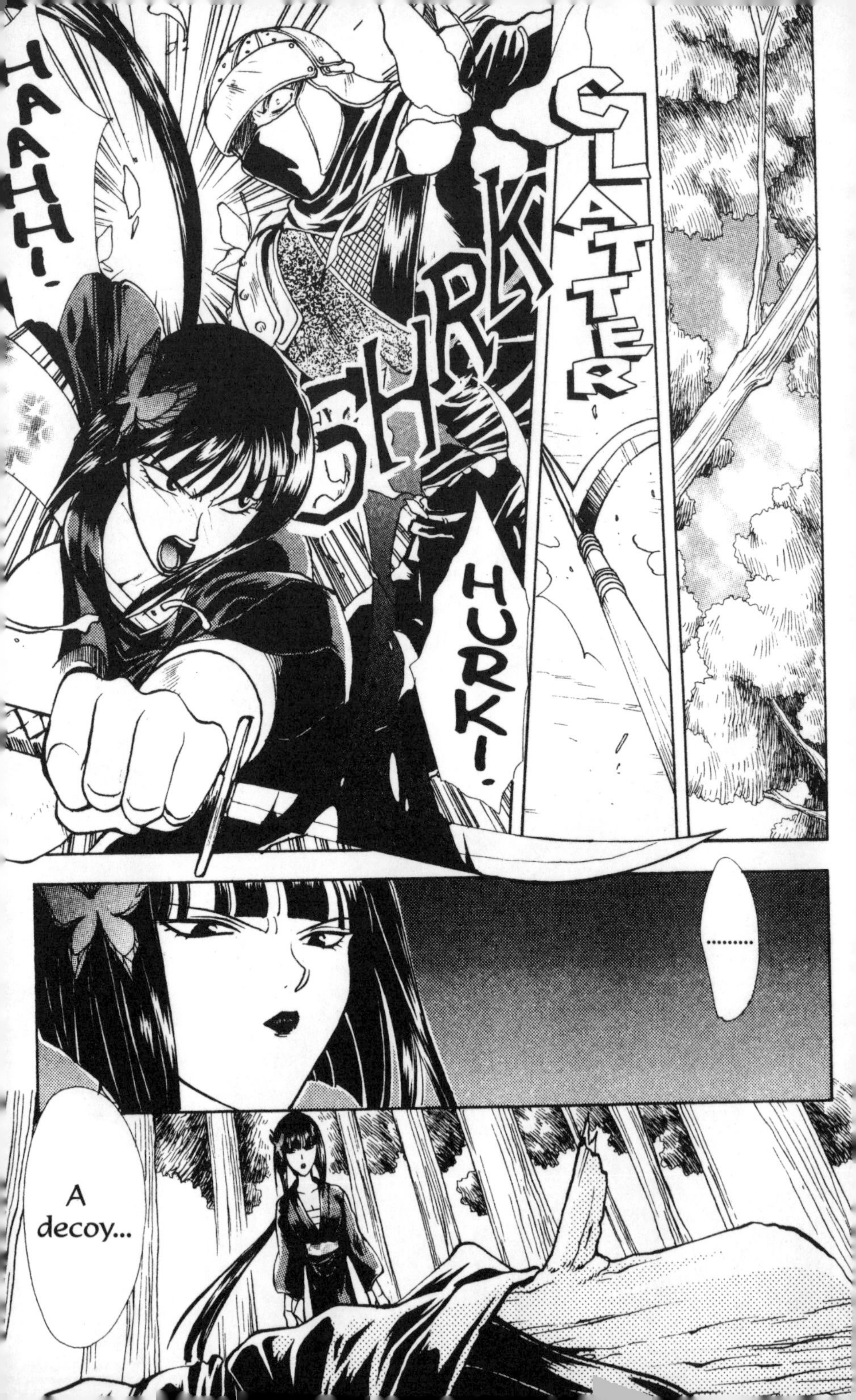
CLATTER
SHRK
HURK!
HAAAHH!
....
A decoy...

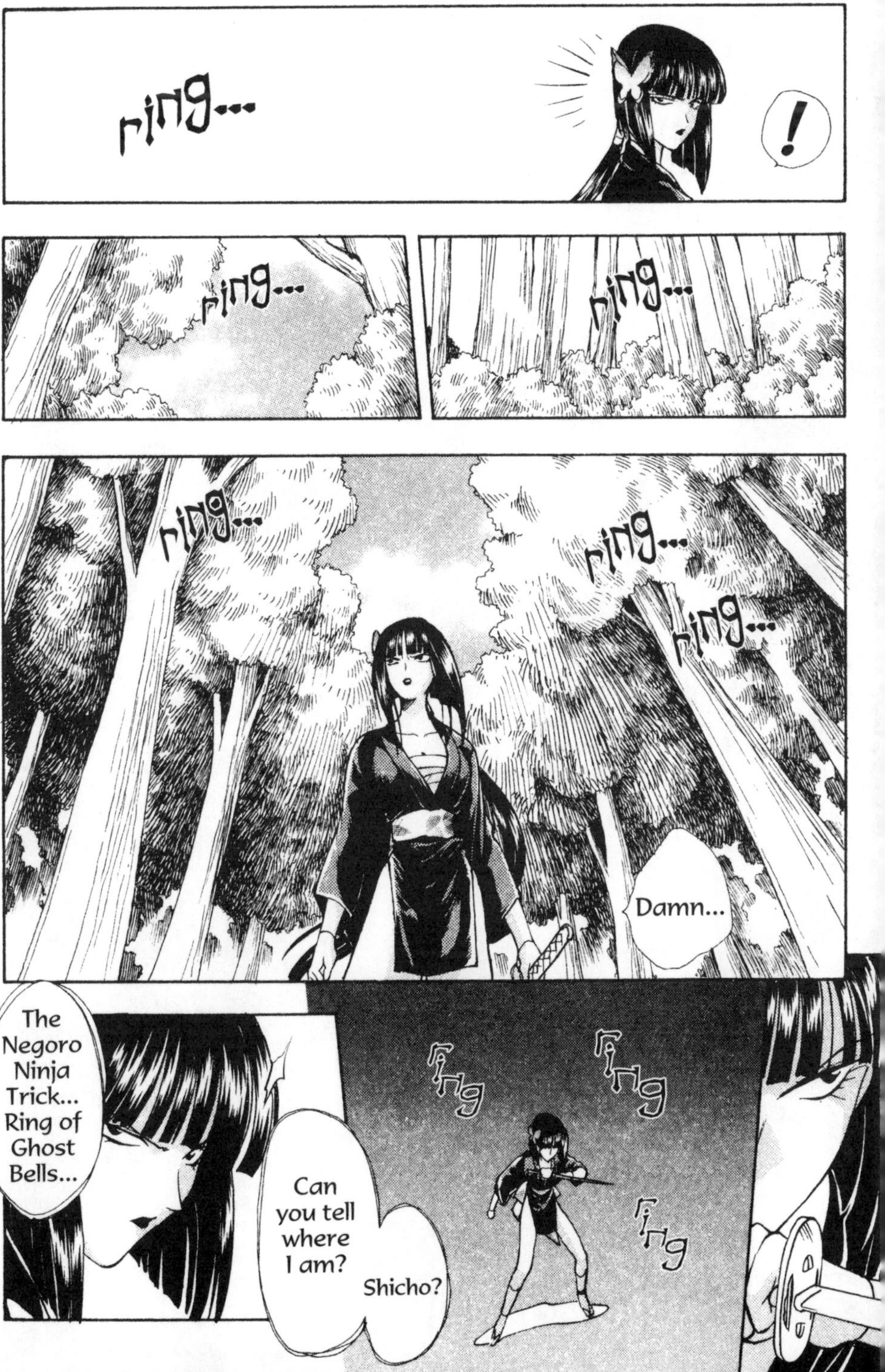

!
ring...
ring...
ring...
ring...
ring...
ring...
Damn...
ring
ring
ring
The Negoro Ninja Trick... Ring of Ghost Bells...
Can you tell where I am?
Shicho?

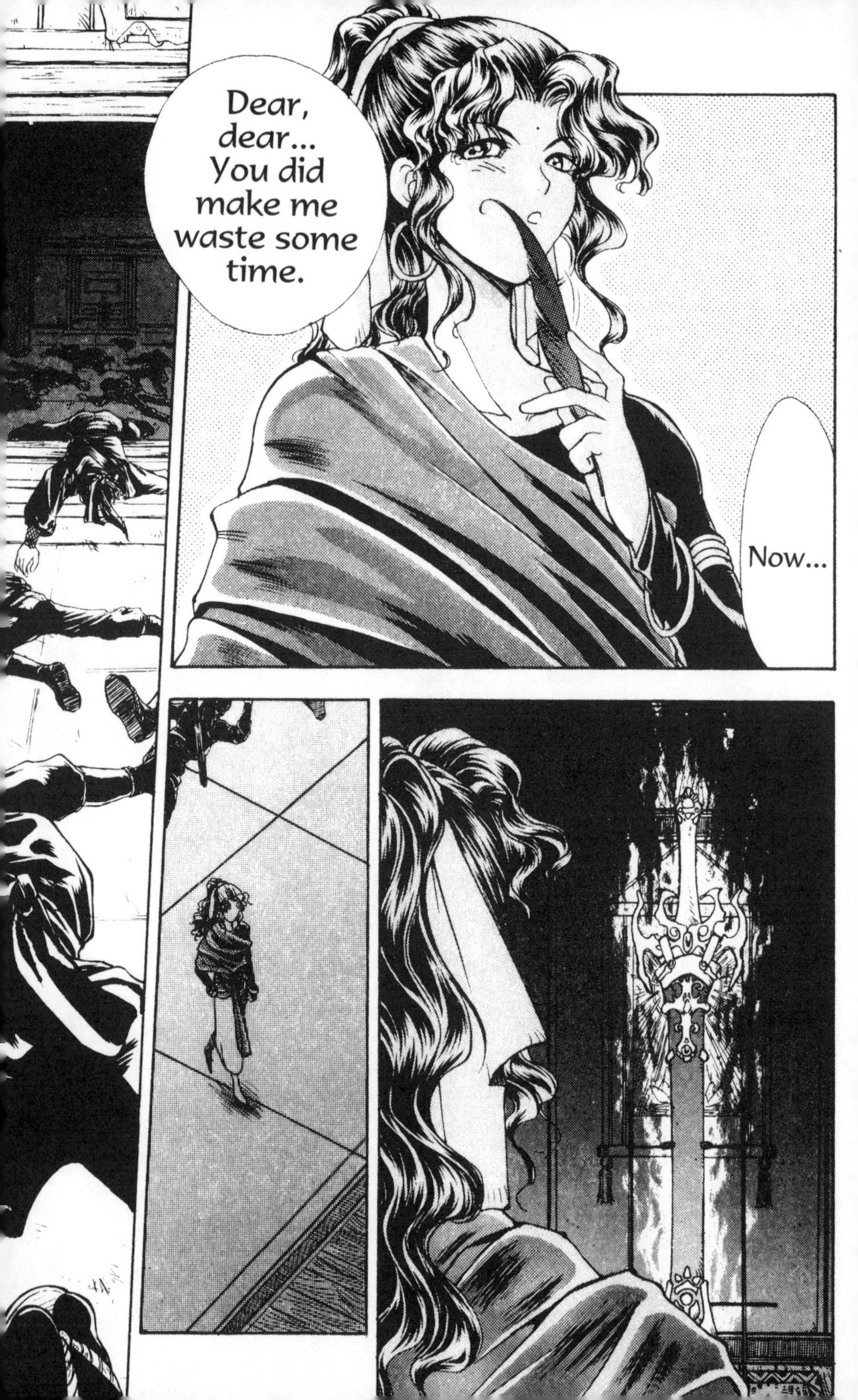
Dear, dear... You did make me waste some time.
Now...

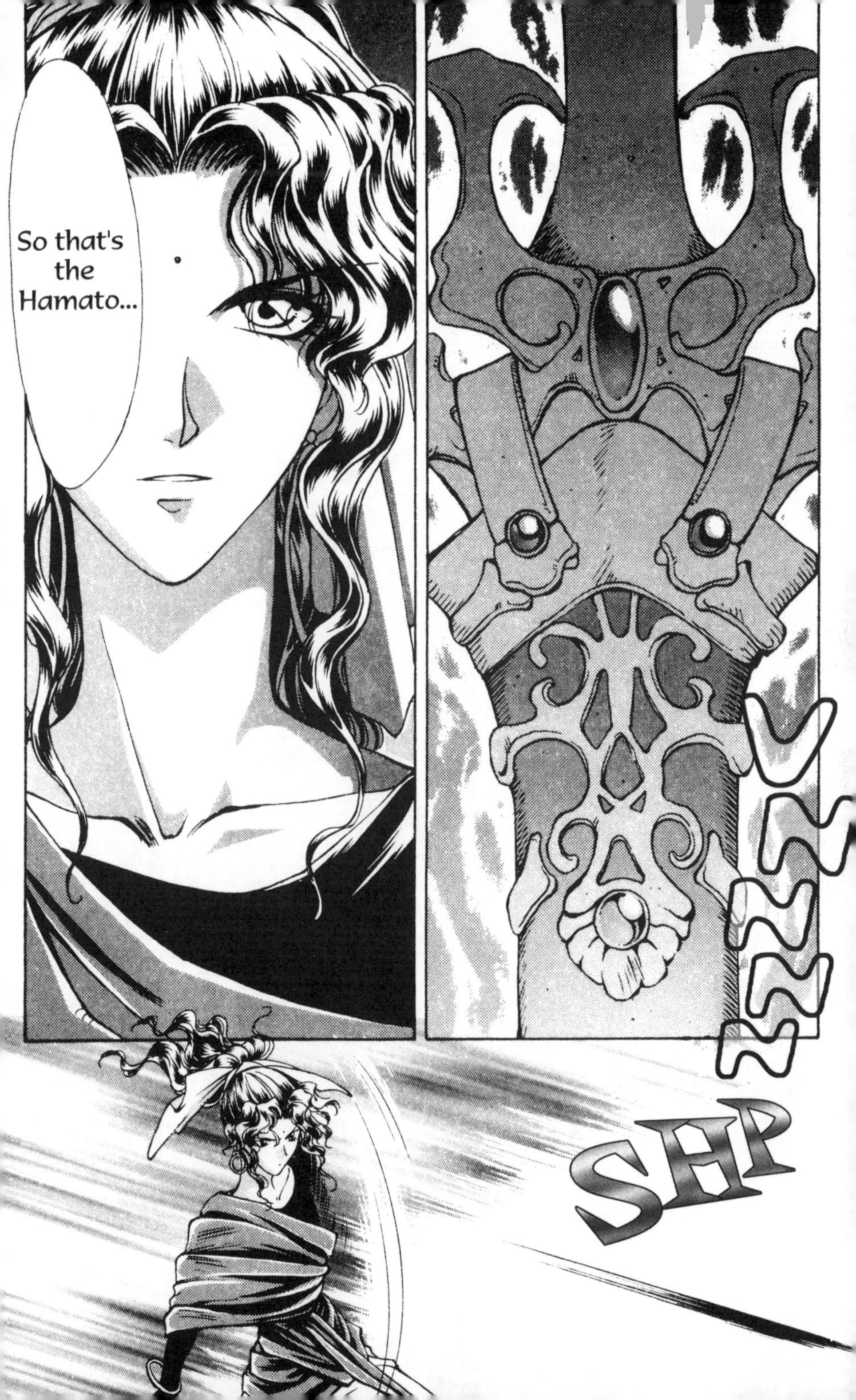
So that's the Hamato...
SHP

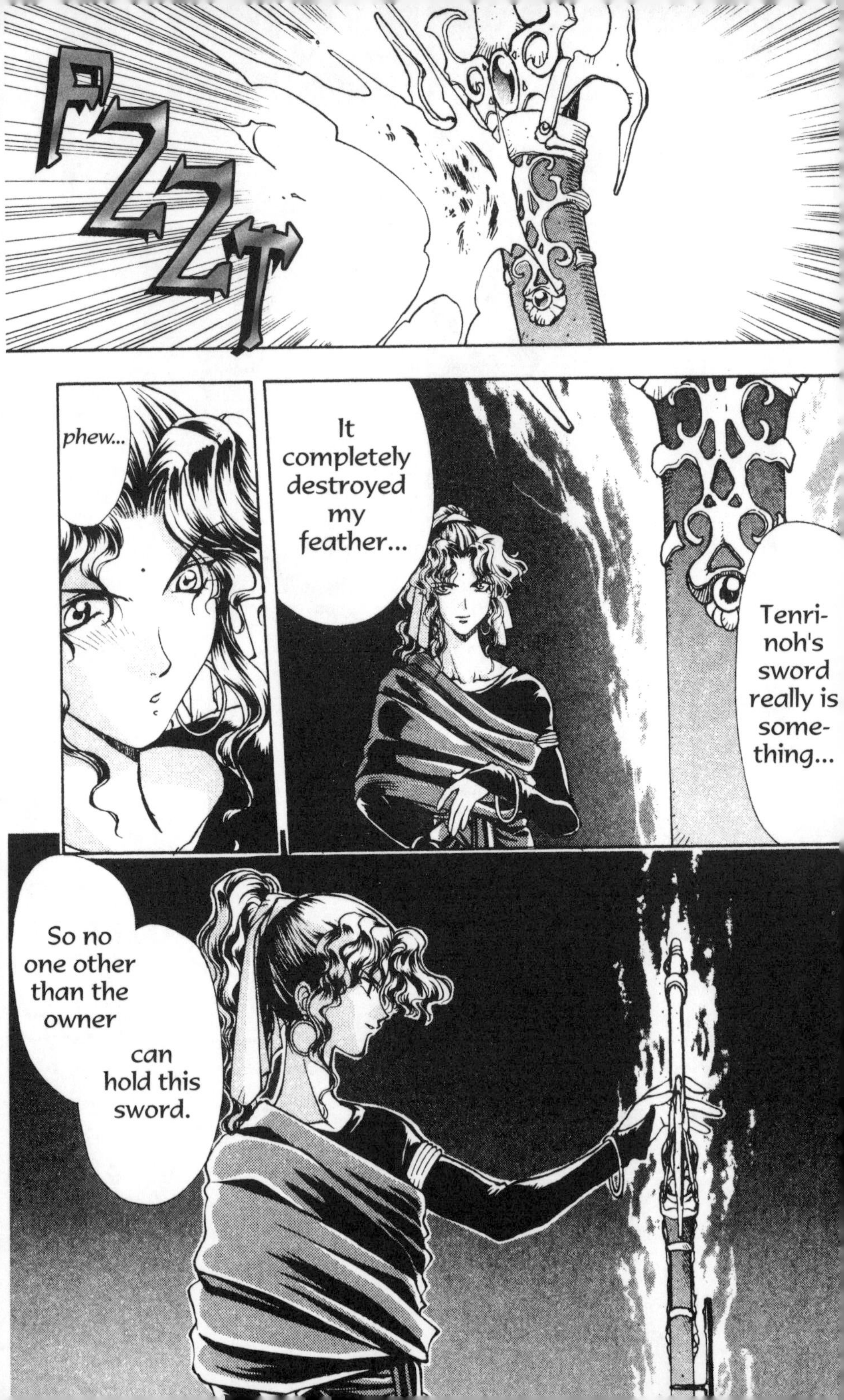
PZZT
Tenri-noh's sword really is some-thing...
It completely destroyed my feather...
phew...
So no one other than the owner can hold this sword.

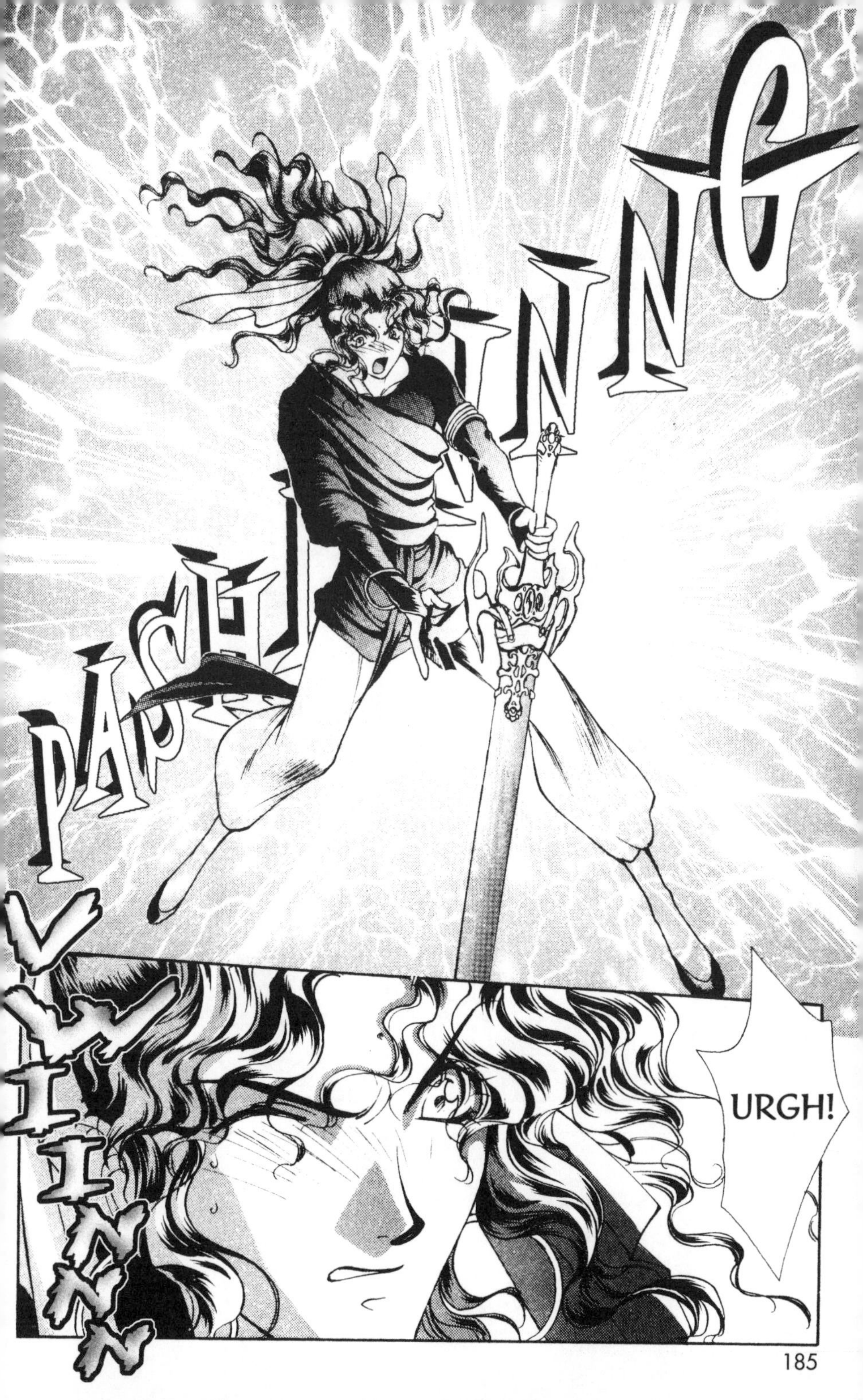
URGH!

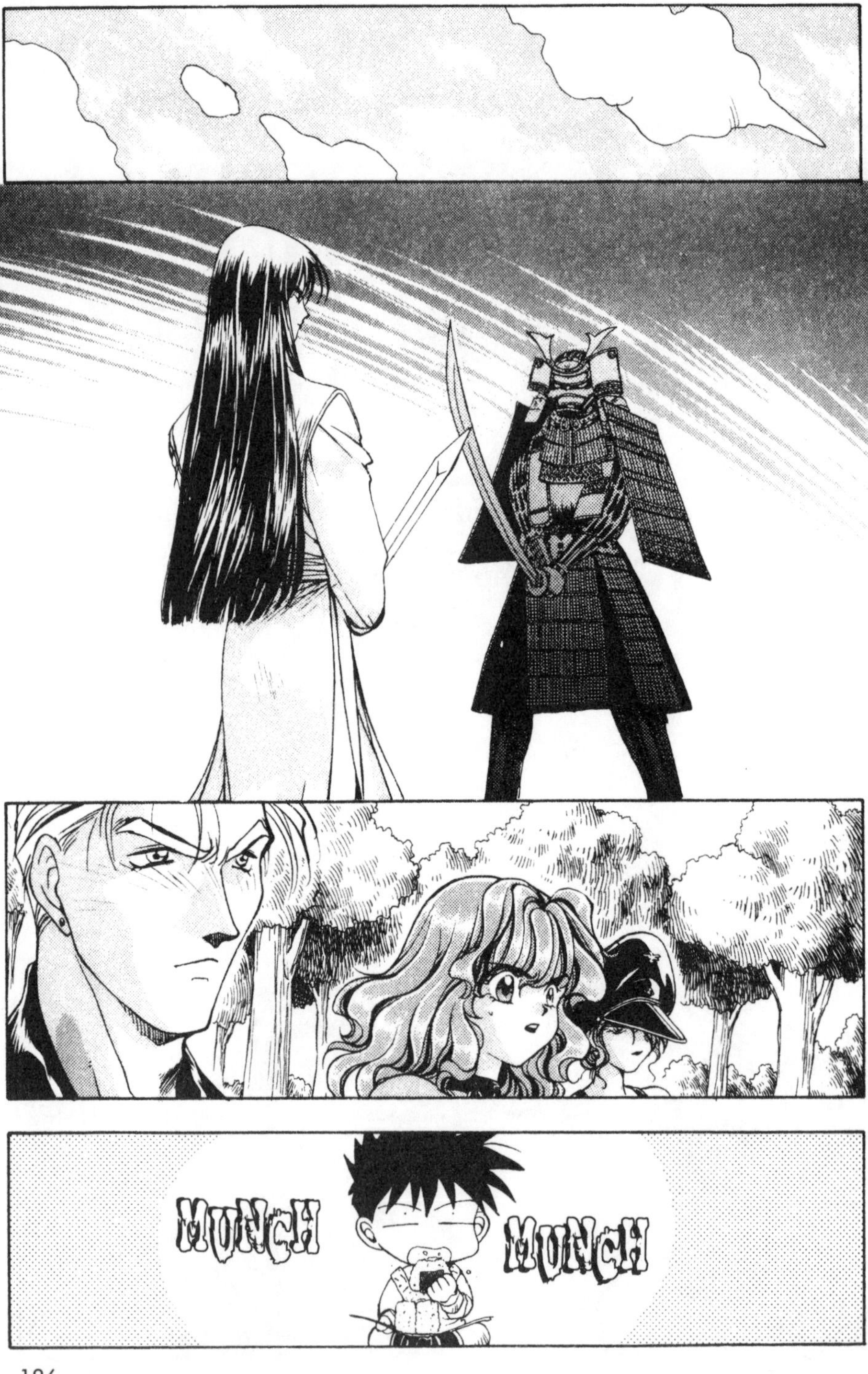
MUNCH
MUNCH

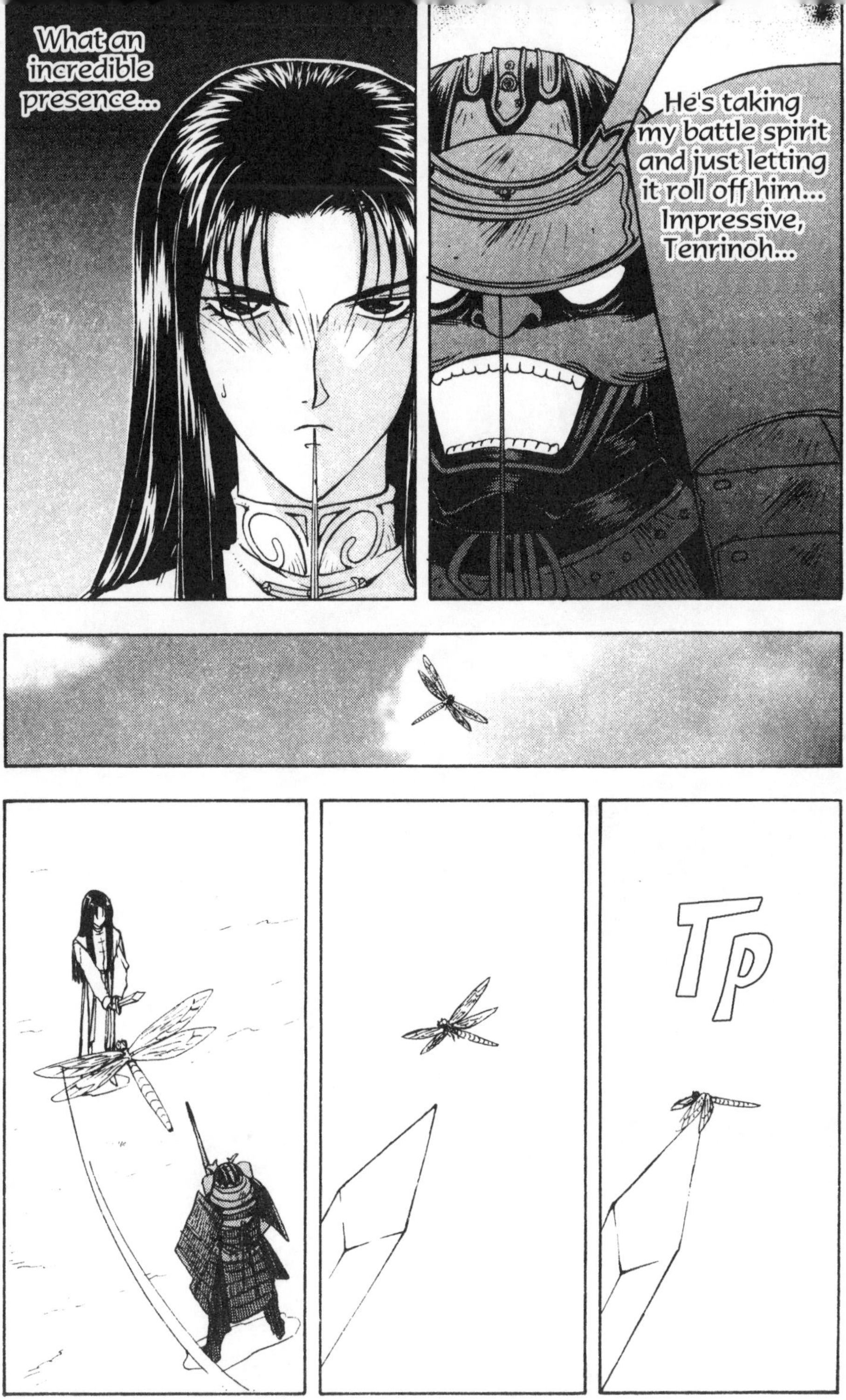
He's taking my battle spirit and just letting it roll off him... Impressive, Tenrinoh...
What an incredible presence...
Tp

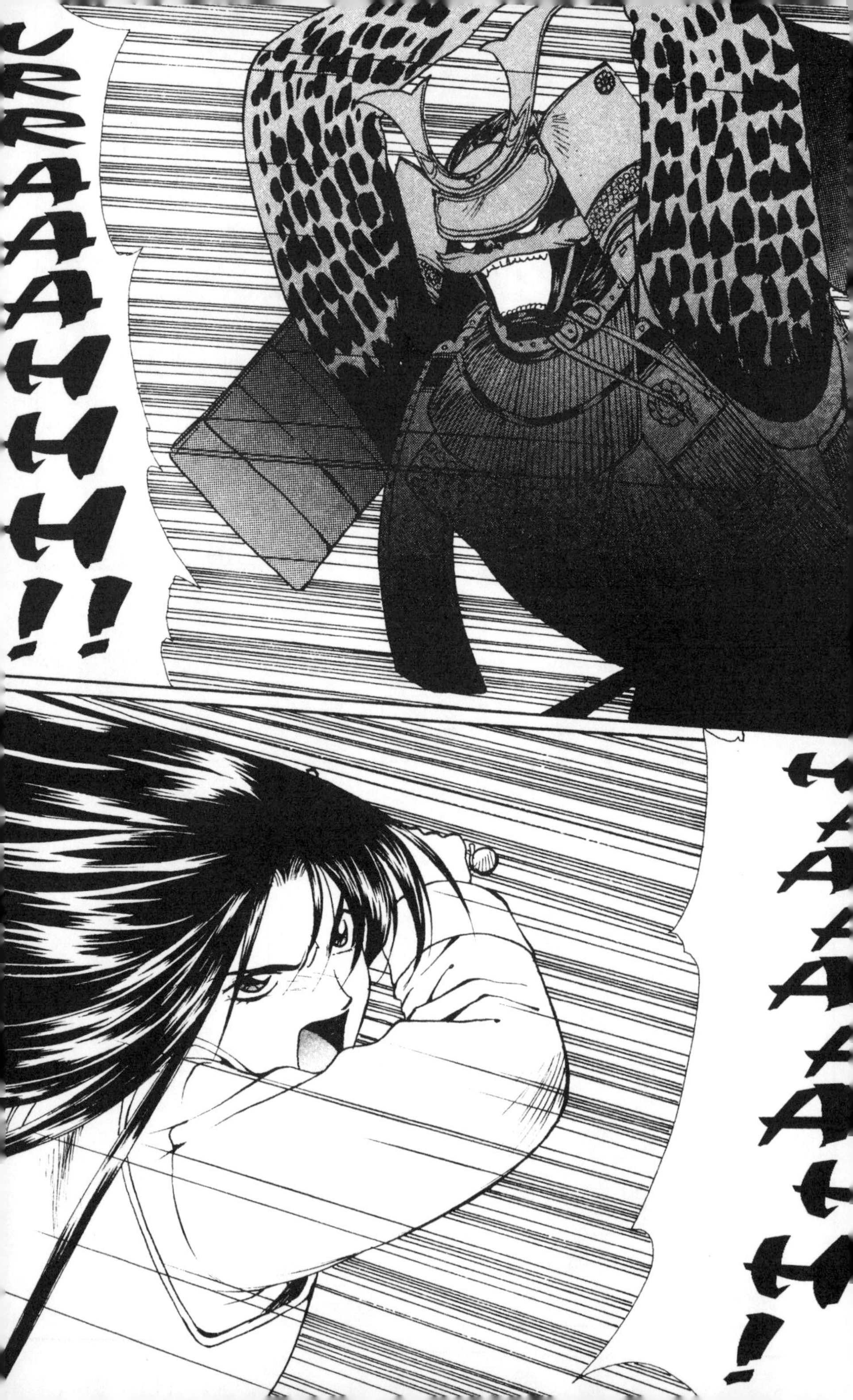
URRAAAHHH!!
HAAAAAAHH!

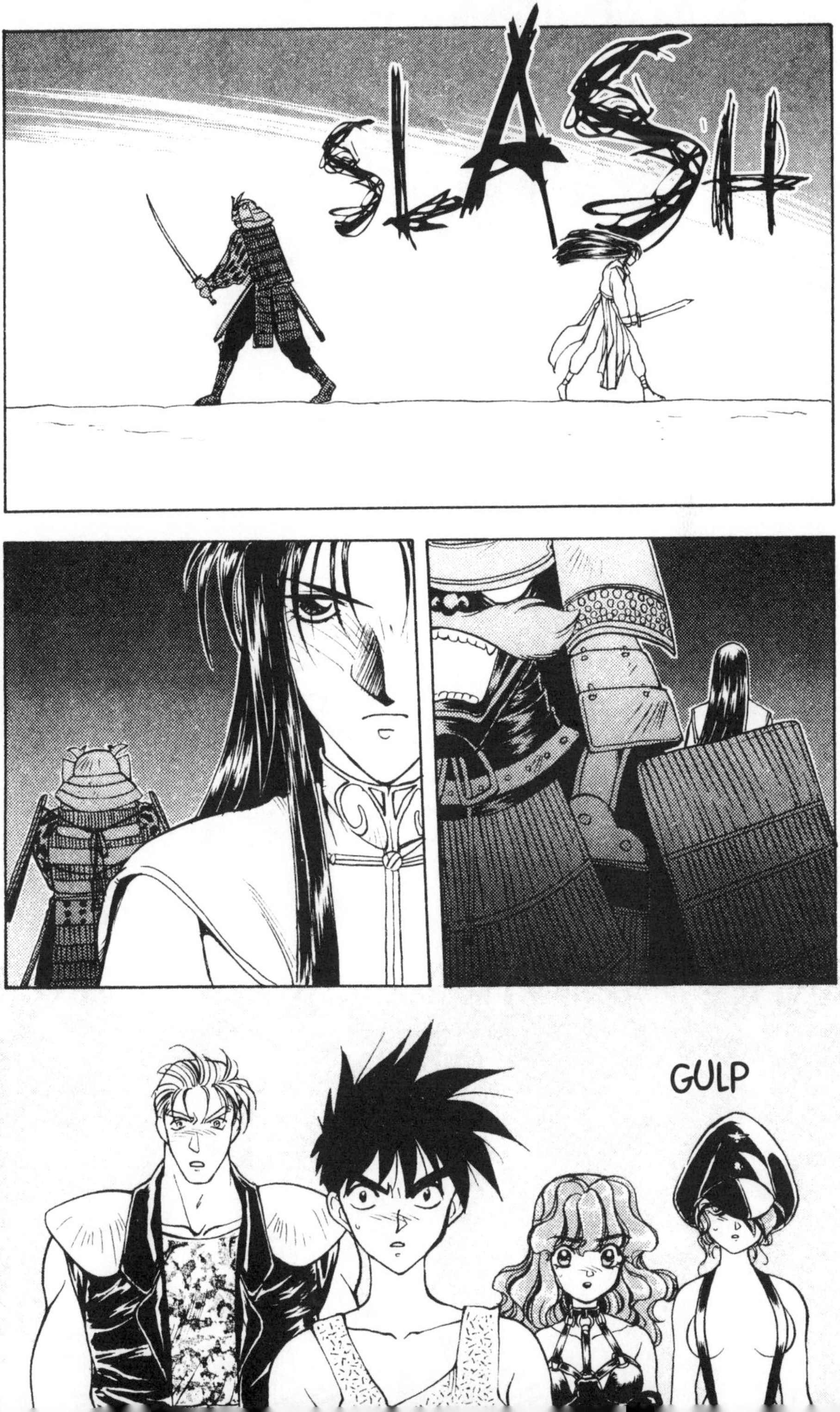
SLASH
GULP

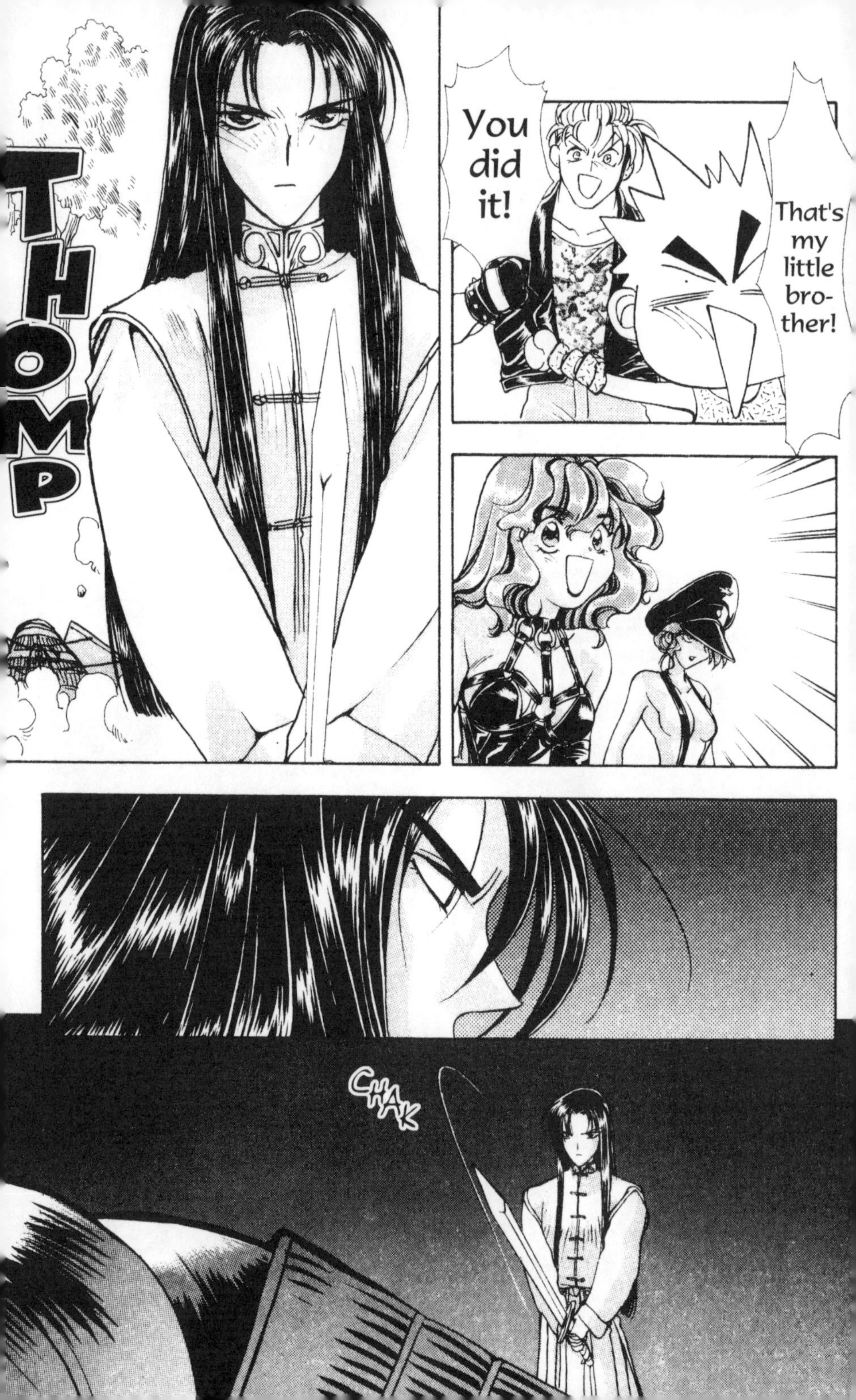
You did it!
That's my little bro-ther!
THOMP
CHAK

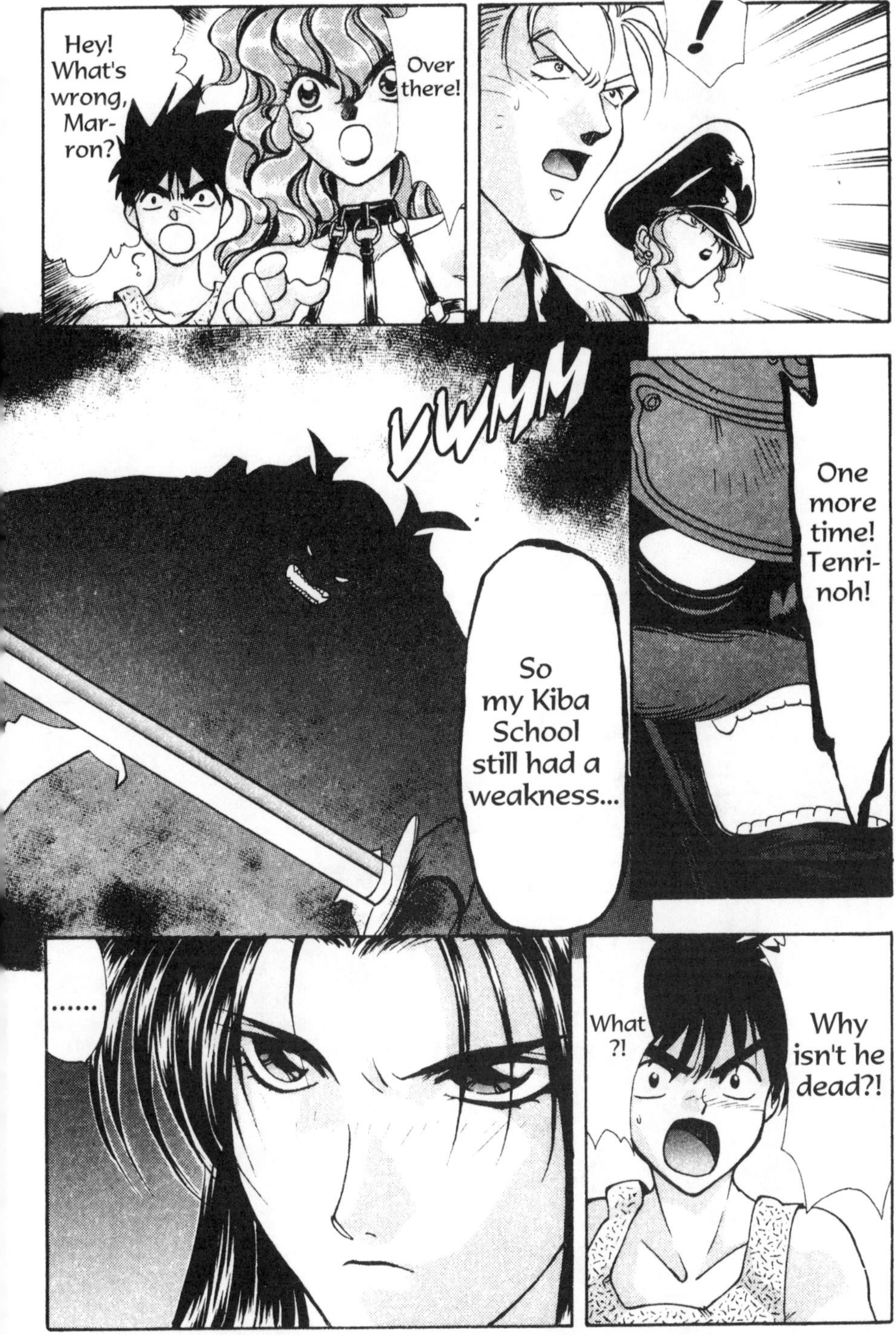
Hey! What's wrong, Marron?
Over there!
!
VWMM
So my Kiba School still had a weakness...
One more time! Tenri-noh!
......
What?!
Why isn't he dead?!

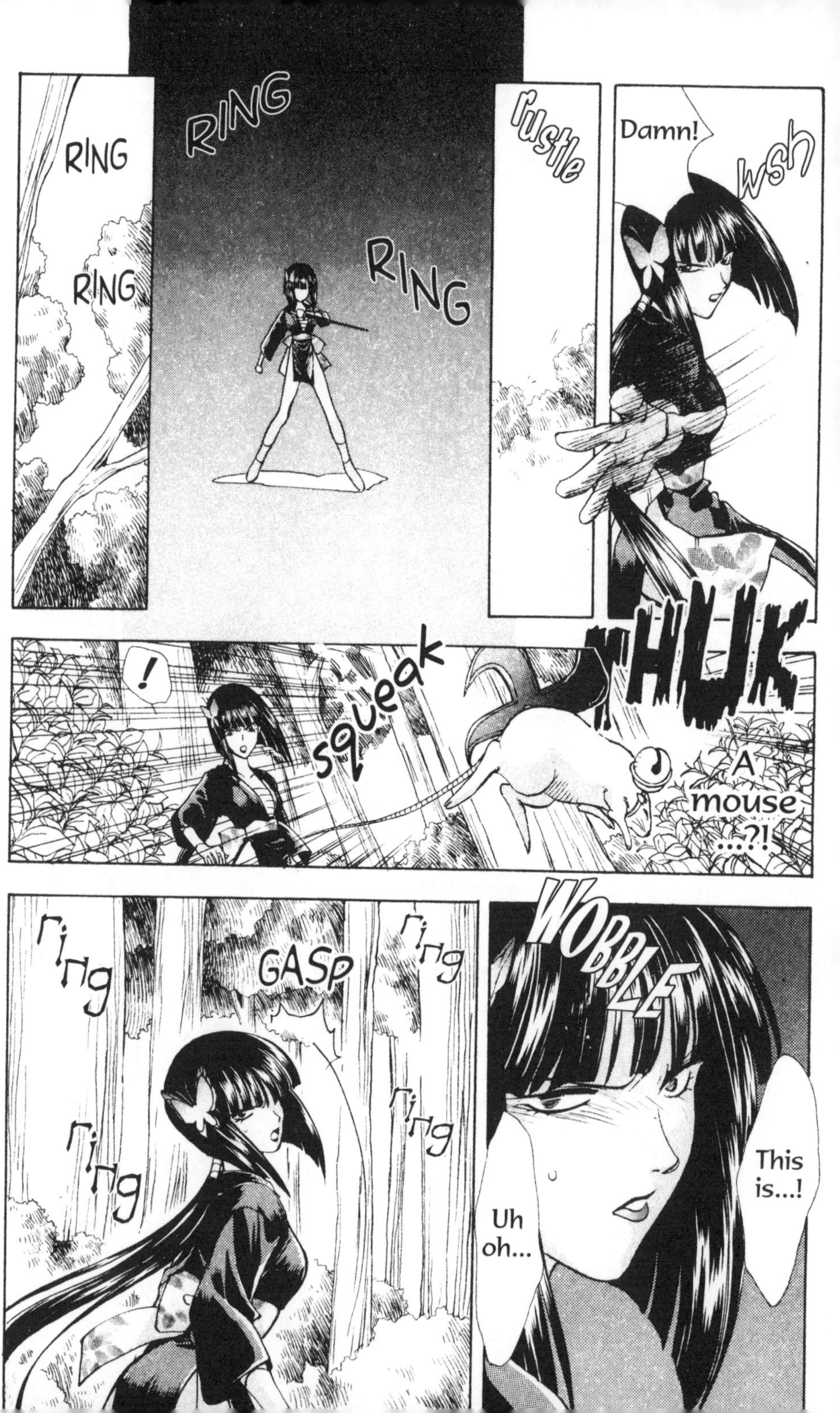
wsh
Damn!
rustle
RING
RING
RING
RING
THUK
A mouse ...?!
squeak
!
WOBBLE
This is...!
Uh oh...
ring
ring
GASP
ring
ring

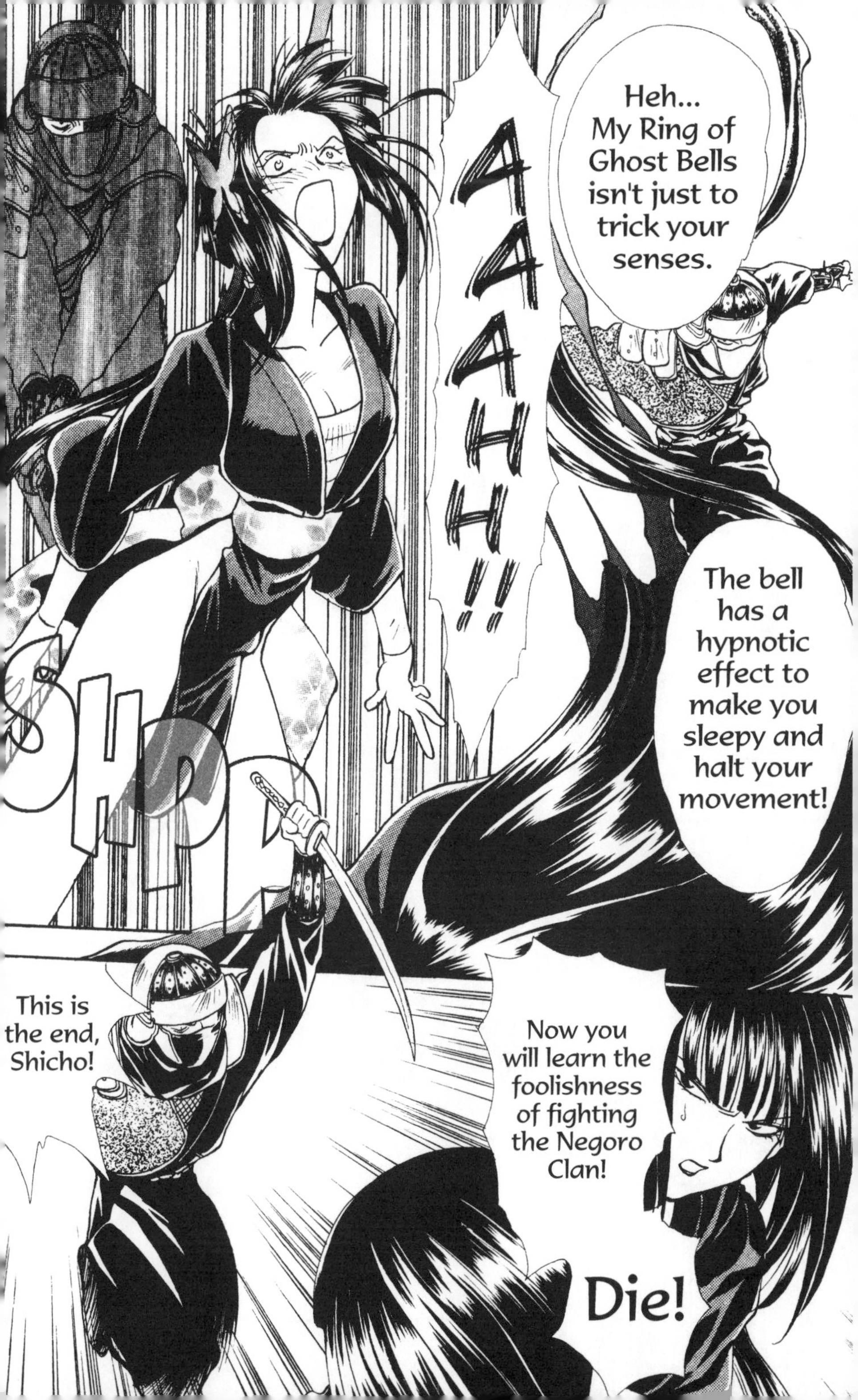
Heh... My Ring of Ghost Bells isn't just to trick your senses.
AAAHH!!
The bell has a hypnotic effect to make you sleepy and halt your movement!
SHP
Now you will learn the foolishness of fighting the Negoro Clan!
Die!
This is the end, Shicho!

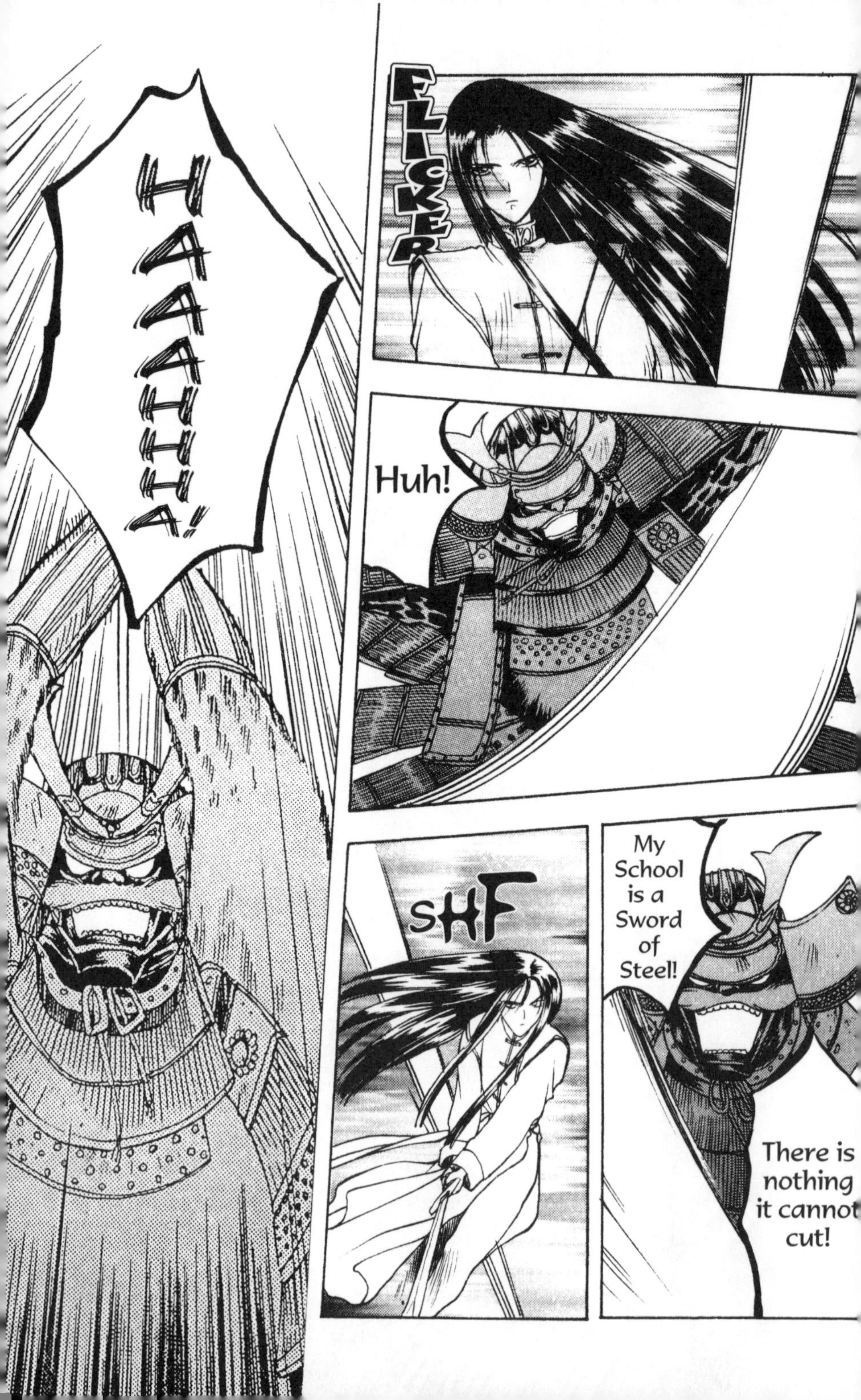
FLICKER
Huh!
My School is a Sword of Steel!
There is nothing it cannot cut!
SHF
HAAAHHHA!

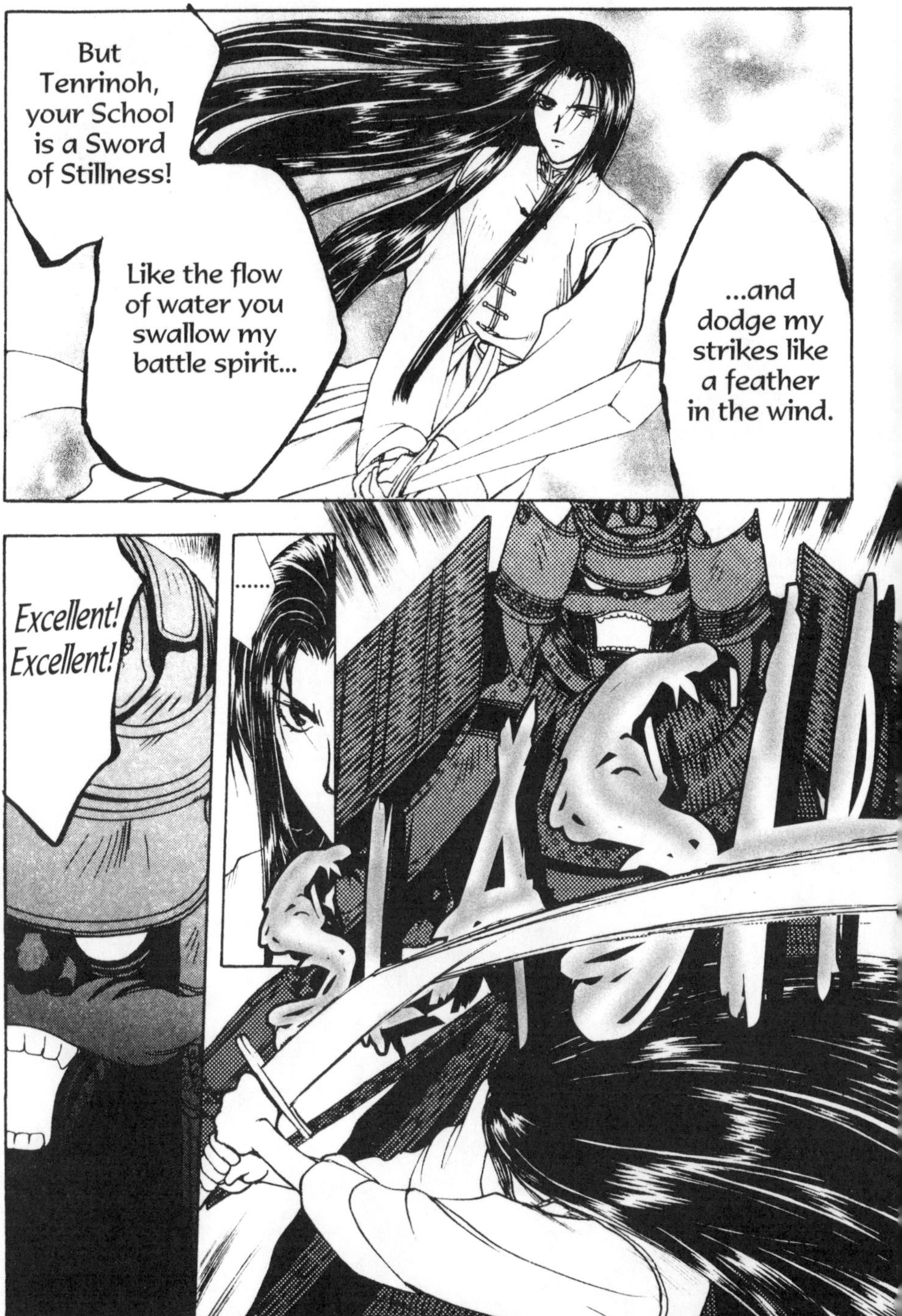
But Tenrinoh, your School is a Sword of Stillness!
Like the flow of water you swallow my battle spirit...
...and dodge my strikes like a feather in the wind.
Excellent! Excellent!
......

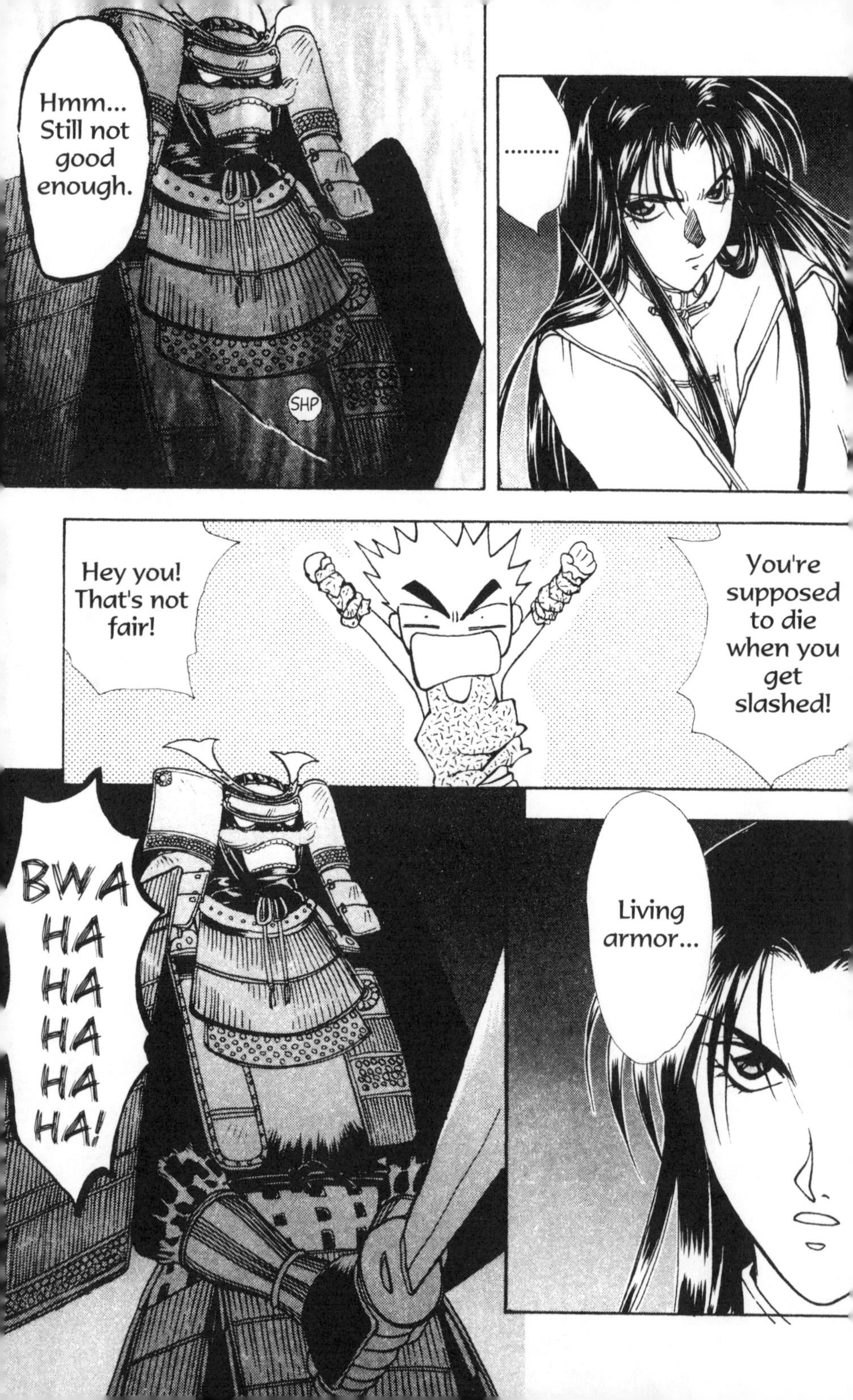
....
Hmm... Still not good enough.
SHP
You're supposed to die when you get slashed!
Hey you! That's not fair!
Living armor...
BWA HA HA HA HA HA HA!

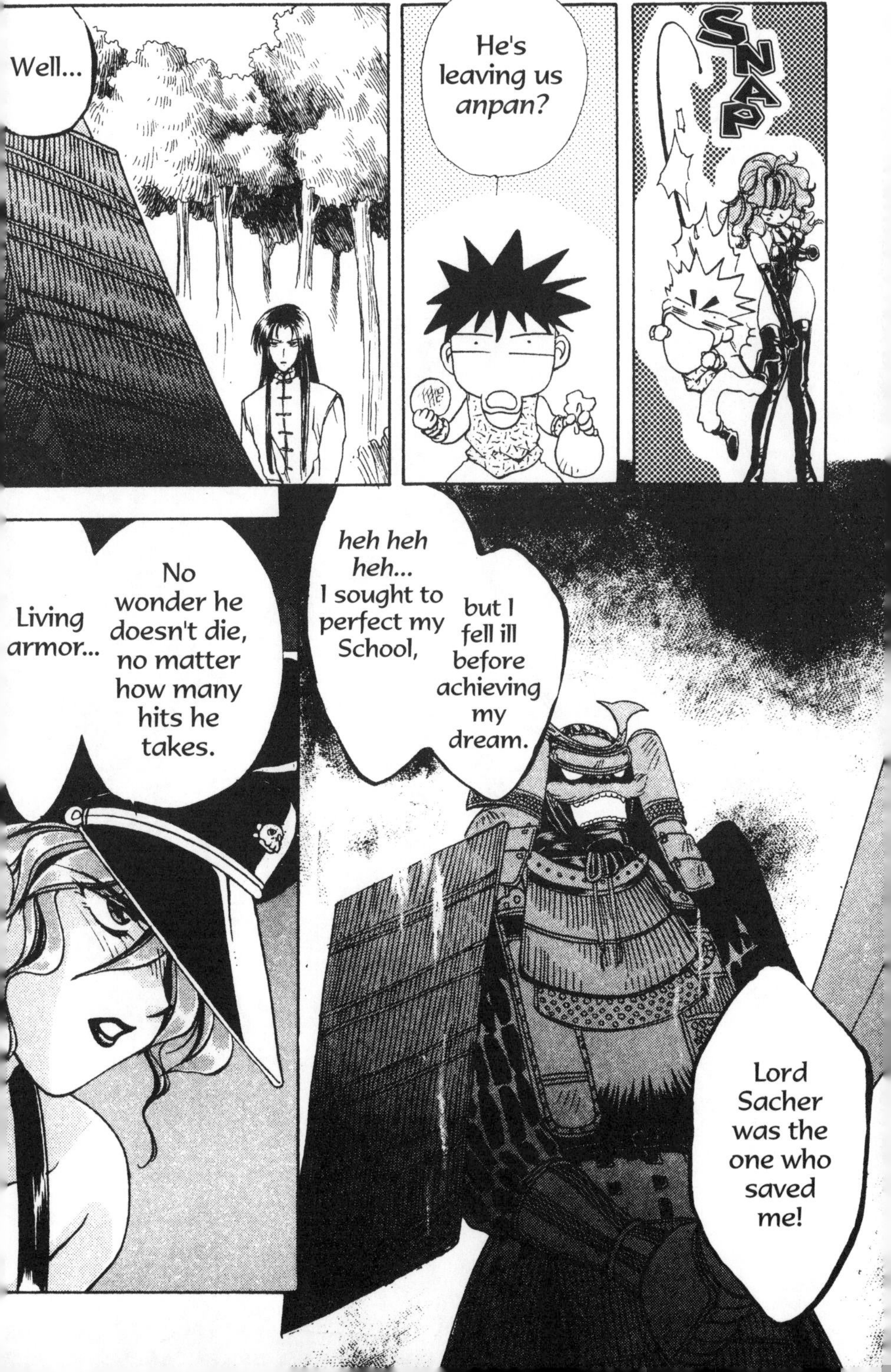
SNAP
He's leaving us anpan?
Well...
heh heh heh... I sought to perfect my School, but I fell ill before achieving my dream.
Lord Sacher was the one who saved me!
Living armor... No wonder he doesn't die, no matter how many hits he takes.

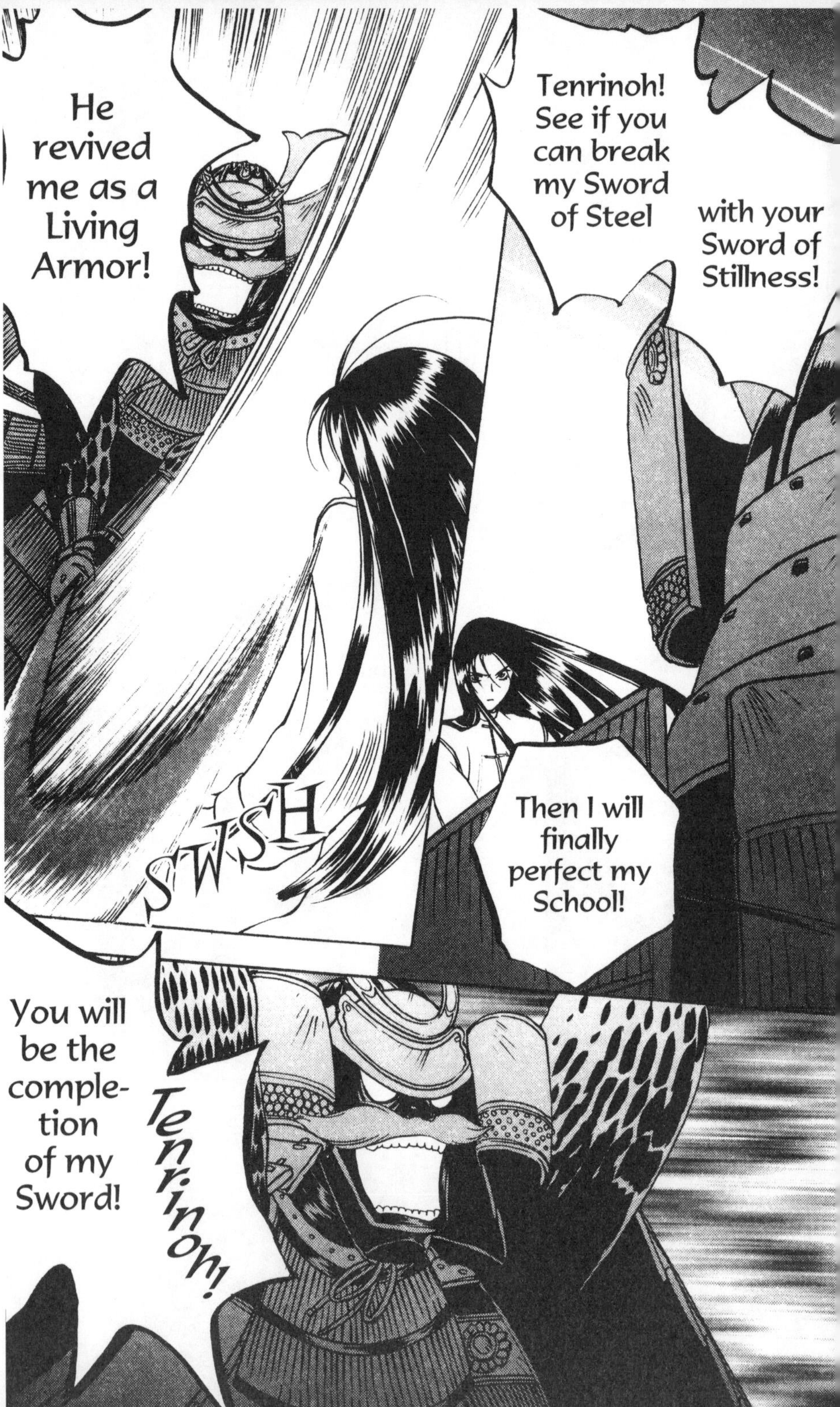
Tenrinoh! See if you can break my Sword of Steel
with your Sword of Stillness!
Then I will finally perfect my School!
He revived me as a Living Armor!
SWSH
You will be the comple-tion of my Sword!
Tenrinoh!

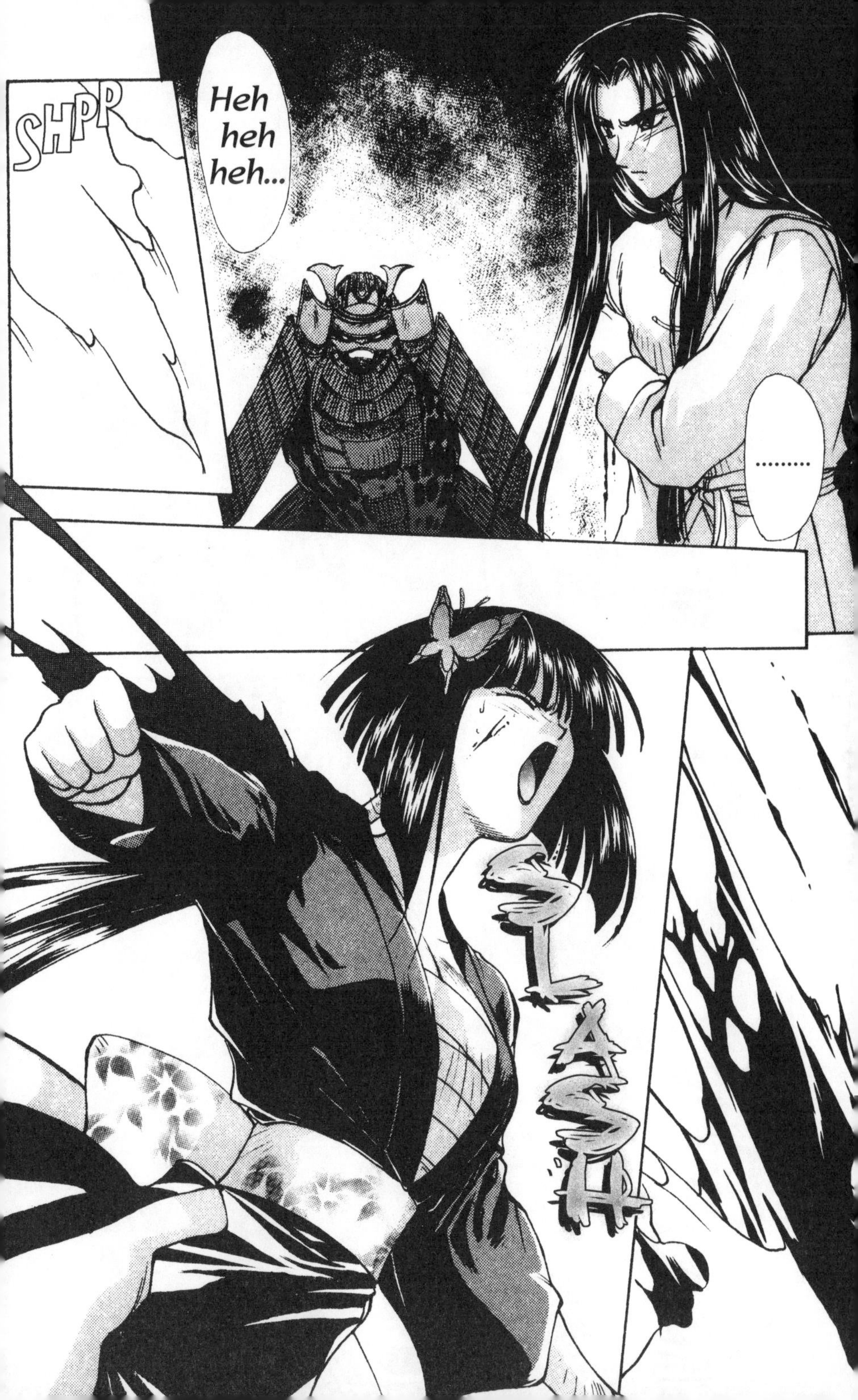
....
Heh heh heh...
SHPP
GASH

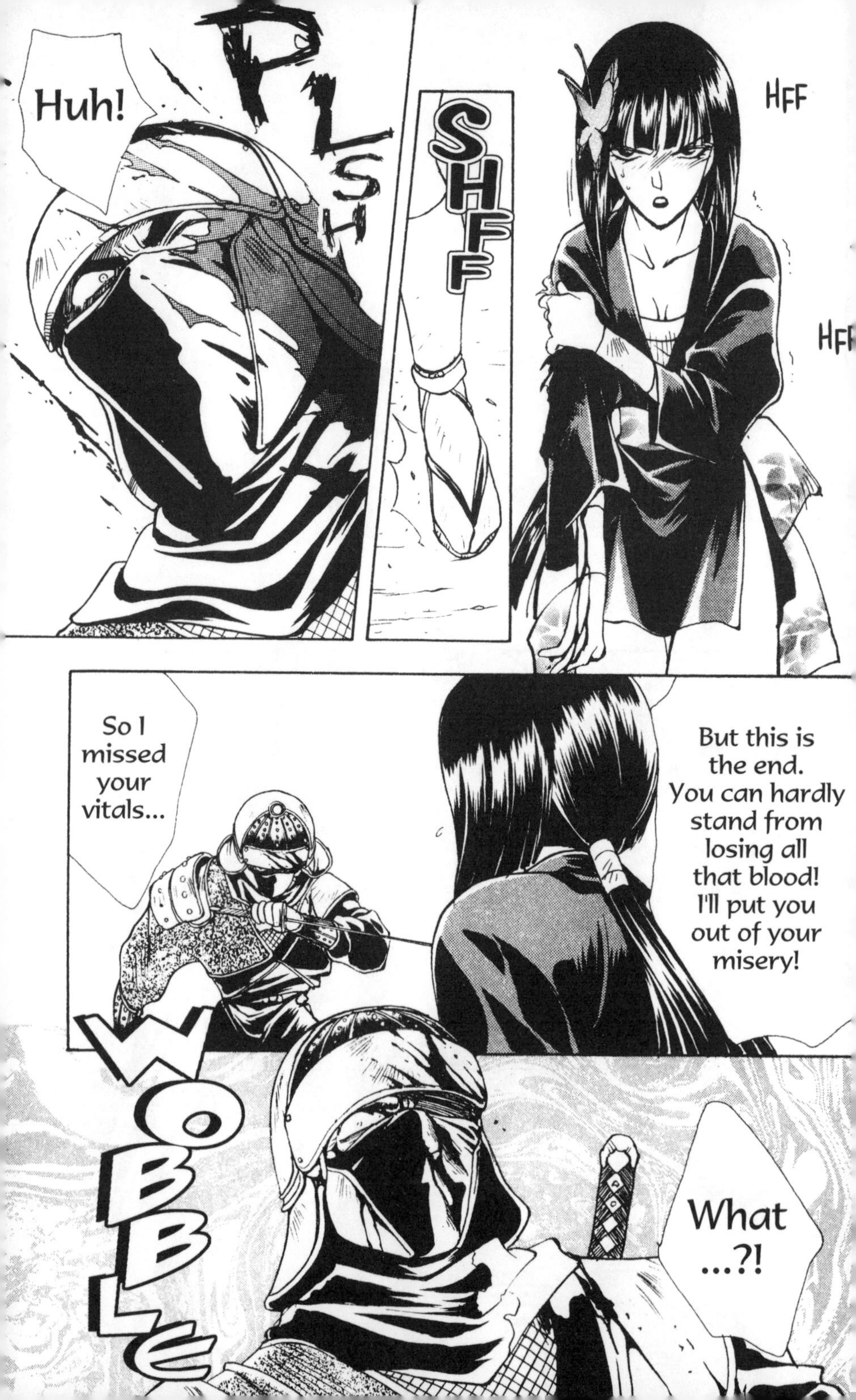
HFF
HFF
SHFF
Huh!
PLSH
So I missed your vitals...
But this is the end. You can hardly stand from losing all that blood! I'll put you out of your misery!
WOBBLE
What ...?!

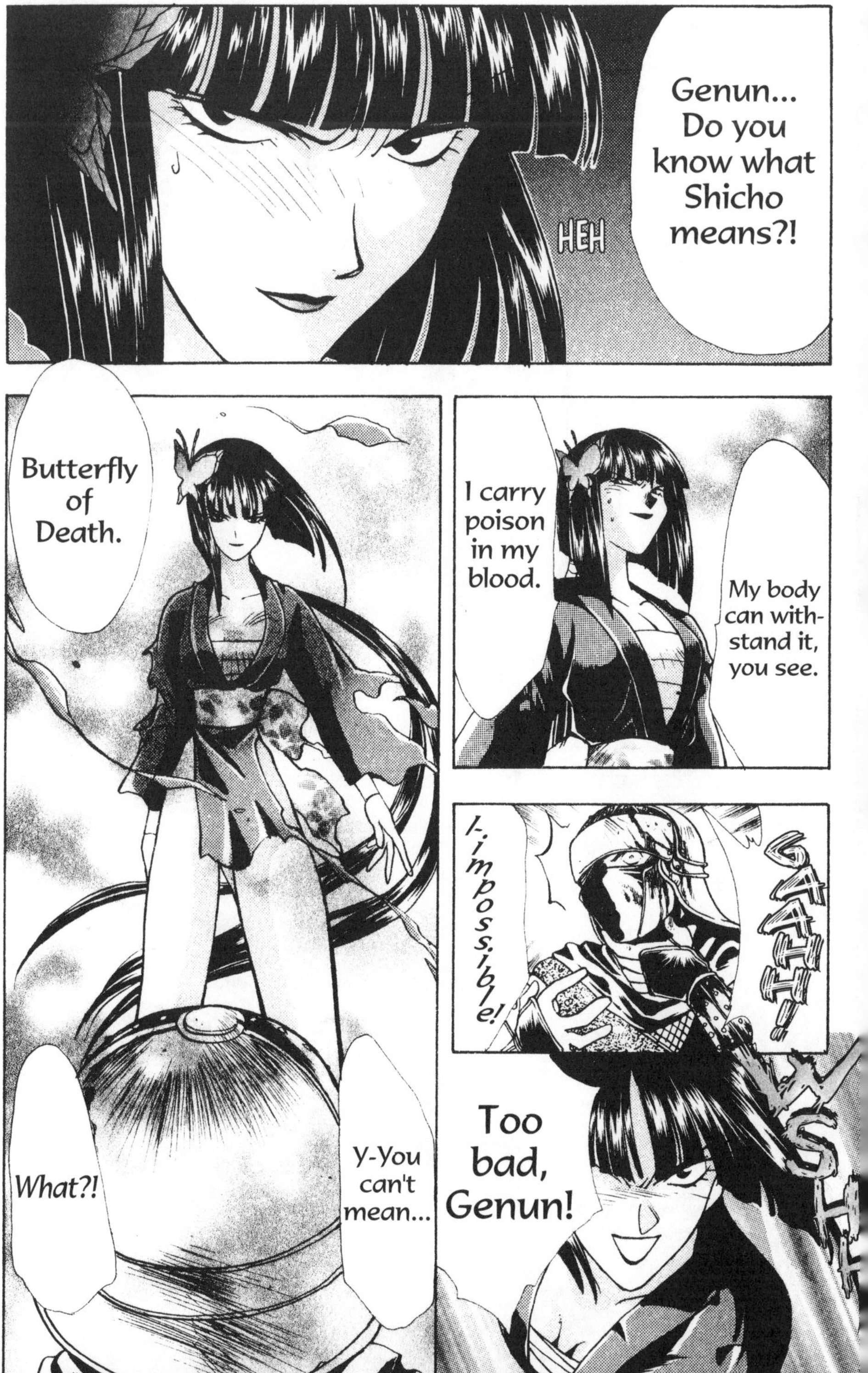
Genun... Do you know what Shicho means?!
HEH
Butterfly of Death.
What?!
Y-You can't mean...
I carry poison in my blood.
My body can withstand it, you see.
I-impossible!
GAAHH!!
Too bad, Genun!

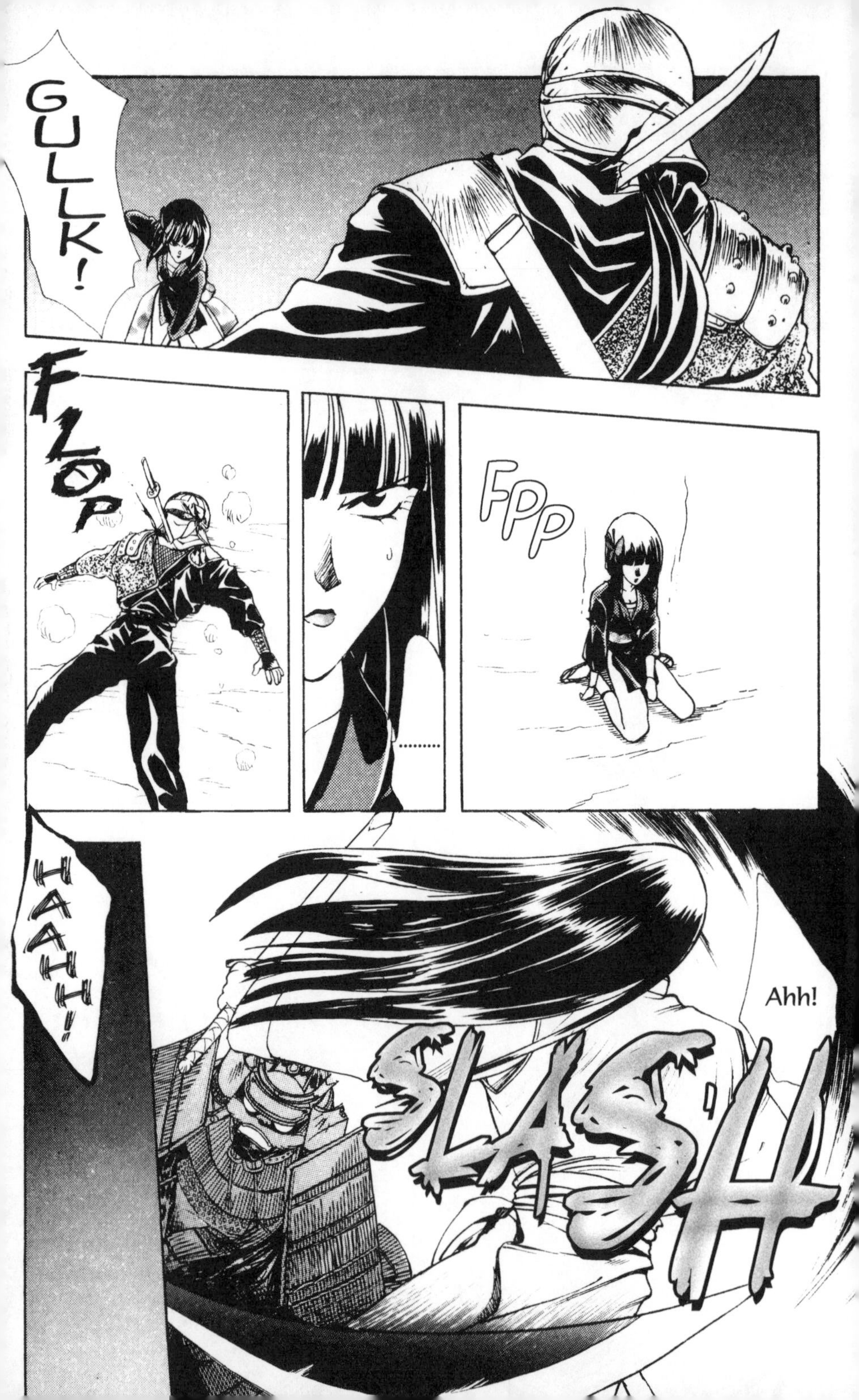
GULLLK!
FPP
....
FLOP
Ahh!
SLASH
HAAAH!!

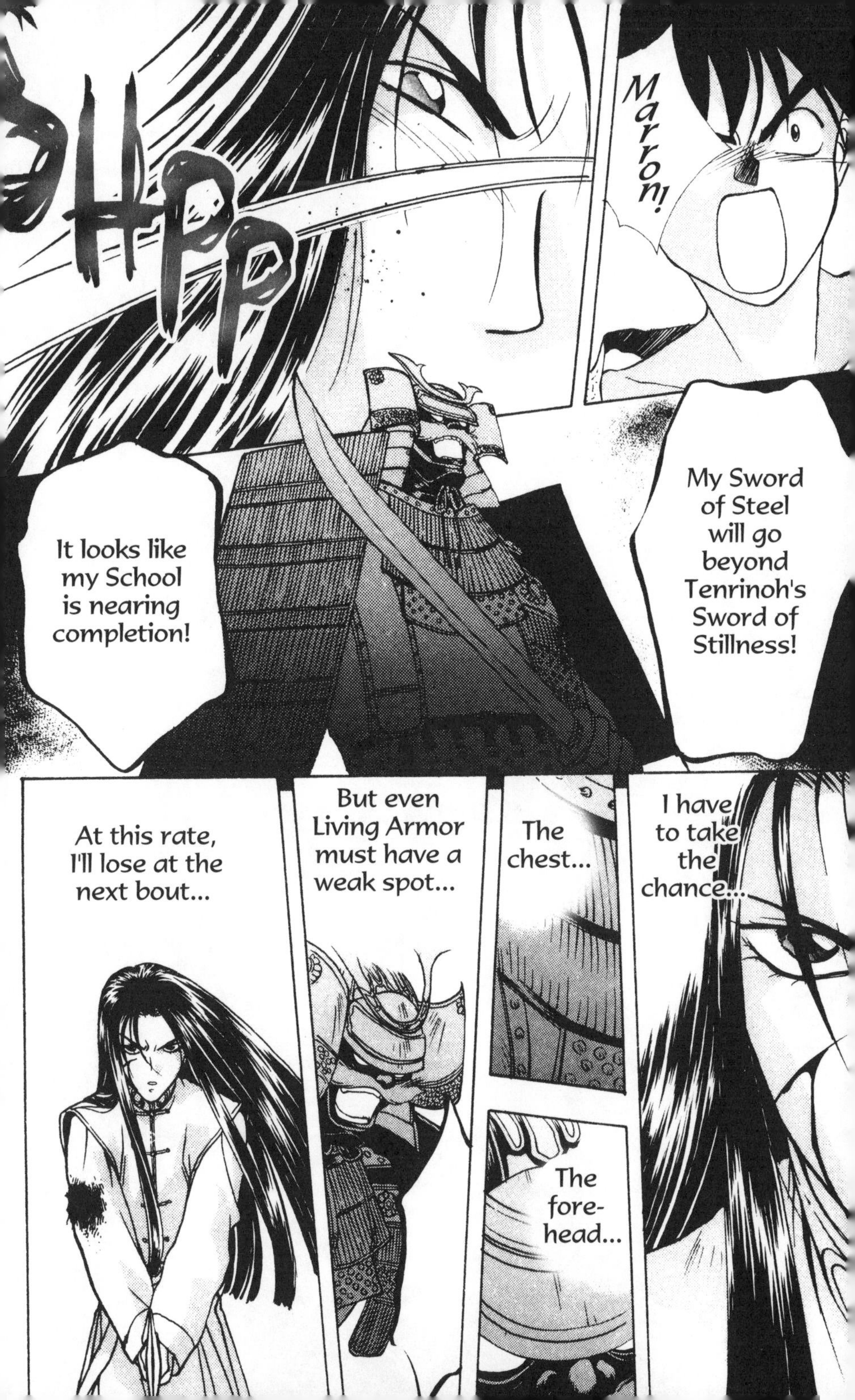
HPP
Marron!
It looks like my School is nearing completion!
My Sword of Steel will go beyond Tenrinoh's Sword of Stillness!
At this rate, I'll lose at the next bout...
But even Living Armor must have a weak spot...
The chest...
The fore-head...
I have to take the chance...

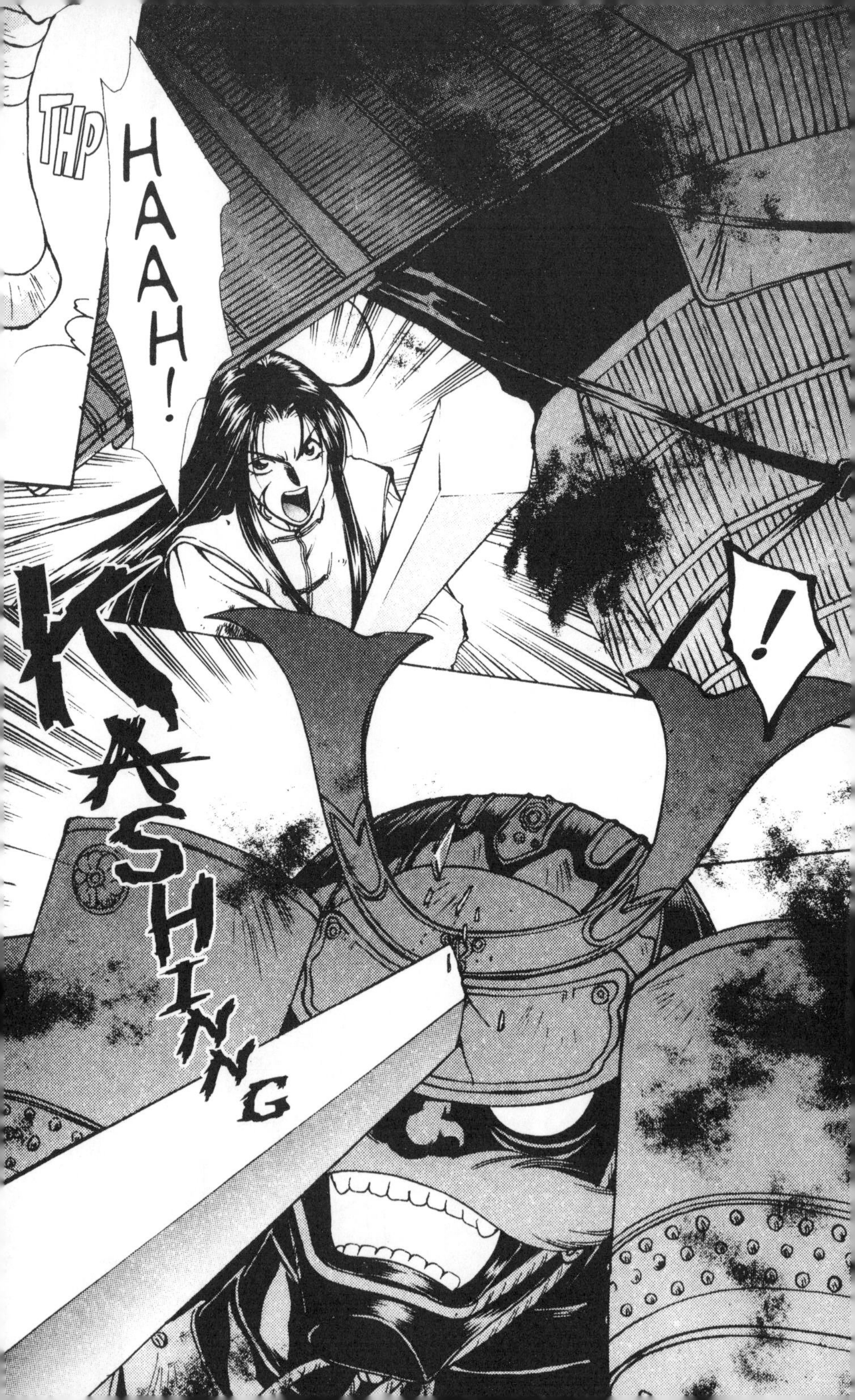
THP
HAAH!
!
KASHING

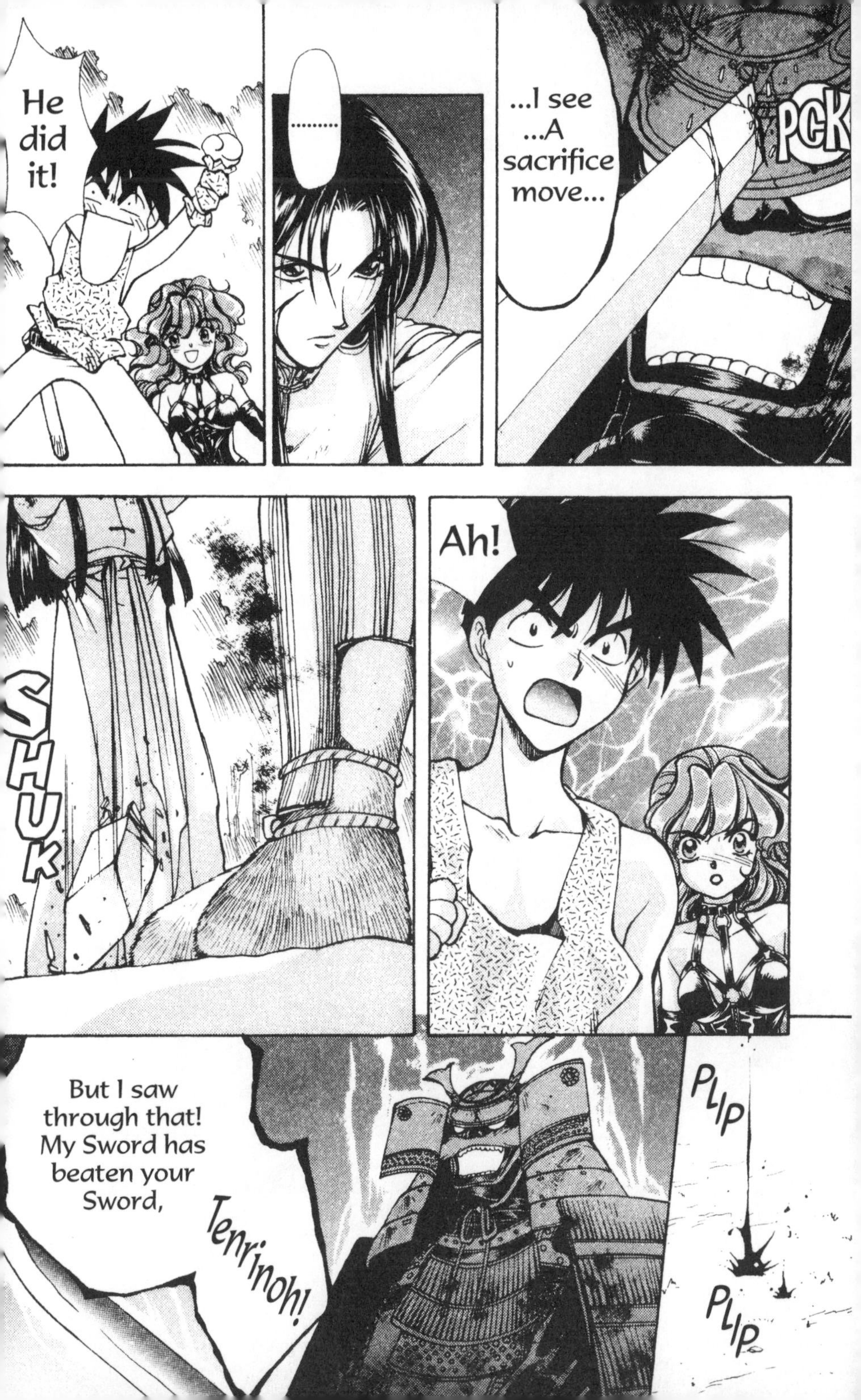
He did it!
....
...I see ...A sacrifice move...
PCK
SHUK
Ah!
But I saw through that! My Sword has beaten your Sword,
Tenrinoh!
PLIP
PLIP

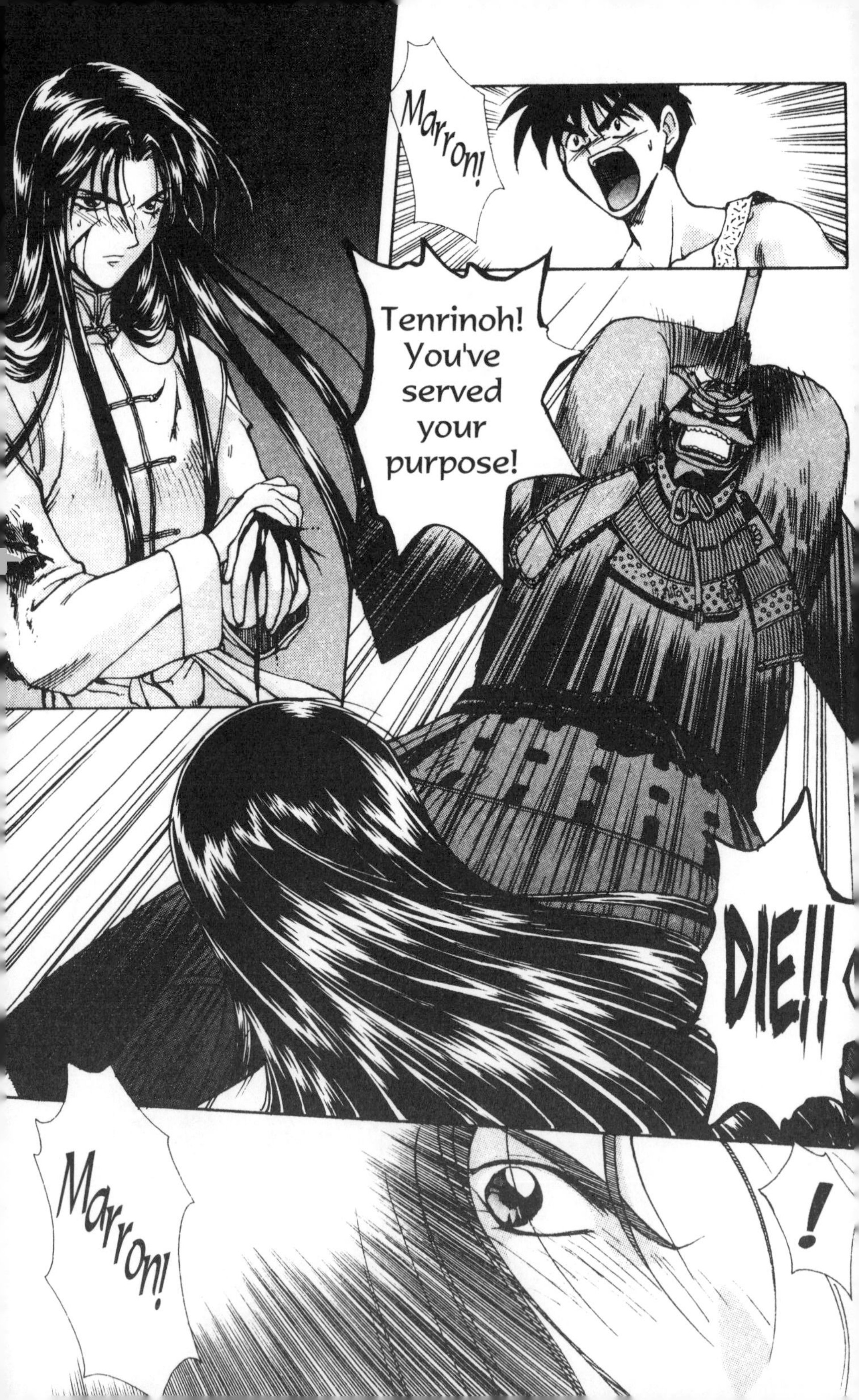
Marron!
Tenrinoh! You've served your purpose!
DIE!!
!
Marron!

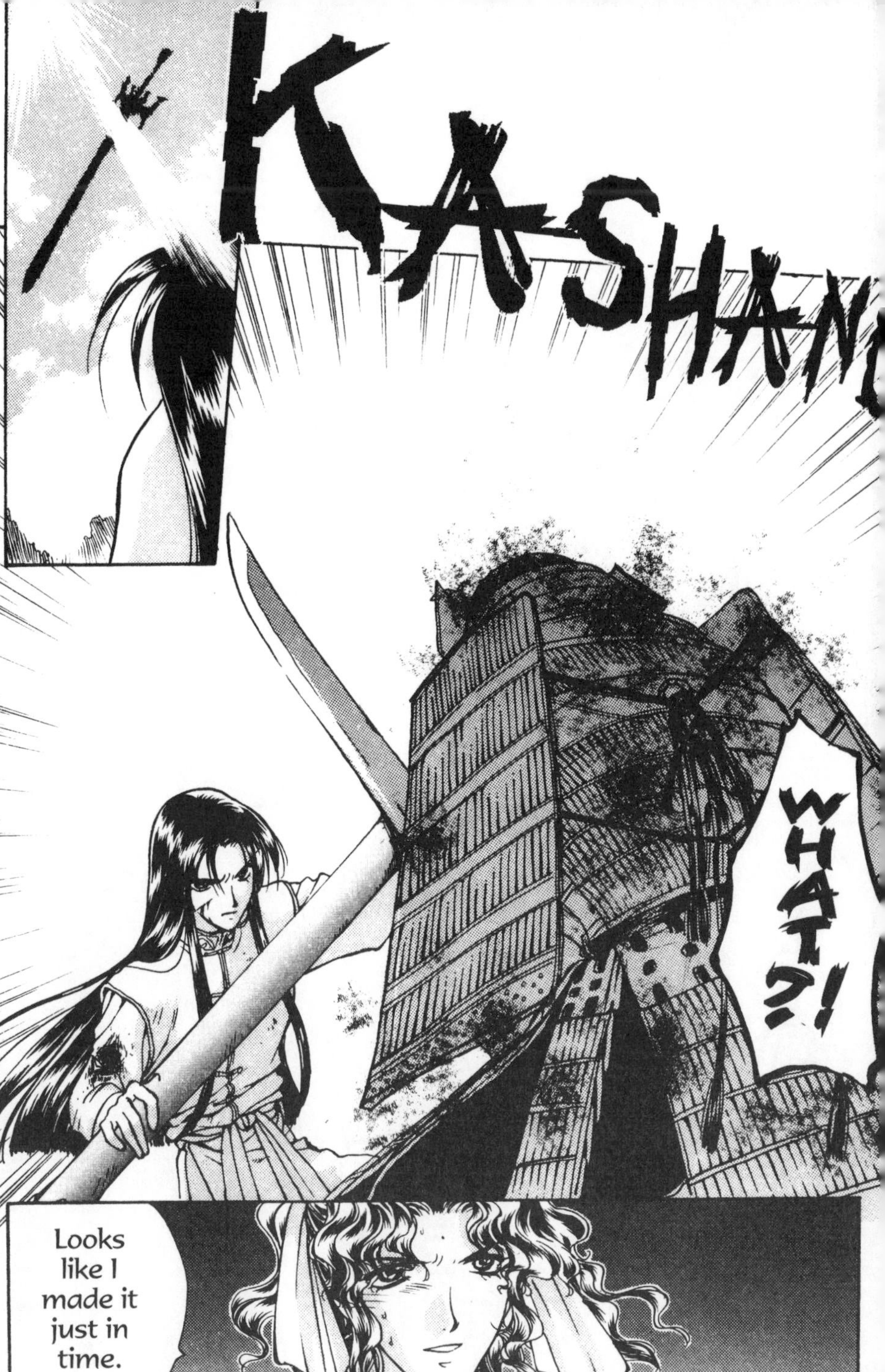
KASHAN
WHAT?!
Looks like I made it just in time.

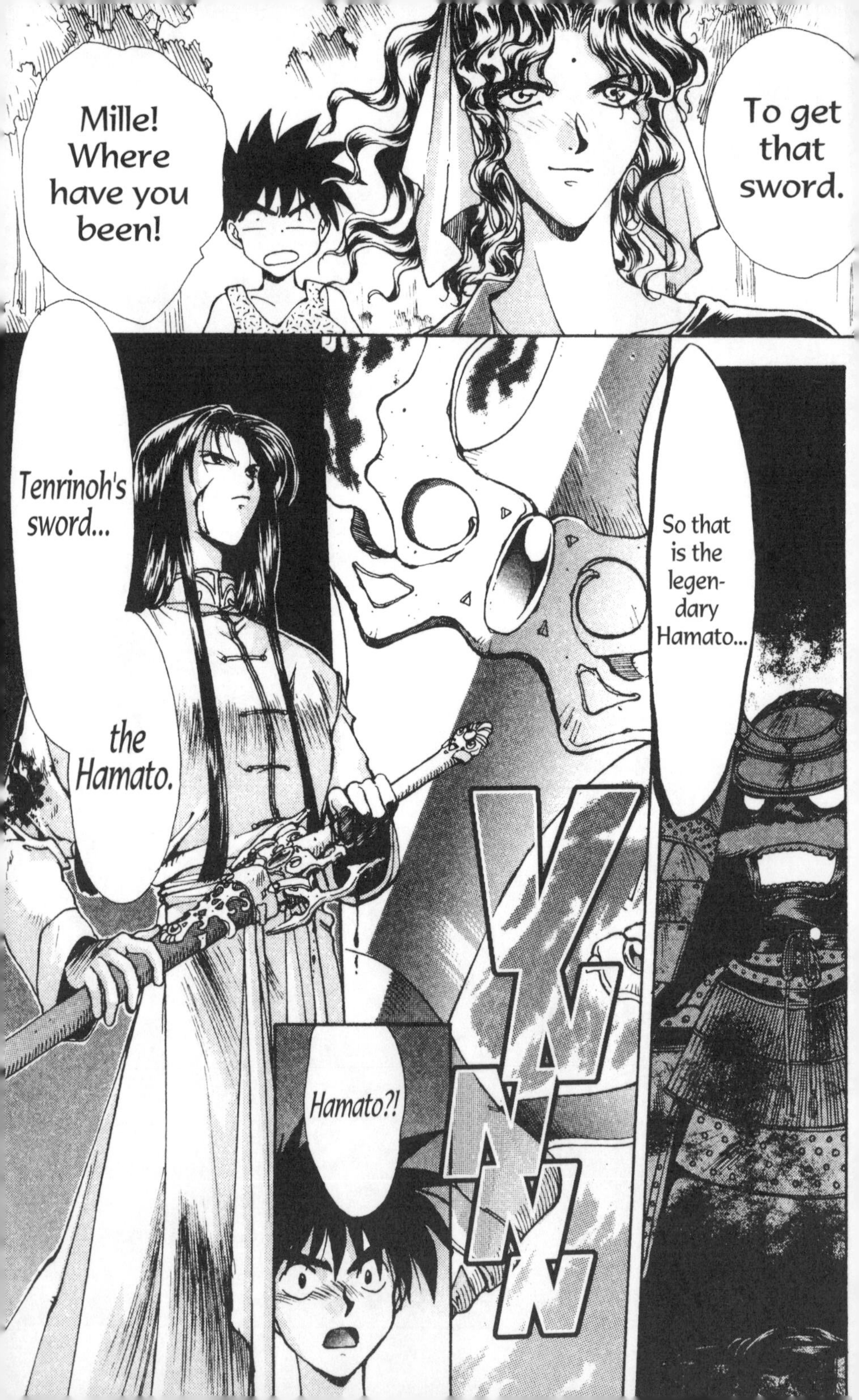
Mille! Where have you been!
To get that sword.
Tenrinoh's sword...
the Hamato.
Hamato?!
So that is the legendary Hamato...

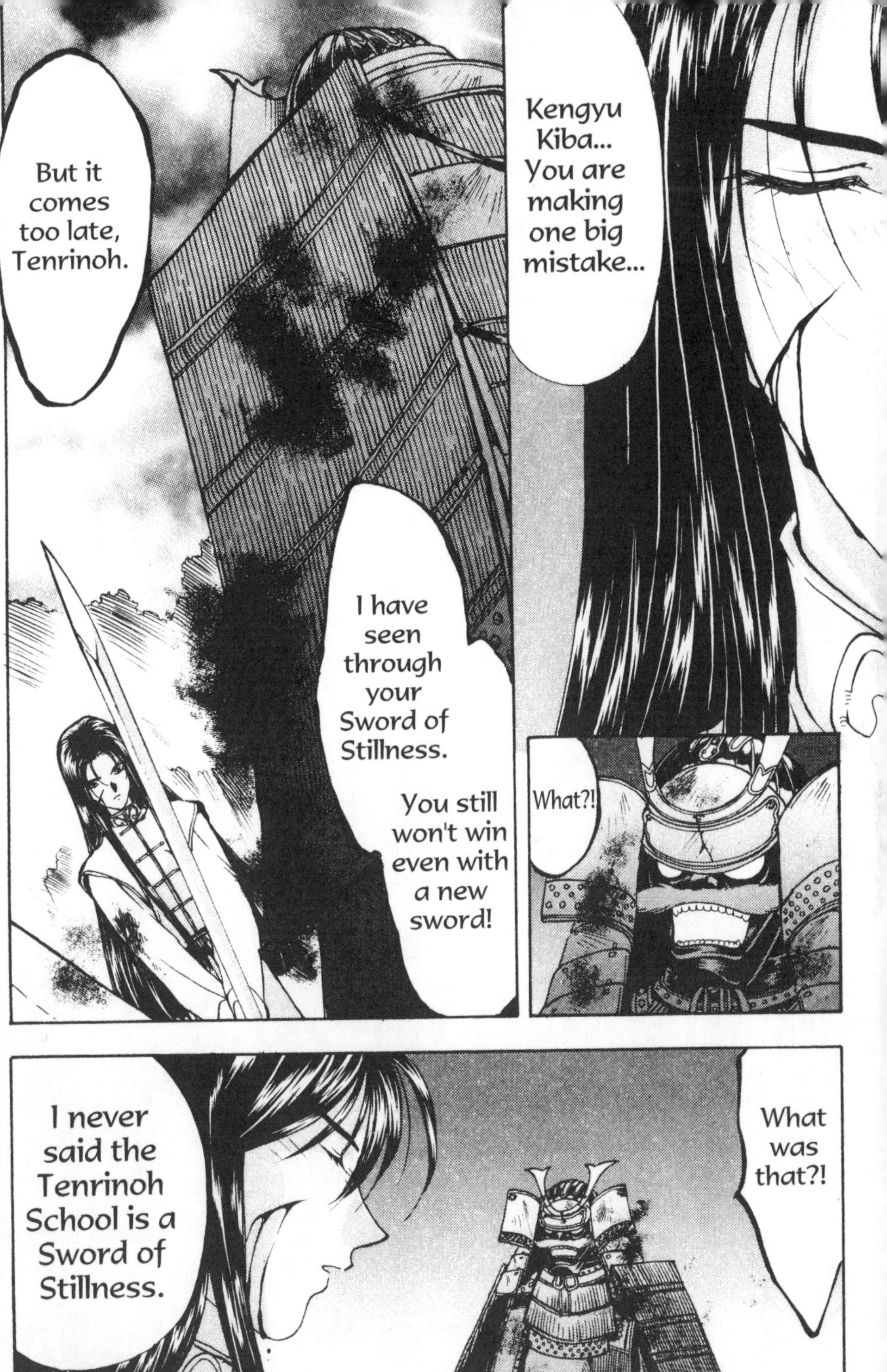

But it comes too late, Tenrinoh.
I have seen through your Sword of Stillness.
You still won't win even with a new sword!
Kengyu Kiba... You are making one big mistake...
What?!
I never said the Tenrinoh School is a Sword of Stillness.
What was that?!

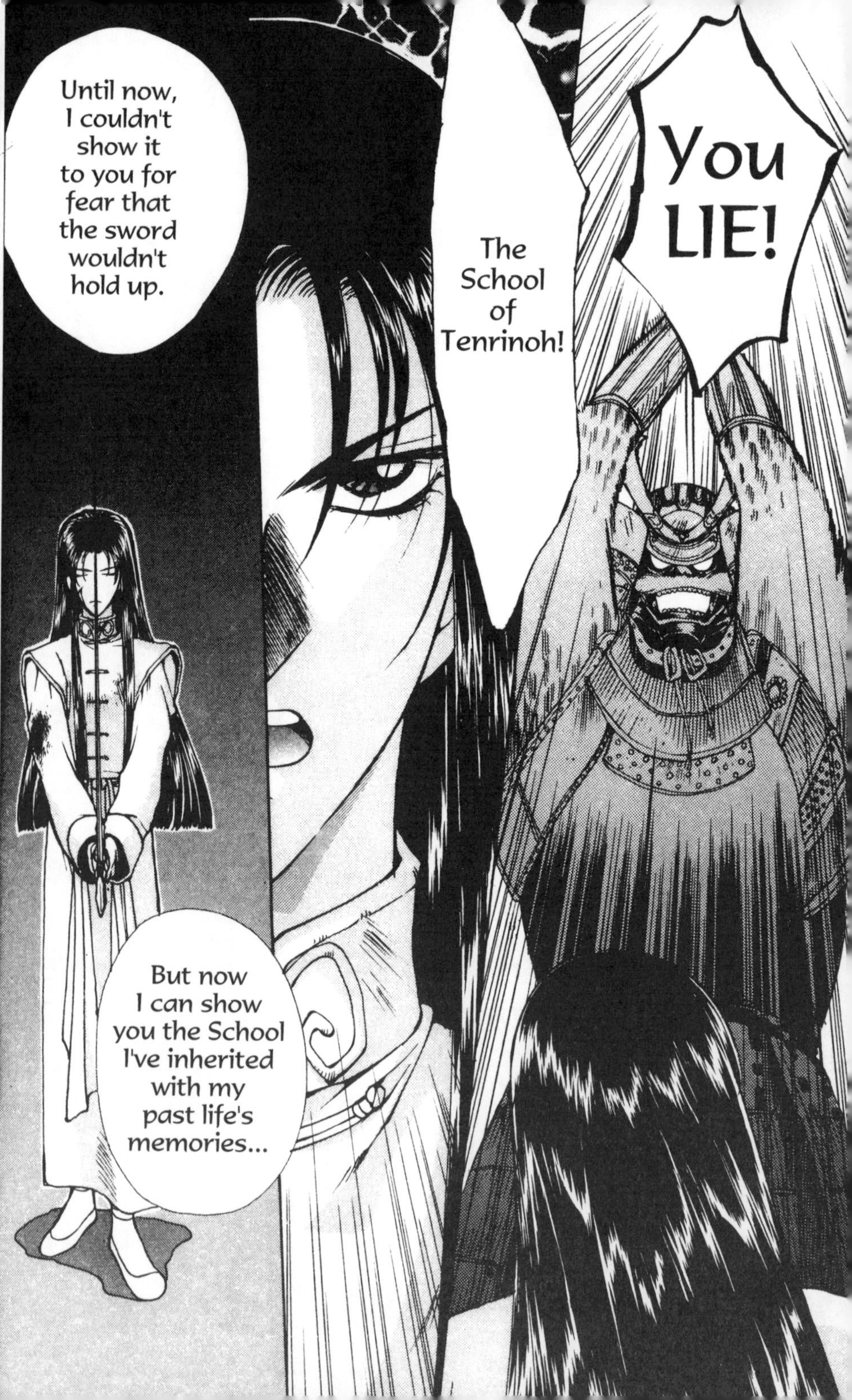
You LIE!
The School of Tenrinoh!
Until now, I couldn't show it to you for fear that the sword wouldn't hold up.
But now I can show you the School I've inherited with my past life's memories...

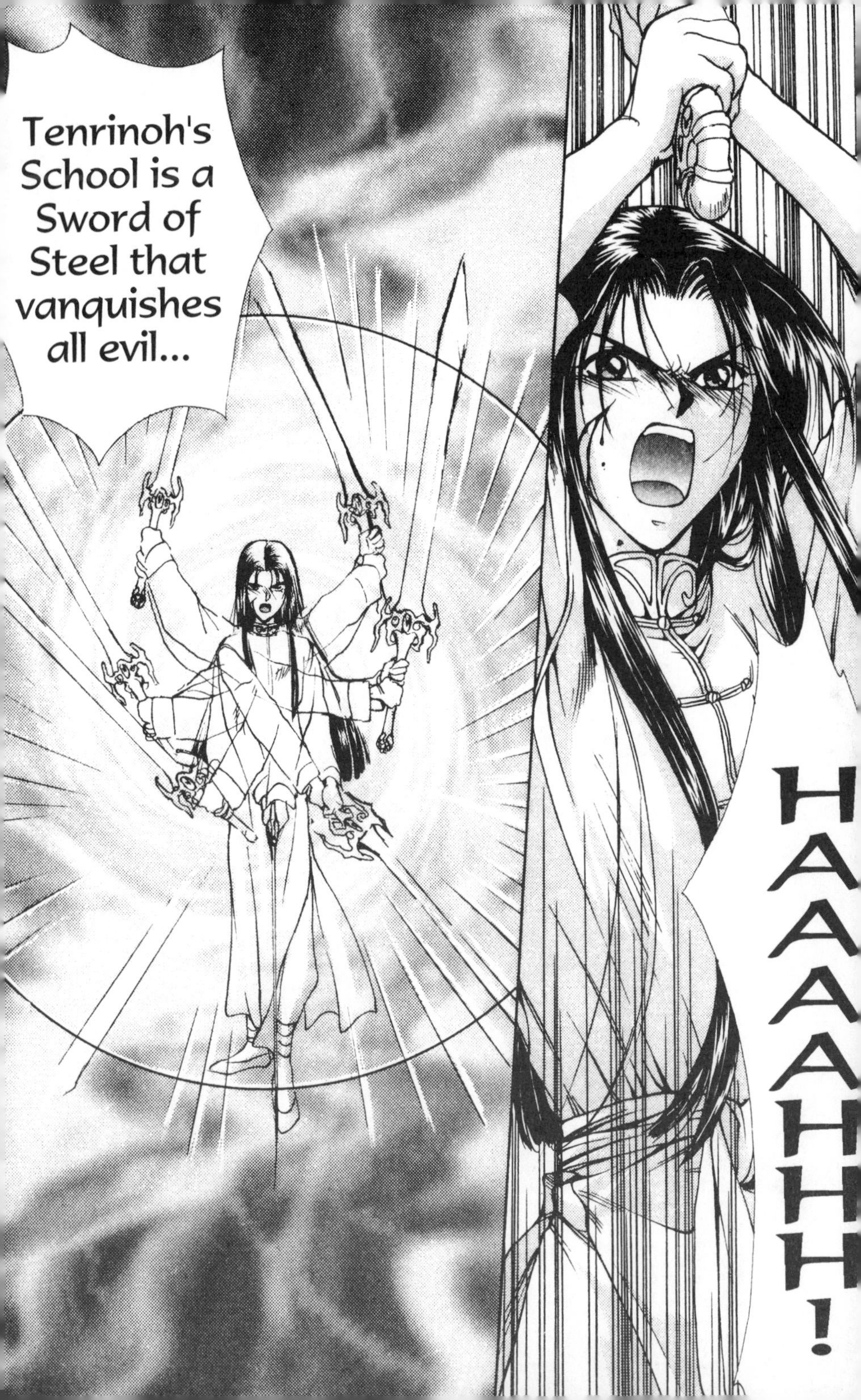
HAAAAAHH!
Tenrinoh's School is a Sword of Steel that vanquishes all evil...

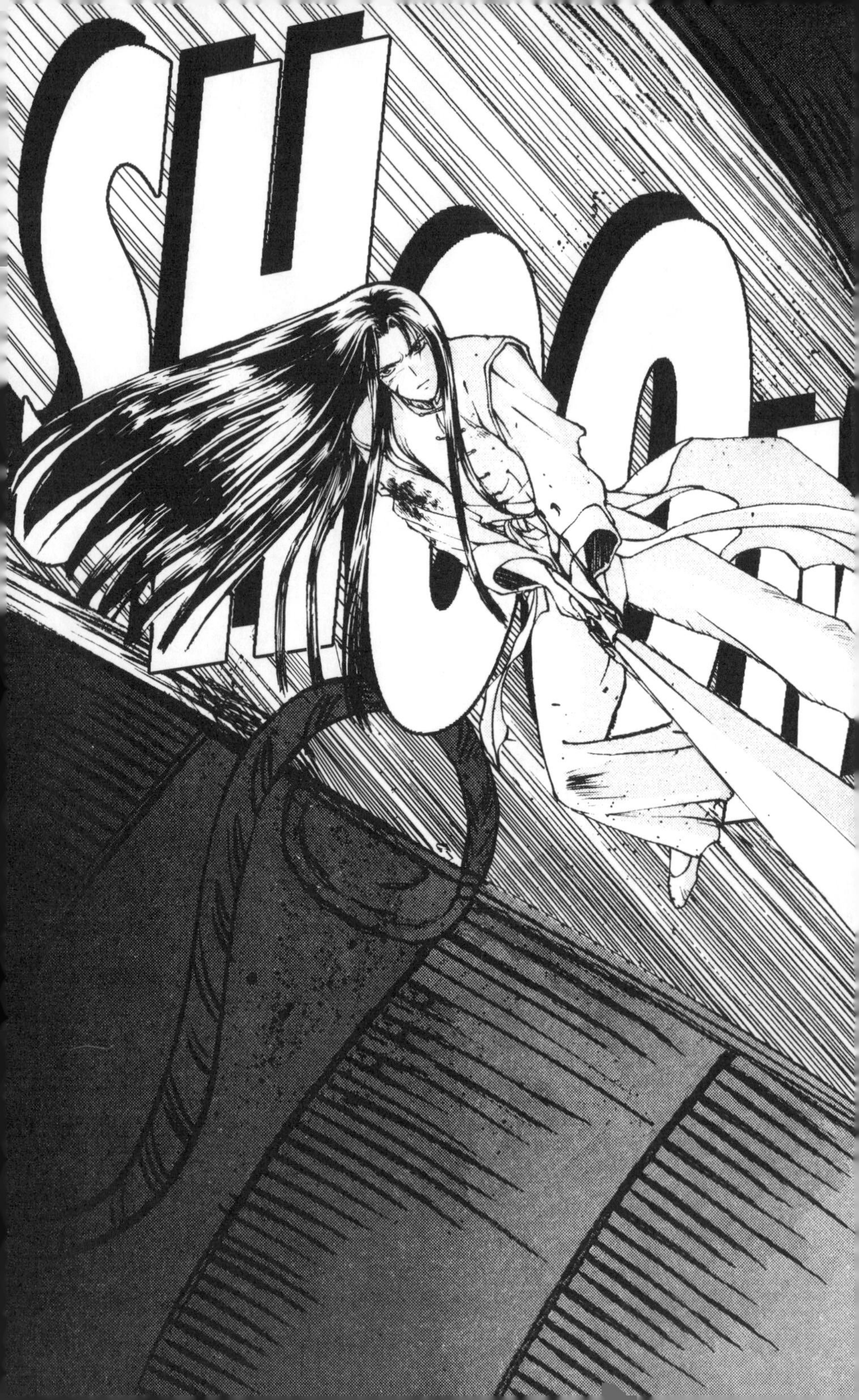
SHOO

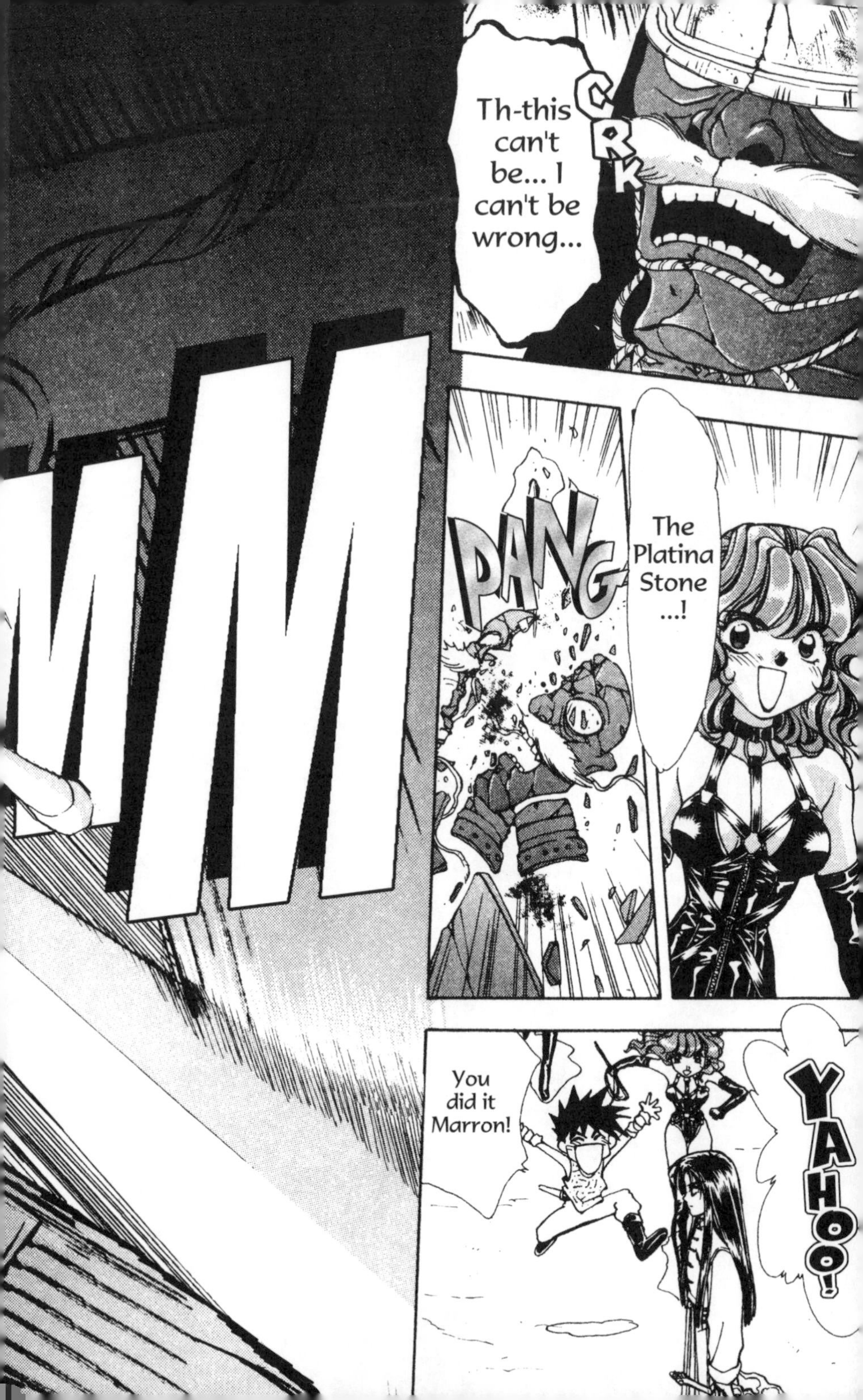
CRK
Th-this can't be... I can't be wrong...
The Platina Stone ...!
PANG
YAHOO!
You did it Marron!
MM

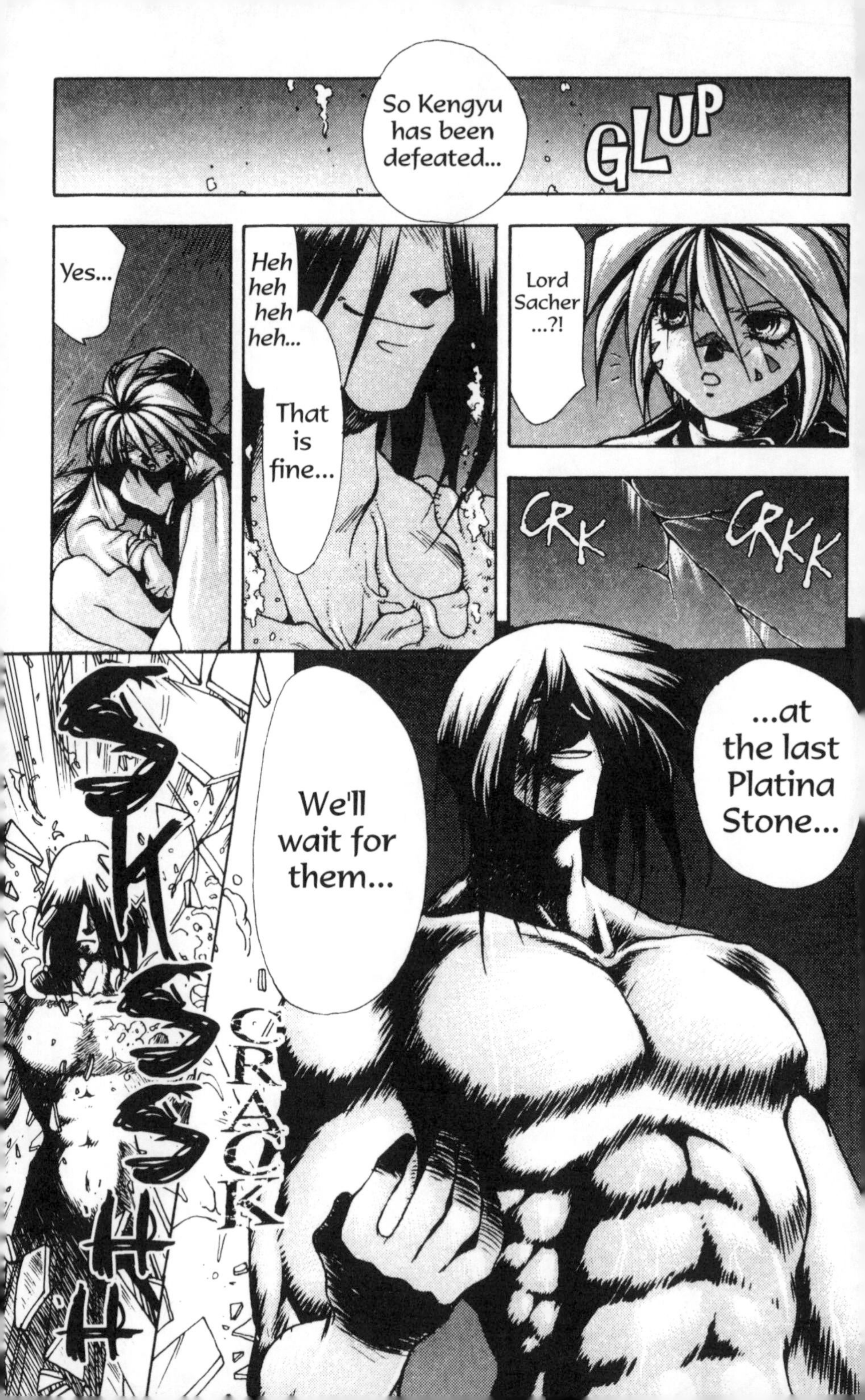
So Kengyu has been defeated...
GLUP
Yes...
Heh heh heh heh...
That is fine...
Lord Sacher ...?!
CRK
CRKK
SHASSHH
CRACK
We'll wait for them...
...at the last Platina Stone...

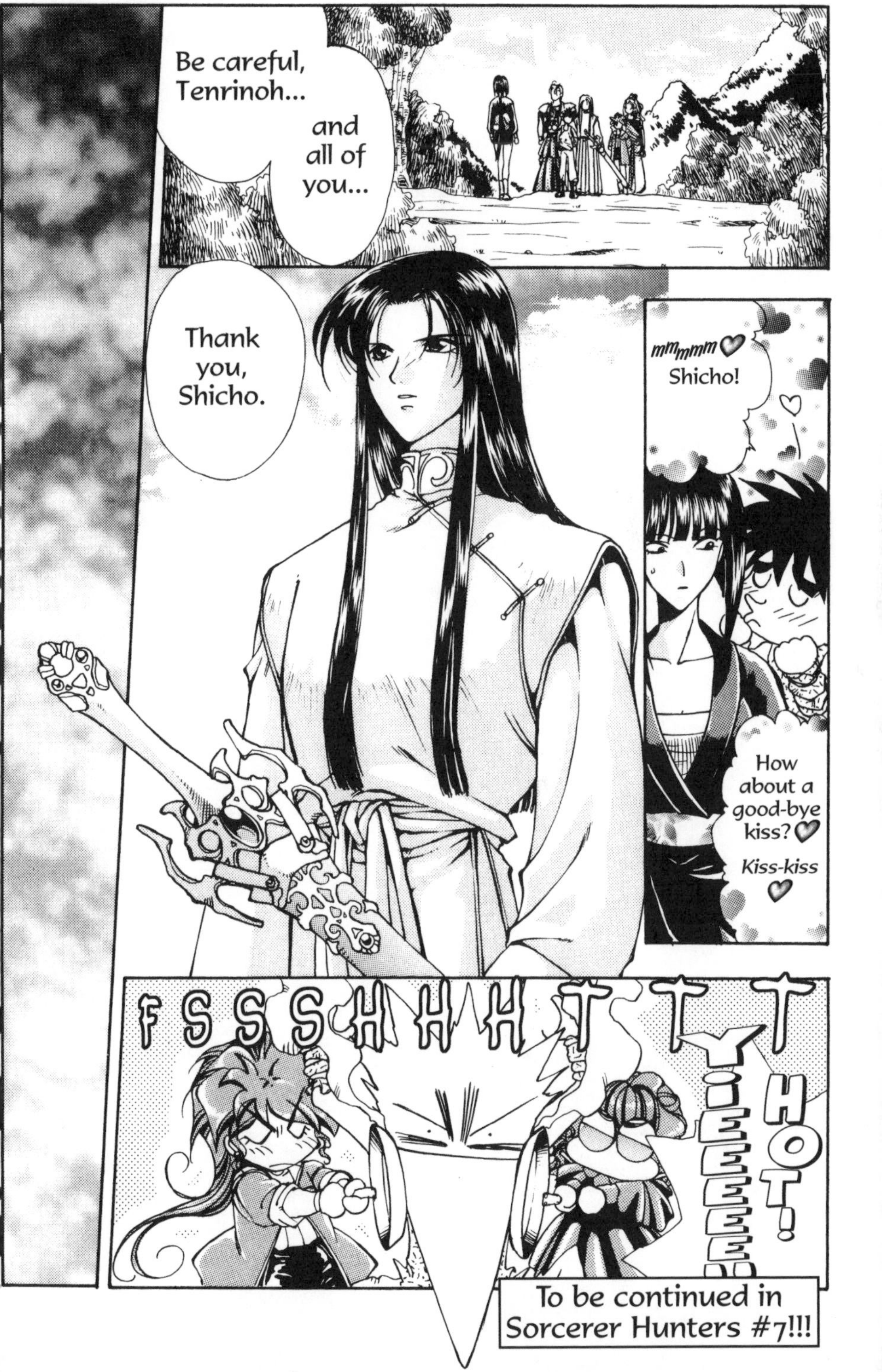
Be careful, Tenrinoh... and all of you...
Thank you, Shicho.
mmmmm Shicho!
How about a good-bye kiss?
Kiss-kiss
FSSSHHHTTT
YIEEEEE!!
HOT!
To be continued in Sorcerer Hunters #7!!!